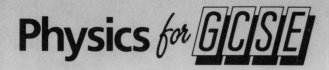

Physics for GCSE

Physics *for* GCSE

Digby Swift

Basil Blackwell

© 1988 Digby Swift

First published 1988

Published by Basil Blackwell Ltd
108 Cowley Road
Oxford OX4 1JF
England

British Library Cataloguing in Publication Data

Swift, Digby G.
  Physics for GCSE.
  1. Physics — For schools
  I. Title
  530

  ISBN 0–631–90072–1

Illustrated by Chris Evans, Nick Hawken, Anne Langford and Trevor Mason

Typeset in Plantin and Frutiger by Opus, Oxford
Printed in Hong Kong by Wing King Tong Co Ltd

Preface

One of the ways in which GCSE physics and science courses differ from earlier exam courses is in the stress that is laid on the relevance of physics to everyday life. There is a new emphasis on technological applications and on social, economic and environmental implications. This book covers the physics syllabuses of all the GCSE examination boards and takes full account of the new emphasis. Applications and implications pervade each chapter and are used to introduce most of the physics content.

Practical work is another major emphasis of GCSE physics (and science), especially problem-solving and open-ended investigations. This book contains many brief suggestions for such activities. But to do full justice to the new practical approach, there is a need for a range of experiments presented in a form suitable for practical assessment. There is also a need for more information-handling exercises, and a wide range of other supporting activities. To have included all these in the present textbook would have overburdened and distorted the text. They have therefore been included in a separate, photocopiable activity pack.

The structure of this book is based on the development of several major themes: force, motion, energy, waves, electromagnetism, electronics and the particulate nature of matter. The treatment of these varies. Forces and motion, electromagnetism and electronics are presented as fairly discrete sections. Energy and waves are presented as topics in their own right, and are then developed through applications (heat, light etc.). The particulate nature of matter is developed in a more subtle way — as a component of most chapters of the book.

Energy is developed in a manner that emphasises the link between energy in physics and energy in everyday life. The concept is developed through examples of energy, especially kinetic energy, rather than through a formal definition (the ability to do work). Heat is treated as a *process* of energy transfer, analogous to work. The term 'heat energy' has been avoided as this can lead to confusion, particularly in relation to internal energy.

In addition to covering the GCSE physics syllabuses, this book covers most of the physics content of dual-award science courses. An attempt has been made to cover the needs of the full ability range. The chapters are presented as double-page spreads (further divided by subheadings) to enable the order of presentation to be changed, and to enable an easy selection of the material needed by individual students.

Some additional special interest topics have been added to the main syllabus topics. These include 'Hyperspace and ham sandwiches' (a brief and simple introduction to relativity), 'A thunderstorm', 'A message from space', 'A thermonuclear future' and 'The world of the computer'. In addition, there are separate sections dealing with three very important, yet often overlooked, issues: 'Physics and faith', 'Science, technology and the world' (including a multicultural perspective) and 'Physics and defence'.

Finally, there are appendixes covering SI units, guidance on the mathematical aspects of the GCSE syllabus, and a brief treatment of the constant acceleration formulae (as an example of this mathematical approach).

A main aim throughout has been to show the importance of science for all, and to encourage students to think more about the world around them.

Digby Swift, 1988

Contents

Acknowledgements

It would be impossible to list all those who have contributed to this book. However, I would particularly like to thank David and Anne Smith for their careful review of the book as a whole, Tom Jenkins and Norman Howe for their helpful advice on several individual sections, and Martin Hollins and Josiah Martin for advice with the section on Science, technology and the world. While some errors almost certainly remain (there is no such thing as an error-free textbook!), they are far fewer in number as a result of their help. Any errors that remain are my responsibility, not theirs.

Many people have generously helped with the photographs, either by posing to be photographed (often repeatedly), or by providing photographs. The following credits include the latter and are, regrettably, an inadequate response on my part. At the risk of singling out individuals, I feel I must particularly thank the editor and staff of the *Sheffield Star* for help with, and repeated free use of, the newspaper's photographic library.

Organisations which have kindly supplied photographs and given permission for their use are:

AA Photo Library 5.2.1, 6.9.1, 6.9.5, 11.3.1; ACE Centre, Ormerod School, Oxford 18.1.2; Acorn Computers Ltd 2.2.4(c); All-Sport (UK) Ltd 1.1.1, 3.2.1, 4.2.1, 4.7.4, 6.2.5, 6.6.2, 6.6.4, 9.1.3; Ames Research Centre 2.6.5; Antiference Ltd 14.5.3(a); Associated Press 14.3.5; Barclays Bank Ltd 13.1.4; Barnaby's Picture Library 4.1.1, 6.5.4, 7.9.2, 11.5.1, 14.4.1, 14.6.2, 14.6.3, 14.12.2, 16.3.5, 19.5.3; BBC Hulton Picture Library 2.6.1, 3.4.3, 4.6.4, 8.7.4, 8.8.1, 17.1.4, 19.8.1, p.28, Fig. 2; BP Ltd 6.8.1; Beekeepers Annual/JD Phipps 2.5.1; British Aerospace 5.7.7; British Airports Authority 3.7.1; British Alcan Aluminium 5.8.1; British Coal 17.8.5; British Railways Board 2.1.4, 2.1.5; British Steel/Port Talbot Works 4.1.3(a), 7.7.3(a); California Institute of Technology 2.6.2; Camera Press 3.3.5, 4.4.2, 4.5.6, 6.6.1, 7.2.1, 7.5.5, 9.2.1, 11.5.4, 11.8.5, 12.1.1(a), 16.5.1, 17.6.1; Cement and Concrete Association 8.9.3; Central Electricity Generating Board 7.1.1, 7.4.1, 7.6.4, 7.7.1, 11.9.3, 13.5.1, 13.9.1(b), 17.7.5, 17.10.1, 17.11.1; Central Office of Information 8.7.5, 11.6.1; Bruce Coleman Ltd 6.4.1, 14.4.4, 15.2.1; Data General/Team Tyrrhel 4.7.1; De Beers Consolidated Mines Ltd 1.6.3; Dimplex Heating Ltd 6.5.5; ERF Plastics Ltd 4.1.4(a); Electrolux 12.1.1(c); Farmers Weekly Picture Library 10.2.4; Ferranti plc 19.6.5; Merlin Firman 5.1.4; Food Research Association 17.8.2; Ford Photographic Unit 3.5.4; Geological Museum 5.3.3(a); James Gilbert 7.8.1; The Griffith Institute 17.9.1; Philip Harris Ltd 1.2.4, 2.2.4(b), 2.4.5, 5.4.2, 5.5.6(a), 15.5.2; Haynes Publishing Group, 1981 6.9.3, 13.8.1; Heath Navigational Ltd/WF Stanley & Co Ltd 12.2.1; Hong Kong Tourist Association 2.5.6; Hydraulics Research Ltd 14.2.1; Imperial War Museum 8.2.6, 14.10.3, p.252, Fig. 2; International Business Machines Co 8.4.1; Iscor Ltd 13.1.1; Tom Jenkins 3.3.3; Eric Kay 7.5.2; Kenwood Ltd 7.1.2(c); Kinderland (Scarborough) Ltd 6.1.1; Kuka Robots 19.2.1; Land Infra Red Ltd 8.6.6; Frank Lane Picture Agency 6.4.5, 9.3.1, 14.1.1, 15.5.5; Lever Bros 14.9.4; Leybold Heraeus Ltd 16.6.4; London Fire and Civil Defence Authority 3.2.6; London Transport Museum 3.1.1; Manchester University, Department of Physics 17.3.1; Mansell Collection 9.1.1; Mary Evans Picture Library p.115, Fig. 3; Meteorological Office/HMSO 5.6.1; Microwave Marketing Ltd 14.6.1; Midlands County Council Planning Department 10.3.4; Ministry of Defence p.252, Fig. 1; Moorfields Eye Hospital 12.3.1; NASA 1.4.1, 1.4.3, 1.4.4, 3.8.4, 4.4.1, 7.3.1; National Optical Astronomy Observatories 1.3.1; Christina Newman 9.1.4, 15.3.3; Ontario Science Centre 10.3.1; Sally Oram 9.3.3; Oxfam 6.2.6, p.29, Fig. 3; Philips Electronics Ltd 7.1.2(b), 11.4.1, 14,5,3(b), 19.3.1; Pilkington Insulation Ltd 9.4.3; Pilkington plc 5.7.1, 9.4.1, 14.8.1; Plessey Telecommunications and Office Systems Ltd 10.5.3, 19.4.1; Popperfoto 5.5.4, 17.4.1; Derek Pratt/Waterways Photo Library 4.3.5; The Press Association Ltd 3.4.1, 11.1.4, 13.4.1, 17.1.1; Prestige Group plc 8.9.2; Rank Xerox Ltd 10.1.3; Rodenstock GmbH 16.2.2; Rolls Royce plc 1.2.5; Royal Astronomical Society 15.5.1; Science Photo Library Ltd Cover, 2.2.1, 5.3.3(b), 14.7.1, 14.8.6, 16.3.2, 17.8.2, 19.8.2(b); The Sheffield Star 3.4.2, 3.5.1, 5.3.1, 6.5.3, 9.4.5, 9.5.4(a), 10.4.1, 11.7.2, 15.2.5, 17.2.1, p.253, Fig. 3; Shell UK Ltd 3.31, 5.5.1, 6.3.1; R Skillman 8.5.1, 6.10.3(a), (c); Sporting Pictures (UK) Ltd 19.5.1; Steel Foundations Ltd 3.4.4; Swan Housewares Ltd 7.1.2(a); Swift Picture Library 6.10.2; Team Advertising and Marketing Ltd/Unigate 14.9.5; Telefocus 15.1.1; The Telegraph Colour Library 1.3.4, 14.7.2; Thames Valley Police/Roy Campbell 2.1.1; Graham Topping 3.3.2, 4.1.4(b), 6.2.1, 6.7.1, 6.10.3(b), 8.8.4, 10.4.4, 11.5.3, 11.10.1, 18.1.1, 19.1.1; Travel Photo International 5.4.4, 6.5.1, 7.3.4, 9.5.4(b), 14.9.1, p.115, Fig. 2; Jeremy Tremaine 7.8.2, 12.5.1; Trustees of the Science Museum, London 6.10.3(d), 12.4.1, 14.12.1, 17.2.3(a), (b), 17.5.5(a); Unipart Group Ltd 3.1.2, 7.9.3; United Kingdom Atomic Energy Authority 17.2.1, 17.5.1, 17.6.4, 17.7.1, 17.8.1; United Nations 17.12.4; US Department of Energy 17.10.4; Water Authorities Association 1.5.5; Water Pressurisation Systems Engineering Ltd 5.2.5; Welbeck Public Relations Ltd 7.8.5; Yorkshire Brick Co. 7.6.3; Yorkshire Post Newspaper Ltd 19.8.2(a); GH Zeal Ltd 8.6.2, 8.6.3(b).

I would like to thank the staff of Basil Blackwell for their helpful advice at all stages, and their care with the editing, illustrating and production of the book.

Finally, I must thank my family for putting up with, and supporting, this literary monster that has for so long taken priority over their more domestic but equally important needs.

Digby Swift, 1988

Introduction

Physics is a human activity. It isn't just something that happens in laboratories. It's about people seeking to learn more about their world, and to come to terms with it.

Physics shows us the marvels of nature, from the tiniest parts of the atom to the furthest reaches of the universe. The study of physics can alter our understanding of ourselves and of our environment.

The use of physics has radically changed our world. Physics has helped us to control our environment through technology. In the past, physics has brought great benefits, but also great harm. In the future, physics will have just as much impact — for good or ill.

We need physics for a wide range of activities (for industry, for medicine, for agriculture, for sport and much else). Physics is important for all of us, and for our world. If (while supporting GCSE studies) this book can make you think more about the world around you, and give you a sense of wonder, understanding and involvement, then it will have succeeded in its task.

1 FORCES

1.1 Pushes and pulls

Pushed around by the wind

Fig. 1 A windsurfer is pushed through the water by the wind. Where are the forces on the surfboard acting? Are they pushes or pulls?

Have you seen windsurfers being pushed through the water by the wind? Beginners find it difficult to balance their sails and are pulled or pushed off their surfboards into the water.

Most sports involve pushes and pulls. Indeed, everything that we do involves pushes and pulls. **How many examples can you think of?**

Forces

Scientists and engineers don't talk much about pushes and pulls. Instead, they talk about forces. What does the word 'force' mean to you? Forcing someone to do something? The police force? The Royal Air Force?

In physics and engineering the word 'force' can only mean one of two things. It is either a **push** or a **pull** (Figure 2).

Feeling different types of force

Weight is a force. It is the pull of gravity on an object. **Lift a heavy weight, and imagine that you are having a tug-of-war with the ground.**

Magnets attract steel with a **magnetic force**. They also push against, or repel, each other with a magnetic force. **Try this—feel the force.**

A rubbed plastic comb attracts water from a tap with an **electrostatic force. Try this. What else can you attract with a rubbed plastic comb?**

Air bubbles in water rise to the surface. The water pushes them with an upwards force called an **upthrust. Hold a cork under water and feel the upthrust—feel the water pushing the cork upwards.**

Fig. 2 In physics, a force is either a push or a pull
Scientists choose their words very carefully.

Sky-divers, speedboats and saws

As well as forces that cause movement, there are forces that stop or reduce movement.

Air resistance is a force that stops or reduces movement. It pushes against moving cars and aircraft, and makes them travel more slowly (Figure 3). Sometimes this drag force is useful. Sky-divers spread out their arms and legs so that they are slowed down by the air as they fall to the ground. Eventually they open a parachute. The drag force on this parachute slows them down still further, allowing them to land safely.

Fig. 3 A cab with a strange hood
What is the purpose of the hood?

Water resistance makes ships and boats travel more slowly. Cross-channel ferries cannot go much faster than about 25 miles per hour (mph) even with careful streamlining. Above this speed, the water resistance becomes too great. Hydrofoils (like aircraft wings) are used on some boats to lift the main part of the boat out of the water. This reduces the water resistance and enables the boat to travel faster. Hovercraft avoid the problem altogether by staying up out of the water.

Frictional forces act whenever two surfaces rub against each other. They make it more difficult for surfaces to slide over each other. Frictional forces can be useful. When you apply the brakes of a bicycle, brake shoes are forced against the wheels. The frictional forces between the brake shoes and the wheels slow the wheels down. Frictional forces can also be a nuisance. For example, when you use a saw to cut wood, there is a frictional force between the blade and the edges of the saw cut. To reduce this force, the teeth of woodsaws are splayed out so that they cut a wider groove. **Why are the teeth of bread knives not splayed out in this way?**

The effects of forces

Forces can pull or attract things, push or repel things, lift things, speed things up and slow things down. They can also make things change their direction of motion (Figure 4).

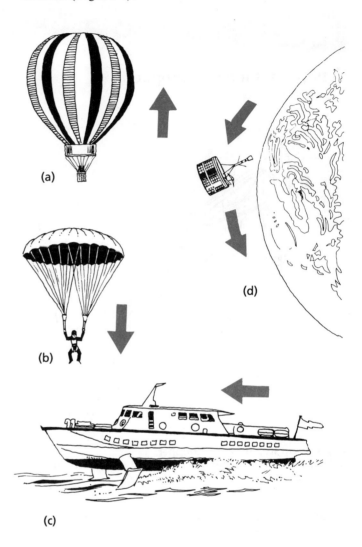

Fig. 4 Pushes and pulls
In each of these diagrams, the arrows show the direction of motion. Copy each diagram, and draw another arrow to show the direction of
(a) the upthrust on the balloon
(b) the air resistance on the free-fall parachutist
(c) the water resistance on the hydrofoil
(d) the weight of the satellite. (If you don't think it has any weight, see Section 1.4.)
Which of these forces is
  (i) speeding things up?
  (ii) slowing things down?
  (iii) changing the direction of motion?

All forces are pushes and pulls. If it isn't a push or a pull, then it isn't a force!

3

How much force?

A big step for a grasshopper

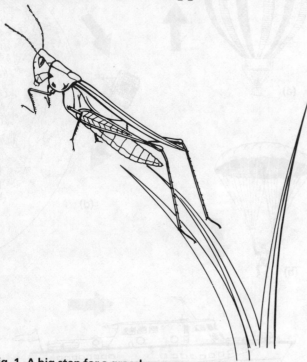

Fig. 1 A big step for a grasshopper
Where do the forces that push the grasshopper into the air act?

A grasshopper leaps high into the air. It feels its muscles pushing upwards with an enormous force. But a small baby can put its hand over the grasshopper and stop it from jumping. A big force for a grasshopper is a very small force for a human (Figure 1).

To say whether a force is large or small, we need something to compare it with. In physics, we have a unit of force called the **newton** as our standard of comparison. In other words, we measure forces in newtons. One newton (1 N) is about the weight of an apple. Figure 2 shows examples of people using different amounts of force. **Try to estimate the force in newtons.** (The forces listed in Figure 3 are intended only as a very rough guide—what we call an **order of magnitude** guide. For example, the force needed to peel an actual banana may be anywhere between, say, 0.5 N and 5 N.)

Fig. 2 How much force are they using?
Estimate the force in newtons that each of these people is using. (Use Figure 3 as a guide.)

Fig. 3 Some examples of forces measured in **newtons**

The force of a grasshopper's legs	0.001 N
The force when you cough against your hand	0.01 N
The force on your tongue when you lick a stamp	0.1 N
The force needed to peel a banana	1 N
The force of a racket hitting a tennis ball	10 N
The force used when kicking a football	100 N
The force of a car engine	1000 N
The force of a train engine	10 000 N
The force of a jet engine	100 000 N
The force of a rocket engine	1 000 000 N

A newton meter

Figure 4 shows a newton meter. These simple measuring instruments (often called spring balances) can be used to measure forces of between about 0.1 N and 100 N.

Fig. 4 A newton meter
What happens when you pull on the lower hook?

● **Try using a newton meter to measure the force needed to double the length of an elastic band, and the force needed to tear some paper. Does it matter which way round you use the newton meter? Do you have to have the scale upright, or can it be upside down or on its side? Why is this so?**

Other units of force

The newton isn't the only unit of force. Engineers sometimes use the **kilogram-force** (kgf), which is approximately equal to 10 N, and the **pound-force** (lbf or just p) which is equal to 4.5 N. For example, you may read in a magazine that an aircraft engine has 'a thrust of 20 000 pounds'. This means that it pushes with a force of $(20\,000 \times 4.5)$ N or 90 000 N (Figure 5).

Fig. 5 A Rolls-Royce RB211 jet engine
This engine produces a thrust of 42 000 lbf. What is this force in newtons?

Whenever you come across units such as the kilogram-force in science or engineering, the safest thing to do is to change them into newtons. For example, think of 10 kgf as 100 N. In this book, we will only use newtons.

Force fields, gravity and a man called Newton

Sir Isaac and his book

Fig. 1 Halley's comet
This came near Earth in 1986. Newton's book, the *Principia*, allows us to tell when it will be back again. See if you can find out when that will be.

Sir Isaac Newton (1642–1727) is often said to be the world's greatest scientist. Yet he wasn't particularly brilliant at school, and towards the end of his life he was more interested in parliament and in running the Royal Mint than he was in science. So why do people call him the world's greatest scientist? Because of a book that he wrote.

It nearly didn't get written. The university where Newton worked was closed because of the plague, and this gave him time to think up the ideas for his book. However, if Edmond Halley (the person the comet is named after) had not begged Newton to write the book and even paid for it to be published, it would have stayed as some of the thousands of scraps of paper that littered Newton's office.

However, the book was written, and later in his life Newton was knighted and made President of the Royal Society. When he died, he was carried to a grave in Westminster Abbey by the Lord High Chancellor, two dukes and three earls. Newton had made science important among the aristocracy, and because of his book the whole world (not just England) now names forces after him.

Apples, gravity and force at a distance

What Newton showed in his book was that there are forces on the heavenly bodies—Sun, Moon and planets—in much the same way as there are forces on us. The planets are pushed around in much the same way as we are. Forces are, in a way, the 'key to the universe'. (Some people say that this idea first dawned on Newton when an apple fell from a tree and hit him on the head.)

Newton showed that the movements of the planets and of the Moon, the tides and even the wobbling of the Earth in its orbit round the Sun, could be explained in terms of a single force: the force of gravity.

Gravitational force acts between all objects. It even acts between us and the things around us. However, only if one of the objects is very large indeed, like the Earth, Sun, Moon and planets, is the force large enough to be noticeable.

Fig. 2 The Moon and an apple
According to Alexander Pope
'Nature and Nature's laws lay hid in night;
God said, let Newton be! and all was light.'
What did Newton 'bring to light' about the Moon and an apple?

The force of gravity keeps the Earth trapped in orbit round the Sun and prevents it from drifting off into space. It also keeps the Moon and satellites trapped in orbit round the Earth (Figure 3).

Fig. 3 Our planet doesn't need a lifeline tied to the Sun
So what stops the Earth from wandering off into space?

Scientists still marvel over (and can't really explain) this astonishing fact—that the force of gravity acts at a distance, with nothing in between.

Force fields

We use a special name for the region in which a gravitational pull acts. We call it a **gravitational field**. (A 'field' in this case is just the wide, open area in which the force is acting—somewhat poetic language!) The gravitational field extends into space, and stops the Moon and artificial satellites from wandering off to some other part of the solar system.

As well as gravitational fields, we have **magnetic fields** around magnets. For example, magnets pull on steel nails even when there is nothing (except air) between them. We also have **electric fields** where electrostatic forces are acting. For example, a piece of rubbed plastic will pick up small pieces of paper even when it is not actually touching the paper.

The nearer you get, the larger the force

If you lower a magnet towards a paper clip, the magnetic force between them gets steadily larger. Eventually the paper clip will jump up to the magnet. **Try this.** Similarly, the further you go into space, the weaker the gravitational force becomes.

If you bring a charged nylon rod near any hairs on your body, the nearer the rod is, the more it affects the hairs. **Try this.**

> Magnetic, electrostatic and gravitational forces all vary with distance.

Fig. 4 Aurora borealis (or Northern Lights)
These are caused by the Earth's magnetic field.
'Saint Elmo's Fire' is produced by an electric field. What is 'Saint Elmo's Fire'?

Losing weight (but not mass!)

Reducing your weight

Fig. 1 Mass and weight on the Moon
Edwin Aldrin steps from the lunar module on to the surface of the Moon during the first Moon landing. Why is the pack on his back not as heavy as it looks?

Do you know someone who is trying to lose weight? The theory of gravitation can help them! If they climb to the top of a mountain, they will be further from the centre of the Earth, and so the gravitational force will be less. Unfortunately, the weight that they will lose will be far too small to show on their bathroom scales (Figure 2).

Fig. 2 One way of losing weight
His mass will get less—he will lose some fat by climbing. What is the other reason why he will be lighter at the top of the mountain? Why can't he lose a lot of weight in this way?

A better plan would be to take a space flight to the Moon. The gravitational pull (the **field strength**) is much less there because the Moon is much smaller than the Earth. People weigh much less, and so does their equipment. Those huge backpacks that the American astronauts carried around so easily on the Moon would have flattened them on Earth!

Mass

On the Moon a heavy astronaut wouldn't hurt you if he stepped on your toe. However, if he bumped into you, it would hurt just as much as it would on Earth. The effect that things have when they collide depends not on their weight, but on the amount there is of them (Figure 3). We call the amount there is of something its **mass**. (This isn't the same as volume—you can change the volume of something just by compressing it. You can't change the mass—the amount there is of it.)

Fig. 3 Moon rocks
Imagine that you are on the Moon. What difference would you notice, compared with on Earth, if you (i) lifted these rocks, (ii) kicked them?

Mass (not weight) is measured in kilograms . . .

. . . and sometimes in pounds. **How many pounds are equal to a kilogram? How many kilograms are there in a tonne?**

When you buy a pound (or, on the Continent, a kilogram) of cheese, you are not really concerned about its weight. It would be better if it weighed less—it wouldn't be so heavy to carry! What you are concerned about is how much cheese there is or, in other words, the mass of the cheese. Strictly speaking, it is wrong to say that some cheese has a *weight* of one kilogram; weight is not measured in kilograms, but in newtons. We should say that the cheese has a *mass* of one kilogram.

The relationship between mass and weight

The more there is of something, the greater is its weight. The weight also increases with the gravitational field strength:

> weight = mass × gravitational field strength

If w = weight in newtons (N)
      m = mass in kilograms (kg)
and g = gravitational field strength in N/kg

then

$$w = mg \qquad (1)$$

The gravitational field strength g on the Earth's surface is 10 N/kg. Thus, on Earth, a 1 kg mass has a weight of 10 N. **1 tonne ≡ 1000 kg. How many newtons is this?**

- **If you have bathroom scales, use them to find your mass. (You may need to know that 1 lb ≡ 0.45 kg.) What is your weight in newtons? What would it be on the Moon where the gravitational field strength is 1.6 N/kg? If the largest mass you can carry on Earth is 50 kg (the mass of a 'hundredweight' bag of cement or sack of coal), what would be the largest mass you could carry on the Moon?**

Weightlessness

People say that astronauts in orbit round the Earth are **weightless**. This isn't really true—the gravitational pull of the Earth is still quite strong. However, the astronauts *feel* weightless because they are falling. The astronauts and their spacecraft are constantly being pulled down to the ground—they experience the same sensation as someone in a falling lift. However, whereas the lift will finally hit the ground, the spacecraft never hits the ground. The reason is that it is speeding round the Earth so fast that it falls 'beyond the horizon'. Although it is constantly falling, it never gets any nearer to the ground—the Earth bends down away from it (Figure 4).

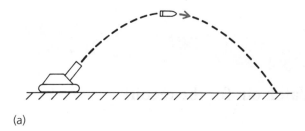

(a)

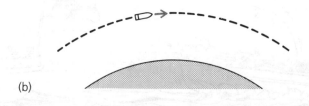

(b)

(c)

Fig. 4 'Weightlessness'—falling but never hitting the ground
(a) A shell falling and hitting the ground
(b) A rocket fired so fast that it falls over the horizon, and therefore stays in orbit round the Earth, never reaching the ground
What would happen if the rocket were fired even faster?
(c) An astronaut floating in space
Like the rocket, he is constantly falling towards the ground but never gets there—he falls over the horizon.

- **How would you like to be in an orbiting spacecraft, constantly falling but never hitting the ground?**

9

There's always a reaction

Watch out for the recoil!

Fig. 1 Recoil can be a problem
On ancient warships like HMS Victory the cannons were on wheels and were fastened to the deck by strong but slack lengths of rope. Why was this? (Why isn't it necessary on modern warships?)

In 1915 the British Navy was testing some launches on the River Thames. These launches were to be used against German warships on Lake Tanganyika in East Africa. They were small boats but they were fitted with large, three-pounder guns (guns which fired 3 pound shells). In his book *Battle of the Bundu*, Charles Miller describes a problem that they had with this unusual kind of gunship:

> 'When the three-pounders were tried out, the first shot saw one of the guns and its gun layer hurled into the river: someone had forgotten to secure the weapon's locking ring.'

Later, when *HMS Fifi* with its overweight gun was speeding after a German warship, the captain unwisely ordered the gun to be fired.

> 'The gun crashed out and *Fifi* stopped dead in her tracks with the recoil . . . the braking effect of the recoil from every shot helped widen the distance between the two ships.'

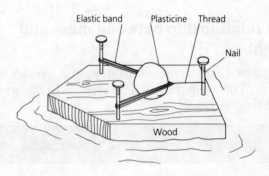

Fig. 2 A floating catapult
What happens when you burn the thread with a match?
Why?
What happens if you alter the mass of the plasticine?

- Figure 2 shows how you can demonstrate the behaviour of *Fifi* with a catapult 'gun' firing plasticine 'shells'. This will also work if you put the wooden platform on, for example, cotton-reel rollers.

Equal and opposite forces

Recoil has always been a problem with guns. Whenever a bullet or shell flies out one way, the gun recoils back the other way. The force is the same—the force on the gun is the same as the force on the bullet.

> As Newton put it, 'to every action, there is an equal and opposite reaction'. This is sometimes called *Newton's Third Law of Motion*.

Aerospace and sewage farms

Reaction forces can be very useful. Jet engines and rockets work by forcing gas out at high speeds from the rear. The recoil from the gas pushes the engine forwards. In a jet engine, the high-speed gas is produced by heating air to a very high temperature (Figure 3). Space rockets carry their own oxygen to burn the fuel and produce a high-speed jet of gas (Figure 4).

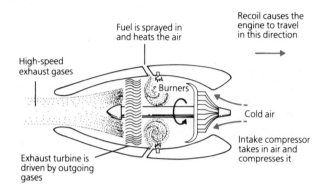

Fig. 3 How a jet engine works
Why can't this method be used for spacecraft?

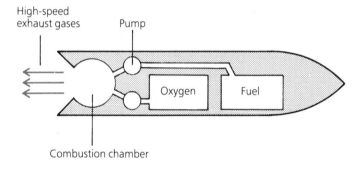

Fig. 4 How a rocket works

Propeller planes and helicopters use the same principle, with propellers to produce the high-speed jet of air.

● **How can you make a simple cold-air 'rocket' using a balloon?**

Reaction forces are also used in the filter beds at sewage farms. The water to be filtered is pumped into four long pipes joined in the shape of a cross. This cross is suspended over the filter bed from a central pivot. Each of the four pipes has holes down one side. As the water pours out of these holes, the reaction causes the cross to rotate. This spreads the water evenly over the whole area of the filter (Figure 5). Many dishwashers and garden sprinklers use the same principle.

Fig. 5 Reaction at a sewage farm
What causes the water sprinkler to rotate?

A less obvious reaction

When we push things, they push back. This allows us to feel that they are there. **Try pushing something with your fingers and feel the reaction forces.**

Sometimes the reaction force is large enough to cancel the pushing force. For example, when we sit on a chair, the reaction force from the chair cancels our weight. If it didn't we would end up on the floor!

Imagine a world where there was no reaction—where you could push objects without them pushing back. You wouldn't be able to sit down on anything. You wouldn't even be able to feel anything. If you tried to walk along a path, your feet would push the path backwards but you would stand still. If you ever did manage to move, you'd have no way of stopping yourself. Life would be very difficult!

Fortunately, there is always a reaction.

Fig. 6 A world where there was no reaction
What other problems would we have if there weren't any reaction forces?

11

Exercises

1 Which of the following has a weight of about 1 N?

   A A drawing pin

   B An orange

   C A dog

   D A cow

   E A bus

2 Which of the following is *not* an example of the effect of a force?

   A A steel nail being attracted to a magnet

   B A beaker of water being heated by a gas flame

   C Air being pumped into a bicycle tyre

   D A hot-air balloon rising into the air

   E A car skidding to a halt

3 A nylon shirt or blouse tends to stick to your body on a hot, dry day. Which of the following is the main cause of this?

   A Air resistance

   B Friction

   C An electrostatic force

   D A reaction force

   E Animal magnetism

4 A large rifle is used to fire a very small bullet. Which of the following best describes the relationship between the force on the bullet and the reaction force on the rifle?

   A The two forces are equal.

   B The force on the bullet is the larger.

   C The recoil force on the rifle is the larger.

   D There is no reaction force because the bullet is so small.

   E It depends on the way the rifle is being fired.

5 The gravitational field strength on a particular planet is 20 N/kg, while on Earth the gravitational field strength is 10 N/kg. A rock weighs 50 N on that planet. What would it weigh if it were brought back to Earth?

   A 100 N

   B 50 N

   C 25 N

   D 20 N

   E 10 N

6 Complete these sentences:

   a Weight is the _____ acting on a mass in a _____ field. It is measured in _____.

   b A rubbed balloon is attracted to the wall by an _____ force.

   c A cork rises to the surface of a liquid because of the upward force or _____ produced by the _____ .

   d It is difficult to pull a balloon through the air because of the _____ of the air on the balloon.

   e The _____ of an astronaut gets less as he gets further away from the Earth, but his _____ remains the same. This is because the _____ _____ strength decreases as he gets further away from the Earth.

   f The force exerted by an object A on an object B is _____ in magnitude, _____ in direction, and in the same straight line as the force exerted by B on A.

   g The force needed to lift a 50 g mass, assuming a gravitational field strength of 10 N/kg, is _____ .

7 State three examples of forces that act at a distance and vary with distance.

8 State one advantage and one disadvantage of frictional forces to the motorist.

9 List four possible effects of a force acting on a rubber ball.

10 Why do you have to hold a magnet close to drawing pins before it will pick them up?

Fig. 1 She's got a problem
How can she move without getting off the trolley?

11 The girl shown in Figure 1 has a problem. As she moves one way, the trolley moves the other way. Why? How can she move without touching anything other than the ball or the trolley?

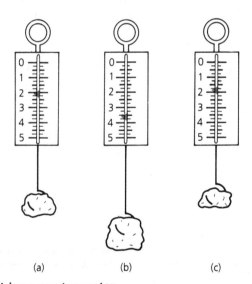

(a)   (b)   (c)

Fig. 2 Using a newton meter

12 **a** What is the weight of each of the lumps of plasticine shown in Figure 2?

b What is the mass of each of the lumps of plasticine, assuming that the gravitational field strength is 10 N/kg?

Fig. 3 The 3100 carat Cullinan diamond
This is the largest diamond ever found

13 The mass of gems is measured in **carats**.
1 carat ≡ 0.2 g.

a What is the mass in grams of the Cullinan diamond shown in Figure 3?

b What is the mass of the most expensive gem in the world, the 43 carat Terestchenko blue diamond, sold in 1984 for U.S. $4 580 000?

c What is the weight of each of these diamonds?

14 Why is it unwise to step off a small boat before first tying it to the jetty? (State and explain what is likely to happen.)

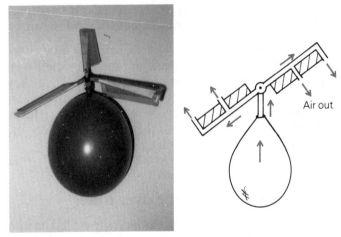

Fig. 4 A toy that makes use of the air from a balloon
How does it work?

15 Figure 4 shows a toy that uses a propeller. The balloon forces air to travel up the central pipe and out through the trailing edge of each propeller blade.
Why does this cause the propeller to turn?
Why does the rotating propeller lift the toy into the air?

2 SPEED AND VELOCITY

2.1   How fast?

Is that car speeding?

Fig. 1   Keeping our roads safe
Cars should not travel faster than 70 mph on a British motorway. What speed is this in (i) km/h? (ii) m/s?

How do motorway police check that a car is speeding? **Think about this for a minute before reading on.**

What the police do is to follow the car for a mile or so. They drive at the same speed and measure their own speed using the police car's speedometer. Then they check their speedometer to make sure that it is accurate. To do this, they drive the car at a steady 60 mph from one milepost to the next. If this takes one minute, then their speedometer is correct.

Speed equals distance over time

'Miles per hour' actually means 'miles travelled *divided by* hours taken. In general,

$$\text{speed} = \frac{\text{distance}}{\text{time}} \tag{1}$$

In our case,

$$\text{speed} = \frac{1 \text{ mile}}{1 \text{ minute}} = \frac{60 \text{ miles}}{60 \text{ minutes}} = 60 \text{ mph}$$

SI units

Feet, miles, minutes, hours and seconds—why do we have all these units? Why not just have one unit for distance and another for time?

Most scientists do use only one unit for distance and one for time. They have decided to use only SI (Système International) units—metres, kilograms and seconds (Figure 2). Other SI units like the newton are based on these three units. So from now on *in all calculations* we will use only

> **metres** for distance
> **seconds** for time
> **metres per second** for speed
> **kilograms** for mass
> **newtons** for force
> etc.

The advantage of this is that the *result* of the calculation will also be in these SI units. So when you've calculated your result, you can just write down the appropriate unit.

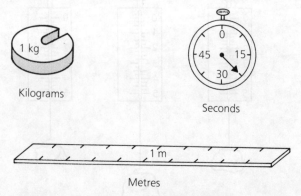

Kilograms

Seconds

Metres

Fig. 2   The basic SI units: metre, kilogram and second
The gram is also an SI unit, but in calculations we write it as 0.001 kg. Why?

When you are *not* carrying out calculations, you can also use units such as milliseconds, millimetres, kilonewtons and meganewtons. (You will find some other prefixes in Appendix 1.) You will have noticed that the basic SI unit for mass—the kilogram—already uses the prefix 'kilo'. If you wish, you can show

14

measurements and results in grams, but for calculations you must use kilograms.

In calculations, we write 1 km as 1000 m, 1 mm as 0.001 m, 1 g as 0.001 kg, 1 MN as 1 000 000 N etc.

Speeds in m/s

One mile is 1625 metres. One minute is 60 seconds. So in SI units one mile per minute is

$$\text{speed} = \frac{\text{distance}}{\text{time}} = \frac{1625\,\text{m}}{60\,\text{s}} = 27\,\text{m/s}$$

On a normal road, a car that is travelling faster than 27 m/s is speeding. Figure 3 shows some more examples of approximate speeds in m/s. **Can you add to the list?**

Fig. 3 Examples of approximate speeds in m/s

Walking speed	= 1 m/s
Running speed	= 4 m/s
Cycling speed	= 10 m/s
Speed of a fast train	= 50 m/s
Speed of most jet aircraft	= 230 m/s
Speed of sound	= 330 m/s
Speed of Concorde at Mach 2*	= 660 m/s
Speed of lightning	= 130 000 000 m/s
Speed of light	= 300 000 000 m/s

* Mach 2 means '2 × speed of sound'

- **Next time you are on a motorway, check your speed by timing how long it takes to drive from the first warning of an exit to the exit itself. (This is usually a distance of one mile.)**

- **Try measuring your walking and running speed between two lamp-posts. Estimate the distance by pacing it out and then measuring the length of your pace.**

Inter-city 83s?

An inter-city 125 train takes 4 hours 45 minutes (17 000 seconds) to travel the 640 km (640 000 metres) from Edinburgh to London. Its speed from Edinburgh to London is therefore

$$\text{speed} = \frac{\text{distance}}{\text{time}} = \frac{640\,000\,\text{m}}{17\,000\,\text{s}} = 38\,\text{m/s}$$

Now 38 m/s is 83 mph. So the train only goes at 83 mph! But British Rail call it the inter-city 125 because it goes at 125 mph (Figure 4)! How can this be explained?

Fig. 4 An inter-city 83?
A typical inter-city 125 train has an average speed of 83 mph. Yet it is said to travel at 125 mph. What is the explanation?

The answer is that we have calculated the **average speed** from Edinburgh to London.

$$\text{average speed} = \frac{\text{total distance travelled}}{\text{total time taken}} \qquad (2)$$

For parts of the journey, the train is travelling at its top speed of 125 mph. At other times, it is travelling more slowly or standing at a station.

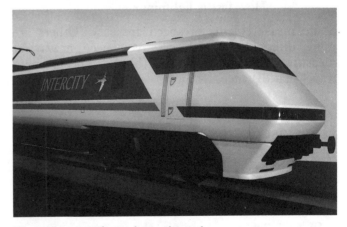

Fig. 5 The new Electra inter-city train

- **The new Electra trains being introduced by British Rail have a top speed of 225 km/h (Figure 5). What is this speed in m/s? If their average speed over a journey of 300 km is 40 m/s, how long will the journey take?**

2.2 Measuring speed

How fast?

Fig. 1 Polevaulting
Which were the fastest moving parts of this man's body?
How do you know?

> How fast do you walk?
> How fast is the stream flowing?
> How fast does your cat move?
> How fast is lightning?

Some measurements of speed are easy. Others are more difficult. In each case you need a way of measuring (a) a distance and (b) the time taken to travel that distance.

How fast do you walk? Simple estimates of speed

You can estimate your walking speed by using your body as a measuring instrument. **Try this.**
1 **Pace out a distance and then measure the length of your pace.**
2 **Find the time it takes you to walk that distance by using your pulse. (Your pulse beats approximately once a second.)**

• **How could you measure the speed of water in a stream? Try out your method if you have access to a stream.**

How fast is a train?

On local lines you can use the fact that the rails are 18 m long, and time the interval between the clicks as the train goes over the gaps in the rails. On main lines, the rails are welded together but you can time yourself between mileposts (as with motorways).

Using a camera to find the speed of a cat

Figure 2 shows how you could use **stroboscopic photography** to measure the speed at which a cat moves. You open the shutter of a camera and operate a flash gun or flashing **stroboscope** several times a second. From the series of photographs, you can work out how far the cat has moved over the time interval between flashes. You can use this method to measure the speed of other objects—even the speed of a bullet fired from a gun!

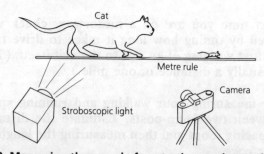

Fig. 2 Measuring the speed of a cat using stroboscopic photography
What would be a suitable number of flashes per second if the cat were (i) walking, (ii) chasing after a mouse?

Measuring speed using a ticker timer

A **ticker-timer** (Figure 3) is a device which is used to measure speed in the school laboratory. It makes a dot or tick on a strip of tape every 0.2 seconds (50 dots per second). One end of the tape is attached to the moving object. The rest of the tape is pulled through the timer.

To work out the time taken by the object in seconds, all you have to do is to count the number of dots on the tape and divide by 50.

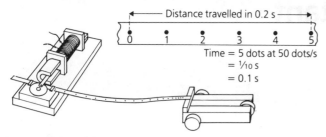

Fig. 3 A ticker-timer
At what speed was the trolley moving to make this trace of dots? (The ticker-tape is drawn full size.)

To find the distance travelled by the object in this time, you measure the distance between the first and the last dot. (Usually there is a mess at the start of the tape, so measure the time and distance from, say, the tenth dot.)

Suppose, for example, that the distance between the tenth dot and the thirtieth dot is 80 cm (or 0.8 m). The time interval between these dots is

$$20 \text{ dots} \equiv \frac{20}{50} \text{ seconds} \equiv 0.4 \text{ seconds}$$

The speed of the object is therefore:

$$\text{speed} = \frac{\text{distance travelled}}{\text{time taken}} = \frac{0.8 \text{ m}}{0.4 \text{ s}} = 2 \text{ m/s}$$

- **If you have a ticker-timer, use it to measure the speed of a trolley moving down a ramp. Try to adjust the angle of the ramp so that the trolley rolls down at constant speed. How can you tell from the ticker-tape when the speed is constant?**

Fig. 4 Examples of electronic timers
You may be wearing another type of electronic timer, though you will not be able to plug wires into it. What is its usual name?

Using a computer or an electronic timer

Figure 4 shows three examples of electronic timers: a VELA, a scaler timer, and a BBC microcomputer. Figure 5 shows some of the ways in which a moving object can operate the timer automatically by switching a current on or off.

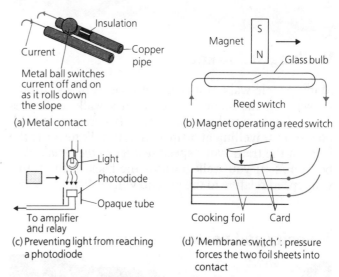

(a) Metal contact

(b) Magnet operating a reed switch

(c) Preventing light from reaching a photodiode

(d) 'Membrane switch': pressure forces the two foil sheets into contact

Fig. 5 Examples of electrical switches for use with electronic timers

Other methods of measuring speed

Radar speed checks measure the change in the frequency of radar signals reflected from a moving vehicle. This change depends on the speed of the vehicle. Radar installations at airports also use this method.

In car speedometers, a magnet is caused to rotate by a cable connected to the wheels. This moves a pointer across the dial (Figure 6).

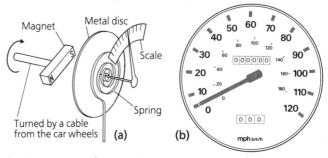

Fig. 6 A car speedometer
The top speed on many speedometers is 110 mph. What is this in (i) km/h? (ii) m/s?

Both these methods are less complicated than they sound but they are, nevertheless, beyond the scope of this book.

17

Direction is important

Walking at 200 km/h

Many people walk at a speed of about 1 m/s (2 mph). In walking races, people sometimes walk as fast as 4 m/s. Imagine walking at 50 m/s. It's easy! Just walk on a train travelling at 50 m/s. If you walk towards the front of the train, your speed *relative to the ground* will be 51 m/s. If you walk towards the back of the train, your speed relative to the ground will be 49 m/s. **Why?**

Velocity and vector diagrams

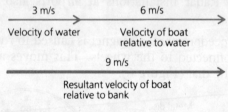

(b) Boat going downstream

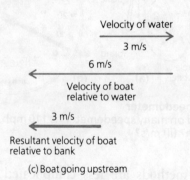

(c) Boat going upstream

Fig. 1 Vector diagrams for river barges

Figure 1 shows a similar situation: barges going up and down a fast-flowing river. The lines with arrows represent the speed and direction of the barges. The lines are drawn in the direction of motion. The lengths of the lines represent the speeds at which the barges are travelling. For example, the line representing a speed of 6 m/s is 6 cm long. We say that the lines and their arrows represent the **velocity** of the barges.

> Velocity is speed in a particular direction.

Note: Constant velocity means constant speed *and* constant direction. The Moon is travelling at constant speed but *not* at constant velocity. **Why not?**

The lines in Figures 1(b) and 1(c) are called **vectors**. The diagrams themselves are called **vector diagrams**.

- **Draw a vector diagram for someone walking at a speed of 1 m/s towards the back of a train travelling at 10 m/s.**

Crossing the river

Fig. 2 Crossing the river
This ferry is crossing the river at right-angles, from one bank to the other. Why are the bows pointing at an angle up the river?

Figure 2 shows the car ferry which crosses the River Rhine near the Lorelei. This is a particularly dangerous stretch of the river. Ships have often run aground on the rocks and been wrecked. (If you have studied

German, you will probably know the song about the beautiful river goddess called the Lorelei who lured sailors on to these rocks.)

The landing stage is directly across the river, but there is a current of about 3 m/s. The crew (and passengers!) don't want to get carried downstream away from the landing stage. **How can this be avoided? Think about this for a moment before reading on.** To stay on a straight line across the river, the ferry will have to travel upstream at the same rate as the current is flowing downstream. So the pilot must point the ferry at an angle upstream.

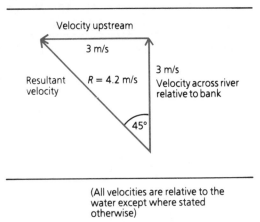

(All velocities are relative to the water except where stated otherwise)

Fig. 3 Vector diagram for the ferry in Figure 2
What is the velocity of the ferry relative to the water?

This part of the river is very busy with lots of barges travelling up and down. To cross safely between these barges, the ferry must travel at a velocity of 3 m/s relative to the bank. But the pilot needs to know what velocity the ferry must have *relative to the water*. To work this out, he must add the velocity of the ferry across the river to its velocity upstream (Figure 3). The **resultant velocity** (labelled R in the diagram) tells the pilot what speed the ferry needs, and the direction in which it must point. Figure 3 shows that this velocity is 4.2 m/s at an angle of 45° to the bank.

● **What would this velocity have to be if the river flowed at 4 m/s?**

Displacement

Figure 4 is a vector diagram for another situation: a girl's journey to school. In this case, the vectors (the lines with arrows) represent **displacements**.

Displacement is distance in a particular direction.

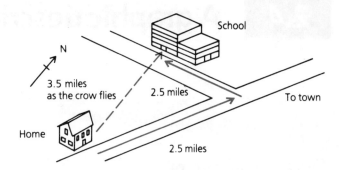

Fig. 4 Distance or displacement?
What distance does the girl travel from home to school:
(i) as the crow flies (in a straight line)?
(ii) by road?
What is the resulting displacement of the girl going from home to school?

Just as

$$\text{speed} = \frac{\text{distance travelled}}{\text{time taken}}$$

so

$$\text{velocity} = \frac{\text{displacement}}{\text{time taken}}$$

Figure 4 shows that, whereas the girl walks 5 miles to school, her resultant displacement is only 3 miles due north.

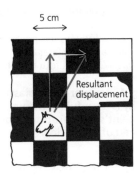

Fig. 5 The knight's move

● **Figure 5 shows one of the more complicated moves in a game of chess. The knight moves two squares forwards and one square sideways. If, on moving once, the knight travels 5 cm, what is (a) the total distance moved, (b) the resultant displacement?**

Displacement, velocity and other quantities that have magnitude (size) *and* direction are called **vector quantities**. We will look at vectors again in Section 4.4.

The need for a graph

'This patient doesn't look very happy, nurse.'

'No, doctor. He says his mouth's sore, and he's having difficulty eating and breathing.'

'How's his temperature doing?'

'Well, I took his temperature at 6 o'clock and it was 37.1 °C. I took it a minute later and it was 37.0 °C. At three minutes past six it was 37.1 °C. At four minutes past six . . .'

Fig. 1 An over-enthusiastic nurse
Why is it useful for a doctor to see a graph of his or her patient's temperature? How do doctors get an idea of the speed of blood flow?

This nurse was rather too enthusiastic! The doctor didn't really want a long list of times and temperatures. What she needed was a temperature–time graph which would show the general trend.

It's the same with motion—a graph makes things much clearer.

Displacement–time graphs

Figure 2 gives the times and positions of a piston moving inside the engine of a car. Figure 3 shows the same thing in graphical form.

Fig. 2 Displacement of the piston from the bottom of the cylinder towards the top of the cylinder

Time (ms)	0	3	6	9	12	15	18	21	24	27	30
Displacement (mm)	0	2	7	13	18	20	18	13	7	2	0

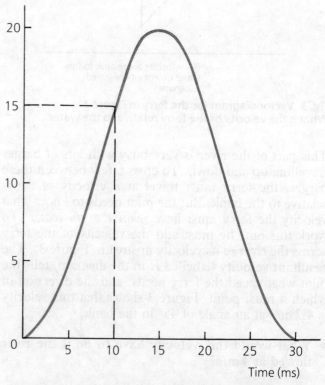

Fig. 3 Displacement–time graph for the data in Figure 2
How far does the piston move up the cylinder?
How long does it take to move from one end to the other?

The graph is much easier to understand. It shows that the piston moves up and down every 30 milliseconds. It also shows that the motion is smooth, not jerky. The piston slows and pauses for a millisecond or so at the top of the cylinder (the position which car mechanics call 'top dead centre'). From the graph we can also see that after 10 milliseconds, for example, the piston has moved through a displacement of 15 mm. (The dotted lines in Figure 3 show you how you can read this off from the graph.) You cannot tell any of this just by looking at the table.

The fact that the lines on the graph in Figure 3 are curved shows that the piston speeds up and slows down gradually. Figure 4 is a displacement–time graph for a lift. The time taken for the lift to speed up and slow down is too short to be shown on the graph. All that we have are the straight-line sections where the lift is moving up or down, and the sections where it is waiting at one of the floors.

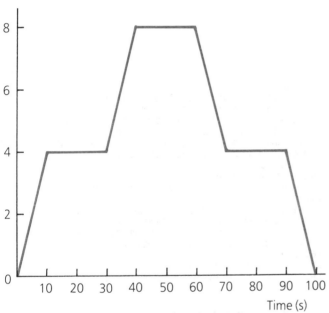

Displacement (m)

Time (s)

Fig. 4 The graph for a lift
How long does the lift wait at each floor?
Can you draw the corresponding graph for a lift in a three-storey building?

Drawing graphs

There are a few things to notice about these graphs which are true of all graphs used in physics:

1 Since they are **displacement–time graphs**, 'displacement' is measured up the page, on the **vertical axis**. 'Time' is measured across the page, on the **horizontal axis**. A **time–displacement** graph would be the other way round, with 'time' on the vertical axis.

2 Both axes are clearly labelled.

3 The units for each quantity are shown in brackets on each axis (e.g. 'Time (ms)').

- **Time yourself over measured distances on a short walk. This should include climbing up stairs or climbing a hill so that your speed changes. Draw the distance–time graph for this walk. (The reason why it will be a distance–time graph rather than a velocity–time graph is that you will not be going in a constant direction: velocity is speed in a particular direction.)**

Chart recorders

Fig. 5 A chart recorder
What is it used for?
Which is the direction of the 'time' axis?

Most research laboratories and large factories use chart recorders to keep a constant check on how things are changing with time (Figure 5).

For example, changes in temperature and pressure can be recorded by the movement of a pen across a sheet of paper. The paper is moved steadily through the recorder, and the pen draws a graph.

The chart recorder is actually producing a displacement–time graph of the movement of the pen. The paper passes under the pen at constant speed and so provides the 'time' axis (as with ticker-tape).

By noting the temperature, pressure etc. needed to move the pen through a certain distance, we can read the displacement–time graph as a temperature–time graph or a pressure–time graph.

21

2.5 Molecules in motion

A surprising discovery

Fig. 1 Bees carry pollen
How else can pollen move from flower to flower?

How many things around us are moving? People. Cars. Bees. The pollen grains in the air that give us hay fever.

The movement of pollen is different from that of bees. Pollen doesn't have wings. It can't move on its own. Or so we believe.

The Scottish botanist Robert Brown also believed this until, one day in 1827, he looked at some very small pollen grains under a very powerful microscope. The pollen grains were suspended in water. The water was quite still but, to Brown's amazement, the pollen grains were jigging about all over the place. How could this be? What was moving them?

- Figure 2(a) shows the type of motion which Brown saw down the microscope. Figure 2(b) is a program for the BBC computer that can draw this sort of motion on the screen. Try using this program, and changing the time and distance for each movement.

Brown couldn't see how anything could be moving the pollen grains. He assumed that they must be alive. **Can you think of any other explanation?**

Maxwell's molecular motion

Thirty years after Brown's discovery, the physicist James Clerk Maxwell explained the motion of the pollen grains in terms of molecules. Maxwell argued

(a)

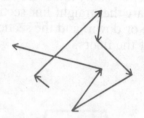

(b)

```
 10 CLS
 20 INPUT'''"DISTANCE (1 TO 10)",D
 30 INPUT'''"TIME (1 TO 10)",T
 40 INPUT'''"DO YOU WANT TRACES (Y/N)",TR$
 50 IF TR$="Y" THEN K=1 ELSE K=0
 60 PRINT'''"HOLD SPACEBAR DOWN TO FINISH PLOTTING"
 70 TIME=0:REPEAT UNTIL TIME>100
 80 MODE 1
 90 PLOT 4,650,500
100 X=RND(40*D)-20*D:Y=RND(40*D)-20*D
110 PLOT K,X,Y
120 PLOT 1,5,0:PLOT 1,0,5:PLOT 1,-5,-5
130 TIME=0:REPEAT UNTIL TIME>10*T
140 PLOT 3,5,0:PLOT 3,0,5:PLOT 3,-5,-5
150 IF INKEY(-99)=0 THEN GOTO 100
160 MODE 7
170 INPUT'''"AGAIN (Y/N)",A$
180 IF A$="Y" THEN GOTO 10 ELSE END
```

Fig. 2 Brownian motion
(a) If all the lines were of equal length, would this mean that the pollen grain was moving at constant velocity, constant speed or neither?
(b) A program for the BBC computer to show Brownian motion. This computer uses the **random number generator** RND in line 100. What is a random number?
Why is Brownian motion sometimes called random motion?

that everything is made up of tiny particles which are far too small to be seen, even with the best microscope.

These **molecules** (from the Latin 'moles', meaning mass) are constantly moving. In a gas, they are far apart, and are moving at very high speeds. In a liquid, they are moving more slowly over each other. In a solid, they are just vibrating.

Maxwell said that the molecules of the water were bumping into the much larger pollen grains and causing them to move.

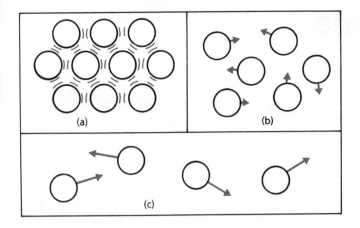

Fig. 3 Solids, liquids and gases
(a) In a solid, the molecules are held together by **bonding forces**, and merely vibrate.
(b) In a liquid, the molecules move over each other.
(c) In a gas, the molecules are far apart, and fly around at high speeds.

Figure 4(a) shows a similar situation in which tiny, moving ball-bearings (like the water molecules) are moving much larger polystyrene balls (like the pollen grains).

Figure 4(b) shows an easier way of seeing real Brownian motion. In this case, smoke particles are being moved by air molecules.

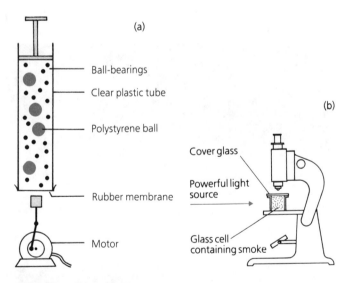

Fig. 4 Showing Brownian motion
(a) A Brownian motion simulator
The motor causes the piston to vibrate the rubber membrane. This causes the ball-bearings (the molecules) to move about the tube. These in turn move the larger polystyrene (pollen) balls.
(b) A smoke cell
Smoke from a burning straw is collected in a glass cell and viewed through a microscope. The smoke particles show up as rapidly moving white specks.

Diffusion

When a drop of ink is put into water, the coloured pigment slowly **diffuses** to all parts of the water. **Try this.** When a crystal of potassium permanganate dissolves in water, the coloured liquid doesn't stay around the crystal but eventually diffuses throughout the water. **Try this.**

You can show what is happening by half-filling a large jar with white polystyrene balls, and then adding a few balls that are painted red. These balls act like the water and permanganate molecules. **What happens when you make them move (by shaking the jar)?**

When someone lights a joss-stick or operates an air-freshener spray, at first only the people nearby smell it. Then, as time goes on, people further and further away can smell it. The molecules carrying the smell take time to diffuse through the normal air molecules. **Try this.**

Fig. 5 Diffusing incense

Diffusion in our bodies and in industry

Oxygen in our lungs diffuses first into our blood and then from our blood into our muscles. Waste products from the cells in our bodies diffuse into our blood and from there into our kidneys.

Diffusion is used in industry too. In the heat treatment of steels, carbon is made to diffuse through the metal. As we shall see in Chapter 19, electronic integrated circuits (microchips) are made by diffusing different chemicals into silicon.

These processes are possible only because solids, liquids and gases are made up of moving molecules.

23

It's the natural state

Galileo *versus* Aristotle

Does everything move? Not according to Aristotle. He said that nothing moves unless it is continually pushed. He said that a ball dropped from a galloping horse would fall vertically to the ground. Do you care what Aristotle said—or who he was, come to that?

Fig. 1 A simple device that changed history
What did Galileo see through his telescope that made him question commonly accepted views?

You are lucky! Had you been studying in Europe a few hundred years ago, you would have heard little else but 'Aristotle said this' and 'Aristotle said that'. Nobody knew much about Aristotle himself, other than that he'd lived in Greece around 350 BC and had written a lot of books. However, in many parts of Europe, his views on many things were the official views. You didn't disagree with Aristotle or you were in trouble.

Galileo was one person who did disagree with what Aristotle had said. He was a brilliant Italian scholar who, around 1600, made one of the first telescopes (Figure 1). When Galileo looked through his telescope, he saw many things that—according to Aristotle—should not happen. He saw that the moons of Jupiter were moving (Figure 2). (Aristotle had said that they couldn't move.) He saw the phases of Venus, showing that Venus was circling round the Sun. (Official view: Venus doesn't move.) He saw, through the movement of sunspots, the rotation of the Sun itself. (Impossible! Dangerous lies!)

Fig. 2 Jupiter and one of its moons
Why does this moon go round Jupiter rather than on its own round the Sun?
What keeps it moving?

Galileo suggested that *motion is the natural state*. He suggested that the Earth itself is moving.

That clinched it! The authorities (at that time, the Pope and the Inquisition) forced Galileo to say that he was mistaken. His books were banned, and he was placed under house arrest for the rest of his life.

It wasn't quite as simple as that (see the section on Physics and faith). But, even today, new ideas based on observation and measurement sometimes clash with the official, traditional, common-sense view of the world. **Can you think of any examples?**

Fig. 3 Is motion the natural state?
If so, why do so many things slow down and stop?

Newton's first law of motion

Newton agreed with Galileo that motion is the natural state. He argued that, although most things slow down in practice, this is only because forces like friction and air resistance are acting on them.

If it wasn't for these forces, things that were moving to start with would continue to move at constant velocity (at constant speed in a straight line). Things that were stationary to start with would, of course, remain stationary if no force acted on them.

In the words of Newton's first law of motion:

> Every object continues in its state of rest or constant velocity unless acted on by a resultant force.

- **Push some model cars along and let them go. Why do some move further than others? Push a model boat gently in some water. What happens when you let go? Why does an *air track* (Figure 4) allow the rider to keep moving for so long?**

- **Spin a raw egg and a hard-boiled egg. Stop them for an instant and let them go again. Try to explain the difference in the behaviour of the eggs.**

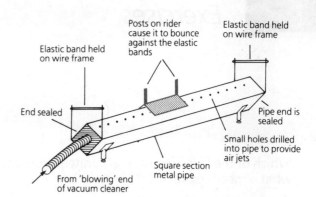

Fig. 4 Floating on air

Moving for ever

In space, there is no air and therefore no air resistance. Things like the Moon and space rockets can keep moving for ever with no force pushing them. (Space vehicles leaving the Earth's atmosphere turn off their engines and drift to where they want to go (Figure 5). They only use rockets again to guide them to the right spot, and to slow them down.)

Fig. 5 The Pioneer 10 interplanetary space probe
This probe was sent deep into space in 1973. Will it ever stop? Why?

At the other extreme, molecules have nothing between them to slow them down. They will keep on moving for ever.

The idea that movement is the natural state of affairs is now one of the basic ideas of physics.

- **Imagine what would happen if Newton turned out to be wrong, if *everything* slowed down when there was no force to keep it moving. What would eventually happen to the things around us?**

Exercises

1 Which of the following most accurately describes
   what is meant by velocity?

   A Displacement per unit time

   B Speed

   C Distance travelled in one second

   D Distance in a particular direction

   E Maximum speed

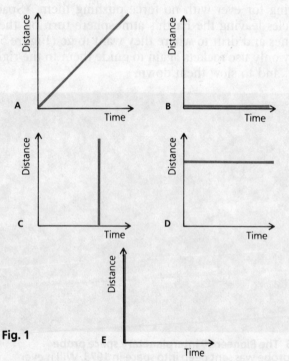

Fig. 1

2 Which of the graphs shown in Figure 1 describes
   an object travelling with a constant, positive
   velocity.

   A   **B**   **C**   **D**   **E**

3 Which of the following is *not* a basic SI unit?

   A Metre

   B Kilogram

   C Second

   D Gram

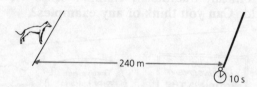

Fig. 2

4 A greyhound can run 240 metres in 10 seconds
   (Figure 2). What is its average speed?

   A 0.24 m/s

   B 2.4 m/s

   C 24 m/s

   D 240 m/s

   E 2400 m/s

5 When brightly lit smoke is viewed through a
   microscope, bright specks are seen moving
   about. These are

   A Particles of smoke moving on their own
        because they are hot

   B Molecules of air moving about

   C Pollen grains

   D Light passing between the smoke particles

   E Particles of smoke that are moved by
        molecules of air

6 On a train travelling at 30 m/s, a passenger walks
   back to the buffet car at 1 m/s relative to the
   train. The passenger then returns forward to his
   seat at 1 m/s relative to the train. What is his
   average velocity relative to the ground?

   A 30 m/s

   B 1 m/s

   C −1 m/s

   D 0 m/s

   E 30.5 m/s

7 The basic SI units for mass, length and time are the _____, the _____ and the _____.

8 Complete these sentences:

    a Speed means _____ per unit time.

    b Velocity means _____ per unit time.

    c The SI unit for speed is _____.

    d The SI unit for velocity is _____.

9 Another gas is added to natural gas to give it a smell. This makes it easier to detect leaks. Only a small quantity of this gas is added, yet it is soon smelt over a wide area when there is a leak. Explain this in terms of molecules.

10 Sharks can smell blood a long way away. If there were a wounded animal on the water surface, which would smell the blood first: a shark in the water or a bloodhound the same distance away but on a boat. Why? (Explain your answer in terms of molecules.)

Fig. 3

11 The sign in Figure 3 shows the distance to the police station. How long would it take you to reach it if you were cycling at 6 m/s?

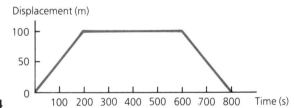

Fig. 4

12 Figure 4 shows the displacement–time graph for a ferry crossing a river.

    a How wide is the river?

    b How long does the ferry take to cross?

    c How long does the ferry wait on the far bank?

    d What is the average speed at which it returns (relative to the bank)?

Fig. 5

13 The speed limit sign shown in Figure 5 was photographed in Europe.

    a What is wrong with the unit of measurement?

    b What is this speed limit in SI units?

14 The **air speed** (the speed relative to the air) of an aircraft is 150 m/s. The plane is pointing due north. However, there is a 50 m/s wind blowing from the west. Draw a diagram to find the resultant velocity of the aircraft relative to the ground.

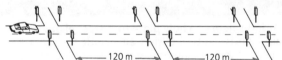

Fig. 6

15 A road has three sets of traffic lights 120 m apart (Figure 6). They are to change to green in turn, so that a car travelling at 12 m/s (just under 30 mph) reaches each light just as it switches to green. (This will discourage traffic from going faster than 30 mph on this road.) What should the time interval be between one set of lights changing to green and the next set changing to green?

16 Briefly describe how you would measure the speed of each of the following (use a different method in each case):

    a a model train

    b a caterpillar (without upsetting it)

    c a bird in flight

17 A boat on a river has to struggle to move upstream but can travel easily downstream. A river is like a moving train. However, it's just as easy to walk to the back of a train as it is to walk to the front. Explain this apparent contradiction.

18 The morning Concorde flight from London to New York takes off at 10.30 am and arrives at 9.20 am the same day. In other words, it arrives more than an hour before it sets off, even though it takes several hours to make the journey! Explain this apparent contradiction.

Physics and faith

Fig. 1 Jerusalem — a holy place for three religions
Judaism, Christianity and Islam all include the idea of progress, of things changing and needing to change. What effect has this had on the growth of science?

Science and religion

In the days before modern science, people who couldn't understand the way things worked used to say 'God did it!' When someone was struck by lightning, this was called an act of God. Today, we use science to explain lightning, and to protect people from it using lightning conductors. Few present-day scientific books and articles make any mention of God.

The Bible talks about the world being created in six days. But modern scientific discoveries suggest that the world has been around for thousands of millions of years. Does this (and other examples like it) mean that science has replaced religion, and that religious beliefs are outdated?

Some scientists feel that science *has* disproved religion, but many others do not. In fact, many scientists have strong religious beliefs, and see no conflict between their science and their religion. Scientists are no different from other people — many are religious and many are not.

How and why

How do scientists reconcile their scientific knowledge with their religious beliefs? One way is to say that science is concerned with *how* things happen, whereas religion is concerned with *why* things happen.

Science can show us

- how the universe has developed from the first big bang
- how our muscles and brains work
- how to make machinery and computers to help us in our work
- how disease and famine occur and how we can help to overcome them
- how to make weapons to fight each other and to defend ourselves.

In general, science asks the question 'How?' We use science to explain *how* things happen. Sometimes science appears to ask the question 'Why?', but this is really the question 'How?' in disguise. For example, the question 'Why does a gas expand when it is heated?' is the same question as 'How does heating a gas cause it to expand?'.

Science cannot show us 'why' in the sense of 'What is the point of it all?'. Science cannot give us a reason for living, a reason for helping others, or a reason for doing most of the things we do (including carrying out scientific research). Only our religious, or non-religious, beliefs can do this. These questions are very important to many scientists, but you will not find them in any scientific book or article.

Galileo versus the church?

Some disagreements which at first appear to be clashes between science and religion aren't quite what they seem. For example, Galileo's dispute with the Pope (see Section 2.6) had more to do with politics than with religion. In fact, the Pope at first welcomed Galileo's discoveries. It was Galileo's colleagues, the university professors, who ridiculed him. They disliked Galileo because his teachings were in conflict with the accepted science of the time.

The main reason why Galileo ran into trouble with the Pope was because he didn't understand politics. The

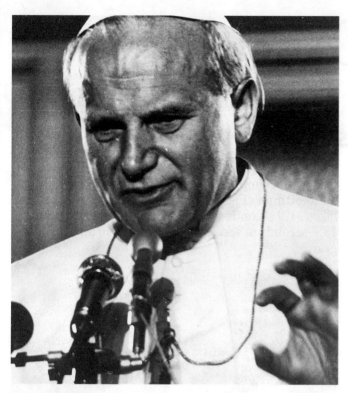

Fig. 2 Science and the papacy
What was the background to Pope Urban VIII's quarrel with Galileo?
Try to find out what Pope John Paul II has said about the responsibility of scientists.

Pope had been Galileo's friend. But Galileo wrote his book in such a way that he played into the hands of the Pope's political enemies. It was this, and not a conflict between science and religion, that turned the Pope against him.

- **Read more about this, for example the article by Lerner and Gosselin in the *Scientific American*, November 1986, pp.116–123.**

Links between science and religion

Modern science started with people's belief in God. The early scientists believed that God had created an orderly universe and that they could 'think God's thoughts after him'. Robert Boyle (who discovered the gas laws) said that the orderliness of nature proved the existence of God. Sir Isaac Newton also held this view, and some people still use this argument today.

Few scientists now refer to religion in the course of their research, but religion does still affect the work of many scientists. An interesting example is the use of Buddhist philosophy by some scientists in an effort to make sense of some of the curious discoveries of modern physics.

The discoveries of modern physics have made other religious scientists re-think what sort of a God they believe in. In the nineteenth century, most scientists believed in a God who had made the world and then left it to run (perhaps occasionally intervening with miracles). Nineteenth-century physics supported this view, but twentieth-century physics has made many religious scientists reject this idea of God. Instead, they believe that God is behind everything, constantly running the universe. The laws of science merely describe what God is doing.

A useful partnership

Fig. 3 Science and religion working together to help people

Science can solve many problems. Some uses of science (like healing and feeding people) are obviously good. Others (like military science and genetic engineering) can be used for good or evil. Our beliefs (religious or non-religious) help us to decide what it is right to investigate and develop, and what it is not.

Science helps us to see what *can* be done. Our faith (religious or otherwise) tells us what *should* be done.

3 ACCELERATION

3.1 Speeding up and slowing down

Stopping buses

Fig. 1 Buses stopping and starting
What would happen to the passengers if the deceleration was too large? Why?

City buses are always stopping and starting (Figure 1). No sooner have they speeded up from one bus stop than they are slowing down again for the next.

In physics, speeding up is called **accelerating**. Slowing down is called **decelerating**. A bus accelerates away from one bus stop and decelerates as it reaches the next stop.

In aircraft and in powerful cars, you can feel the acceleration caused by the powerful engines. You can also feel the deceleration produced by the powerful brakes.

Acceleration in m/s²

Acceleration is a measure of how rapidly things increase their velocity. Car brochures state the number of seconds it takes for the car to get from 0 to 60 mph, or to go from 30 to 50 mph in fourth gear. For example, a Rover 800 takes 7.8 seconds to accelerate

from 0 to 60 mph, and 8.3 seconds to accelerate from 30 to 50 mph (Figure 2). In contrast, an Austin Mini takes 21.9 seconds to accelerate from 0 to 60 mph, and 13.7 seconds to accelerate from 30 to 50 mph in fourth gear.

Fig. 2 8.3 seconds from 30 mph to 50 mph
What is this acceleration in m/s²?

Scientists and engineers prefer a different way of stating acceleration. They use the following definition:

$$\text{acceleration} = \frac{\text{gain in velocity}}{\text{time}}$$
$$= \frac{\text{new velocity} - \text{old velocity}}{\text{time}}$$

(1)

Since velocity (and therefore gain in velocity) is measured in metres per second and time is measured in seconds, the SI unit for acceleration is metres per second per second, or m/s².

- Acceleration, like velocity, is a vector quantity: the direction is important.
- If the acceleration is not constant, then Equation (1) gives the *average* acceleration. In practice, a car's acceleration is far from being constant (Figure 3).

30

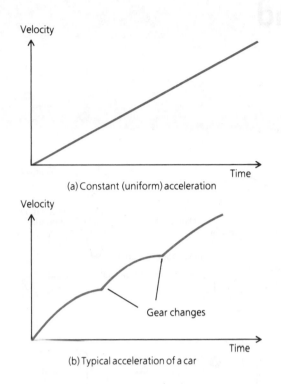

(a) Constant (uniform) acceleration

(b) Typical acceleration of a car

Gear changes

Fig. 3 Cars don't have constant acceleration
When you talk about the acceleration of a car, you are talking about the *average* acceleration.

Calculating the acceleration

Consider, for example, a Rover 800 accelerating from 0 to 60 mph (0 to 27 m/s) in 7.8 seconds:

$$\text{acceleration} = \frac{(27\,\text{m/s} - 0\,\text{m/s})}{7.8\,\text{s}}$$

$$= 3.5\,\text{m/s}^2$$

⦿ **What is the corresponding acceleration of the Mini in m/s²? What is the acceleration of each of the cars from 30 to 50 mph in fourth gear? Why is the acceleration from 30 to 50 mph not the same as that from 0 to 60 mph?**

Measuring the acceleration

The velocity is measured at two different times (using any of the methods discussed in Section 2.2). All that is then needed is the time interval between the two measurements.

Figure 4 shows ticker-tape being used to measure the acceleration of a trolley. (The ticker-tape can also be used to produce a velocity–time graph—see Section 3.6.)

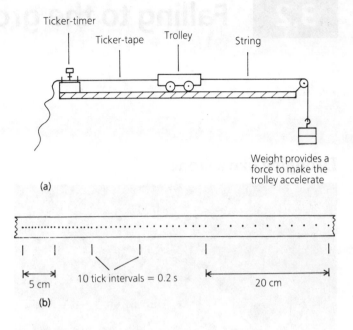

(a)

10 tick intervals = 0.2 s   5 cm   20 cm

(b)

Fig. 4 Using a ticker-timer to measure acceleration
(a) A typical experimental arrangement.
(b) The dot pattern on the ticker-tape. What is the acceleration?

Figure 5 shows an electrical method for measuring the acceleration of a metal ball.

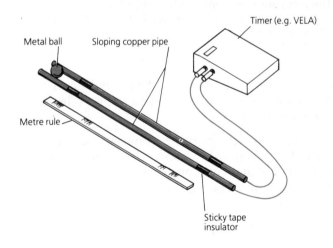

Fig. 5 Measuring the acceleration of a metal ball
The ball conducts electricity between the two copper pipes *except* when it is passing over the strips of tape. The acceleration can be found by measuring
   1 the lengths of tape
   2 the lengths of time for which current is *not* flowing and
   3 the time interval between these disconnections.
How?

● **Try using one of these methods to measure the acceleration of a cyclist.**

31

3.2 Falling to the ground

Dropping like a stone

Fig. 1 'Jump out of an aeroplane and make a lot of people very happy!'
This headline appeared in an advertisement for a sponsored parachute jump in aid of charity. What difference does a parachute make?

Suppose that you jumped out of an aeroplane without a parachute? You would drop 'like a stone'. What would this mean in practice?

As soon as you left the plane, you would start to travel vertically downwards. Your velocity would rapidly increase, but at a constant rate (at least to start with). You would accelerate downwards with **gravitational acceleration**.

Gravitational acceleration

Would your rate of acceleration depend on your mass? Do heavier things fall faster?

- **Try dropping steel balls of different masses and check how long they take to hit the ground. Figure 2 shows two possible ways of timing the fall. Do the balls fall with the same acceleration? How can you tell? Think of another accurate method of timing the fall.**

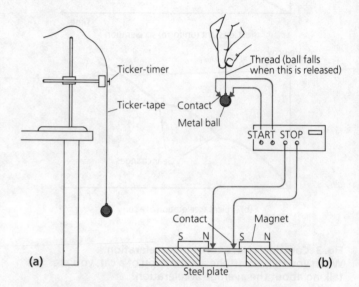

Fig. 2 Measuring gravitational acceleration by free fall
(a) Using a ticker-timer
(b) Using an electronic timer. (How does the ball switch the timer on and off?)
Which of these two methods is likely to be the most accurate? Why?
Try to design another method of timing.

Near the Earth's surface, *everything* starts to fall with the same acceleration: $10 \, \text{m/s}^2$. **Where have you come across the number 10 before in connection with gravity? As we shall see in Section 3.4, this is not just a coincidence.**

This gravitational acceleration varies very slightly from place to place depending on the rocks under the ground. Scientists looking for oil and minerals study these rocks by measuring variations in gravitational acceleration using very sensitive instruments.

Stones and feathers

As objects start to fall faster, the air resistance increases. The air resistance of feathers is greater than the air resistance of stones, so feathers fall more slowly than stones do. Galileo argued that if there were no air resistance everything would continue to fall with the same (gravitational) acceleration. **You can show this for yourself by dropping a stone and a feather in a clear plastic tube from which the air has been removed (Figure 3).**

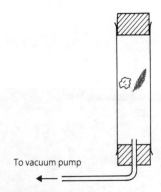

Fig. 3 Galileo's experiment
When the air is removed, the stone and the feather fall at the same rate. Does this mean that the gravitational force on each of them is the same?

Terminal velocity

If you were falling from an aircraft, the air resistance would increase as your speed increased. Eventually, the air resistance would prevent your speed from increasing any further. You would continue to fall downwards with constant **terminal velocity**. **Raindrops, hailstones and snowflakes all fall with terminal velocity. Which falls the slowest? Why?**

If you jumped out of an aircraft without a parachute, *you* would soon be terminated. Your terminal velocity as you hit the ground would be several hundred miles per hour! If you spread out your arms and legs, you would reach terminal velocity earlier. **Why?** You would not fall so fast. (Free-fall parachutists use this technique—mainly to stay stable in the air rather than toppling head over heels.) You would still need a parachute nearer the ground to make your terminal velocity slow enough for a safe landing.

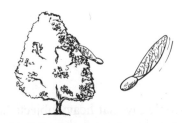

Fig. 4 Falling slowly to the ground
Why does the sycamore seed fall so slowly?
See if you can make a card and plasticine 'sycamore seed' that falls even more slowly.

- **Try making a model parachute using cloth and string, or paper and thread. Can you make one that will allow an egg dropped from a high window to fall to the ground without breaking?**

- **Drop some tiny ball-bearings into some glycerine. They reach terminal velocity very quickly. Why?**

'It matters not how far you go'

You may have seen cartoons where the cartoon character runs off the edge of a cliff. He keeps travelling horizontally for a while—then stops, looks down—and falls vertically at high speed.

In reality, it's a bit different. Your horizontal velocity has no effect at all on your vertical velocity. A coin thrown horizontally falls at the same rate as one dropped vertically. Figure 5 shows a method of launching two coins at the same time—one horizontally and the other vertically.

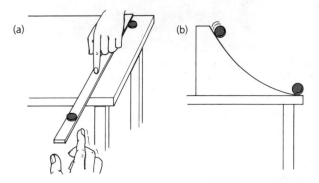

Fig. 5 Which coin or ball will reach the ground first?

When you throw an object, it falls to the ground in the same way as water falls from the end of a hose (Figure 6). All projectiles follow this **parabolic** curve: water from a hose, a bullet from a gun, a tennis ball, and even a person jumping out of an aircraft.

Fig. 6 Projectile motion

Stopping a supertanker—the importance of mass

Supertankers have right of way

Fig. 1 Supertankers have the right of way
Why is a supertanker so difficult to stop?

The rule used to be 'power boats give way to sail'. If you were sailing a yacht in the Channel, it was up to power boats to get out of your way. They could stop and turn more easily than you could. That rule has now been changed.

The captain of a supertanker is cruising up the Channel. He sees your boat less than a mile dead ahead. What should he do? Slam on the brakes? Put the engines into reverse? It's too late! The ship will not stop in time. A supertanker needs far more than a mile in which to stop, even with its powerful engines full astern. The rule is now 'power boats give way to sail, but both give way to supertankers'!

The importance of mass

The larger the mass is, the less acceleration you get for the same force. For example a supermarket trolley is more difficult to control (to start, stop and steer) when it's full of food (Figure 2).

Dragsters are racing cars with very high acceleration (Figure 3). They consist of little more than their exceptionally powerful engines. Their mass is as small as possible.

Fig. 2 Difficult to control
Why is a supermarket trolley so much more difficult to control when it is full of shopping?

Fig. 3 A drag racer
What steps have been taken in the design of this racing car to give it maximum acceleration?

What is a multi-stage rocket? Why are rockets designed in this way?

Inertia

Sometimes, people say that heavy objects have a lot of inertia, and that this is why they are so difficult to move. **Inertia** here is just another word for mass.

- **Inertia is the basis of many party tricks. One such trick is to pull a (low mass) tablecloth off a table,** leaving the (higher mass) dishes still in place. Rather than smashing the best crockery, use the similar but safer trick shown in Figure 4(a).

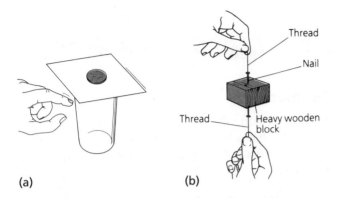

Fig. 4 Tricks that use inertia
(a) What happens when you flick the card? Why?
(b) Choosing which string to break.

- Figure 4(b) shows another trick. Ask your friends which string they want you to break. If they say 'the upper string', then pull *slowly* on the lower string. If they tell you to break the lower string, then pull *rapidly* on (jerk) the lower string. Why does this work?

Newton's second law of motion

Newton summed up these experiences in his second law of motion:

$$\boxed{\text{force} = \text{mass} \times \text{acceleration}}$$
or
$$F = ma \tag{1}$$

where F is force, m is mass and a is acceleration.

For example, we saw in Section 3.1 that the 945 kg Rover 800 has a maximum acceleration of 3.5 m/s². The maximum force of the engine is therefore

$$\begin{aligned} \text{force} &= \text{mass} \times \text{acceleration} \\ &= 945\,\text{kg} \times 3.5\,\text{m/s}^2 \\ &= 3300\,\text{N} \end{aligned}$$

- The *Globtik Tokyo* supertanker has a mass of 480 000 000 kg and engines that produce a force of just over 4 000 000 N (Figure 5). What is its maximum acceleration? How long will it take to reach a speed of 1 m/s—the speed at which a person can swim?

Fig. 5 One of the world's largest tankers
The *Globtik Tokyo*

- Describe how you could find the mass of a trolley just by pulling it with an elastic band. How would you keep the force constant, and how would you measure it? How would you compensate for friction so that you didn't have to apply a force just to keep the trolley moving? (See Sections 2.2 and 2.6.) How would you measure the acceleration? (See Section 3.1.)

Falling objects

If we ignore air resistance, then the only force on a falling object is its weight (the force due to gravity). Remember Equation (1):

$$\text{force} = \text{mass} \times \text{acceleration}$$
or
$$\text{acceleration} = \frac{\text{force}}{\text{mass}}$$

Then

$$\frac{\text{gravitational}}{\text{acceleration}} = \frac{\text{force}}{\text{mass}} = \frac{\text{weight}}{\text{mass}}$$

But
$$\text{weight} = \text{mass} \times \text{gravitational field strength}$$
So
$$\frac{\text{gravitational}}{\text{acceleration}} = \frac{\text{mass} \times \text{gravitational field strength}}{\text{mass}}$$

$$\boxed{\frac{\text{gravitational}}{\text{acceleration}} = \text{gravitational field strength} = 10\,\text{m/s}^2}$$

- How could you use this result to measure the gravitational field strength g? Try your method, if you can.

Bumping into things—the importance of momentum

Rubber bullets

Fig. 1 Even rubber bullets can kill
Why?

Simply throwing a rubber at someone—even a rubber bullet—will not do them much harm. But if rubber bullets are fired at short range from a gun, as they sometimes are in riots, they can seriously hurt or even kill people (Figure 1). It is the speed of the rubber bullets that makes them dangerous. (At short range, they have not been slowed down by air resistance.)

In contrast, molecules of air are hitting us millions of times a second at speeds very much greater than that of any rubber bullet. Yet these molecules do not hurt us at all. The reason for this is that molecules have a very tiny mass.

Momentum

When it is difficult to stop something from moving, we say that it has a lot of **momentum**. Moving objects are difficult to stop if they have a large mass and a high velocity:

$$\text{momentum} = \text{mass} \times \text{velocity} \qquad (1)$$

Note that momentum, like velocity, is a **vector** quantity. **What does this mean? See Section 2.3.**

To take an example, for a 5000 kg lorry travelling at 20 m/s,

$$\text{momentum} = 5000\,\text{kg} \times 20\,\text{m/s}$$
$$= 100\,000\,\text{kg m/s}$$

- **Find the momentum of**
  (a) a 100 g rubber bullet travelling at 100 m/s
  (b) a 1 kg cricket ball travelling at 10 m/s
  (Figure 2).

Fig. 2 Catching a cricket ball
How can you catch a ball so that you remove its momentum without it hurting you?

Conservation of momentum

Consider again the example of the lorry. If no force acts on the lorry, then it will continue to have a momentum of 100 000 kg m/s. Even if the lorry collides with a car then, provided that no other force is acting, the momentum will still be conserved (will not change). Suppose that the car has a mass of 1000 kg and that after the collision the car and the lorry are locked together. Their velocity immediately after the accident will be

$$\text{velocity} = \frac{\text{momentum}}{\text{mass}}$$

$$= \frac{100\,000\,\text{kg m/s}}{6000\,\text{kg}} = 17\,\text{m/s}$$

Fig. 3 Lots of momentum
Which is the most dangerous, a light lorry travelling at 60 mph or a lorry which is twice as heavy travelling at 40 mph?
Why?

Other examples of the conservation of momentum

You use the conservation of momentum when you hammer a nail into a wall. As you swing the head of the hammer, it gains a lot of momentum. When the hammer hits the nail, this momentum is transferred to the nail, and drives it into the wall.

Fig. 4 A pile-driver
This raises a heavy weight, and lets it fall on to the end of a pile or girder. Why does this force the pile or girder into the ground?

The conservation of momentum is also used at building sites when steel or concrete piles (vertical posts) are driven into the ground. A pile-driver is placed on top of the pile. Compressed air lifts a heavy hammer that forms part of the pile-driver. The hammer is then allowed to fall and hits the top of the pile. The momentum of the hammer is transferred to the pile, and drives it into the ground (Figure 4).

Tachographs and other velocity–time graphs

What is a tachograph?

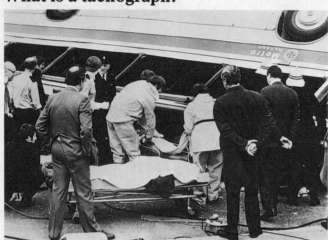

Fig. 1 Tachographs make such accidents less likely to occur Why?

A party of schoolchildren were on a school trip to France. The children were tired, but excited. They had been travelling since early morning, and now it was late evening. The driver was very tired. He was also driving far too fast—he was anxious to finish the journey and get to bed. Suddenly a car stopped unexpectedly ahead. The coach driver tried to brake and steer out of the way, but lost control. The children screamed as the coach veered off the road and crashed down the embankment.

Fortunately, such accidents are now rare. A device called a **tachograph** is now fitted to buses and lorries (Figure 2). It shows whether drivers have been driving too fast or for too long. Tachographs must already have prevented many accidents.

The tachograph consists of a speed–time graph (or a velocity–time graph if the direction is constant) drawn on a thin plastic disc. A clock makes the disc rotate at a slow, constant speed. If the vehicle is stationary, a pen resting on the disc draws a circle. As the vehicle starts to move, the pen moves outwards towards the edge of the disc. By measuring the distance of the ink mark from the centre of the disc, you can find out how fast the vehicle was travelling at any particular time.

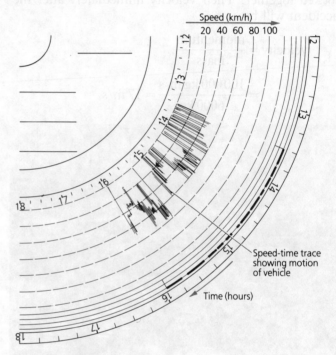

Fig. 2 A tachograph

- See if you can get hold of an old, used tachograph. Work out the fastest speed at which the vehicle was travelling. How long was it on the road for? (When did the motion start and finish?)

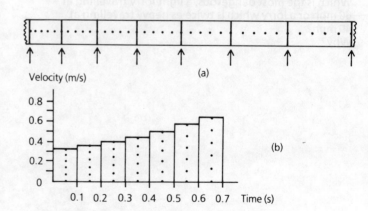

Fig. 3 A velocity–time graph using ticker-tape
If the tape is cut at every fifth dot, then each strip represents $5/50\,s = 0.1\,s$. The length of each strip will be the distance travelled in 0.1 s, so the velocity scale is just the length of the scale multiplied by 10 (i.e. a 10 cm length represents 1 m/s).

- You can produce your own tachograph velocity–time graph using ticker-tape. Figure 3 shows how. What are the differences between this graph and the real tachograph?

A simple velocity–time graph

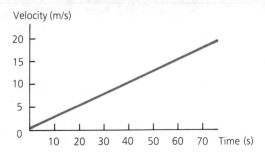

Fig. 4 A lorry accelerating
What is the highest velocity reached by the lorry?
How many seconds does it take to reach this velocity?

Figure 4 is a velocity–time graph for a lorry accelerating. It is a straight-line graph which shows that the velocity is increasing at a regular rate. **What does this show about the acceleration?**

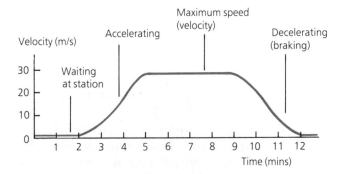

Fig. 5 A velocity–time graph for a train
Is the rate of deceleration (slowing up) the same as the rate of acceleration? How do you know?

Speeding up and slowing down

Figure 5 is a velocity–time graph for a train travelling between stations. In this case, the acceleration and deceleration are not constant, since these sections of the graph are curves rather than straight lines. **How long does the train wait at the first station? How long does it take to accelerate to maximum velocity? What is this maximum velocity?**

- Draw a velocity–time graph for a lift going from the ground floor of a building to the first floor and back again. The maximum speed is 1 m/s and the lift takes 10 s to reach this speed. It travels at this speed for 20 s, decelerates during the next 10 s, and then pauses at the first floor for 20 s.

Gravitational acceleration

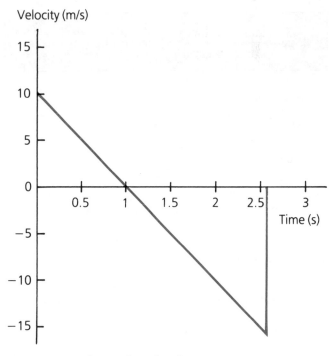

Fig. 6 A stone thrown into the air
What is its speed as it hits the ground?

Figure 6 is a velocity–time graph showing the *upwards* velocity of a stone thrown into the air. Note that the acceleration is constant and negative (i.e. downwards) throughout. **Where is the upwards (positive) velocity greatest? Where is the downwards (negative) velocity greatest? Where is the velocity zero? What part of the flight does this represent?**

- Draw a velocity–time graph to show the *downwards* velocity of a stone that is dropped down a well and takes 3 seconds to hit the bottom.

39

Getting the most from your graph

Using the slope to find the acceleration

The slope or **gradient** of a graph, like the slope of a hill, is the vertical height divided by the horizontal distance. For example, consider the slope of the velocity–time graph shown in Figure 1. This is equal to BC divided by AB. The distance from B to C represents the gain in velocity. The distance across from A to B represents the corresponding period of time. Hence:

$$\text{slope} = \frac{\text{gain in velocity}}{\text{time interval}} = \text{acceleration}$$

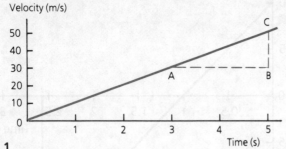

Fig. 1

In this particular graph,

$$\text{acceleration} = \frac{\text{BC}}{\text{AB}} = \frac{50\,\text{m/s} - 30\,\text{m/s}}{5\,\text{s} - 3\,\text{s}} = 10\,\text{m/s}^2$$

i.e. the acceleration of gravity.

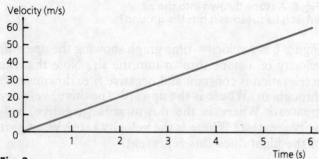

Fig. 2

- **What was the acceleration of the rocket represented by the velocity–time graph in Figure 2?**

Using the area to find the displacement

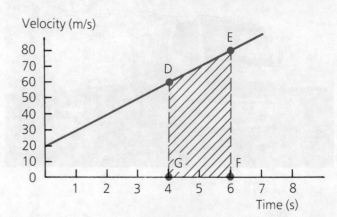

Fig. 3

Consider the area under section DE of the graph in Figure 3 (in other words, the area of the trapezium DEFG). This area is equal to the average height (DG + EF)/2 multiplied by the base GF.

But the average height represents the average velocity, and the base GF represents the time that has elapsed.

Thus the area represents

    average velocity × time

This is equal to the distance travelled.

In this particular graph, the distance travelled is given by

$$\text{distance} = \frac{\text{DG} + \text{EF}}{2} \times \text{GF}$$

$$= \frac{60\,\text{m/s} + 80\,\text{m/s}}{2} \times 2\,\text{s} = 140\,\text{m}$$

- **The fastest rate at which a car can decelerate is approximately 7 m/s². Use a velocity–time graph to find the minimum stopping distances for cars travelling at 18 m/s and 27 m/s. Compare these with the stopping distances given in the Highway Code.**

3.7 Hyperspace and ham sandwiches

How fast can you go?

According to Albert Einstein's **theory of relativity**, the fastest we can go is 300 000 000 m/s—the speed of light.

This many seem pretty fast! However, even at this speed, it would take four years to reach the nearest star, Alpha Centauri, and centuries to reach all but a few other stars. So it looks as though we will have problems if we want to travel through the galaxy looking for alien life.

Fig. 1 Concorde travels faster than sound. Why can't we build a spaceship that travels faster than light? A thermonuclear spaceship, Starship Daedalus, was proposed by the British Interplanetary Society. If it travelled at 80 000 000 mph, how long would it take to reach the nearest star?

In many science fiction books and films, spacecraft get to distant stars by going into **hyperspace**. They pop out of the universe into another dimension (outside space and time) and then pop back in again near the distant star. This is a nice idea, but unfortunately it is far removed from present day scientific reality!

But why can't we build a very powerful spaceship that can 'break' this 'light barrier' in the same way as Concorde 'breaks' the sound barrier?

Travelling at the speed of light

According to the theory of relativity, if we travelled at anywhere near the speed of light, a lot of strange things would happen:

1 Our mass would increase tremendously, making it impossible to keep accelerating.

2 Our time would slow down. If we flew round the solar system at nearly the speed of light, time would go so slowly for us that (according to one writer) all that we would need for food would be a ham sandwich. However, time would stay the same for those on Earth. When we got back, we'd find that everyone else was many years older!

Fig. 2 What happens if you go at nearly the speed of light?

For things travelling at the speed of light, time stops altogether. More remarkable still, *if* anything does travel faster than light (and some scientists think that there may be tiny particles called **tachyons** that do this), then it actually travels backwards in time!

In the words of a limerick:

'There was a young lady called Bright,
Who could travel far faster than light;
She set off one day,
In a relative way,
And returned home the previous night.'

41

Exercises

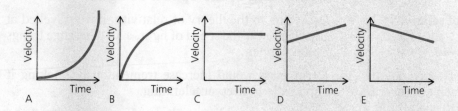

Fig. 1

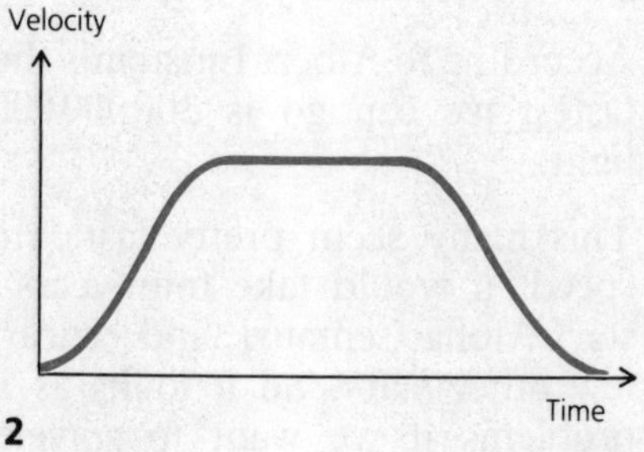

Fig. 2

1 Which of the graphs shown in Figure 1 could represent an aircraft accelerating down a runway with constant acceleration?

2 Which of the following is *not* a vector quantity?

   A Mass

   B Displacement

   C Velocity

   D Acceleration

   E Momentum

3 A stone is thrown into the air. Where is the acceleration greatest?

   A Just after it leaves the thrower's hand

   B At the highest point of travel

   C As it starts to descend

   D Just before it hits the ground

   E The acceleration is constant throughout

4 Which of the following could the graph shown in Figure 2 represent?

   A A stone thrown in the air

   B A car driving over the mountain

   C A train between two stations

   D A hotel lift going up and down

   E A space rocket

5 A strip of ticker-tape is pulled through a ticker-timer making 50 dots per second. Which of the following does the distance between two neighbouring dots represent?

   A 0.2 seconds

   B 0.02 seconds

   C The distance travelled in 1 second

   D The distance travelled in 0.02 seconds

   E The velocity in m/s

6 If you were hit by the following, which would have the biggest effect on your motion?

   A A 10 000 kg lorry moving at 2 m/s

   B A 3000 kg rhino charging at 10 m/s

   C A 1000 kg car moving at 20 m/s

   D A 500 kg meteorite moving at 20 000 m/s

   E A 100 g bullet moving at 2000 m/s

7 Complete this passage:
The acceleration of an object is equal to the increase in its _____ divided by the _____ over which this occurs. It is also equal to the applied force _____ by the _____ of the object. The SI unit for acceleration is _____.

8 It is more painful to kick a brick than a football of the same mass. The harder brick produces a bigger force on your foot. Why?

9 Why does paper fall more rapidly into the waste bin if you screw it up into a ball first?

10 A tile falling from a roof is moving with constant acceleration. A parachutist dropping from a plane is moving with constant velocity.

  a What is the tile's acceleration?

  b What do we call the parachutist's constant velocity?

  c Explain the difference in motion between the tile and the parachute.

11 Figure 3 is the velocity–time graph for a 1000 kg car accelerating from 10 m/s to 30 m/s to join a motorway.

  a How long does this take?

  b How far does the car travel during this time?

  c What is the force of the engine?

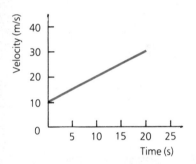

Fig. 3

Fig. 4 The launch of the Saturn V rocket

Fig. 5 How deep is a well?

12 Concorde has a mass of 180 000 kg on take-off. Each of the four engines produces a take-off force of 170 kN. What is the acceleration on take-off under these conditions?

13 The Saturn V space rocket on launch had a mass of 3 400 000 kg, and its rockets produced a total force of 34 MN. What was the vertical acceleration on launch?

14 It takes 3 seconds for a stone dropped down a well to hit the bottom (Figure 5).

  a At what speed is the stone travelling when it hits the bottom?

  b Draw a velocity–time graph for the stone, and use it to find the depth of the well.

15 Figure 6 shows some oil marks on the road after a 'hit-and-run' accident. The marks are 10 m apart between A and B. The police believe that, over this section, the car from which the oil was dripping was travelling at 20 m/s.

  a How could the police tell that the speed was constant from A to B?

  b At what rate was oil dripping from the car?

  c At what position do you think the accident occurred? Why?

  d What was the speed of the car between D and E?

  e A car seen a few miles away shortly after the accident had a maximum speed of 40 m/s and a maximum acceleration of 4.0 m/s^2 (according to the manufacturer's data). Could this have been the car that caused the accident? How do you know?

Fig. 6

43

4 FORCES ACTING TOGETHER

4.1 Moulding things

The work of a potter's hands

Fig. 1 A potter moulding a vase
Can you see where forces are balancing each other?

The potter throws the clay into the middle of the rotating wheel. Gently, he starts to mould it into shape. He applies various forces to the clay with his fingers. He compresses some parts of the clay, and stretches other parts. He may also bend, twist or shear the clay. He is careful to apply all the forces evenly, so that the clay remains in the middle of the wheel throughout. The forces on the clay are then said to be **balanced**.

Few forces act on their own. Few of them produce motion. Most are balanced by other forces, and merely deform the object on which they are acting. Figure 2 shows how several forces acting together can deform a piece of clay or plasticine in different ways. **Try this.**

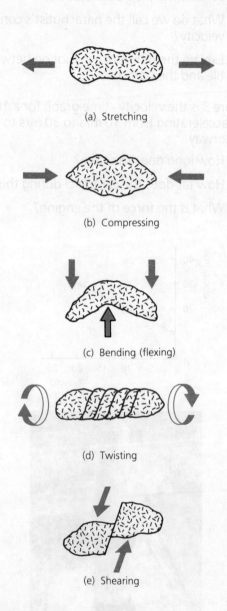

(a) Stretching

(b) Compressing

(c) Bending (flexing)

(d) Twisting

(e) Shearing

Fig. 2 Different ways of deforming clay
Is there any other way in which you can deform a material?

Deforming things

Figure 3 shows several ways in which we deform other materials. **Copy the diagrams and draw on to them arrows showing where the forces are acting. Label each force a push or a pull.**

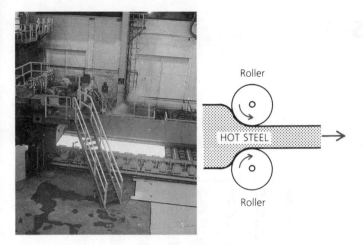

(a) Hot steel being rolled into a strip: compression

(b) Stretching textile fibres

(c) Bending copper pipe

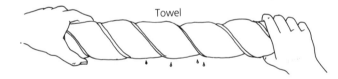

(d) Twisting: wringing out a wet towel

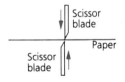

(e) Shearing: cutting with scissors

Fig. 3 Where are the forces acting?

● **Try bending, stretching, compressing, twisting and shearing a piece of rubber tubing. Draw an ink square on the tubing and watch what happens to this as you deform the tube.**

Elastic and plastic deformation

(a)

(b)

Fig. 4 Dough moulding a plastic plate
The materials in (b) are often called 'plastics', but this is misleading. Why?

When you stretch an elastic band and then let it go, it recovers its old shape and size. This is called **elastic** behaviour, and is why we call it an *elastic* band.

When you stretch a length of plasticine and then release it, nothing happens. It keeps its new shape and size. This is called **plastic** behaviour (hence the word *'plasticine'*).

Household plastics are called 'plastics' because of the way in which they are *made*. In dough moulding, a hot plasticine-like dough is compressed. It is plastically deformed into the shape of the final object. Plastic pipes and buckets are made by **extruding** the hot plastic—forcing it through a tube in the same way that cake icing is forced through an icing gun.

Once the dough has cooled and hardened, household plastics deform elastically. Perhaps we should call them 'elastics'!

45

Stretching things

Falling off a mountain

Fig. 1 Why do climbers use nylon ropes?

Sensible people have nylon ropes round them when they fall off a mountain! Nylon ropes are very strong and stretch more than the old-fashioned hemp ropes. With a hemp climbing rope, if you fell off a mountain, you would come to a very sudden (and painful) stop as the rope became taut. With a stretchy nylon rope, you are stopped more gently and therefore less painfully.

A rope acts like a spring. The more you pull on it, the more it stretches. Hemp is like a very stiff spring, whereas nylon is like a less-stiff spring.

Springs

Figure 2 shows what happens when a simple (helical) spring is loaded with standard masses. **Try this.** The graph of length against **load** is a straight line.

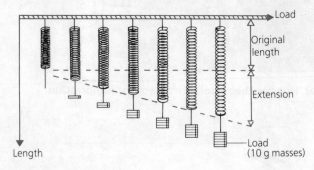

Fig. 2 Loading a spring
The greater the load is, the greater the extension will be. If the spring was originally 10 cm long, how long would it be with 8 weights hanging from it?

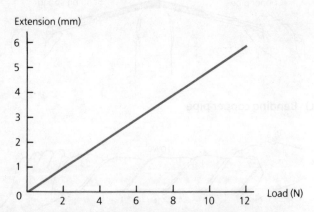

Fig. 3 An extension–load graph for a spring
What is the extension when the load is 12 N?

Figure 3 shows the same graph plotted as an extension–load graph. In this case, the straight line goes through the **origin**. Note that when you double the force (the load), you double the extension. With three times the force, you get three times the extension, and so on.

When things increase together like this we say that they are **proportional**.

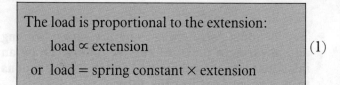

The load is proportional to the extension:

  load ∝ extension   (1)

or load = spring constant × extension

The stiffer a spring is, the larger the **spring constant** is.

- **What happens when you remove the load? Do you get the same result for much larger masses? (Rather than spoiling a bought spring, make your own spring by winding some wire round a pencil.) Does an elastic band behave in the same way when you stretch it? (Wear goggles to make sure it doesn't hit you in the eye as it breaks.)**

Hooke's law

One of the few people to make a lot of money out of the Great Fire of London was a surveyor called Robert Hooke (Figure 4). (He helped to assess the damage and to plan the rebuilding.) Hooke had originally trained for the church, but took up a scientific career since he reckoned that it was less strenuous! Although his wealth didn't appear to do him or anyone else much good (he was a real scrooge!), he did go on to make a lot of discoveries about forces. He even claimed, as an old man, that he had discovered the law of gravity before Newton.

Fig. 4 Hooke's law!
What is Hooke's law?

Hooke discovered that most things (including charred wooden beams!) stretch just a little bit when you pull or bend them. In other words, they deform when a force is applied to them. Moreover, provided that the force is small

$$\text{deformation} \propto \text{force} \qquad (2)$$

This statement is known as **Hooke's law**. Equation (1) is one example of Hooke's law.

For an elastic band, Hooke's law is obeyed (at least approximately) even for quite large extensions. For plasticine, it is only obeyed for extremely small forces.

Figure 5 shows typical **load–extension** curves for steel and copper wire. Notice that Hooke's law is obeyed even for quite large loads. Eventually (beyond the **limit of proportionality**) the metal atoms start to pull apart. If you continue to increase the load, the wire breaks.

- **Which is the stronger of the two wires shown in Figure 5? Which is the stiffer?**

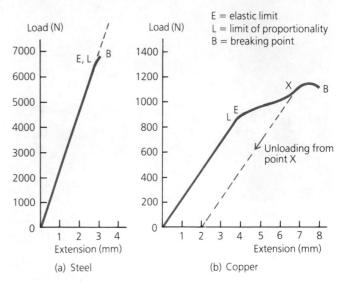

Fig. 5 Load–extension graphs for steel and copper

The elastic limit

Steel piano wires snap as soon as they reach the limit of proportionality. Copper wire becomes plastic at this point—if the load is increased further, it will deform plastically (Figure 5(b)). The point at which a material starts to deform plastically is called its **elastic limit**. This point is usually very close to the limit of proportionality.

When a climbing rope is used in a heavy fall, it may be stretched beyond its elastic limit. It will be permanently deformed, and may be dangerous. It should therefore be replaced with a new rope.

This also applies to car seatbelts. These should always be replaced after a serious accident. If a seatbelt fails in an accident, the person wearing it will continue to move forwards and will be deformed by the windscreen. Unfortunately, human beings don't have a very high elastic limit!

The moment of a force:
'Give me a fulcrum and I can move the world'

Levering up a heavy stone

Fig. 1 Dry-stone walling

When you are rebuilding a dry-stone wall, you often have to re-lay the foundation stones. They are very heavy and very difficult to lift (Figure 1). You need

- a metal rod, called a crowbar, to act as a **lever**

- a rock to act as a pivot, or **fulcrum** (a fixed point about which the crowbar can *turn*). If you try to use the soil as a fulcrum, the crowbar will sink into the ground and will not lift the stone.

Levers are very useful. Figure 2 shows a screwdriver being used to lever up the lid of a tin of paint, and a spanner being used to turn a nut. **How many more example of levers can you think of?**

The turning effect of a force

How do you increase the turning effect (the leverage)?

1 Increase the magnitude (the size) of the force.

2 Make the force act a long way from the fulcrum. (For example, powerful wire cutters have long handles.)

Two thousand years ago, Archimedes reasoned that, if only you could get far enough away from the fulcrum, you could use a lever to move the world (Figure 3). The only problem was what to use as a fulcrum, and as a lever!

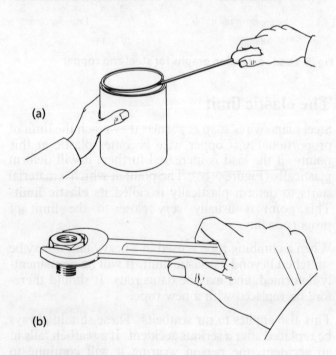

Fig. 2 Using levers
(a) Why is not a good idea to use brittle steel (for example, an old file) to lever up a paint lid?
(b) How can you increase the turning effect of the spanner?

Fig. 3 Give me a fulcrum and I can move the world!
What point was Archimedes making when he said this?

It is the **perpendicular distance** of the force from the fulcrum that is important (Figure 4). The pedal of a bicycle is always the same distance from the fulcrum. (The length of the crank doesn't alter.) However, the *perpendicular* distance from the fulcrum, and therefore the turning effect that you get, depends very much on the position of the pedal. **Try this. What is the best position for the pedal when you start cycling? Why?**

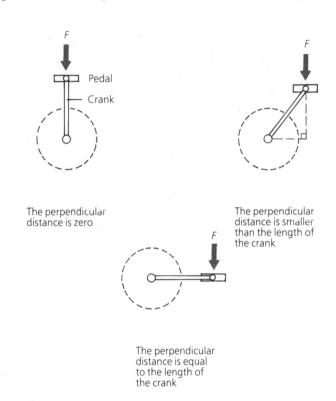

Fig. 4 **It's the perpendicular distance that counts**

Moments

A special name has been given to the turning effect of a force. We call it the **moment** of the force. This isn't the same 'moment' as in 'wait a moment'. It has nothing to do with time. It has more to do with mo-ve-ment. For example, the longer a spanner is, the greater is its turning effect (or moment) making a nut move.

The moment of a force is defined like this:

> moment = force × *perpendicular* distance from fulcrum

For example, the man in Figure 5 is opening the lock gates by pushing 3 m from the fulcrum with a force of 200 N. The turning effect is given by

moment = (200 N) × (3 m) = 600 N m

Fig. 5 **Opening the gates of a lock**
Which is the easiest direction in which to push – at right-angles to the lever or parallel to the side of the lock? Why?

The torque of car engines

'Moment' isn't the only word that is used for the turning effect of a force. Car brochures refer to the **torque** of an engine, meaning the turning effect. For example, an Austin Mini has a maximum engine torque of 70 N m. A Rover 800 has an engine torque of 220 N m.

Car workshop manuals often state the maximum torque that you must use when tightening some of the engine bolts. Some special spanners have a mechanism that automatically prevents you from using too much torque.

For our purposes, 'moment' and 'torque' mean almost the same thing. 'Torque' is used rather than 'moment' when something is being twisted or continually turned.

In practice, mechanical engineers working with engines and other things that involve movement or rotation use the word 'torque'. Civil engineers designing buildings and bridges that are static used the word 'moment'.

Floating on air

Fig. 1 Floating in space
These astronauts feel weightless. They are actually falling towards the Earth, but at the same rate as their spacecraft. Why do they and their spacecraft never get nearer to the ground? (See Section 1.4)

> *I wish that my room had a floor.*
> *I don't so much care for a door,*
> *But this crawling around*
> *Without touching the ground*
> *Is getting to be quite a bore.*
>
> Gelett Burgess

Have you ever had a dream in which you were floating above the ground? To float like this in real life, you would need something to balance your weight—an upwards force.

Figure 2 shows a Maglev train which uses magnetic repulsion to float above a metal track. ('Maglev' stands for '*magnetic levitation*'.) Because the train floats in the air, there are no frictional forces with the ground to slow it down.

A hot-air balloon floats because the **upthrust** (the upwards force) from the outside air balances the weight of the balloon. The air outside the balloon is cooler and denser than the air inside. The upthrust it produces is therefore larger than the weight of the air inside the balloon.

Fig. 2 A Maglev train
What are the advantages of this train?

- Hang a stone from a newton meter (a spring balance) and lower it into water. Notice how the upthrust balances some of the weight. Now try the same thing with a piece of wood. Eventually, the upthrust is equal to the weight and the wood floats.

- Make a *Cartesian diver* as shown in Figure 3. What happens when you squeeze the bottle? Why? (Hint: Watch the level of water in the diver.)

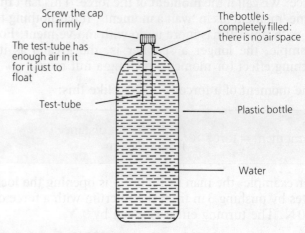

Screw the cap on firmly

The bottle is completely filled: there is no air space

The test-tube has enough air in it for it just to float

Test-tube

Plastic bottle

Water

Fig. 3 A Cartesian diver

'Equilibrium' means 'balance'

'Aequi' is the Latin for 'equal', and 'libra' is the Latin for 'balance'. Rather than saying 'the forces (and moments) on this object are balanced', we say 'this object is in **equilibrium**'. (It doesn't save any words, but scientists think that it sounds better!)

Note that *moving* objects can be in equilibrium provided that they are moving with constant velocity (see Section 2.6).

Forces between atoms

Solids are made up of tiny particles called atoms. (A molecule—see Section 2.5—is several atoms stuck together.) The atoms are held in equilibrium by the forces between them. These are called **interatomic forces**. If you try to push the atoms together, the interatomic forces push back and keep the atoms apart. If you try to pull the atoms apart, these forces hold them together.

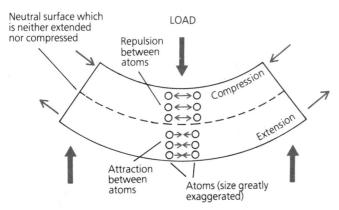

Fig. 4 Forces between atoms in a bent beam
What happens if (i) the attractive forces and (ii) the repulsive forces cannot increase as you increase the applied moment?

Figure 4 shows these forces acting in a bent beam. Thick beams are much better for supporting heavy loads than thin beams are. The thickness of the beam is far more important than the width. This is why roofing beams are always laid on edge. They can support much greater loads like this than they could if they were laid flat. **Suggest a reason for this. Try it for yourself with balsa-wood beams.**

Steel girders have an I-shaped cross-section. This means that most of the atoms in the beam are as far as possible from the neutral axis (the middle of the beam). This makes the beam much stronger for the same amount of metal. **Why is this?**

Fig. 5 Bridge over the Mosel
The beam that carries the A61 autobahn over the Mosel valley is more than 6 m in depth. Why is it so thick?

Using the floor to stop you from falling!

You don't have to be floating above the ground in a balloon, or floating on the sea in a boat, to be in equilibrium. When you sit in a chair, the **reaction** from the chair (see Section 2.5) balances your weight.

Even when you stand, you need a reaction force to balance your weight. For example, if you skate on thin ice, the weak ice may not be able to provide a large enough reaction force, and you may fall through.

If you stood on a floor that was too weak to provide a reaction force because it had been eaten by termites, then you'd be in the same unfortunate condition as Ogden Nash's 'cousin May':

> *'Some primal termite knocked on wood*
> *And tasted it, and found it good,*
> *And that is why your cousin May*
> *Fell through the parlour floor today.'*

51

Fig. 1 Is it in danger of overturning?
How can you tell?

Many people are killed on farms by tractors overturning. Figure 1 shows a tractor on a steep and dangerous slope. How can we tell whether it is about to overturn? What causes it to overturn? What can we do to prevent it? These are the questions that we shall try to answer in this section.

Balancing the moments

A tractor on a slope is a bit like two children on a see-saw (Figure 2). The downhill wheels of the tractor act as a pivot. The weight of the upper part of the tractor provides a clockwise moment. The weight of the lower part of the tractor provides an anticlockwise moment.

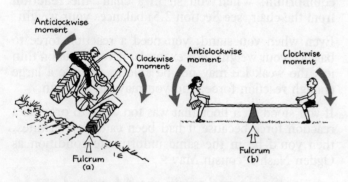

Fig. 2 The tractor will overturn if the moments don't balance
What would happen to the tractor if the anticlockwise moment were greater than the clockwise moment?

52

The see-saw will balance only if the clockwise and anticlockwise moments balance:

> An object can be in equilibrium only if the sum of the clockwise moments about any point is equal to the sum of the anticlockwise moments about that point.

This is called the **principle of moments**. Figure 3 shows some examples. This same principle applies to the tractor.

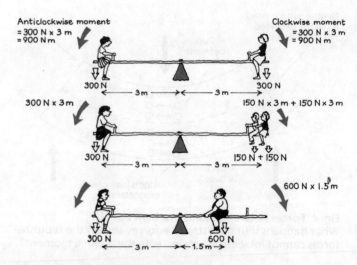

Fig. 3 Balancing a girl on a see-saw

Where does the weight as a whole act?

Rather than considering the weight of different parts of the tractor, we can consider the weight of the tractor as a whole. Like any other object, the tractor behaves as though all its weight were concentrated at one point— the **centre of mass** (sometimes called the **centre of gravity**).

The position of this centre of mass determines whether or not the tractor will topple on the slope:

- If the centre of mass lies vertically above the base of the tractor (in other words, if the weight acts between the wheels), then the tractor will be stable (Figure 4(a)). It will lean in the uphill direction until the moment from the left-hand (uphill) wheels balances the moment from the weight.

- If the centre of mass overhangs the wheelbase, then there is nothing to balance the weight. The tractor will topple (Figure 4(b)).

One way of making this less likely to happen is to give the tractor a wide wheelbase (Figure 4(c)).

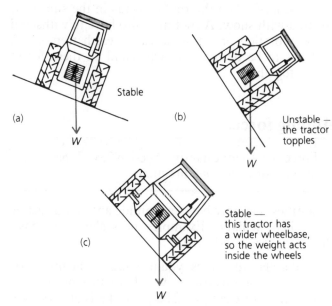

Fig. 4 Making a tractor more stable by extending the wheelbase
How else can you make a vehicle more stable?

- **Stand with your back to a wall. Bend over and try to touch your toes. Why can't you stop yourself from falling over?**

- **Why doesn't the Leaning Tower of Pisa topple over?**

Finding the centre of mass

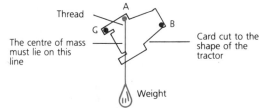

1 Pin the thread and the card to the wall at point A. The card should be able to swing freely
2 When the card has stopped swinging, draw a pencil line where the thread crosses the card.
3 Repeat this for points B and C.

Fig. 5 Where is the centre of mass (or centre of gravity)?

Figure 5 shows a way of estimating the centre of mass of the tractor. A **lamina** (for example, a flat sheet of card, plastic or plywood) is cut in the shape of the tractor. The centre of mass of this lamina is then found by pinning a plumb-line to it and hanging it from three different points.

- **Is this likely to be an accurate method of finding the centre of mass of a tractor? Why? Try it using (a) a low, wide-wheelbase tractor, (b) a high, narrow-wheelbase tractor. Then try using this method to find the centre of mass of mainland Britain by cutting a card to shape. Which town or city is nearest to the centre of mass of mainland Britain?**

The lower the centre of mass, the more stable the tractor

The centre of mass can be kept low by keeping the heaviest parts of the tractor as low as possible. This is common practice with tractors, buses, lorries, trains and, indeed, all other vehicles. In particular, boats and ships have heavy keels well below the surface to stop them from overturning.

- **See if you can find out and explain why the *Herald of Free Enterprise* car ferry capsized (Figure 6).**

Fig. 6 The *Herald of Free Enterprise*
Water flooded on to the car deck of this ferry. Why did this cause it to overturn?

- **Find the mass of**
    (a) a lump of plasticine
    (b) a metre rule
  by two different methods, using only the following additional items: (i) an elastic band, (ii) thread, (iii) a 100 g standard mass. (You may assume that $g = 10 \text{ N/kg}$.)

Problems with roofs: force as a vector

Designing a roof

Fig. 1 Building a roof
What forces does an engineer have to take into account when designing a roof?

The roofs of modern British homes are designed very carefully. The architects take careful account of all the forces acting on the roof. This is very important. In some other countries, steel roofing sheets have been ripped off badly designed schools by the wind and have sliced into, and killed, schoolchildren.

Several forces act on a roof. The weight of the roof acts downwards. The wind acts sideways, and also upwards. (Many accidents have been caused by the **Bernoulli effect**—see Section 5.8.) Additional forces

are produced when the roof expands in the sun, or is covered with snow. A roof may also have to withstand traffic vibration or, in some cases, earth tremors. A roof has to be designed to withstand all these forces added together.

Adding forces

> Force is a vector quantity (Section 2.3). It has magnitude (size) *and* direction.

Quantities that only have magnitude and not direction are called **scalars**. Examples of scalars are mass, distance, speed and time.

To add scalar quantities, you just add up the numbers. To add vector quantities, you have to look at their directions. For example, 2 kg plus 2 kg is always 4 kg. But $2 \, \text{m/s}^2$ plus $2 \, \text{m/s}^2$ could be anything from $0 \, \text{m/s}^2$ to $4 \, \text{m/s}^2$, depending on the direction.

Luckily, all vector quantities can be added in the same way—by drawing lines (vectors) to represent their magnitude and direction. This method was described for displacements and velocities in Section 2.3. It also works with forces.

In Figure 2, this method is used to find the resultant force on the roof of a lean-to shed. The roof has a weight of 400 N and is acted on by a horizontal wind force of magnitude 300 N. The vector diagram can be

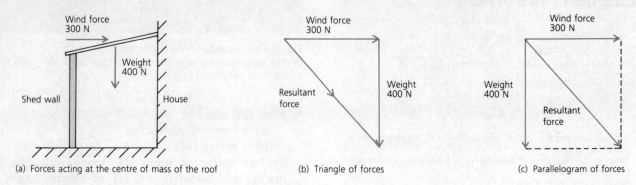

(a) Forces acting at the centre of mass of the roof

(b) Triangle of forces

(c) Parallelogram of forces

Fig. 2 Adding the forces on a shed roof
Does the wind force alter the downward force on the shed wall?

drawn either as a **triangle of forces** (Figure 2(b)) or as a **parallelogram of forces** (Figure 2(c)). Both methods give the same result (500 N at an angle of 53° to the horizontal). Choose whichever you prefer.

- Use one of these methods to find the resultant force on
  (a) a tile of weight 3 N (mass 300 g) blown off a roof by a horizontal wind force of 4 N
  (b) a 2 g raindrop blown with a sideways force of 0.02 N
  (c) smoke particles being forced upwards with an upthrust of 0.1 N and with a horizontal wind force of 0.2 N.
  What is the acceleration in each case?

A flying buttress

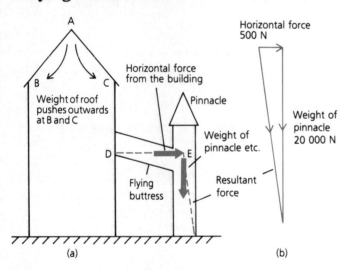

Fig. 3 Forces in a flying buttress
How is the roof of a normal house constructed so that the sides of the roof do not push outwards against the walls?

Some ancient buildings have **flying buttresses** like that shown in Figure 3(a). In the building shown, the weight of the roof at point A is pushing the walls out at points B and C. The flying buttress pushes back at point D, keeping the wall vertical.

The vector diagram (Figure 3(b)) shows the forces that we might expect to be acting at point E. The resultant force is produced by a horizontal force of 5000 N from the building and the weight of a 2 tonne pinnacle. This resultant force acts inside the pillar, and can be balanced by an equal and opposite reaction force inside the pillar. (If the resultant force acted outside the pillar, the buttress and building would fall down.)

Fig. 4 Not just a pretty face!
The pinnacle above this gargoyle has a useful purpose in helping to hold up the structure. What is it? What is the purpose of the gargoyle itself?

When the resultant force is zero

Just because the resultant of several forces is zero, it doesn't necessarily mean that we can ignore these forces (Figure 5). An object with several forces acting on it is being stressed. This may cause parts of the object to weaken and eventually to fail.

Making life simpler

Vectors allow you to add forces, accelerations and a wide range of other vector quantities as though they were simple displacements. They enable you to solve complicated problems in terms of easier, but similar, problems. And that's what most of physics is about!

Fig. 5 Pulled in all directions
How could his wife tell that the resultant force on him was zero?

Exercises

1 Which of the following requires only one force?

A Bending

B Stretching

C Accelerating

D Twisting

E Shearing

2 Which of the following objects must be in equilibrium?

A An object which is not moving.

B An object which is not rotating.

C An object on which no forces are acting.

D An object on which the resultant force is zero.

E An object on which all the forces and moments are balanced.

3 Which would be the best reason for calling an elastic band 'elastic'?

A It stretches.

B It regains its original size after being stretched and then released.

C It obeys Hooke's law.

D It extends by a very large amount when stretched by only a small force.

E It bounces.

Fig. 1

56

4 Which of the following can remain constant as a car goes round a corner?

A Its velocity

B Its acceleration

C Its momentum

D Its speed

E The force of the wheels on the road

5 Plasticine normally sinks in water. But if it is moulded into the shape of a hollow boat it will float because this:

A Reduces its mass

B Reduces its weight

C Makes it less able to cut into the water

D Increases the upthrust

E Increases the interatomic forces

6 A 2 m cable that obeys Hooke's law is used to lift a 600 N load. It extends by 3 mm. By how much would it extend if it were used to lift an 800 N load?

A 2 mm

B 4 mm

C 5 mm

D 8 mm

E 240 mm

7 Complete these sentences:

a When a small load is hung from a spring, the extension of the spring is _____ _____ the load. This is an example of _____ law.

b Force is called a _____ quantity because it has magnitude and _____ .

8 The racing car shown in Figure 1 can go round corners at much higher speeds than an ordinary car can without toppling over. State two reasons for this.

9 In a serious accident, the seatbelts of a car are likely to exceed their elastic limit. What does this mean?

10 Explain in terms of moments why the pushchair shown in Figure 2 overturned.

Fig. 2 Why did this happen?

11 Describe how you would find the centre of mass of each of the pieces of metal sheet shown in Figure 3. Copy the diagrams and on each of them mark where you would expect to find the centre of mass.

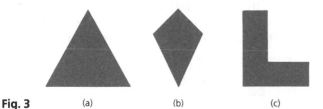

Fig. 3   (a)   (b)   (c)

12 What is wrong with the following statement? 'The moment of a force is always equal to the magnitude of a force multiplied by the distance of its point of application from the fulcrum.' Sketch one example of a situation in which this statement is not true.

13 **a** Why are the yachtsmen in Figure 4 leaning so far out of their yachts?

 b If the wind force provides a moment of 1000 N m and a yachtsman has a mass of 50 kg, what should be the horizontal distance between the yachtsman's centre of gravity and the centre of the boat?

 c Why do many yachts have a heavy broad section at the bottom of their keels?

Fig. 4 A racing yacht

14 Use a diagram or diagrams to explain why it is dangerous to stand up in a small boat.

15 Compare the wheelbarrow designs shown in Figure 5, giving reasons why you might expect some of them to be easier to use than others.

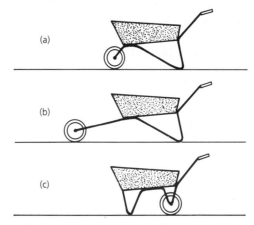

Fig. 5 Can you design a better wheelbarrow?

16 When a 60 kg parachutist opens her parachute, the upward wind resistance on her increases to 1000 N. There is also a horizontal wind force of 100 N. What is

 a the resultant force acting on her?

 b her acceleration?

5 PRESSURE

5.1 Under pressure

Earth movers and stiletto heels

Fig. 1 Machines with giant tyres
The tyres of heavy, juggernaut lorries are not as large as this. How do juggernauts avoid putting too much pressure on the road?

Earth-moving machines have large tyres or caterpillar tracks (Figure 1). Why? How do skis and snow shoes prevent people from sinking into snow? Why should you use a ladder when going on to thin ice to rescue someone who has fallen through? Why do stiletto heels damage floors more than ordinary heels (Figure 2)?

Fig. 2 Ten million pascals!
The pressure under a stiletto heel.
People tiptoe when they want to move silently. Why? Does it make loose floorboards less likely to creak?

In each case, spreading the weight over a larger area reduces its effect.

Pressure

To most people, **pressure** means the same as force. In science, pressure means more than this.

$$\text{pressure} = \frac{\text{force}}{\text{area}} \qquad (1)$$

The greater the pressure on a surface, the more the surface is deformed.

Pascals

Force is measured in newtons. Area is measured in square metres. The units of pressure are therefore newtons per square metre (N/m^2). Since N/m^2 looks complicated, it is often replaced by **pascals** (Pa).

$$1\,\text{Pa} = 1\,\text{N/m}^2$$

The French mathematician, Blaise Pascal, was born in 1623, about 20 years before Newton. He was the first person to show that the air around us is under pressure. He is also remembered for having a very kind brother-in-law. Pascal's sister's husband agreed to test his theories by carrying a heavy glass barometer filled with mercury 1000 metres up a mountain (Figure 3)!

Fig. 3 Pascal had a very kind brother-in-law

You may come across other units for pressure (for instance on air pumps in garages, and on weather maps). Examples are bars, millibars (mb), kgf/m² and pounds per square inch (psi).

$$1 \text{ bar} \equiv 100\,000 \text{ Pa} \qquad 1 \text{ mb} \equiv 100 \text{ Pa}$$
$$1 \text{ kgf/m}^2 \equiv 10 \text{ Pa} \qquad 1 \text{ psi} \equiv 6900 \text{ Pa}$$

Building a wall

Fig. 4 Sinking into the marsh
Over the centuries, the pressure of this church has pushed it down into the soft, marshy soil.
How could this have been avoided?

The foundation of a wall is always made wider than the wall itself. This spreads the weight of the wall over a large area of soil, and so reduces the pressure on the soil. If you don't provide a good foundation, the wall is likely to sink into the ground, and may topple over.

Suppose, for example, that a wall 10 m long and 20 cm (0.2 m) wide has a mass of 6000 kg. Suppose also that the greatest pressure that the soil can stand without giving way is 20 000 Pa. Will the wall be all right on its own, or does it need a foundation?

$$\text{force} = \text{weight} = \text{mass} \times g$$
$$= 6000 \text{ kg} \times 10 \text{ N/kg} = 60\,000 \text{ N}$$

$$\text{area} = \text{length} \times \text{width}$$
$$= 10 \text{ m} \times 0.2 \text{ m} = 2 \text{ m}^2$$

Therefore

$$\text{pressure} = \frac{\text{force}}{\text{area}}$$

$$= \frac{60\,000 \text{ N}}{2 \text{ m}^2} = 30\,000 \text{ Pa}$$

This is greater than the pressure that the soil can withstand. The wall will sink into the ground. Examples of places where this has happened are the Leaning Tower of Pisa, some ancient churches built on marshy ground (Figure 4) and some badly designed garden walls!

- **Carry out this calculation for the same wall built on foundations 50 cm (0.5 m) wide and 12 m long. Can the ground withstand the pressure of the wall in this case?**

- **Devise a test to measure the pressure at which objects sink into sand to a depth of more than 1 cm. A 5000 kg earth-moving machine must not sink more than 1 cm into soft sand. Use your result to find the total area of contact that the tyres of the machine must have with the ground. What should the pressure in the tyres be?**

Getting the point

Fig. 5 Getting the point
Why is it that you can push a drawing pin with your (soft) finger into a (hard) piece of wood?

Extremely high pressures occur at sharp points, such as the point of a drawing pin or the edge of a knife or saw. The area of contact is so tiny that even a small force produces an enormous pressure.

- **Try gently pressing a drawing pin between your thumbs so that the point is pressing into one of them. The force on each thumb is the same (otherwise the pin would move) but the pressure is very different.**

> *There was a faith-healer of Deal*
> *Who said: 'Although pain isn't real,*
> *If I sit on a pin,*
> *And it punctures my skin,*
> *I dislike what I fancy I feel.'*

59

Spongy brakes: pressure in gases and liquids

Air in the brakes

Once a car is 3 years old, it must have its brakes tested every year in an MOT test. One reason why your car might fail this test is if the brakes feel spongy and not hard. With spongy brakes, you can push the brake pedal down quite easily. But even when the brake pedal is pushed down to the floor, the brakes don't come on fully. If you needed to stop in an emergency with brakes like this, you could have a problem!

Spongy brakes are the result of air getting into the brake pipe. The brake pipe contains hydraulic fluid, which like all liquids cannot be compressed. But air— a gas—can easily be compressed. So it is much easier to push down the brake pedal when there is air in the brake pipe. To remove the air bubbles, you have to bleed the brakes. This means allowing the fluid that contains the bubbles to leak out.

- **Try making up your own hydraulic system using syringes as shown in Figure 2. How well does it work when filled (a) completely with water, (b) with air, (c) with water containing air bubbles?**

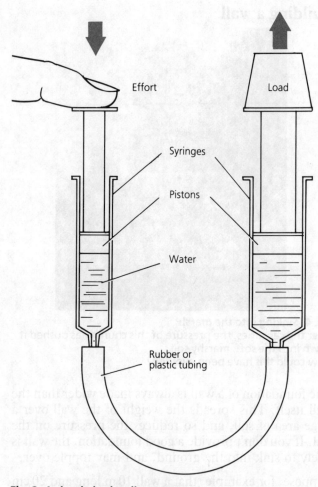

Fig. 2 A simple hydraulic system

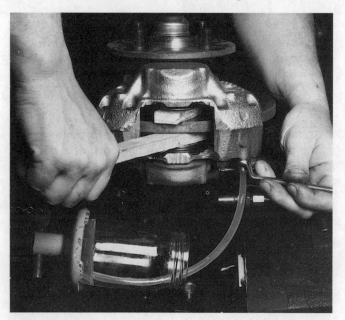

Fig. 1 Bleeding the brakes to remove the air bubbles
Why do we use hydraulic fluid for brake systems? Why don't we use water?

Pressure of gas and water jets

The pressure produced by jets of gas or liquid can be very large indeed. The jets of compressed air used in some factories can be dangerous if they are not used carefully. Air and sand jets used for sand-blasting cause the dirty surface of stone buildings to crumble under the pressure, revealing the clean stone underneath. Water jets from garden hoses need to be spread out using a sprinkler. Otherwise, they can damage plants. The water cannon used in some countries to stop riots can knock people over and badly hurt them. Liquid jets are sometimes even used for cutting.

Why are gases more compressible than liquids?

Gases and liquids are made up of tiny particles called **molecules** (see Section 2.5).

In a liquid, the molecules are close together. If you try to force them even closer together, strong repulsive forces between the molecules keep them apart (see Section 4.4).

In a gas, the molecules are moving much faster than they are in liquids, and this keeps them much further apart. Because they are so far apart, it is much easier to push them together.

You can actually turn some gases into liquids just by forcing the molecules closer together. Butane and propane, the bottled gases used in caravans, are stored as high-pressure liquids. When you open the cylinder, the molecules escape and fly apart to form a gas.

Bombarded by molecules

Fig. 3 Bombarded by molecules
The molecules hit us at speeds of about 400 m/s (900 mph). Why don't we feel them?

Our bodies are constantly being bombarded by millions of air molecules (Figure 3). We don't feel the individual molecules because they are too small. Instead we feel this bombardment as a constant pressure. (Even then, because the pressure is always there, we seldom notice it.)

- **Try sucking the back of your hand. All you are doing is removing the air molecules, stopping them from hitting your skin. What does the skin of your hand feel like?**

Similarly, the air pressure in a bicycle tyre or balloon is caused by air molecules bombarding the walls, trying to make them expand.

- **You can demonstrate the link between pressure and molecular bombardment using the equipment shown in Figure 4. The ball-bearings represent the molecules of a gas. When you switch on the motor, the balls hit the underside of the piston. They provide a pressure, pushing the piston up the tube. Push down on the piston and feel the pressure caused by these moving 'molecules'.**

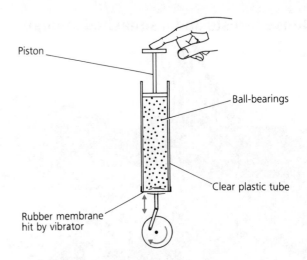

Fig. 4 How air molecules produce air pressure
The ball-bearings represent air molecules.
What happens to the pressure if
  (i) you increase the rate of vibration?
(ii) you push down, or put weight on, the piston?

Fig. 5 Cleaning with a high-pressure water jet

Dense forests and a squashed sponge

Fig. 1 Crushed like a sponge
Some car crushers can compress a car into a cube. If a car has a mass of 512 kg at the start, and ends up as a cube of side 80 cm, what is the density of the cube?

Some woods and forests are very dense—the trees are very close together. Dense crowds build up in shopping centres just before Christmas—the people are very close together. In the same way, there are some very dense materials in which the atoms and molecules are very close together.

Foam rubber isn't very dense. However, you can make it denser by crushing it with your hands. **Try this. What happens to the holes in the sponge? What happens to the mass of the sponge? What happens to the volume? If you had a 1 cm cube of squashed sponge and compared it with a 1 cm cube of ordinary sponge, would there be a difference in mass?**

Density

- **Which is heavier, a tonne of feathers or a tonne of lead?**

People say that lead is a 'heavy' material. What they mean is that, for the same volume, lead has a greater mass than most other materials. You could carry a cubic metre box of feathers on your shoulders. A cubic metre of lead would squash you flat! **What is the mass of a cubic metre of lead?** Scientists say that lead is **denser** than feathers:

$$\text{density} = \frac{\text{mass}}{\text{volume}} \qquad (1)$$

The correct SI unit for density is kg/m^3.

As a cubic metre is such a large volume, we sometimes use g/cm^3 instead. $(1\,g/cm^3 \equiv 1000\,kg/m^3.)$

An example

The fewer cracks there are in concrete (and thus the greater its density is) the stronger it is likely to be.

A concrete manufacturer wishes to check the strength of his 3 by 2 paving slabs. The slabs are of length 90 cm (0.9 m), width 60 cm (0.6 m) and depth 5 cm (0.05 m). They should have a density of at least $2300\,kg/m^3$. The manufacturer finds that his slabs have a mass of 65 kg. We can find their actual density as follows:

$$\begin{aligned} \text{volume} &= \text{length} \times \text{width} \times \text{depth} \\ &= 0.9\,m \times 0.6\,m \times 0.05\,m \\ &= 0.027\,m^3 \end{aligned}$$

Therefore

$$\text{density} = \frac{\text{mass}}{\text{volume}} = \frac{65\,kg}{0.027\,m^3} = 2400\,kg/m^3$$

The slabs are acceptable!

- **Carry out the same calculation using centimetres and grams to give the final result in g/cm^3.**

Fig. 2 Densities of some common solids

Solid	Density (in kg/m³)	Density (in g/cm³)
Balsa-wood	200	0.20
Oak	700	0.70
Butter	900	0.90
Ice	920	0.92
Ebony	1200	1.2
Sand (dry)	1600	1.6
Concrete	2400	2.4
Glass (soda glass)	2500	2.5
Clay (china clay)	2600	2.6
Aluminium	2700	2.7
Steel	7800	7.8
Copper	8900	8.9
Lead	11000	11
Gold (9 carat)	11000	11
Gold (22 carat)	18000	18
Uranium	19000	19

The densities of some common solids are listed (in kg/m³ and g/cm³) in Figure 2.

- **Find the densities of some other solids by measuring and weighing small rectangular blocks.**

Why is lead denser than aluminium?

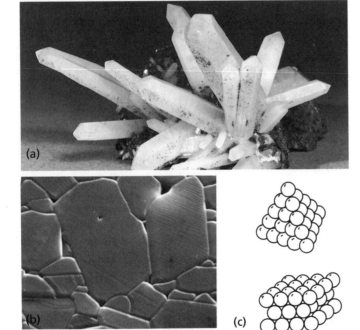

Fig. 3 Lead and aluminium are made of crystals
(a) A large crystal of quartz. Lead and aluminium crystals are too small to be seen without a microscope.
(b) Metal crystals seen through a microscope.
(c) In crystals, the atoms are stacked neatly like these polystyrene balls.

Lead is denser than feathers because the atoms are much closer together in lead than they are in feathers. However, in aluminium, the atoms are just as close together as they are in lead. So why is lead denser than aluminium?

The reason is that the atoms themselves are heavier. Lead atoms have about ten times the mass of aluminium atoms. Uranium atoms are even more massive. Uranium is one of the densest materials in the world. But elsewhere there are even denser materials.

Neutron stars

Neutron stars are much greater in mass than our own Sun. Their gravitational field is far greater than anything that we can imagine. This tremendous force of gravity crushes the atoms of which the star is made.

In neutron stars, each atom is compressed down to the size of its nucleus (Figure 4). A matchboxful of dust from a neutron star has a mass of a thousand, million tonnes!

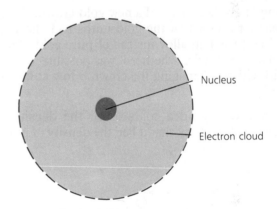

Fig. 4 Atoms have hard, dense centres

Black holes

Black holes are stars whose gravitational field is so great that they pull in everything that gets anywhere near them. They even pull in light from other stars, which makes them appear as black holes in the universe. (It has been suggested that our whole universe could one day be sucked into a giant black hole and disappear, like water down the drain.) Inside these black holes, atoms and the nuclei of atoms are completely crushed to (apparently) infinite density. And that's about as dense as you can get!

- **How many reasons can you think of why it would be impossible to bring some of this very dense material back to Earth?**

Archimedes and King Hiero's crown

Archimedes was a scientific genius who lived in Sicily more than 2000 years ago. Everyone took their scientific and engineering problems to him. 'How can I repel this naval invasion?' asked an admiral. (Legend has it that Archimedes set fire to the enemy ships with sunlight reflected from highly polished metal shields.) 'How can I get a better water pump?' asked the farmers. (Archimedes invented a screw-like device for raising water.) And then there was the problem brought by King Hiero of Syracuse: 'Have I been cheated by the goldsmiths?'

King Hiero had ordered a new gold crown. There was a nasty rumour that the goldsmiths had cheated him, and had used an alloy instead of pure gold. The King asked Archimedes whether it was possible to check the gold without damaging the crown. **How could you do this?**

Archimedes decided to measure the density of the crown and to check that it had the density of pure gold. **What is this density?**

Fig. 1 One way of measuring your volume
How could you use a bath to find the density of your whole body *without* flooding the bathroom floor?

Measuring the density of a crown

To find the density of the crown, Archimedes needed to know the volume. It's easy to calculate the density of a regular object like a cube or sphere, but how do you find the density of an irregular object? **Think about this.**

It is said that Archimedes discovered the answer while he was sitting in the public baths. In his excitement, he ran home naked shouting 'Eureka! Eureka!' ('I've found it!')

If you put a crown (or any other object) into water, the water level will go up. If the container was full to start with, then the water will overflow. The volume of water that overflows is equal to the volume of the crown (provided that the crown is completely under water). If you measure the volume of the displaced water, you will have found the volume of the crown. (Actually, Archimedes went a stage further and measured the upthrust on the crown, but this much will do for our purposes.)

● **Use this method to find (a) the volume, (b) the density of some stones or other irregular-shaped objects. Do all stones have the same density?**

Archimedes was eventually killed by a soldier while he was studying a scientific problem. He was unaware that his country had been invaded, and was busy sketching some ideas in the sand. A soldier came and stood in the sand, messing up his diagram. Archimedes—somewhat unwisely—shouted at him!

Checking the wine

Fig. 2 A hydrometer

You can use the density of homemade wine to tell whether it is ready for bottling. A typical homemade wine starts with a density of $1100 \, kg/m^3$. When it is properly fermented, it has a density of $1000 \, kg/m^3$. (Wine-makers call this the **specific gravity** of the wine.)

You could check the density by weighing the wine and then finding its volume with a measuring jug. A better way is to use a hydrometer (Figure 2). The denser the wine is, the higher the hydrometer floats. **Why is this a better method?**

Figure 3 shows the densities of some common liquids. The easiest to remember, and the one that you are likely to use most, is that of water. Pure water has a density of $1 \, g/cm^3$ ($1000 \, kg/m^3$).

Fig. 3 Densities of some common liquids

Liquid	Density (in kg/m³)	Density (in g/cm³)
Water	1000	1.0
Paraffin (and petrol, and alcohol)	800	0.8
Olive oil	900	0.9
Milk	1030	1.03
Sea water	1030	1.03
Glycerine	1300	1.3
Brine (and the Dead Sea)	1800	1.8

Fig. 4 Swimming in the Dead Sea
Why is it so difficult to swim in this sea?

Gases also have density

Air at normal atmospheric pressure (100 kPa) has a density of just over $1 \, kg/m^3$, i.e. one-thousandth the density of water. **How could you measure this?**

Figure 5 shows the densities of some other gases. **Compare these with the densities of the liquids in Figure 3.** You will see that carbon dioxide is denser than air. Figure 6 shows a way of demonstrating this.

Fig. 5 Densities of some common gases at standard temperature and pressure

Gas	Density (in kg/m³)
Air	1.30
Hydrogen	0.09
Helium	0.18
Methane (natural gas)	0.72
Nitrogen	1.25
Carbon monoxide	1.25
Oxygen	1.43
Carbon dioxide	1.98
Propane	2.02
Butane	2.65

- **Some people have been killed by poisonous carbon monoxide fumes from faulty gas appliances. Are these fumes likely to be worse near the ceiling or near the floor?**

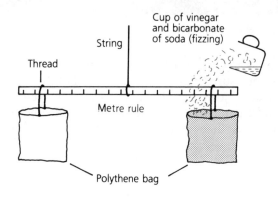

Fig. 6 Carbon dioxide is denser than air
Oxygen is also denser than air. Yet one-fifth of ordinary air is oxygen, and air contains carbon dioxide. Why is air as a whole less dense than these two gases?

In 1986, some carbon dioxide bubbled out of a volcanic lake in Africa and lay on the surrounding land, forcing out the oxygen. More than a thousand people and many thousands of cattle were killed. **Why is carbon dioxide often used for putting out fires? (There are at least three reasons.)**

Pressure under the ocean

North Sea divers

Fig. 1 A deep-sea diver

Divers going down below oil rigs in the North Sea are under pressure (Figure 1). The weight of the sea above them acts down on them. Because the water is all around them, it also pushes against their chests, and their backs. It even presses against the soles of their feet.

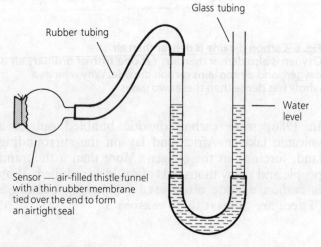

Glass tubing

Rubber tubing

Water level

Sensor — air-filled thistle funnel with a thin rubber membrane tied over the end to form an airtight seal

Fig. 2 A simple pressure sensor
How can this device be used to show that pressure at a given depth within a liquid is the same in all directions?

Water pressure is the same in all directions.

If the pressure on the rubber membrane in Figure 2 increases, then water is pushed round the U-tube. The water level rises. The sensor can be put into water, and its direction altered while the depth is kept constant. **Try this if you can.**

Going deeper

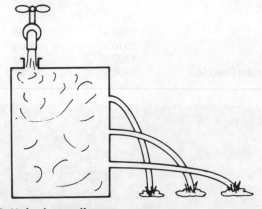

Fig. 3 Holes in an oil can
Water comes out of the bottom hole at higher pressure than it comes out of the top hole. Why?
Why does water often flow much faster from a cold water tap than it does from a hot water tap?

The deeper the divers go, the greater the pressure becomes. Figure 3 shows a way of demonstrating this. If the divers went too deep, the pressure would crush them—their rib cages would collapse! (You can feel the pressure building up if you swim deep under water in a swimming pool.) The water pressure forces some of the air in the divers' lungs to dissolve in their blood. If they then come to the surface too quickly, this air bubbles out of their blood all over their body. This dangerous and very painful condition is known as 'the bends'. North Sea divers take great care to avoid it.

The pressure also depends on the density of the water. It's worse under the dense, cold waters of the North Sea than under a warm freshwater lake.

In fact the pressure under a liquid is given by

$$
\boxed{
\begin{aligned}
\text{pressure} &= \text{depth} \times \text{density} \times g \\
\text{or} &\qquad\qquad\qquad\qquad\qquad (1)\\
P &= h\rho g
\end{aligned}
}
$$

where g is the gravitational field strength, h is the depth and ρ is the density of the liquid.

For example, the pressure at the bottom of a 20 m deep freshwater lake (water density, $1000 \, \text{kg/m}^3$) is

$$
\begin{aligned}
\text{pressure} &= \text{depth} \times \text{density} \times g \\
&= 20 \, \text{m} \times 1000 \, \text{kg/m}^3 \times 10 \, \text{N/kg} \\
&= 200\,000 \, \text{N/m}^2 \\
&= 200\,000 \, \text{Pa}
\end{aligned}
$$

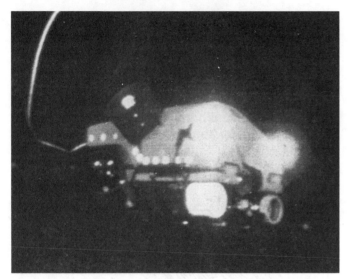

Fig. 4 Jason-Junior – the robot submarine that discovered the Titanic
The Titanic lies on the bed of the Atlantic ocean, approximately 2 kilometres below the surface. What is the pressure at this depth if the density of seawater is $1030 \, \text{kg/m}^3$?

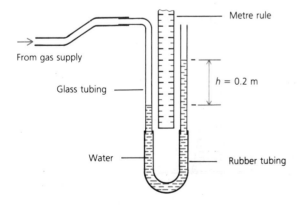

From gas supply

Glass tubing

Water

Metre rule

$h = 0.2 \, \text{m}$

Rubber tubing

Fig. 5 A manometer for measuring pressure
What is the pressure of the gas supply (above atmospheric pressure) in this case?

● **What is the pressure at the bottom of a 3 m deep swimming pool? What is the force due to the water on each cm^2 of your body at this depth?**

Measuring pressure

You can use water pressure to measure the pressure of a gas. In Figure 5, a U-tube manometer is being used to measure the pressure of a gas supply. Since the gas has pushed the water 0.2 m higher on the far side of the manometer, the pressure of the gas must be

$$
\begin{aligned}
\text{pressure} &= \text{depth} \times \text{density} \times g \\
&= 0.2 \, \text{m} \times 1000 \, \text{kg/m}^3 \times 10 \, \text{N/kg} \\
&= 2000 \, \text{N/m}^2 \\
&= 2 \, \text{Pa}
\end{aligned}
$$

● **How could you use this method to measure the pressure of the water supply? Try it if you can.**

Although U-tube manometers are sometimes used in research laboratories (for example, to measure the air pressure inside a wind-tunnel), the most common instrument for measuring pressure is the **Bourdon gauge**.

Figure 6 shows how a Bourdon gauge works. The gas or liquid forces open a flattened tube, causing it to uncoil (against a spring)—just like the fairground toy that uncoils as you blow into it. You may have a Bourdon gauge at school for measuring air pressure.

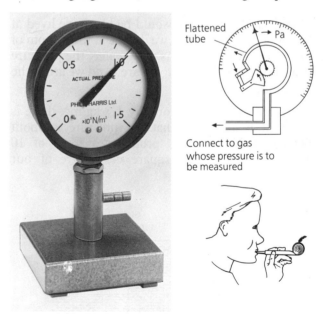

Fig. 6 How a Bourdon gauge works

● **How could you measure the pressure of a water supply using a Bourdon gauge without letting water enter the gauge? Try this if you can.**

67

Under an ocean of air

Pressure from above

Fig. 1 Launching a weather balloon to go high up into the atmosphere
Why has the balloon been only partly filled with gas?

Imagine what the pressure would be like if we lived at the bottom of an ocean. Yet we do live at the bottom of an ocean: an ocean of air. As with water, the pressure of the air is greater the lower you are. And we are at the very bottom.

Although air has a density of only 1.3 kg/m³, there is so much of it above us that the pressure is about 100 000 Pa (100 kPa). This produces a force of 10 newtons (1 kgf) on each square centimetre of our bodies!

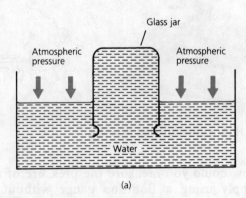

Fig. 2 Why doesn't the water run out?

- Estimate the height of the atmosphere using Equation (1) from Section 5.5. Assume the density of air to be 1 kg/m³ throughout. Do you think that your result is anywhere near the true height of the atmosphere? Why?

Demonstrating atmospheric pressure

Figures 2, 3 and 4 show some ways of demonstrating atmospheric pressure. Water is kept in the upside-down jar and the drinking cup by atmospheric pressure. There is no pressure inside the jar or the cup to push the water out. **What would happen to the cup in Figure 2(b) if you took your finger off the hole? Why?**

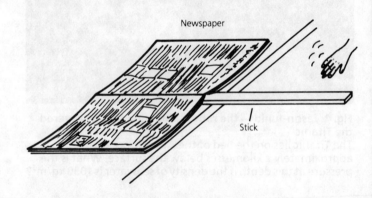

Fig. 3 Using atmospheric pressure to break a stick

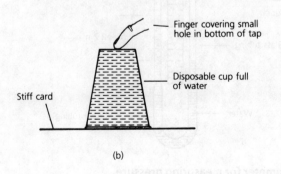

In Figure 3, atmospheric pressure on the newspaper holds the stick down. This allows you to break the stick just by hitting the far end. **What would happen if the paper were not there?**

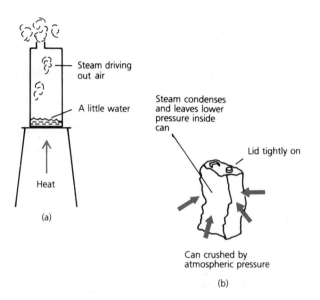

Fig. 4 Using atmospheric pressure to crush an oil can
What force does atmospheric pressure produce on each 30 cm by 20 cm side of the oil can? Suppose that you provided the same force by getting people to stand on the can. How many people of mass 60 kg would be needed?

Figure 4 shows a way of getting atmospheric pressure to crush a can. (*This can be dangerous, and it is not something you should try yourself.*) A little water is boiled in the can so that the steam drives out the air. The can is then corked and allowed to cool. As it cools, the steam condenses to water and leaves a vacuum (or very low pressure) inside the can. The atmospheric pressure outside then crushes the can.

Fig. 5 The Magdeburg hemispheres

In 1645, the Mayor of Magdeburg in Germany wished to demonstrate his new air pump, and the effect of atmospheric pressure. He made two hemispheres a little over a metre in diameter. When these were placed together with an air-tight seal (using grease) and the air was pumped out, two teams of eight horses were needed to pull them apart (Figure 5). **Your school laboratory may have some model *Magdeburg hemispheres* that you can use. If not, use two rubber plungers—the type used for unblocking drains—or, failing that, use rubber suckers.**

Sipping cider through a straw

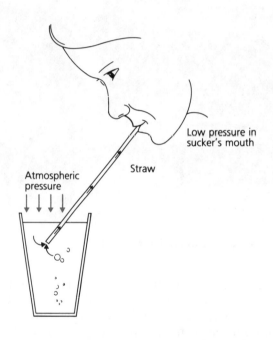

Fig. 6 There's no such thing as suction!
The water isn't pulled up the straw, it's pushed. (Why then do you have to suck harder with a longer straw?)

Strictly speaking, in physics there's no such thing as suction! When you drink with a straw, you don't really suck the liquid into your mouth. There's nothing actually *pulling* on the liquid. What you do is to remove the air, and therefore the pressure, from the top of the straw. Atmospheric pressure then *pushes* the liquid up to your mouth (Figure 6).

If the straw was very long, atmospheric pressure wouldn't be enough to do this. For example, you can't get water from a very deep borehole just by positioning a pump at the top and using it to suck up the water. The pump has to go at the bottom. **Estimate the depth of the deepest borehole from which you could obtain water using a pump at the top.**

5.7   Making use of atmospheric pressure

Rubber suckers

Fig. 1 Suckers lifting a sheet of glass

Rubber suckers are used in industry for lifting flat surfaces like panes of glass or roofing sheets (Figure 1). The sucker is placed gently against the surface. Air is then removed with a pump, until there is no pressure inside the sucker. Atmospheric pressure then pushes the sucker hard against the sheet, and keeps it in place.

Small rubber suckers are sometimes used in people's homes. For example, they may be used to clamp a mincer to a work surface. In this case, the air is removed from inside the sucker just by pressing the sucker against the work surface (Figure 2). **Why do these suckers eventually lose their grip?**

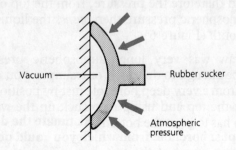

Vacuum — Rubber sucker

Atmospheric pressure

Fig. 2 A rubber sucker

- **Devise a simple method for comparing two of these suckers. Use your method to compare two rubber suckers of different sizes. Which sucker sticks for the longest time? Does it make a difference if you wet the suckers? Why?**

Pumps

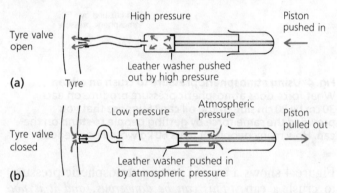

High pressure

Piston pushed in

Tyre valve open

Leather washer pushed out by high pressure

(a)   Tyre

Low pressure

Atmospheric pressure

Piston pulled out

Tyre valve closed

Leather washer pushed in by atmospheric pressure

(b)

Fig. 3 How a bicycle pump works
In diagram (b), the tyre valve prevents the air from coming back out of the tyre into the pump. (A car foot-pump works in the same way. Explain why it isn't identical in its design.)

Figure 3 shows how a simple bicycle or car pump is refilled by atmospheric pressure. Figure 4 shows a lift pump. **Explain how it works and how it makes use of atmospheric pressure.**

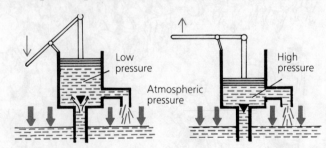

Low pressure

High pressure

Atmospheric pressure

Fig. 4 A lift pump
Why does it have this name?
When it is pumping liquid from a deep borehole, the pump should be at the bottom of the borehole. Why?

Barometers

Atmospheric pressure changes as the weather changes. In a deep **depression**, atmospheric pressure can fall to 96 000 Pa. In an **anticyclone**, it can rise to, say, 104 000 Pa. We can forecast the weather by measuring atmospheric pressure using a barometer. For example, when the pressure rapidly falls, you know that a storm is brewing.

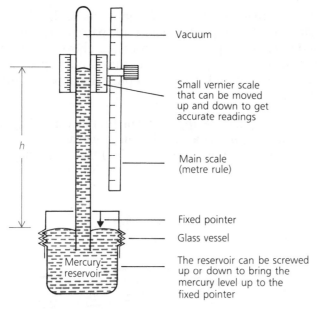

Fig. 5 A Fortin barometer
What is the pressure in pascals when the barometer shows that the difference in mercury levels is 750 mm? (Density of mercury = 14 000 kg/m^3 = 14 g/cm^3.)

Figure 5 shows a Fortin barometer. This was the earliest type of barometer, but it is still the most accurate. Atmospheric pressure pushes mercury up into an evacuated glass tube. The higher the pressure is, the higher the mercury level will be. Mercury is used because it is a very dense liquid—you don't need a large column of mercury to balance atmospheric pressure. (A water barometer would need a pipe more than 10 metres long!)

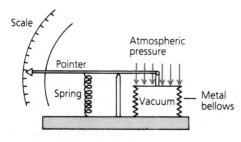

Fig. 6 An aneroid barometer
Why must there be a vacuum inside the bellows?

Today, most barometers are **aneroid barometers** (Figure 6). These contain metal bellows from which most of the air has been removed. ('Aneroid' is an Ancient Greek word meaning 'no air'.) The bellows are held open by a spring. At the same time, they are compressed by atmospheric pressure. The greater the atmospheric pressure, the more the bellows are compressed.

Altimeters

Altimeters enable aircraft pilots to work out their height above the ground. An altimeter is like an aneroid barometer but with a scale showing feet above sea-level. The higher you go, the lower the atmospheric pressure becomes. (Pascal got his brother-in-law to demonstrate this by carrying a Fortin barometer 1000 m up a high mountain!)

An altimeter compares the atmospheric pressure outside the plane with the atmospheric pressure at ground level (Figure 7). Pilots flying above 18 000 ft use an agreed value of ground atmospheric pressure (1013.2 millibars (101 kPa)). Below 18 000 ft, pilots adjust their altimeters to use the atmospheric pressure at the nearest airport.

Fig. 7 An altimeter in an aircraft
What do you think the numbers in the boxes labelled 'IN HG' and 'MG' are?

Pilots also have to remember that some airports are well above sea-level! In 1974, a Boeing 747 was approaching Nairobi airport through a bank of cloud. The captain misheard the ground control and began a descent to 5000 feet. This could have been disastrous—Nairobi airport is at 5327 feet! Luckily the plane came out of the cloud just in time for the captain to take action. But the plane came within 70 feet of crashing into the ground!

Why does an aircraft fly?

Fig. 1 What keeps the plane up in the air?

What causes the aircraft wings to lift the plane into the sky?

- **Hold a thin sheet of paper horizontally on the tips of your fingers. Imagine this to be the wing of an aircraft. Now create a draft of air over the top of the paper using the palm of your other hand. This is like the air flowing over the top of an aircraft wing. What happens to the paper?**

> When air (or any other gas or liquid) flows at high speed, its pressure becomes less.

The faster the air flows, the lower is the pressure. This is called the **Bernoulli effect** after the Swiss mathematician, Daniel Bernoulli, who first explained it.

When a gas or liquid hits something head on, the Bernoulli effect no longer applies. You then have high pressure at the point of impact. For example, the pressure inside a jet of water from a hose is very low. But the jet will compress the soil when it hits the ground. (You can sometimes see the water jet get narrower as it leaves the hose. This shows that there is a region of low pressure inside the water jet.)

Suppose that you create a draught to make the air flow fast over the top of a sheet of paper and slower underneath the paper. The pressure above the paper will then be less than that underneath the paper. The extra pressure underneath will push the paper up into the air.

The same principle applies to an aircraft wing (Figure 2). The wing is shaped so that air flows faster over the top of the wing than underneath it. This creates higher pressure under the wing, which pushes it up into the air.

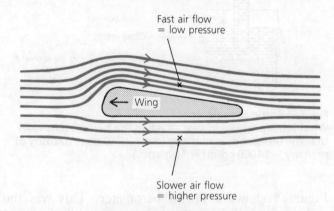

Fast air flow = low pressure

Slower air flow = higher pressure

Fig. 2 Air flow over an aircraft wing
What must the difference in pressure be to lift an aircraft with a mass of 100 tonnes (100 000 kg) and wings of area 1000 m²?

Demonstrating the Bernoulli effect

Two simple ways of demonstrating this effect are shown in Figure 3. When you blow through the cotton reel in Figure 3(a), you expect to blow the card away. In practice, the card stays in place. **Try this!** The fast-moving air blowing over the top of the card produces low pressure. Atmospheric pressure pushes up on the underside of the card and keeps it in place.

If you blew between the balloons in Figure 3(b), you would expect them to move apart. **Try this. What happens in practice? Why? If the air is moving fast through point X, will the pressure here be higher or lower than atmospheric pressure?**

(a)

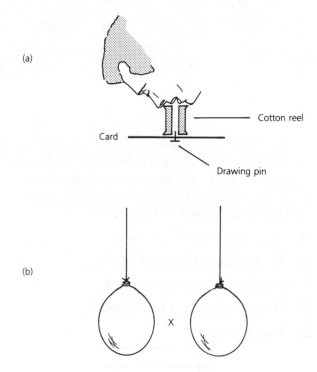

Cotton reel

Card

Drawing pin

(b)

X

Fig. 3 Two tricks using the Bernoulli effect

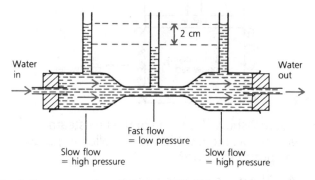

2 cm

Water in

Water out

Fast flow = low pressure

Slow flow = high pressure

Slow flow = high pressure

Fig. 4 Demonstrating the Bernoulli effect
What is the difference in pressure in this case? What would happen to the water levels if you turned off the water supply and at the same time closed the outlet tube?

Figure 4 shows a way of measuring the change in pressure produced by the Bernoulli effect. The water levels rise as the pressure at the bottom of each pipe increases. As water flows through the horizontal pipe, it flows fastest through the narrow central part. The pressure in this narrow part of the pipe is therefore lower than the pressure at each side. This means that the water level in the central vertical pipe is lower than that in the outside pipes.

How a carburettor works

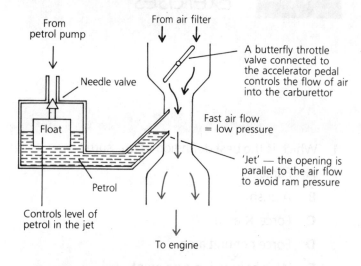

From petrol pump

From air filter

Needle valve

A butterfly throttle valve connected to the accelerator pedal controls the flow of air into the carburettor

Float

Fast air flow = low pressure

Petrol

'Jet' — the opening is parallel to the air flow to avoid ram pressure

Controls level of petrol in the jet

To engine

Fig. 5 How a carburettor works
Why is the end of the jet parallel to the air flow rather than across the air flow?

The Bernoulli effect is used in car engines. The air entering the engine is mixed with petrol in the carburettor. Inside this carburettor, the air passes through a narrow section of pipe which makes it flow faster. Its pressure decreases, and this allows petrol to squirt into the pipe from a small jet. The petrol evaporates and mixes with the air. The petrol/air mixture then passes into the engine cylinders. We will see what happens there in Section 6.9.

- **Figure 6 shows the structure of an airbrush. Use the Bernoulli effect to explain how it works.**

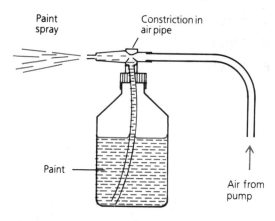

Paint spray

Constriction in air pipe

Paint

Air from pump

Fig. 6 Painting with an airbrush
How does it work?

Exercises

1 Which is the best definition of pressure?

  A   Force

  B   A push

  C   Force × area

  D   Force per unit area

  E   Weight pressing on a point

2 A manometer is used to measure:

  A   Pressure

  B   Density

  C   Depth

  D   Altitude

  E   Temperature

3 You can easily compress a balloon filled with air but not one filled with water. This is because air molecules are:

  A   More compressible

  B   Less dense

  C   Further apart

  D   Moving

  E   Smaller

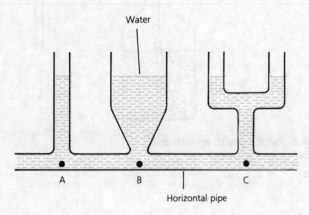

Fig. 1

4 Figure 1 shows three different shapes of waste-pipes containing water. How do the pressures at A, B and C compare with each other?

  A   The pressure at A is the lowest.

  B   The pressure at B is the highest.

  C   The pressure at B is the lowest.

  D   The pressure at C is the highest.

  E   They are equal.

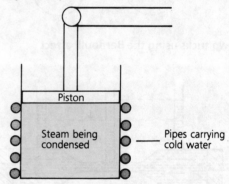

Fig. 2

5 Figure 2 shows how one of the first steam engines worked. Which of the following causes the piston to move?

  A   The pressure of the steam

  B   Atmospheric pressure

  C   Suction produced by the vacuum

  D   The increase in temperature

  E   The Bernoulli effect

6 The pressure in the cylinder of a motorbike engine is 6 MPa (6 000 000 N/m²). This acts on a piston of area 0.003 m². What is the force on the piston in newtons?

  A   18 000

  B   5 000 000

  C   6 000 000

  D   2 000 000 000

  E   18 000 000 000

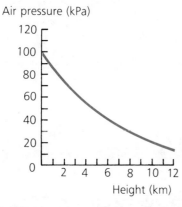

Air pressure (kPa)

Fig. 3

7 Figure 3 shows a graph of air pressure against height above the ground.

a What is the air pressure at 5500 m (18 000 feet)? (See Section 5.7 for the importance of this height to aircraft.)

b Why is the graph not a straight-line graph?

8 If you operate a bicycle pump with your finger over the end to stop the air coming out, what happens

a to the spacing between the air molecules in the pump?

b to the pressure of air in the pump?

c to the density of the trapped air?

9 Explain why:

a a dam is thicker at the base than at the top

b evaporated milk flows out of a tin more easily if you make a second hole in the lid

c a rubber sucker will not stick to the outside of an orbiting satellite

d you should rest a plank or ladder on the ice when rescuing someone who has fallen through, and lie full length on it

e a cushion makes a chair more comfortable to sit on

f most bicycle tyres are pumped up to a higher pressure than most car tyres.

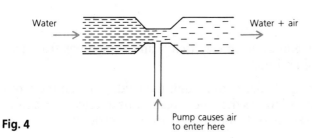

Fig. 4

10 Figure 4 shows a simple **suction pump** that uses the flow of water from a tap to 'suck' air through a pipe. Explain how it works.

11 Calculate the pressure under each of the following, assuming that all the weight is acting on the area indicated:

a An elephant's foot (mass of elephant = 3000 kg; area of elephant's foot = 0.5 m^2).

b A stilletto heel (mass of wearer = 60 kg; area of heel = 0.0001 m^2).

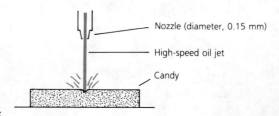

Fig. 5

12 Figure 5 shows an oil jet used at a factory making chocolate bars with honeycombed candy centres. The jet cuts through the brittle sheet of candy without causing it to crumble. The jet has a diameter of 0.15 mm and hits the sheet with a pressure of 18 000 000 Pa (i.e. 180 MPa).

a What is the force on the sheet of candy?

b What is the pressure on the underside of a sheet 50 cm long and 10 cm wide while it is being cut by this oil jet?

c A pressure of 180 MPa inside a tin would cause the tin to explode, yet the oil remains as a narrow jet. Explain this.

13 Our teeth can bite with a force of 1000 N. What is the pressure between them if the total area in contact is 2 cm^2? Suggest a method for measuring this pressure.

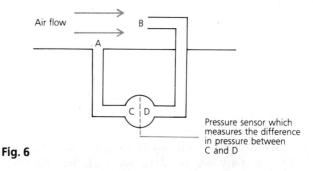

Fig. 6

14 Figure 6 shows a **Pitot tube** which is used to measure the speed of an aircraft relative to the air. Explain how it works. (Hint: What happens to the air pressure at A, B, C and D?)

6 ENERGY

We need energy

Full of energy

Fig. 1 Full of energy
From where did these children get their energy?

Some people are very lively. They play sports, and move around a lot. They are full of **energy** (Figure 1). Where do they get this energy? From their **food**!

Nearly all foods contain energy. Some foods, like unsweetened black coffee, contain very little energy. Others, like lemonade and chocolates, contain a lot of energy. Egg yolk has four times as much energy as egg white.

Our food provides us with energy in the same way as petrol provides a car with energy. Food gives us energy to walk about and to move all our muscles. People in famine-stricken countries don't get enough energy from their food. They quickly become tired and can't move about energetically.

The energy in our food also keeps our bodies warm. What is the outside temperature today? It is unlikely to be higher than 27 °C. What is the temperature inside your body? For the average person, it is 37 °C. Our bodies are usually much hotter than the surrounding air. This is why we need to wear clothes to keep ourselves warm. Our high body temperature helps us to move about quickly. (Lizards have to bask in the sun to raise their body temperature before they can make rapid movements.)

I prefer carbohydrates. They don't leave that burnt taste in your mouth!

Fig. 2 Food to keep ourselves warm
Why do we need to stay warm?
How, and why, do lizards warm their bodies?

A high temperature also helps us to fight disease. People who don't take in enough energy in their food can easily become ill. If their body temperature drops well below 37 °C, they may die of **hypothermia**. (This happens to some old people in this country who aren't properly looked after.)

- **How can tortoises and some other animals survive through the winter without eating?**

Energy from fuel and electricity

We need energy to travel long distances quickly—we can't get very far in an hour on foot. The cars in which we travel get their energy from petrol.

- **Where do lorries get their energy from? What about aircraft? And rockets? And electric trains? Nuclear submarines can stay under water for more than a year (at least so far as the engines are concerned). Where do they get their energy from?**

We need energy to heat and light our homes. We get this energy from electricity, and sometimes from gas, coal and oil.

We need energy to plough the fields, to reap the crops and to process the food. Again, this energy comes from diesel oil and, sometimes, from electricity.

We need energy to mine the minerals, to smelt the metals and to produce the cement, plastics and other materials that we use in vast quantities.

A lot of energy is used up just in obtaining more energy. For example, coal mines and oil refineries use large quantities of electricity. But most of the coal produced in this country is used to generate electricity. Even to build a power station, a large amount of energy is needed. Electricity is sometimes called **secondary fuel** whereas coal, oil and gas are called **primary fuels**. Why do you think this is?

Slaves, oxen and horses

In past centuries, in some parts of the world, slaves did the heavy, manual work for their owners. They supplied a lot of the extra energy needed for large-scale agriculture.

In many parts of the world today, animals provide the energy, at least for transport and agriculture.

Britain's energy needs

We can get some idea of Britain's energy needs by looking at the way in which Britain uses its energy, in particular its electricity, gas, coal and oil. This is shown in Figure 4.

- **Where is most of Britain's oil used? Who are the biggest users of electricity? What other sources of Britain's energy are there that are not shown in Figure 4? Do we really need all this energy? Think of some ways in which we could reduce the amount that we need.**

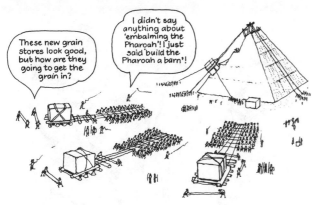

Fig. 3 Slaves – an ancient source of energy
Only today, with other large sources of energy, can we have civilisation without slavery.
What do we mean by civilisation? What has it got to do with energy? (See the section Science, Technology and the World)

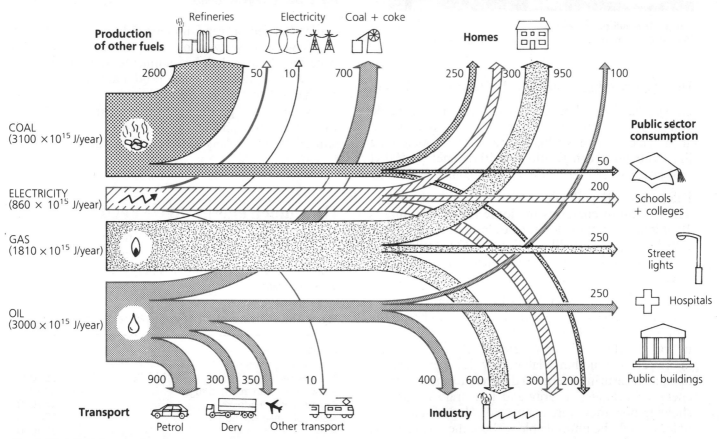

Fig. 4 How Britain uses its energy

77

Kilojoules and killer calories

A million joules of cream cake

Fig. 1 One million joules!
Why are too many slices of cream cake bad for us?

Have you heard someone on a diet talk about calories?

Do you have cereal or crispbread for breakfast, or do you eat low-fat spread? Next time you do, have a look at the label. There is usually a note saying something like 'Nutritional composition per 100 g: energy 1400 kJ (335 kcal)' or '28 kilocalories (117 kilojoules) per slice'.

Kilojoules (kJ) and kilocalories are units of energy. The SI unit of energy is the **joule (J)**. A **kilojoule** is 1000 joules. (A kilocalorie, or Calorie as it used to be called, is equal to 1000 calories and 4200 joules. It is only used in nutrition and not in other branches of science.)

The joule is named after James Prescott Joule who was born near Manchester in 1818. Because of ill health, he didn't go to school but was brought up at home until he was 15. He loved experimenting, and got his father (a brewer) to build him a laboratory. He spent much of his time measuring energy in different forms (electrical energy, mechanical energy and heat transfer) and in showing how they were connected. Modern-day technology would be unthinkable without the results of his experiments.

Fig. 2 Dedication to science

Joule married a very understanding wife! On his honeymoon in Switzerland he came across a beautiful waterfall. Rather than just admiring it, Joule saw this as a way of measuring the production of heat from mechanical energy. He decided to find how much heat the waterfall was producing by measuring the temperature at the top and at the bottom (Figure 2). **Why should there be any difference in these temperatures?**

How much energy do we need?

Figure 3 shows the amount of energy (in joules) in some of the foods that we eat. Figure 4 gives some examples of the amount of energy that we need for various tasks.

Fig. 3 The energy content of some typical foods

A stalk of celery	12 500 J
The white of an egg	67 000 J
The yolk of an egg	250 000 J
A cup of tea with milk and sugar	320 000 J
A glass of lemonade	440 000 J
A slice of bread and butter	500 000 J
A slice of cream cake	1 250 000 J

Fig. 4 The energy needed for various tasks

Lying in bed for 1 hour	250 000 J
Sitting writing for 1 hour	480 000 J
Driving a car for 1 hour	700 000 J
Going for a 20 minute walk	700 000 J
Running for 10 minutes	700 000 J
Swimming for 10 minutes	850 000 J

● Why do you need energy just to lie in bed?

To have enough energy to move and to work and to keep warm, an average adult should eat food containing about 13 MJ of energy every day. (1 MJ (megajoule) is 10^6 J. We could write 13 MJ as 13 000 000 J. The joule is really a very small unit of energy.) Many people in the world today cannot get enough food to provide this much energy.

Fig. 5 Removing excess stores of energy
How can exercise reduce people's weight?

Fig. 6 Not enough stored energy
How have science and technology helped to cause famines?
How could they, instead, help to overcome famines?

Too many joules

In Britain and the industrialised world, most of us eat far more than we need. We take in more energy than is needed to keep us warm, to fight disease, or for physical work and exercise. The excess energy is stored as fat. (6.5 MJ of excess energy is stored as 1 kg of fat.) And too much fat in our bodies is bad for us. Indeed, the increased mass of our bodies makes us reluctant to do the sort of energetic work that would get rid of our fat (Figure 5). Fat puts a strain on our hearts that can lead to heart failure. This is why 'weight-watchers' are always 'counting the calories'. To a weight-watcher, kilocalories become killer calories!

Too many joules of energy in our food—more than we can use—are bad for us. But we must eat enough joules (enough energy) to carry out our normal work, and more if we do any form of vigorous exercise.

79

6.3 Buying energy

A tank-full of energy

Fig. 1 A tank-full of energy
What do we call the form of energy that is present in petrol?

Just as food contains energy, so does petrol. A 50 litre tank of petrol in a car contains about 2000 MJ of energy. This is sufficient for the car to travel up to 800 km (500 miles).

● **How much energy is there in a litre of petrol?**

What about an electric milk-float? This gets its energy from electricity. The electricity comes from chemicals in the batteries that the milk-float uses. (In other words, it comes from chemical energy.) The two huge batteries of a milk-float contain only about 15 MJ of energy each. This is why a milk-float cannot travel very far.

Coal, oil, electricity and gas bring energy into the home. A kilogram of coal contains about 30 MJ of energy.

Electricity boards use their own unit of energy. It is called a kilowatt hour (kW h). 1 kW h ≡ 3.6 MJ. A kilowatt hour is the amount of energy converted by a 1 kW fire in 1 hour.

The gas boards' unit of energy is called a therm. 1 therm ≡ 105 MJ.

Fig. 2 This lump of coal has a mass of 2 kilograms
How many megajoules of energy does it contain?

Energy costs money

Food, coal and oil cost money. You have to pay for the gas and electricity that you use (Figure 3).

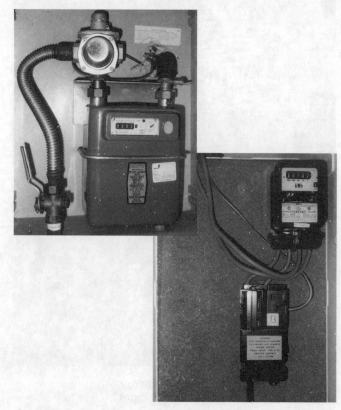

Fig. 3 Meters to measure your usage of energy
What unit do the electricity boards use to measure energy? What unit do the gas boards use? How many joules are equal to each of these units?

When this book was written (1987), coal cost just over 15p per kilogram, a kilowatt hour of electricity cost just under 6p and a therm of gas cost 37p.

- **How much did it cost to use a 2 kW electric fire for 1 hour at this price?**

- **How many joules could you get for a pound with**
  - **(a) coal?**
  - **(b) gas?**
  - **(c) electricity?**
  - **(d) petrol?**

- **How much (on average) does a litre of petrol cost now? How much does a kilogram of petrol cost? (The density of petrol is about 800 kg/m³?)**

- **Have a look at some fuel bills, particularly gas and electricity bills. What is the cost of**
  - **(a) a kilowatt hour?**
  - **(b) a therm?**

  What is the cost of a joule of
  - **(a) electricity?**
  - **(b) gas?**

  What reasons might someone have for using the more expensive of these sources of energy?

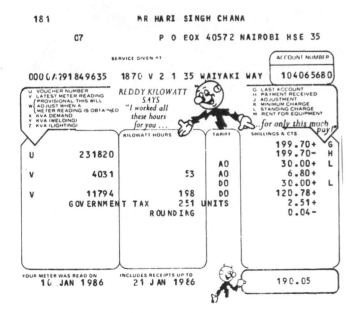

Fig. 4 Mr Reddy Kilowatt
This Kenyan electricity bill represents energy by a man who does work for you 'for only this much pay'. Are there any jobs that a man could do that couldn't be done using electricity? Are there any jobs that can be done by electricity but not by a man?

- **On average, how many kilowatt hours of electrical energy does your family use**
  - **(a) in the winter months?**
  - **(b) in the summer months?**

How many therms of gas? How many joules is this?

Some people have more money to spend than others. In the same way, some people have more energy to use than others. People in North America use the most energy, but those in other industrialised countries use quite a lot. In Africa and Asia, most people don't use very much energy at all. They cannot afford it. Figure 5 shows how the usage of energy varies throughout the world.

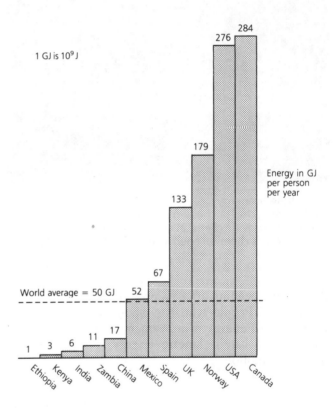

Fig. 5 How the world uses its energy
Zambia has large copper mines and processing plants. This is why it uses more energy (per person) than Kenya. Why do you think that people in Canada use more energy than people in the USA?
Is it right that we should use so much more energy than most people in the world?

- **Could people in Britain survive on the energy used by a typical African family? What extra needs are there in a country like Britain? Think of some ways in which we could save money by using less energy, without making life too unpleasant.**

81

What is energy?

Fig. 1 Kinetic energy
The speeding cheetah has kinetic energy (energy of motion). Its prey will provide chemical energy in the form of food. Where did this chemical energy come from in the first place?

A cheetah speeding after its prey has plenty of energy (Figure 1). People who run about a lot are full of energy. This energy of movement is just one kind of energy. We call it **kinetic energy** (KE). ('Kinetic' means 'of motion'.)

Internal energy

The moving molecules of which everything is made (see Chapter 2) have kinetic energy. Since this energy is hidden inside the solids, liquids and gases around us, we call it **internal energy**. The hotter an object is, the faster the molecules move. A hot object therefore has more internal energy than a cold object.

Some people (incorrectly) call this 'heat' energy. **Heat** is the transfer of energy from a hot object to a cold object. A hot cup of tea doesn't contain heat energy—it contains internal energy. However, it heats you when you drink it. We will look at heat in more detail in Chapter 8.

Chemical energy

A firework has **chemical energy** stored in the gunpowder. When you light the touch paper of a rocket, this chemical energy turns to kinetic energy as the rocket shoots into the sky (Figure 2).

Petrol tanks, cornflakes, lumps of coal and the food that we eat all contain chemical energy.

Fig. 2 Chemical energy about to turn to kinetic energy
What happens to this kinetic energy as the rocket shoots up into the air?

Nuclear energy

This is the energy that is stored in the nucleus of an atom. The nuclear energy of uranium heats water in a nuclear reactor. The nuclear energy of hydrogen is the source of the Sun's energy. We will look at nuclear energy in more detail in Chapter 17.

Potential energy

Where there are forces, there is also stored energy. This **potential energy** (PE) has the potential (the possibility) of turning into kinetic energy. There are several forms of potential energy depending on the forces involved: magnetic potential energy, electric (or electrostatic) potential energy, gravitational potential energy and elastic potential energy.

Magnetic potential energy

Fig. 3 Magnetic potential energy
What other form of potential energy is Sir Lancelot about to gain?

This form of potential energy changes to kinetic energy when a piece of steel moves towards a magnet. Pulling the 'keeper' from a magnet increases the magnetic energy, making the magnet appear more powerful.

Electric (or electrostatic) potential energy

A comb that has been rubbed contains **electric energy** (sometimes called **electrostatic energy**). This enables it to attract someone's hair.

A thundercloud contains a vast amount of electric energy.

Gravitational potential energy

This is the energy that, say, an apple on a branch has because of its position above the ground. Eventually, the apple will fall. The gravitational energy will then change to kinetic energy.

A bicycle at the top of a hill has gravitational potential energy. This potential energy turns to kinetic energy as the bicycle speeds down the hill.

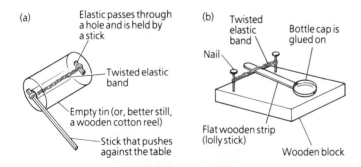

Fig. 4 Elastic energy
(a) A 'tractor' made using an elastic band and a tin (or a cotton reel).
(b) A model hippocaust or catapult made using an elastic band.

Elastic potential energy

A stretched elastic band has **elastic energy**. It can be used to catapult an object, or to make something move (Figure 4). **Try competing with your friends to see who can make the elastic-band tractor that climbs the steepest slope, or the elastic-band catapult that throws a lump of plasticine through the greatest distance.**

Compressed springs also contain elastic energy, and so do the gases in a car engine just after ignition (see Section 6.9).

Electrical energy

Electricity carries energy from one place to another along electric cables. In a torch, electrical energy flows from the batteries to the bulb.

Energy carried by waves

Sound waves carry sound energy from a speaker to your ears.

Light, microwaves, solar radiation, X-rays and gamma rays carry energy. For example, they carry heat radiation from the Sun. (See Chapter 8.)

Ordinary water waves carry energy, so do seismic (earthquake) waves. Seismic waves are produced when rocks suddenly break under the ground. They can carry enough energy to destroy towns and cities on the surface of the Earth. They also make enormous waves on the ocean called tsunami.

Fig. 5 The result of seismic energy
A city destroyed by an earthquake

The many forms of energy discussed in this section are very different from each other. Yet all are measured in joules.

Switching on a million lights

Fig. 1 Switching on a million lights – the Blackpool illuminations
Suppose that there were a million lights each using 40 joules every second. How much would this cost per hour at 6p per unit? (1 unit ≡ 1 kW h ≡ 3.6 MJ)

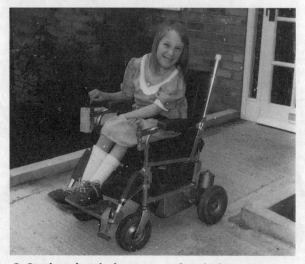

Fig. 2 Storing electrical energy as chemical energy
When the battery under this wheelchair is charged, electrical energy is converted into chemical energy. It is converted back again when electrical energy is needed to drive the wheelchair.

The Central Electricity Generating Board (CEGB) has to cope with a demand for electricity that is far from constant. Consider, for example, what happens when a popular television programme ends. A million lights are switched on in homes throughout the country. A million kettles are switched on. Billions of joules of extra electricity are suddenly needed, but only for a short time.

It is too expensive to have extra power stations just for this short period of high demand. What is needed is some way of storing energy, so that the energy is there waiting for us when we need it.

Batteries

One possibility is to store the energy in batteries (Figure 2). Car batteries and rechargeable radio batteries convert electricity to chemical energy and store this chemical energy. The electricity flowing into the car battery causes a chemical reaction to occur. The new chemicals produced (lead and lead oxide) have more energy than the original chemical (lead sulphate). Later on, when the electrical energy is needed, the chemical reactions occur in the opposite direction. **Why does a car need to store energy in this way?**

The Dinorwig pumped storage scheme

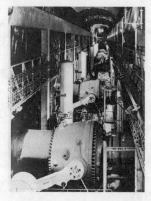

Fig. 3 The Dinorwig pumped storage scheme—the turbine room deep in the mountain
The giant pipes carry water from the high-level reservoir. How does this scheme store energy?

It would be far too expensive for the CEGB to use batteries to store billions of joules of energy for times of peak demand. Instead, the CEGB uses **pumped storage** schemes. At Dinorwig in Wales, the CEGB has created an artificial lake high up in the mountains. When there's a sudden need for electricity, water flows down from the lake through huge turbines which generate electricity. Gravitational potential energy is turned into electrical energy. When the sudden demand is over, electricity is used to pump the water back up to the lake. In other words, the electrical energy is stored as gravitational potential energy until it's needed.

Cuckoo clocks and model cars

Cuckoo clocks also store their energy as gravitational potential energy. You 'wind up' the clock by raising some weights. These keep the clock going as they slowly drop to their lowest position. Most mechanical clocks use springs to store their energy.

Fig. 4 Storing energy as gravitational potential energy
How is the energy stored in a digital watch?

Model cars use clockwork springs as a store of energy. **Make a toy car that uses an elastic band to store energy. Starting from a standstill, how far can you get such as car to go with just one small elastic band?**

Stores of internal energy

Electric storage heaters use cheap off-peak electricity. They are supplied with electricity only when other people are using very little—in the early hours of the morning. This electrical energy has to be stored in the heater until it is needed later in the day. Again, batteries would be too expensive to store such a large amount of energy.

In this case, the energy is stored as internal energy. The off-peak electricity heats a well-insulated ceramic material (like brick) to a very high temperature. This slowly heats the room for the rest of the day (Figure 5).

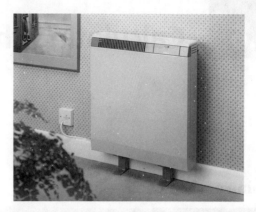

Fig. 5 A storage heater stores heat as internal energy
Ceramic (brick) inside this storage heater is raised to a high temperature by electric heating. For the same increase in temperature, water can store more internal energy than ceramic. Why, then, do these storage heaters use ceramic rather than water?

Regenerative braking

Cars, buses and trains waste a lot of their energy by heating up the brakes as they slow down. On some electric trains, the brake consists of an electricity generator. The brakes slow the train down by converting the kinetic energy of the train to electrical energy. This is stored as chemical energy in a battery. When the train speeds up again, it uses the electricity from this battery.

Some buses are now using flywheels for regenerative braking. When the driver applies the brakes, the flywheel is connected to the bus wheels. This slows the wheels down, and stores energy as the kinetic energy of the spinning flywheel. When the bus is ready to move off again, the flywheel transfers its kinetic energy to the wheels of the bus (Figure 6).

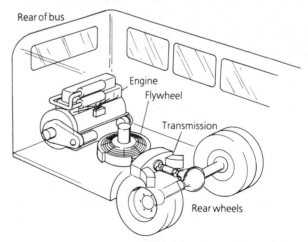

Rear of bus

Engine

Flywheel

Transmission

Rear wheels

Fig. 6 Regenerative braking

● **List some other examples of stored energy.**

Calculating the energy

Pushing a wheelchair

Fig. 1 How much work is he doing?
Why would he do less work if he were taller?

How much energy are you using when you push a wheelchair? This is something that the manufacturers of electric wheelchairs need to know. They can then decide what size of battery they need to use to drive the electric motors.

The energy that you use (or rather **convert**) is equal to the pushing force multiplied by the distance that the wheelchair moves in the direction in which you are pushing it. This is called the **work done** by the pushing force.

> work done = force × distance moved in direction of force (1)
> or
> $$W = Fs$$

For example, if you (or an electric motor) push a wheelchair a distance of 100 m with a force of 100 N, then

work done = force × distance
= 100 N × 100 m
= 10 000 Nm
= 10 000 J = 10 kJ

- How much work would you do pushing a child's pushchair 5 km to town if you pushed with a force of 50 N?

> *Remember:*
> 1 The joule is defined as the work done (or the energy converted) by a force of one newton moving something through a distance of one metre in the direction of the force.
>
> 2 In physics, work is the name given to the energy converted from one form to another by means of a force, and nothing else. (Homework, however difficult, is not 'work' so far as the physicist is concerned.)
>
> 3 Energy is usually defined as 'the ability to do work'. (If you don't have any energy to start with, you won't be able to convert it!)

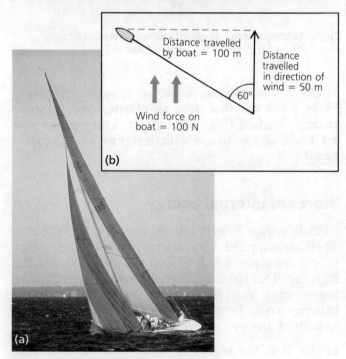

Distance travelled
by boat = 100 m

Distance
travelled
in direction of
wind = 50 m

60°

Wind force on
boat = 100 N

(b)

(a)

Fig. 2 Moving at an angle to the force
(a) A yacht being blown at an angle to the wind.
(b) Calculating the work done by the wind on the yacht. (Work = force *f* × distance *d*.)

Blown by the wind

The distance s in Equation (1) must be in the direction of the force. For example, suppose that a yacht is blown 100 m by a wind of force 100 N at an angle of 60 degrees to the wind direction. As shown in Figure 2, the yacht only travels 50 m in the direction of the wind. The work done by the wind on the boat is therefore only

$$\text{work} = \text{force} \times \text{distance in direction of force}$$
$$= 100\,\text{N} \times 50\,\text{m}$$
$$= 5000\,\text{J}$$

● **What will the work be if the force of the wind increases to 200 N and the boat is blown 200 m at 45 degrees to the wind? Draw a scale diagram to help you to calculate this.**

Lifting paving flags on to a lorry

Fig. 3 How much work is he doing?

How much work is done when you lift a 50 kg paving flag 2 metres on to the back of a lorry (Figure 3)?

work = force × distance moved in direction of force
  = weight × distance
  = (mass × gravitational field strength) × distance
  = 50 kg × 10 N/kg × 2 m
  = 1000 J

This energy is converted into the gravitational potential energy (PE) of the paving flag. Hence

$$\text{change in gravitational potential energy} = \text{mass} \times g \times \text{height}$$
$$\text{or}$$
$$E = mgh \tag{2}$$

● **What is the potential energy of the water in the Dinorwig reservoir if it contains 200 000 000 kg of water and is at a height of 500 m?**

Calculating kinetic energy

Equation (1) can be used to find the kinetic energy (KE) of a moving object. The method is beyond the scope of this book, but the result is as follows:

$$\text{kinetic energy} = \frac{\text{mass} \times \text{speed}^2}{2}$$
$$\text{or}$$
$$E = \frac{mv^2}{2} \tag{3}$$

(Here v represents the *magnitude* of the velocity, i.e. the speed.)

For example, a car of mass 500 kg travelling at a speed of 20 m/s, has kinetic energy

$$\text{KE} = \frac{mv^2}{2} = \frac{500\,\text{kg} \times 20\,\text{m/s} \times 20\,\text{m/s}}{2}$$
$$= 100\,000\,\text{J}$$

● **What is the kinetic energy of a 500 g football travelling at 5 m/s?**

Fig. 4 What is the energy of this football?

Heat and electricity

We shall see in later chapters how to calculate the internal energy gained when something is heated (see Chapter 8) and the electric energy being carried along a wire by an electric current (see Chapter 11).

Digging the garden – using levers and inclined planes

Increasing the force by using a spade

Fig. 1 Why use a spade?
How does a spade make it easier to turn the soil?

How could you dig a garden without a spade? And how could you use a spade that didn't have a handle? The handle of a garden spade is as important as the blade. It acts as a lever – one of the hundreds of levers that we come across every day.

In this case, the lever increases the force. You apply a small 'effort' force to the handle, and the spade turns this into a much larger 'load' force pushing against the soil.

However, there is a drawback: you have to move the handle further than you move the soil. To see why this is so, we need to consider the energy involved:

energy in = energy out

The work that you do on the spade is the same as the work that the spade does on the soil. In each case, work = force × distance (Section 6.6, Equation (1)). Hence, for this and any other lever,

> effort × distance effort moves
> = load × distance load moves   (1)

The smaller the effort force is, the further you have to push the lever to get the same effect (Figure 2).

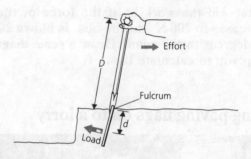

Fig. 2 The spade as a lever
Because the length *D* of the handle is much greater than the length *d* of the blade
(i) the load force is much greater than the effort force
(ii) the handle moves through a much bigger distance than the blade.
What is the ratio of load force to effort force for a spade with handle length $D = 1$ m and blade length $d = 0.1$ m?

Fig. 3 Hoeing – another use of the lever
How is the handle of this woman's hoe helping the blade to travel faster? (One hand is acting as the fulcrum.) The soil here is lighter (less dense), but with a harder surface, than most English soil. Why is a hoe more efficient than a spade in this case?

Increasing the speed by using a hoe

The handle of a hoe acts as a lever, but in this case it is used to increase the speed of movement (Figure 3). The blade moves much faster (and therefore much further in a given time) than the handle. However, in this case, you need a large 'effort' force to move the fairly light blade.

Your forearm works in a similar way (Figure 4). **Estimate the distances D and d in Figure 4 for your own arm. What is the force in your muscle when you lift a 1 kg load as shown? What mass, hanging from your muscle, would produce the same force? Why are our arms designed in this way? What advantages does this design have for, say, throwing a stone into the air?**

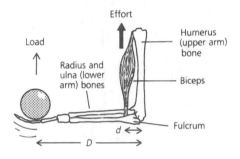

Fig. 4 Your arm as a lever

Inclined planes (or sloping surfaces)

One way of making it easier to climb a hill is to choose a more gently sloping path. You have to walk further, but it is easier.

You are using what is called an **inclined plane.** This isn't a special type of aircraft! An inclined plane is a

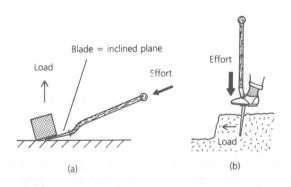

Fig. 5 Using the spade as an inclined plane
(a) Lifting a sod of earth.
(b) Cutting a sod of earth.
Why, in each case, is the load force greater than the effort force?

sloping surface which, like a lever, allows us to turn a small effort force into a large load force.

For example, when you push a spade into a pile of earth, the soil rides up the slope of the blade (Figure 5). The force pushing the soil is much larger than the force on the handle. Figure 5 shows how the spade also acts as an inclined plane when you push it down into the soil.

A wedge used to stop a door from opening acts as an inclined plane, as does a screw. The head of the screw moves (round and round) through a large distance. The point of the screw only goes a short way into the wood. However, the downward force into the wood is much greater than the force on the head of the screw.

- **What other examples of inclined planes can you think of?**

Changing the direction and point of application

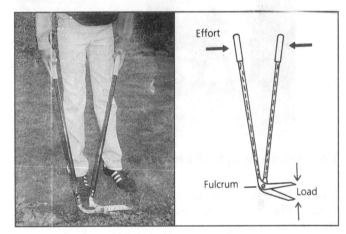

Fig. 6 Using levers to trim the lawn
Each half of the shears works as a lever.
What other common tools use the same principle?

Shears designed for cutting the edges of lawns have long handles. This increases the cutting force. Perhaps more important, the handles change the direction of the force and its point of application. This enables you to cut the edge of the lawn without bending down. Most tools are designed so that the force that we apply is at the most convenient place and in the most convenient direction. **What other examples can you think of?**

Although tools don't give us extra energy, our lives would be much more difficult without them. Some people call man 'the tool-using animal' – it's one of the things that gives us the edge over our animal cousins!

Pulleys, gears and hydraulics

Lifting a heavy load

Fig. 1 Using a pulley to lift a load on to an oil rig

Cranes have pulley systems to enable them to lift heavy loads. The pulley reduces the force that the crane's motor has to apply.

In the pulley system shown in Figure 2, the bottom block is held by four lengths of rope. The tension (the force) in the rope is constant throughout. This means that if you pull the rope with a force of 1 N, each of the ropes supporting the bottom block is also pulled with a force of 1 N. Thus the bottom block is lifted with a force of 4 N. The pulley multiplies by 4 the force that you apply. (In practice, some force is lost in overcoming frictional forces in the pulley wheels.)

As with levers, there's a price to pay: you have to pull four times as much rope. To get the bottom block to rise 1 cm, you have to shorten each of the four ropes by 1 cm. So you have to pull the rope a distance of 4 cm.

- **Where else are pulleys used? Try making a pulley system that will lift a 300 g load with a force of just over 1 N.**

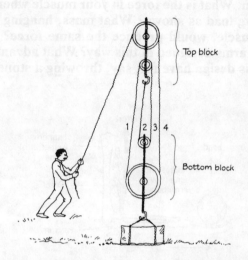

Fig. 2 Four ropes supporting the bottom block
(The pulley wheels of each block are drawn under each other for clarity. In practice, they would lie one behind the other.) How heavy a load can you lift by pulling on the rope with a force of 100 N?

Whisking an egg

The beaters of an egg whisk need to turn very fast. However, they don't need much force to turn them. Egg whisks have gears that enable you to turn the handle slowly (but with a large force) and make the beaters turn at high speed.

Car gears enable a car to go fast, or uphill, without putting a strain on the engine. When a car is going uphill, a large force is needed. The driver selects a low gear, which allows the engine to rotate much faster than the wheels. The gearing increases the effect of the turning force (torque) supplied by the engine. When the car is going at high speed on the level, less force is needed. The driver selects a high gear, making the wheels go much faster than the engine (Figure 3).

Bicycle gears work in the same way, although (in the case of derailleur gears) the gear wheels aren't touching each other. Instead, they are connected by the bicycle chain. **Where else are gears used?**

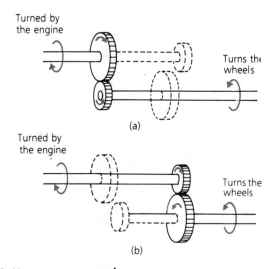

Fig. 3 How car gears work
(a) Top gear is used for high speeds.
In case (a), which turns faster, the engine or the car wheels?
Where is the torque greatest, at the engine or at the wheels?
What about case (b)?
(b) First gear is used for going up a hill.

Wheel and axle

The steering wheel of a car uses wheel-and-axle gearing. The handle has a much larger diameter than the shaft. The force that you apply to the steering wheel is therefore much less than the force changing the direction of the wheel (Figure 4). Similarly, the handle of a screwdriver allows you to tighten a screw using a much smaller force than that applied to the screw. **What other examples can you find?**

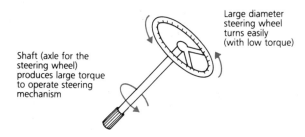

Fig. 4 The wheel-and-axle principle

- Design and make a buggy powered by an elastic band that uses wheel-and-axle gearing. How far can you get it to travel?

Hydraulic systems

The force on a piston is equal to the area of the piston multiplied by the pressure of the air or liquid in the cylinder. To increase the force, all that you need do is to increase the area (use a larger piston).

- Connect two disposable syringes of different sizes with some plastic tubing. Push on each piston in turn, and notice any difference in (a) the force, (b) the distance that the piston moves.

A hydraulic press has a small pump pushing fluid into a very large cylinder (Figure 5). Similar hydraulic systems are used in road diggers and on industrial robots. **Where else are they used?**

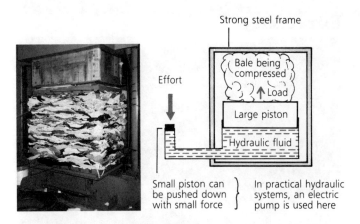

Fig. 5 A hydraulic baling press
This press is compacting rags ready for transport.
The diagram shows how it works, with fluid being forced from a small cylinder into the large cylinder.

In the braking system of a car, the master cylinder drives four similar-sized slave cylinders connected to the brakes. A small force on the brake pedal therefore causes four times this force to be applied to the brakes. The piston of the master cylinder has to move four times as far as each slave cylinder piston (Figure 6).

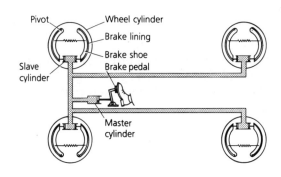

Fig. 6 The hydraulic system for car brakes
Why is it dangerous if air gets into the brake fluid?
(See Section 5.2.)

You can use a wide variety of mechanisms to increase either a force or a speed. However, in each case, increasing one decreases the other. In science, as in life, 'you can't get owt for nowt'!

Under the bonnet

Extra energy

Fig. 1 Under the bonnet
Can you see the air filter on top of the engine to let in clean air?
Can you see the cables supplying electricity to the spark plugs of each cylinder?
Under the air cleaner is the carburettor. What does this do? (See Section 5.8.)

A bicycle doesn't give you any extra energy. It just allows you to use your energy more efficiently. A car does give you energy. Petrol provides this as chemical energy. Petrol burns in the engine to give heat, which drives the engine. We call this an **internal combustion engine.**

The four-stroke petrol engine

This is the most common form of petrol engine. The four strokes are as follows (Figure 2).

1 Inlet stroke (*suck*) – At the start of the stroke, the piston is at the top of the cylinder. The inlet valve is opened. The piston then moves down the cylinder, allowing an explosive gas consisting of air and petrol vapour to enter the cylinder.

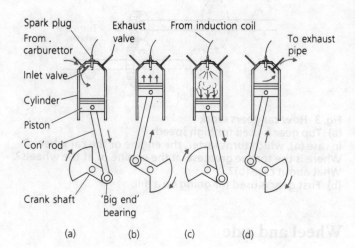

Fig. 2 The four-stroke petrol engine—suck, squash, bang, blow
(a) Inlet stroke
(b) Compression stroke
(c) Power stroke
(d) Exhaust stroke
What causes the piston to move in steps (a), (b) and (d)?

2 Compression stroke (*squash*) – The inlet valve closes. The piston moves up the cylinder and compresses the gas.

3 Power stroke (*bang*) – The spark plug produces a spark which sets fire to the gas. (This is called **ignition.**) The gas burns rapidly, reaches a very high temperature and expands, pushing the piston down the cylinder.

4 Exhaust stroke (*blow*) – The exhaust valve opens and the piston moves up the cylinder, pushing the burnt gases out to the exhaust pipe.

The power stroke is the only stroke that turns the engine. In the other three strokes, the piston is moved by the turning engine. Because of this, car engines contain at least four cylinders. (Some cars have six cylinders and some racing cars have twelve.) At any time, one of the pistons is being pushed down on its power stroke. This piston pushes the car forwards and also pushes the other pistons on their inlet, compression and exhaust strokes (Figure 3).

Fig. 3 Inside the engine block
Can you see the cylinders?
Can you see a piston?

Diesel engines

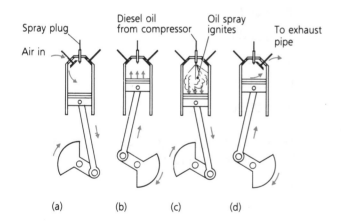

Fig. 4 The four-stroke diesel engine
(a) Inlet stroke – air (only) enters through the inlet valve
(b) Compression stroke – the air is very highly compressed and reaches a high temperature
(c) Drive stroke – diesel oil (DERV) is sprayed into the cylinder. It ignites, heats the air further and pushes down the piston
(d) Exhaust stroke – the waste gases are pushed out through the exhaust valve.

Diesel engines are similar to petrol engines except that no spark plug is used. Also, no fuel is added until the last minute. In the compression stroke, the piston compresses air alone, heating it as it does so. Oil is then injected (squirted) into the cylinder. The oil catches fire immediately because of the high temperature and pressure (Figure 4).

Because diesel engines work at higher pressure than petrol engines, they need to be stronger (and this makes them heavier). They do not produce such good acceleration as petrol engines. However, diesel engines are more efficient. They use much less fuel, especially when they are just 'ticking over'. Although in the past they were mainly used for lorries and buses, they are now increasingly being used in cars.

Fig. 5 A car that uses a diesel engine
What are the advantages?
What are the disadvantages?

- Look through some advertising leaflets for various cars, including diesels. Compare the fuel usage, compression ratio, weight and acceleration for diesel cars and petrol cars with the same capacity (the same cylinder volume).

Heat engines

Car and diesel engines are **heat engines.** Steam engines and steam turbines are also heat engines. A heat engine takes energy from a high temperature gas (or, in some cases, a liquid) and pushes the gas out through the exhaust at a lower temperature. Work is done in the process. It was the study of heat engines that made physics so important at the time of the industrial revolution. Even today, this is a very important branch of physics.

Exercises

1 The unit of electrical energy used by electricity boards is the

  A   Joule

  B   Calorie

  C   Therm

  D   kWh

  E   Kilowatt

2 Which of the following cannot be measured in joules?

  A   Magnetic energy

  B   Potential energy

  C   Kinetic energy

  D   Work

  E   Moment

Fig. 1

3 Figure 1 shows a pulley which is about to be used to lift a machine up to a first-floor workshop. At present, the machine is not moving. How will the energy of this machine have changed once it is at rest in the workshop?

  A   Its kinetic energy will have decreased.

  B   Its kinetic energy will have increased.

  C   Its potential energy will have decreased.

  D   Its potential energy will have increased.

  E   Its elastic energy will have increased.

Fig. 2   What is the energy of this eagle?

4 A 5 kg eagle flies at a height of 100 m. What is its gravitational potential energy?

  A   500 J

  B   2500 J

  C   5000 J

  D   25 000 J

  E   500 000 J

5 The 5 kg eagle of question **4** flies at 10 m/s. Its kinetic energy is equal to

  A   25 J

  B   50 J

  C   250 J

  D   500 J

  E   1000 J

6 Which of the following is true of water flowing at a constant rate along a drain?

  A   Its gravitational PE is decreasing.

  B   Its kinetic energy is increasing.

  C   There is no force acting on it.

  D   Its thermal energy is decreasing.

  E   It is producing energy.

7 Complete these sentences:

a Fat in our bodies is a store of _____ energy. Uranium contains _____ energy.

b The work done in lifting a crate on to the back of a lorry is equal to the _____ of the crate multiplied by the _____ of the back of the lorry.

c When lizards warm themselves in the sun, they are converting the _____ energy from the sun to _____ energy in their bodies. This enables them to move about faster, converting the _____ energy of the food stored in their bodies to _____ energy.

8 Show how the objects in Figure 3 act as levers. To do this, draw each of the levers as straight lines, and show the position of the fulcrum, the load (force) and the effort (force):

a Nutcrackers or pliers

b Scissors

c A wheelbarrow (with the wheel at the front)

d Your lower jaw

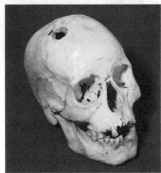

Fig. 3

9 Explain the connection between the following:

a A path up a hill

b A wedge-shaped chisel being hammered into a piece of wood

c A wood screw

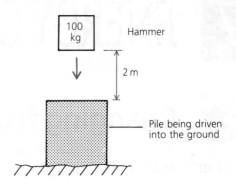

Fig. 4 A pile-driver

10 Figure 4 shows the hammer of a pile-driver at a building site being used to drive a steel pile into the ground. (The pile-driver lifts the hammer and then drops it.)

a What is the change in the gravitational potential energy of the pile as it falls?

b What is its kinetic energy when it is about to hit the pile? (Ignore air resistance.)

c What happens to this kinetic energy once the hammer has hit the pile?

11 A pulley system is to be used on a crane to raise loads of up to 1000 kg as quickly as possible. The maximum effort force with which the motor can pull is 2000 N. Draw a suitable pulley system.

12 It has been suggested that you use more energy chewing a piece of celery than you get from eating it!

a What work do you do in biting the celery once if your teeth move a distance of 1 cm and bite with a force of 10 N?

b Suppose that it takes 100 bites to chew a stick of celery. How much energy is needed for this?

c Suppose that your digestive system takes 1000 J of energy from the celery (about 10% of its total chemical energy). Calculate the energy that you gain or lose when eating the celery, and state whether it is a gain or a loss.

13 Low-octane (2-star) petrol explodes at a lower pressure than high-octane (4-star) petrol. Use the four stroke cycle of the petrol engine to explain why a high compression engine is less powerful (and can be damaged) if low-octane petrol is used.

95

7 ENERGY CONVERSION

7.1 Changing from one form to another

Power plants don't make energy

Fig. 1 Two types of 'power plant'
Power stations convert chemical or nuclear energy to electrical energy.
What energy conversion happens in the grass that these horses are eating?

Power stations do not *make* energy. They convert it into a form that we can use. They change some other form of energy into electrical energy. Most British power stations take in chemical energy (coal or oil) or nuclear energy (uranium). Some power stations use the gravitational potential energy of water piled up behind a dam. It is these forms of energy that are converted into electrical energy in the power station (Figure 1).

Americans call power stations 'power plants'. The other type of plants—the green ones that you find in the garden—are rather like power stations. They don't make energy either. Instead, their leaves convert solar energy to chemical energy. They produce (high-energy) sugar out of carbon dioxide and water. This conversion process is called **photosynthesis**. Without it, we would have no food to eat, and no coal, oil or peat to dig out of the ground.

- Why are grapes grown in the south of Europe, or on south-facing slopes, usually sweeter than grapes grown elsewhere?

Using energy

When you use energy, it isn't used up. It is just converted into some other form (Figure 2). For example, when you use petrol in a car, the energy isn't lost. It is partly converted to kinetic energy and partly to internal energy. (The engine rotates, and gets hot.) When you apply the brakes, they get hot—the car's kinetic energy is converted into internal energy.

When you use energy to dig a hole, this energy isn't lost either. The soil gains some gravitational potential energy and you gain some internal energy.

- **Where do batteries get their energy from? (See Section 6.3.) In what form does energy enter a wind-powered generator?**

Fig. 2 Converting electrical energy to other forms
What forms of energy are given out by (i) the toaster? (ii) the television? (iii) the food mixer?

Energy chains

Energy is seldom changed directly from its initial (starting) form to its final form. It usually goes through a chain of energy conversions.

Figure 3 shows our weather system as an energy chain, starting with solar energy from the Sun.

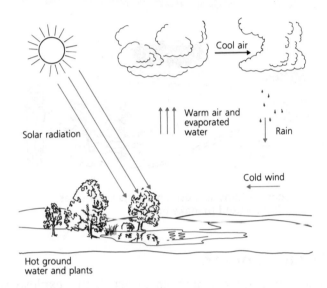

Fig. 3 An example of an energy chain
Explain what is happening in this diagram, and list the energy changes involved.

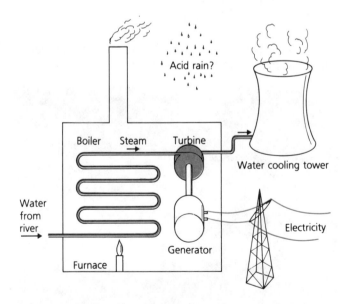

Fig. 4 How a power station works
A coal or oil furnace, or a nuclear reactor, heats water. The water turns to steam under high pressure. This causes a turbine to rotate, which turns a generator attached to the same shaft. The generator produces electricity.

Figure 4 shows the processes which take place in a power station.
● List the energy changes that occur in
   (a) **the furnace**
   (b) **the boiler**
   (c) **the turbine**
   (d) **the generator.**

You can't make energy and you can't get rid of it!

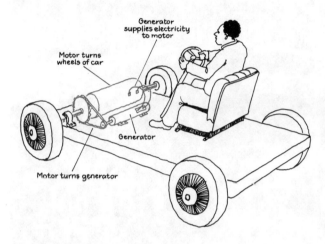

Fig. 5 Why won't it work?

Many people have tried to design machines that will keep on working for ever, without an energy source (Figure 5). Other people would like to find a way to destroy energy. For example, people have tried to design brakes that will slow a car down without heating up in the process. Unfortunately, neither is possible.

> Energy can be neither created nor destroyed, but only turned into other forms.

This is called the principle of **conservation of energy**. It's a nuisance when you want to run a car. But without this law the universe itself wouldn't work—and that's rather more important!

Power for the people

People want power

Fig. 1 (What sort of) power for the people?
Protestors at the new Brockdorf power station in West Germany. Why do you think they were protesting? (See Section 17.10.)

Most people don't talk much about energy. Instead, they talk about power. A lot of people want things to happen in a hurry. For example, they want a powerful car so that they can drive faster and overtake the car in front. In other words, they want a car that converts chemical energy to kinetic energy very rapidly.

Of course, a powerful car needs powerful brakes, so that it can stop quickly, but safely. The brakes must convert kinetic energy to internal energy as fast as possible.

At home, we might want a powerful electric kettle so that we can boil water quickly—that is, the kettle must convert electrical energy to heat energy in a short time.

Power can be dangerous as well as useful. Powerful explosives give out a lot of energy in a very short time. (In fact, a lump of coal contains as much energy as some explosives. But coal isn't much good as an explosive, because it doesn't give out its energy fast enough.)

Fig. 2 Coal contains as much energy as explosives
Why can't it be used to make bombs?

What is power?

The power of a machine, an electric kettle, explosives or anything else, is the rate at which energy is converted from one form to another.

$$\text{power} = \frac{\text{energy}}{\text{time}} \qquad (1)$$

Power is measured in **watts** (W). One watt is equal to one joule per second. (1 W = 1 J/s.)

Fig. 3 One oxpower?
Although the watt is named after the Scotsman James Watt, he actually invented another unit—the horsepower (hp) (1 hp = 750 W).

Examples of power in watts

Every second, a 100 W light bulb converts 100 joules of electrical energy to light energy (and internal energy—light bulbs can get very hot).

A 1 kW (1000 W) electric kettle converts 1000 joules of electricity to internal energy each second. In 1 minute it will have converted 60 000 joules of internal energy, and in 1 hour it will have converted 3 600 000 joules. Thus, as stated in Section 6.3, the electricity boards' unit of energy—the kilowatt hour—is equal to 3 600 000 joules.

- **How long will it take a 100 W light bulb to use 1 kW h of energy?**

Fig. 4 Examples of power ratings

Items	Power	
Click beetle leaping into the air	0.5 W	
Powerful torch	5 W	
Car headlights, TV, microcomputer	50 W	
Swimming (enthusiastically!)	300 W	
One horsepower (hp)	750 W	
One-bar electric fire	1 kW	(1000 W)
Leaping red deer	2 kW	(2000 W)
Central-heating boiler	20 kW	$(2 \times 10^4 \, \text{W})$
Austin Maestro car	50 kW	$(5 \times 10^4 \, \text{W})$
Jaguar car	150 kW	$(1.5 \times 10^5 \, \text{W})$
Railway locomotive	1 MW	$(10^6 \, \text{W})$
World's most powerful tug	10 MW	$(10^7 \, \text{W})$
Saturn V moon rocket	100 MW	$(10^8 \, \text{W})$
Britain's largest power station	10 GW	$(10^{10} \, \text{W})$
Giant flash of lightning (100 kJ)	1 TW	$(10^{12} \, \text{W})$
Most powerful conventional bomb	$10^{19} \, \text{W}$	
One-megatonne hydrogen bomb*	$10^{22} \, \text{W}$	
Krakatoa volcano exploding in 1883	$10^{24} \, \text{W}$	
The Sun	$10^{26} \, \text{W}$	

* A **neutron bomb** has ten times the energy of a hydrogen bomb (for the same power). But it takes ten times as long to explode $(10^{-6} \, \text{s})$. More energy for the same power means more radiation for the same blast. So the bomb is said to destroy people rather than buildings.

Power = force × velocity

work = force × displacement in direction of force

Thus

$$\text{power} = \frac{\text{work}}{\text{time}} = \frac{\text{force} \times \text{displacement}}{\text{time}}$$

$$= \text{force} \times \frac{\text{displacement}}{\text{time}}$$

In other words,

$$\boxed{\text{power} = \text{force} \times \text{velocity}} \qquad (2)$$

Suppose, for example, that a car engine pushes the car with a force of 1000 N at 20 m/s. The power of the engine is

$$\text{power} = \text{force} \times \text{velocity}$$

$$= 1000 \, \text{N} \times 20 \, \text{m/s} = 20 \, 000 \, \text{W}$$

- **What would be the power of a car pulling with a force of 500 N at 30 m/s?**

The new Class 91 *Electra* locomotive pulls at speeds of up to 67 m/s. Its power is 4.5 MW (1 MW = 10^6 W). Using these figures, the pull of the locomotive would be:

$$\text{force} = \frac{\text{power}}{\text{velocity}} = \frac{4 \, 500 \, 000 \, \text{W}}{67 \, \text{m/s}}$$

$$= 67 \, 000 \, \text{N}$$

Human power

Fig. 5 Suppose that our only power supply was from human beings!
Many of the tasks for which we use electricity were in the past carried out by slaves. State some examples.

Imagine what our lives might be like without modern power machinery. It *is* like that for many other people in the world today. The work that we do with power machinery they have to do themselves, with people working at an average rate of about 100 W.

- **How many people would be needed, at this value of power, to do the work of a 50 kW tractor? How many people would be needed to replace a 2 kW washing machine? If human labour were to cost £1 per hour, how much would 1 kW h of human labour cost? How much does this amount of electricity cost at present? Are these fair comparisons (and if not, why not)?**

- **Try measuring your power in running upstairs. (Just consider the work done against gravity.)**

Where does our energy come from?

The 'big bang'

Many scientists believe that, long ago, the whole universe was in the form of a single fireball. This exploded. It threw out into space all the matter now in the universe. All the energy that now exists also came from this fireball. This energy has been estimated at 10^{68} joules.

Energy from the Sun

Fig. 1 Shutting off the source of most of our energy
This total eclipse of the Sun was caused by the Moon passing between the Earth and the Sun.
How does the Moon provide us with energy?

Today we still have our own 'fireball'. We call it the Sun. Every year the Sun gives out 10^{34} joules of energy, of which 10^{25} joules reach the Earth.

Although it gives out all this energy, the Sun doesn't cool down. Its surface temperature remains at about 6000 °C. It is kept hot by **nuclear reactions**—the same type of reactions that occur in a hydrogen bomb. One day, all the hydrogen in the Sun will be used up, but that won't happen for many millions of years.

The Sun provides nearly all the Earth's energy. It controls our weather system and puts chemical energy into the plants that we eat (see Section 7.1). The Sun provided the chemical energy for the plants and sea organisms that, over millions of years, have formed coal, oil and gas deposits (Figures 2 and 3).

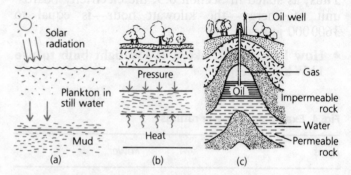

Fig. 2 How petroleum oil was formed
(a) Over millions of years, plankton in shallow seas took in solar energy. When they died, they fell into the mud at the bottom of the sea.
(b) As millions more years passed, layers of sediment built up on the sea bed. These layers pressed down on the mud at the bottom, and heated it until it formed rock. The compression and heat turned the remains of the plankton into oil.
(c) Most of the oil flowed to the surface. But some was trapped underground, often with natural gas above it. We can drill down and recover this gas and oil.
Where are the world's most important oilfields?

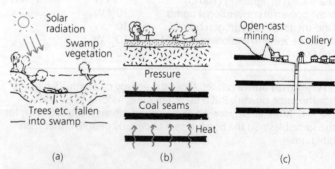

Fig. 3 How coal was formed
(a) Millions of years ago, tropical swamp vegetation, which had grown with energy from the Sun, died and fell into the swamps.
(b) As the vegetation decayed, it formed peat. As millions of years passed, layers of rock built up on top. The rock pressed down on the peat and made it heat up. Eventually, the heat and the pressure turned the peat into coal.
(c) These coal seams can now be reached by open-cast mining, or by drilling mine shafts.
The fact that we have coal seams in Britain shows that this country once lay in the tropics. How can this be? (See Chapter 9.)

- The planets Mercury and Venus are much warmer than Earth. Mars is colder. Why?

Energy from the Earth

Many millions of years ago, the Earth was a fireball, too. Now the surface of the Earth has cooled. But deep inside the Earth it is still very hot—around 4000 °C! (That is why coal mines have to be cooled and ventilated by constant streams of air.)

The Earth has been kept hot by nuclear reactions which happen inside the core or centre of the Earth. A product of these reactions is the uranium used in nuclear power stations. Some scientists are now experimenting to find out whether some of our oil resources were produced deep inside the Earth by these nuclear reactions.

Water which sinks down from the surface is heated up by the hot underground rocks. Some of the water returns naturally to the surface in the form of geysers and hot springs (as in the Roman Baths at Bath). This hot water is a valuable source of energy. In some countries, people drill very deep boreholes to underground lakes. The water in such lakes is much hotter than in the springs and geysers which come naturally to the surface. When the boreholes reach the underground water, high pressure forces the water to boil and rush to the surface as powerful steam jets. This **geothermal energy** is being used to produce electricity in, for example, Iceland, Kenya, New Zealand and the USA.

Fig. 4 The Sodi Geyser in Iceland
What is the source of energy for this geyser?
How can we use this energy source?

- See what you can find out about the Cornish Hot Rocks Project (Cambourne School of Mines) and the growth of tomatoes and other vegetables in Iceland.

Energy from the Moon

Since the 'big bang', the Moon has lost most of its internal energy. But it must still have kinetic energy, since it moves round the Earth. As it circles, its gravitational field affects the Earth's oceans, and produces the tides. On average, the difference between high tide and low tide is only half a metre. However, on some of Europe's western coasts, the difference can be several metres. Britain has plans to harness the tide in the Mersey and Severn estuaries. A tidal scheme in the Severn estuary could meet 12% of the energy needs of England and Wales. France is already using tidal power in the Rance estuary. **Find out what you can about these projects.**

Comparing the three sources

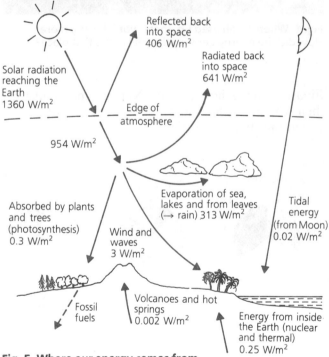

Fig. 5 Where our energy comes from
The energy from the Moon comes from its kinetic energy.
What does this suggest is happening to the Moon?

Taking the Earth as a whole, 99.98% of our energy comes from the Sun. Most of the rest comes from the Earth itself. In comparison, the energy that we get from the Moon is negligible.

101

Britain's sources of energy

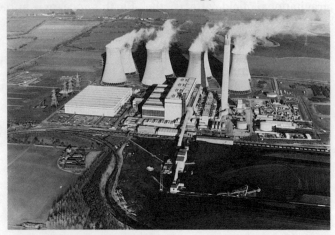

Fig. 1 When it's all used up, there won't be any more!
How did the energy get into the coal in the first place?

Figure 2 shows how Britain, Norway and Kenya get their energy. **What differences do you notice between the three countries?**

Most of Britain's energy comes from underground sources. Much of our oil and gas comes from under the North Sea. Our coal comes from mines in many parts of Britain, and uranium is imported from mines in Canada, South Africa and Australia.

Figure 3 shows Britain's power stations. **How many coal-fired power stations are there? How many oil-fired power stations? How many nuclear power stations? How many hydroelectric power stations?**

Non-renewable resources

It took millions of years to produce the **fossil fuels**—oil, gas and coal—that we use today. It took even longer to produce the reserves of uranium. These are all **non-renewable** sources of energy.

Oil and gas have probably already passed their peak of production. They will not suddenly run out, but they will increase in price (again!) until we can no longer afford them. This may well happen early in the next century.

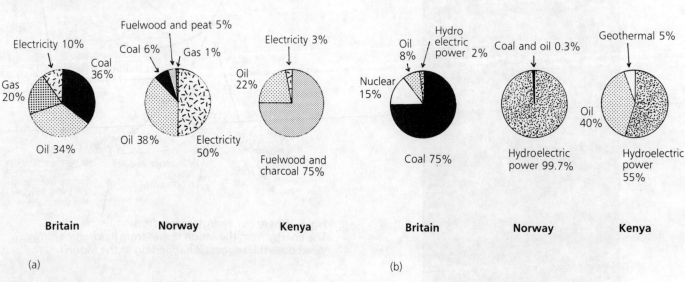

(a)   (b)

Fig. 2 How three countries get their energy
   (a) The main sources of energy
   (b) The sources of energy used for generating electricity
What is the main source of energy in each of the three countries?
What fraction of the electricity in each of the three countries is produced by renewable energy sources?

Fig. 3 Large power stations in Britain

Coal-fired power stations

C1 Longannet	C7 Thorpe Marsh	C13 Drakelow C
C2 Cockenzie	C8 West Burton A	C14 Didcot
C3 Blyth B	C9 Cottam	C15 Tilbury B
C4 Ferrybridge C	C10 High Marnham	C16 Grain
C5 Eggborough	C11 Fiddler's Ferry	C17 Aberthaw B
C6 Drax	C12 Ratcliffe	

Nuclear power stations

N1 Windscale	N7 Trawsfynydd	N13 Hunterston
N2 Calder Hall	N8 Dungeness A	N14 Hartlepool
N3 Chapelcross	N9 Sizewell	N15 Heysham
N4 Berkeley	N10 Oldbury	N16 Dungeness B
N5 Bradwell	N11 Wylfa	N17 Winfrith
N6 Hinkley Point A	N12 Hinkley Point B	N18 Dounreay

Oil-fired power stations

O1 Inverkip	O4 Pembroke	O7 Kingsnorth
O2 Kilroot	O5 Grain	
O3 Ince B	O6 Fawley	

Oil/coal-fired power station

D1 West Thurrock

Hydroelectric power stations

H1 Fasnakyle	H3 Rannoch	H5 Clunie
H2 Errochty	H4 Sloy	H6 Rheidol

Pumped-storage schemes

P1 Ffestiniog	P3 Dinorwig	P4 Foyers
P2 Cruachan		

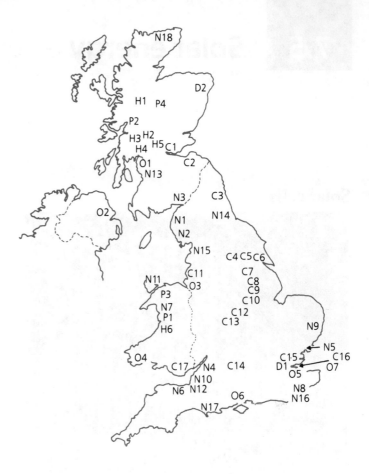

Explain the typical positions of each of these types of power station. (For example, why are the nuclear sites all near the coast?)

Coal will last longer, perhaps for a few hundred years. Then that will also 'run out'. (In other words, it will become too expensive to extract and burn.)

Increased use of nuclear power is sometimes seen as a way of conserving coal, oil and gas. But uranium itself will eventually run out. If we build a lot of nuclear reactors (other than breeder reactors—see Chapter 12), then uranium will run out long before coal.

We are using up these resources at a dramatic rate

Coal, oil, gas and uranium have been buried in the Earth for millions of years, yet in only a few centuries we have almost used them up.

Of course, this may be the right thing to do. Perhaps in the future we will no longer need these resources, so it is sensible to use them now. But we're taking a big risk—once we have used up these resources, that's it!

Some scientists think that within the next 100 years we will have discovered how to build nuclear fusion reactors that use deuterium instead of uranium. All water contains some deuterium, so the ocean could supply all our energy needs for thousands of years. But this is still just a dream—at present, we don't know how to make power stations that run on deuterium.

We need to look at other, *renewable* sources of energy—and to see how we can reduce our need for energy.

103

Solar energy

Solar cells

Fig. 1 Solar cells (photovoltaic cells) for a water pump
Solar cells convert at most one-tenth of the solar energy falling on them into electricity. What happens to the rest of the solar energy?

The Sun shines down on us every day with far more energy than we need. In tropical and sub-tropical regions, around 1000 W of solar energy falls on each square metre of land. Even Britain (believe it or not!) gets many times the solar energy needed to supply all its energy needs. Why can't we use this solar energy directly?

We can. Solar cells (**photovoltaic cells**) can turn solar energy directly into electricity. These solar cells were first used to power space vehicles. They are now used in everything from solar-driven watches and calculators to large water-pumping stations in tropical countries.

Unfortunately, solar cells are expensive. They are only worthwhile if
(a) you don't need much electricity (as in a pocket calculator) or
(b) you want to power something in a sunny but out-of-the-way place.
For example, solar cells are used to power remote telecommunications repeater stations that increase the strength of telephone signals, to drive water pumps, to power electric fences etc.

The price of solar cells is steadily dropping. Before long, they may be a very important source of power in countries where there is plenty of sunshine.

- **You may be able to get hold of a cheap, low-power motor that will run off a solar cell. If not, try connecting a cheap voltmeter across a solar cell and using it as a light meter.**

Solar drying

Fig. 2 Make hay while the Sun shines
What other things do people dry using solar radiation?

This is one way in which we all use solar energy directly. For example, we hang clothes out to dry. Many crops (such as hay) are dried by the Sun. This use of solar energy is simple and costs us nothing.

Solar water heaters

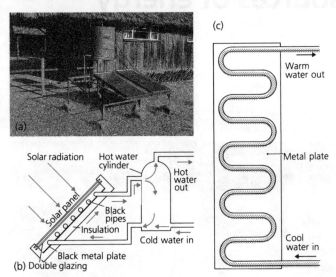

Fig. 3 A solar heater
(a) A low-cost solar heater in use in Africa
(b) How it works—side view
(c) The design of the solar panel as seen from above
The solar panel is always painted black and covered with glass (usually double-glazed). Why? (See Chapter 9.)

Solar water heaters are another way of using solar energy. Figure 3 shows how a typical solar heater works. Even in Britain solar energy can be used to preheat water before using some other form of heat, or to warm water for use in swimming pools. (Unfortunately, solar heaters are usually too expensive for this to be worthwhile.) However, in many parts of the world, solar heaters are very effective. In Israel, for example, they provide hot water for most of the houses.

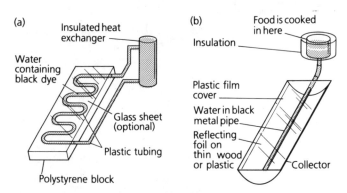

Fig. 4 Home-made solar heater and solar cooking

- Try making one of the simple solar heaters shown in Figure 4. Measure the increase in the temperature of the water.

The main problem with solar heating (apart from the cost of the solar collector) is that you often need energy most (for hot water, heating etc.) when the Sun isn't shining!

Designing for solar energy

Houses can (and should) be designed to make better use of solar energy. For example, most of the windows of houses in Britain should face south. Some 'solar houses' have been built with very good insulation so that they need very little extra heating.

Using solar energy to give high temperatures

A large amount of solar radiation focused on to a small area, can produce very high temperatures. The arrays of reflectors at the French solar furnace shown in Figure 5 produce a temperature high enough for metal to melt.

Fig. 5 A solar furnace
Solar furnaces focus solar radiation from the Sun on to a small area, and can reach very high temperatures. However, no solar furnace will ever exceed the temperature of the surface of the Sun (6000 °C). Why not? (See Chapter 8.)

It has been suggested that a giant solar collector many kilometres across should be built in space. Energy in the form of microwaves could then be focused on to a receiving station on Earth where it could be turned into electricity.

- What might be the benefits and dangers of such a system?

Other renewable sources of energy

Firewood

Fig. 1 The Third World's main source of energy
What happens when the firewood is used at too fast a rate for replacement? How can this problem be (at least partly) overcome?

Firewood is the main source of energy in many parts of Africa and in some other parts of the world (Figure 1). It is a renewable source of energy *provided* that you plant trees as fast as you cut them down.

Unfortunately, in many countries, forests are being cut down much faster than they can be replaced. As the forests disappear, the people have to hunt further for poorer (or more expensive) fuels. Once the trees have gone, the land gradually turns to desert. This is the world's most serious **energy crisis**.

However, with good management, including the correct choice of trees, firewood can be a very effective renewable source of energy.

Biogas

Biogas is a renewable energy source which China and India are starting to use on a large scale. Cow dung or other manure is composted in an air-tight container. Bacteria produce biogas as they turn the compost into fertiliser (Figure 2). Biogas is a roughly equal mixture of methane and carbon dioxide. It can be used for cooking, lighting and driving internal combustion engines. It is particularly useful as a source of energy for sewage works because the sewage can be used to produce the gas. **See what you can find out about the use of biogas in cars during the Second World War. Why couldn't the cars travel very far?**

Fig. 2 Energy from cow manure—a biogas plant
This particular plant supplies all the gas and electricity needs of this farm, and produces all the fertiliser needed for the crops.
How does energy get into the cow manure in the first place?

Fig. 3 Using an alternative energy source
The gas used for firing bricks at this brickworks comes from under a nearby landfill (rubbish dump). The second photograph shows gas pipes being laid. How was the gas produced? How does it differ from North Sea gas?

Hydroelectricity

Hydroelectricity is used more than any other renewable energy source for producing electricity (Figure 4). Norway gets most of its electrical energy from hydroelectric power. **Why can't Britain?**

Fig. 4 Spot the power station!
Hydroelectricity is an almost ideal source of energy. Why? The pipes supplying water to the turbines normally come from halfway up the dam rather than from the top or bottom. What reason can you think of for this?

Wind energy (atmospheric energy)

In past centuries, windmills provided much of Britain's energy (Figure 5). Today, wind generators are used for generating electricity in the windier parts of Britain.

- **Why did Britain stop using windmills—at least, on a large scale?**

Fig. 5 A traditional windmill
Windmills were once considered to be dangerous new technology! They are still used effectively in many places for pumping water from low-lying land.

Other renewable resources

Strong winds produce large waves. Scientists are trying out ways of using wave power to produce electricity (see Section 14.1). Geothermal energy and tidal energy are two other examples of renewable energy sources (see Section 7.3). Another possible future source of energy is the temperature difference between the ocean surface and ocean depths. Alternatively, we might be able to make use of the ocean currents.

The problems

Why don't we make more use of these renewable energy resources instead of using up precious fossil fuels?

One problem is expense. Just to get an output of a few kilowatts from solar power or wind power can cost many thousands of pounds. In addition, hydroelectric schemes and fuel crops can use up vast areas of land that is needed for food.

Another problem is what to do when (for solar power) the Sun isn't shining or (for wind power) the wind isn't blowing.

We have a dilemma. Either we rapidly use up the Earth's non-renewable energy resources or we destroy the world's forests, flood vast areas with huge reservoirs, or spend vast amounts of money producing tens of thousands of wind generators and solar cells. (At present we seem to be doing several of these at once!)

Energy conservation

A better way of solving the problem of energy resources might be to reduce the amount of energy we use. We can do this by reducing heat loss, by improving the efficiency of our machines and factories and by using microelectronic controls. We shall consider ways of doing this later in the chapter.

- **Imagine that you have been marooned on an island on which there are some wild animals, some corn (maize), a forest and a fast-flowing stream. You managed to rescue a motorbike and some tools from the boat, but you have no fuel. To survive, you need heat energy to cook the corn, to warm yourself at night and to dry your clothes. You want some light when it gets dark and you want some fuel for the motorbike so that you can travel about the island. How would you solve these problems?**

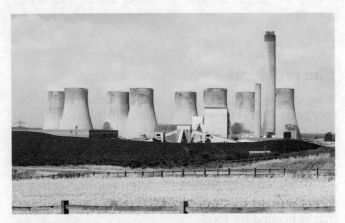

Fig. 1 Where the power station dumps its waste energy

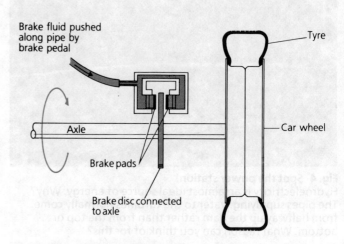

Fig. 2 Friction dissipates the car's energy
How the disc brakes of a car work.

Getting dissipated

The universe started as a big bang. How will it end? We've seen that the energy of the universe can't be destroyed, so what will happen to it?

Let's take as an example the gravitational potential energy of a lump of plasticine held in your hand. What happens to this energy, in the long run, when you drop the plasticine? **Try this. What energy changes are occurring?**

When the plasticine lands, it warms up very slightly. Its potential energy is converted to internal energy. The warm plasticine heats the surrounding floor and the surrounding air. But gradually the energy is **dissipated** (spread out and made less effective) and the amount by which the temperature of the floor and air is raised becomes smaller and smaller.

Friction

When the brakes of a car are applied, the brake pads rub against discs connected to the wheels, as shown in Figure 2. Although the surfaces of the brake pads and the discs look smooth, on a microscopic scale they are covered in pits and peaks (Figure 3). (All surfaces, however smooth they may appear, look rough through a microscope.)

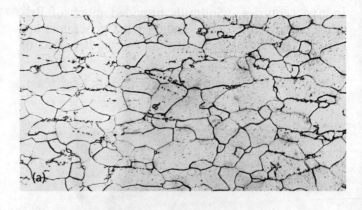

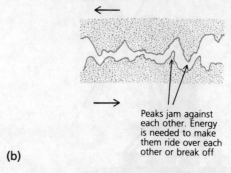

Peaks jam against each other. Energy is needed to make them ride over each other or break off

Fig. 3 The cause of solid friction
(a) All surfaces are rough on a microscopic scale
(b) What happens as the two surfaces slide over each other?

As the brake pads and discs rub against each other, the peaks in the surfaces collide and slow down the motion. The collisions heat the surfaces. They turn the kinetic energy of the wheels into internal energy in the brake pads. From there, the energy is dissipated (by heat conduction) to the surrounding metal and air.

● **Feel the rise in temperature as you rub your hands together. Do they stay at a high temperature or cool down? Explain what is happening.**

This also happens with other forms of energy. In the long run, the energy is turned into internal energy, and is then **dissipated** by heating the surroundings.

● **How is your energy dissipated as you speed down a hill on a bicycle?**

Advantages of energy dissipation

Energy dissipation can be useful. The cooling system of a car dissipates heat that would otherwise damage the engine. Similarly, the pipes at the back of a refrigerator have cooling fins which dissipate energy. (Refrigerators wouldn't work if the heat given out at the back couldn't escape.) Some electronic components also have cooling fins. These components would be spoilt if the heat were not removed.

Fig. 4 Where the fridge dumps its energy
Could you cool a room with a refrigerator if you left the door open? Why?

Power stations have **cooling towers** to dissipate the unwanted internal energy to the surroundings.

● **Where else is energy dissipation useful?**

Disadvantages of energy dissipation

Energy dissipation can be a nuisance. For example, energy is dissipated in the cables which carry electricity from the power station to your house. The cables are heated by the electricity flowing through them. This is a waste of energy.

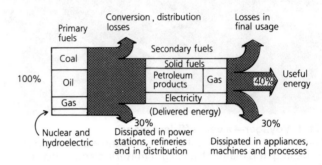

Fig. 5 Most of our energy is dissipated before we can start to use it
How can these losses be reduced? (See Section 7.8.)

Some of the energy of a car is dissipated through friction in the engine, and through heating the air around the car. This is a nuisance. It just wastes petrol.

● **Where else is energy dissipation a nuisance?**

High-grade heat

People who work in the energy business often talk about high-grade heat and low-grade heat (or high-grade energy and low-grade energy). High-grade heat is produced at a temperature much higher than that of the surroundings; low-grade heat isn't. High-grade heat can easily be used to drive machinery; low-grade heat can't.

For example, the Sun produces high-grade heat, as does a gas flame, or a glowing wire filament. A hot-water bottle or a warm pond gives low-grade heat.

As more energy is dissipated, there is less high-grade heat available. It looks as if, eventually, we could end up with a universe full of low-grade heat, with everything at nearly the same temperature. This universe started with a bang. It could end in a whimper!

109

Efficiency as the effective use of energy

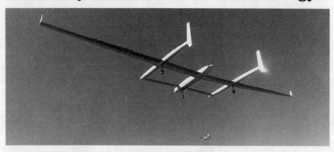

Fig. 1 Voyager—a very efficient plane
This aircraft was designed to fly round the world without refuelling. It is made of very light materials and structures. Why?

Efficiency means different things to different people. For example, to an economist, a more-efficient railway is one which costs less to run. To a passenger, it is one in which trains are cheap and run on time.

● **What do people mean by 'an efficient factory' or 'an efficient coal mine'? List some of the different things that they could mean.**

To a scientist or an engineer, efficiency just means the effective use of energy:

$$\text{efficiency} = \frac{\text{useful energy output}}{\text{total energy input}} \qquad (1)$$

This fraction is usually expressed as a percentage.

● **What would the useful energy be equal to in**
(a) a 100% efficient engine?
(b) a 0% efficient engine?

Most cars have an efficiency of about 30%. Only one-third of the energy from the petrol is used to drive a car along the road. The rest is lost as heat. Cars with diesel engines have higher efficiencies—up to 40%. **Does the efficiency change if you use the car heater? Why?**

Power stations also operate at efficiencies of about 30%. Most of the heat from the furnaces is dissipated in the cooling towers (Figure 3).

Fig. 2 Romantic, but not very efficient
Old steam engines owe part of their attraction to their noise, jets of steam, billowing smoke and other energy losses. You can see and hear the energy seeping out—their efficiency is no more than 10%. In contrast, many electric vehicles are very quiet because they are so efficient.

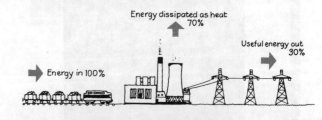

Fig. 3 Energy balance at a power station
What is the efficiency of this power station?

Pulley efficiency

You can work out the efficiency of pulleys just by measuring the forces. The energy input is the work that you do in pulling on the rope. This is equal to the force with which you pull on the rope multiplied by the distance that you pull the rope. (In other words, the energy input is equal to the effort force multiplied by the distance that the effort moves.) The useful energy output is the work done in lifting the load. This is equal to the load force (the weight of the load) multiplied by the distance that the load moves.

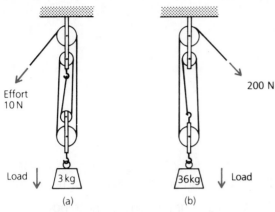

Fig. 4 The efficiency of a pulley system
What is the efficiency of these two systems?

Thus, from Equation (1):

$$\text{pulley efficiency} = \frac{\text{load force} \times \text{distance load moves}}{\text{effort force} \times \text{distance effort moves}} \quad (2)$$

For example, the pulley system shown in Figure 4(a) has an effort force of 10 N and a load force of 30 N (3 kg × 10 N/kg). Since there are four ropes supporting the bottom block, the effort moves four times as far as the load. Hence, using Equation (2):

$$
\begin{aligned}
\text{efficiency} &= \frac{\text{load} \times \text{distance load moves}}{\text{effort} \times \text{distance effort moves}} \\
&= \frac{30\,\text{N} \times \text{distance load moves}}{10\,\text{N} \times (4 \times \text{distance load moves})} \\
&= \frac{30\,\text{N}}{10\,\text{N} \times 4} = 0.75 = 75\%
\end{aligned}
$$

- **What is the efficiency of the pulley system shown in Figure 4(b)?**

Efficiency in terms of power

According to Section 7.2, Equation (1), energy is power × time. Equation (1) above can therefore be rewritten as

$$\text{efficiency} = \frac{\text{useful power output} \times \text{time}}{\text{total power input} \times \text{time}}$$

$$\text{efficiency} = \frac{\text{useful power output}}{\text{total power input}} \quad (3)$$

For example, a typical 100 W light bulb gives out only about 30 W of visible light. Its efficiency is therefore

$$
\begin{aligned}
\text{efficiency} &= \frac{\text{useful power out}}{\text{total power in}} \\
&= \frac{30\,\text{W}}{100\,\text{W}} = 0.3 = 30\%
\end{aligned}
$$

- **What happens to the rest of the 100 W input? How efficient is a 30 W electric motor with an output power of 27 W?**

Fig. 5 Saving energy
Recycling saves energy—less energy is needed to melt old glass than to make new glass.
How else can we save energy?

Energy conservation

In one sense, it is strange that we should worry about conserving energy because energy is always conserved—we can't destroy it. But what people mean by 'energy conservation' is the *efficient use* of energy. Efficiency can be improved by

- avoiding heat losses (e.g. by insulation)
- reducing friction (by lubrication and using ball-bearings)
- streamlining to reduce air and water resistance
- reducing the mass of moving parts
- storing energy when it can be used later on
- choosing the correct engine for the task (engine efficiency depends on load—overloaded or underloaded engines operate inefficiently).

Energy costs money, and obtaining energy sources (for example, by mining) can spoil the environment. The more efficiently we use energy, the better.

111

Exercises

1 Power is measured in

  A Volts

  B Watts

  C Joules

  D Newtons

  E Kilowatt hours

2 Which of the following is a renewable source of energy?

  A Uranium

  B Coal

  C Biogas

  D Oil

  E North Sea gas

3 Torch batteries:

  A create electrical energy

  B store electrical energy

  C convert chemical energy into electrical energy

  D convert chemical energy into light energy

  E convert electrical energy into light energy

4 Your new kettle has a higher power than the old one. This means that it

  A costs more

  B boils more water

  C wastes less energy

  D takes longer to boil

  E uses electricity at a faster rate

5 Which of the following is the most-correct statement of the principle of energy conservation?

  A People should conserve energy.

B Energy can be converted to different forms.

C You can't get energy for nothing.

D You cannot create energy. You cannot destroy it. You can only change it to other forms.

E High-grade energy should be conserved.

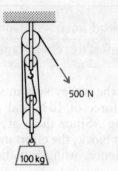

500 N

100 kg

Fig. 1

6 The pulley system shown in Figure 1 is used to lift a 100 kg load. An effort force of 500 N is needed. What is the efficiency of the pulley system?

  A 2

  B 4

  C 20%

  D 40%

  E 50%

7 Copy and complete these sentences:

  a _____, _____ and _____ are called fossil fuels. They are the remains of plants and animals that lived _____ of years ago and got their energy from the _____. Fossil fuels are _____ sources of energy. Solar energy, _____ energy and _____ are _____ sources of energy.

  b The efficiency of an energy conversion process is the _____ energy output divided by the _____ energy input. It is quoted as a _____.

Fig. 2

8 What energy conversion will no longer be possible this coming winter for the tree shown in Figure 2?

9 Suppose that a unit of electricity costs 8p.

    a State the name of this unit.

    b What is the cost of cooking on a 1000 W electric cooking ring for 1 hour?

    c What is the cost of cooking on two of these rings together for 3 hours?

10 A vehicle is pulled horizontally by a winch that uses 500 W of electrical energy (Figure 3). The force pulling the vehicle is 1000 N.

    a If energy losses can be ignored, how much work will the winch do in 1 second?

    b At what speed will the car move?

    c How would your answers to **a** and **b** change if you were told that the winch had an efficiency of 50%?

11 According to one encyclopedia, a man working an Archimedes screw for 1 hour can raise 12 m³ of water to a height of 1 m.

    a What is the gain in gravitational potential energy each hour?

    b At what level of power is the screw raising water?

    c If the man was working at a rate of 100 W, what was the efficiency of the screw?

12 Figure 5 shows a drum brake being used to measure the output power of a toy steam engine. (The 'brake horse power' of a car engine is measured in a similar way.) When the engine rotates at 200 revolutions per minute, the reading on the newton meter falls to zero, and the 100 g mass is just supported by the rotating drum (circumference, 50 cm). The engine is now using up chemical energy (from the fuel) at a rate of 1000 joules per minute.

    a Through what distance does a point on the surface of the drum move in

       (i) one revolution? (ii) 1 minute?

    b What is the force on the brake produced by the engine?

    c What is the work done against friction in 1 minute?

    d What is the output power of the engine?

    e What is the efficiency of the engine?

    f How would you use this method to find how the power output and efficiency depend on the load?

Fig. 3

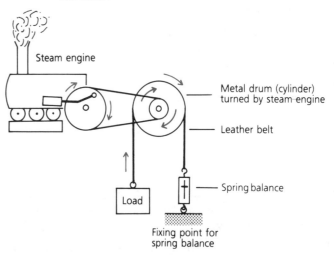

Fig. 4 An Archimedes screw for raising water

Fig. 5

113

Science, technology and the world

Newton, Boyle, Hooke, Watt, Joule and Kelvin were all British. Pascal, Ampère and Charles were French. Ohm and Hertz were German. Galileo and Volta were Italian, and Archimedes came from Sicily. Weren't there any famous scientists outside Europe?

Of course there were. Our scientific knowledge is the result of discoveries made in many different countries, and today scientific research is carried out all over the world. But despite the worldwide importance of science and technology, our units and laws are named (mainly) after Europeans.

- Before you read on, think of some reasons why this is the case.

Science owes its origins to the whole world

Thousands of years ago, the Greeks made great discoveries in science and technology. The ancient Romans made use of Greek science to build huge structures and other technological wonders. We still make use of this science today.

What many people forget is that the Greeks weren't the only ancient civilisation interested in science:

- 2600 years ago, Kanada was telling people in India about atoms.

- More than 2000 years ago, a Chinese group called the Mohist made many discoveries about motion, mechanisms and the behaviour of light.

- Around 1500 years ago, people living on the shores of Lake Victoria in East Africa were producing high-quality carbon steel in blast furnaces which reached a temperature of 1800°C. (This temperature is far higher than anything achieved in Europe until quite recently!)

- What other ancient civilisations have you heard of? See what you can find out about their science and technology.

The Dark Ages in Europe (AD 500–1100) were only 'dark' so far as European science was concerned. In the Islamic world, scientists were still making discoveries and inventions and further developing the discoveries of ancient civilisations. So were scientists in China.

- How many Chinese discoveries and inventions can you name? Two examples (to get you started) are paper and gunpowder.

- See what you can find out about the Arabic scientists Jabir, Al-Kindi and Alhazen of Basra.

You could say that 'nothing' was invented in India! The number 'zero' on which all present-day mathematics depends was invented in India around AD 700.

- What other scientific or technological discoveries occurred in India?

Modern science is a global task

Today, famous scientists come from all over the world. For example, the Nobel Prize winner, Hideki Yukawa, comes from Japan. His explanation of force at a distance is one of the bases of modern particle physics.

Another famous Asian scientist — the discoverer of the **Raman effect** in the scattering of light — is the Indian Sir Chandrasekhara Venkata Raman. He was also a Nobel Prize winner.

- Find out about some other famous scientists from other parts of the world.

The scientific revolution

During the Dark Ages, science had little effect on life in Europe. But after about 1500 things started to change. European governments set up teams of scientists to work on national problems. James II of England set up the Royal Society. The Society had as some of its early members Boyle, Hooke and Newton. Most of the physics in this book owes its present form to the work of such societies.

Fig. 1 Where three cultures met
In the centuries before Galileo, Moslem, Christian and Jewish scholars shared their scientific knowledge here in Cordoba.

See if you can find out how this (and other factors) led to Galileo's discoveries and to the scientific revolution? Why did this revolution occur in Europe?

The Industrial Revolution

The Industrial Revolution grew out of the scientific revolution. It started with the cotton industry. Raw cotton was imported from India, and later America, and was woven into cloth in Lancashire mills. From there it was sold to the world. At first, water power was used to drive the cotton mills, then coal-fired steam power was used. Later, other industries, including steel-making, followed the example of the cotton trade.

• See what you can find out about the causes of the Industrial Revolution. What part did physics play? How did the Industrial Revolution affect countries outside Europe, including their science and technology? Some people think that we are going through a second industrial revolution at the moment. What do you think are their reasons?

Good and bad

The scientific and industrial revolutions have brought about most of the benefits that we now take for granted: better health, better working conditions, better leisure and comfort. Unfortunately, not everyone has been able to enjoy these benefits. Indeed, these revolutions have brought with them some massive problems:

• The 'dark satanic mills', and the coal mines that fed them, produced terrible conditions for many people in Britain.

• Better weapons helped Europeans to conquer other countries. Many Europeans then started to look down on the people of these countries.

• European technology came to dominate and destroy local technologies and economies in many parts of the world, particularly in India.

• Perhaps worst of all, the cotton trade brought about a massive trade in African slaves to work in the plantations.

We need to make sure that modern science and technology bring benefits to *all* mankind.

Fig. 2 Children working in a coal mine— was science to blame?
Through the Industrial Revolution, science-based technology first provided, and then removed, the demand for large-scale slavery. How?

What are the good and bad effects of science and technology in today's world?

115

8 HEAT AND TEMPERATURE

8.1 Staying cool: the meaning of temperature

How hot is it?

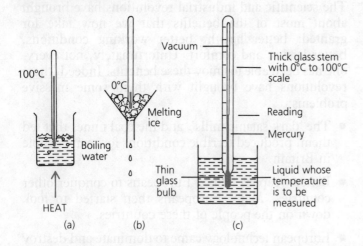

Fig. 1 The Celsius temperature scale
What is the temperature of the liquid?

What is a hot day? One on which you feel hot? Not necessarily—you may have a slight fever. Your senses aren't a reliable guide. You need to measure the temperature using a thermometer.

- **Put your right hand into water as hot as you can bear, and your left hand into very cold water (with ice in it). After a minute or so, put both hands into some ordinary tap water. What do you notice?**

The Celsius temperature scale

Thermometers show whether something is hotter than something else. To understand temperature and temperature scales, you need first to understand thermometers.

> A thermometer can be made of anything that changes in some way as it gets hotter.

The most common type of thermometer consists of a liquid that rises up a tube as the thermometer gets hotter. To make such a thermometer:

1 Mark the position of the liquid when the thermometer is in melting ice, and call this 0 °C.

> The temperature at which ice normally melts is the *lower fixed point* of the Celsius temperature scale (0 °C).

2 Mark the position of the liquid when the thermometer is in boiling water, and call this 100 °C.

> The temperature at which pure water normally boils is the *upper fixed point* of the Celsius temperature scale (100 °C).

3 Divide the space between the two marks into 100 equal sections and label these from 1 to 100.

You now have a thermometer. If you put this thermometer into a cup of tea and it reads '50', then your tea is at a temperature of 50 °C. That's all that we mean by 50 °C!

Fig. 2 Bathing baby
How can you check that the bath temperature is correct?
Why is a baby more affected by changes in temperature than an adult? (See Section 8.3.)

- **Try making your own thermometer with coloured water, starting with a narrow glass tube with a bulb at one end.**

116

Temperature and molecular motion

Fig. 3 Higher temperature, faster molecules
Why is it wrong to talk about 'the temperature of a molecule'?

The hotter a solid gets, the faster its molecules vibrate. The hotter a liquid or gas becomes, the faster its molecules move around.

> The higher the temperature of a solid, liquid or gas, the greater the kinetic energy of its molecules.

- Look back at the apparatus shown in Section 2.5, Figure 4. What do you think would happen if you increased the speed of the motor? If possible, try this. This has the same effect as increasing the temperature of a gas.

Temperature and heat flow

> Temperature shows the direction in which heat travels.

Heat always travels from a hot object to a colder object. If you stand in the sunshine or near a stove, heat enters your body from the hotter surroundings. If you stand in the snow, heat escapes from you to the colder surroundings (Figure 4).

Fig. 4 Heat flows from high temperatures to low temperatures
Why is the man in (b) wearing more clothes than the man in (a)?

> Heat is the transfer of energy from a hot object to a cold object caused by the difference in temperature.

Temperature is *not* the same thing as heat (Figure 5). You get more heat from a bowl of *warm* soup than you do from a teaspoon of *hot* soup. (The hot soup just burns your tongue!)

Fig. 5 Heat isn't the same thing as temperature
Which has the higher temperature, the washing-up water or the freshly-made tea?
Which gives out the most heat?

- Put one hand in very cold water and the other hand in hot water for a minute or so. Now quickly dry them and put them very close to your cheeks. Can you feel the heat coming from your warm hand? Can you feel heat leaving your cheek near your cold hand?

117

8.2 Getting hotter, getting bigger

Space to move about

At a disco, some dancers are doing a slow smoochy dance, very close together. A faster record is put on, and the dancers move more energetically and further apart. Then someone puts on a record for some break-dancing. The break-dancers now have to be some way from each other (Figure 1).

Fig. 1 Dancing molecules
The faster the dancing is, the further the dancers move apart.

This is the sort of thing that happens when you heat something. The faster the molecules move, the further apart they get. This makes the solid (or liquid, or gas) expand.

Fig. 2 An expansion joint on a bridge
What is the purpose of this gap between the two sections of roadway?
Why do you think it has this shape? (Why isn't it straight?)

118

Bridges and railway lines need gaps to allow for expansion (Figure 2). **What would happen otherwise? Where else do we have to make allowances for thermal expansion?**

Thermal expansion can be useful. One use that we have already come across is the thermometer. **What other uses can you think of?**

Different solids expand at different rates

Metal expands more than glass. For example, one way of removing a tightly fitting metal cap from a glass bottle is to place the top of the bottle under the hot tap. The cap expands more than the glass and can easily be unscrewed.

Brass expands more than steel. If you stick a strip of steel and a strip of brass together and then heat them, this bimetallic (two-metal) strip bends in the direction of the steel.

Bimetallic strips are used in the flashing bulbs of Christmas lights. As the bulb filament heats up, it

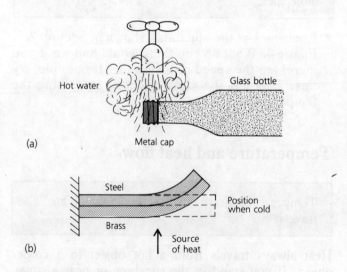

(a)
Hot water   Glass bottle
Metal cap

(b)
Steel
Brass
Position when cold
Source of heat

Fig. 3 Different solids expand at different rates
(a) The metal cap expands more than the glass bottle
(b) The brass part of the bimetallic strip expands more than the steel part

warms the bimetallic strip. This bends and breaks the circuit. As the bulb cools down, the bimetallic strip straightens, and the bulb is switched on again.

Thermostats

Thermostats are used for keeping the temperature constant in ovens, heating systems and elsewhere. They work by switching the electricity (or gas) supply on and off automatically as the temperature changes. Figure 4 shows some examples of thermostats.

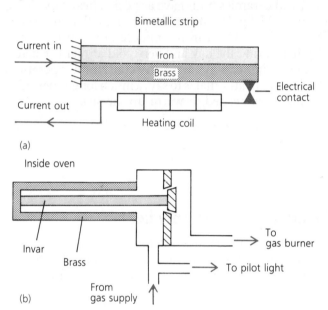

(a)

(b)

Fig. 4 Thermostats
(a) A bimetallic strip controlling an electric heater
(b) A brass tube controlling the gas supply to a gas heater
(invar expands much less than brass)
Explain how these thermostats work.

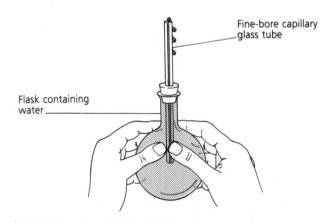

Fig. 5 Expansion of a liquid
Warming the flask in your hands causes water to expand out of the flask.
What would happen if the glass expanded more than the water?

The expansion of liquids

Liquids expand more than solids. Figure 5 shows one way of demonstrating this. If water in a heating system is not allowed to expand, it will burst one of the pipes. To avoid this, central-heating systems that use water have a **feed and expansion tank** (see Section 8.3, Figure 2). Water feeds into the system through this tank. Water can also expand up into this tank when it gets hot.

Danger—unexploded bottles

Gases expand more than liquids. People have been injured by exploding bottles of fizzy drink. When this has happened, it has often been because the bottle has been left in the sun, and because there has been a large space at the top of the bottle. The gas in this space has been heated by the sun and, in trying to expand, has produced such a high pressure that the bottle has exploded. This could be prevented by having a much smaller gas space. (There should be just enough room for the liquid to expand. The amount of gas should be small enough for it to be able to dissolve in the liquid.)

Bombs make use of the expansion of gases. A bomb is just something that gets very hot very quickly. As the air is suddenly heated, it expands, producing a blast wave. This applies to everything from an explosive firework to a hydrogen bomb explosion (Figure 6).

Fig. 6 One result of the thermal expansion of gases
The picture shows Hiroshima after the atomic bomb had exploded. This damage was caused by blast waves as the air, heated by the bomb, suddenly expanded.
Thunder is also caused by thermal expansion. How? (See Chapter 10.)

The expansion of solids, liquids and gases has many more important applications in everyday life—some of them useful, some of them downright dangerous. We must be wary of thermal expansion whenever something is changing its temperature.

119

Treating a burn

Fig. 1 What to do when you burn your finger

What should you do if you burn your finger? Put it straight under the cold tap (Figure 1). The cold water will remove the internal energy in the burn before it can do any more damage.

- **Most car engines have water cooling systems. Why? How do they work?**

How much heat?

The heat lost from your finger (or gained when you burn your finger) depends on you finger's mass and specific heat capacity and on the change in temperature.

> heat transferred
>
> = mass × specific heat capacity × change in temperature   (1)
>
> $= mc(\theta_2 - \theta_1)$

This applies to any object warming up or cooling down. For example, when a kettle containing 2 kg of water (specific heat capacity 4200 J/kg °C) cools from 40 °C to 20 °C, the heat given out by the water is

$$\text{heat} = mc(\theta_2 - \theta_1)$$
$$= 2\,\text{kg} \times 4200\,\text{J/kg}\,°C \times (40\,°C - 20\,°C)$$
$$= 168\,000\,\text{J}$$

- **How much heat energy is needed to warm 200 kg of water (the amount needed for a bath) from 15 °C to 45 °C?**

Sand and ceramics

Sand and ceramics both have a specific heat capacity of about 700 J/kg °C—much lower than that of water. This is why a desert in the middle of a continent gets very hot during the day and very cold at night, whereas land near the sea stays at a fairly constant temperature. Much more heat—that is to say, a much longer period of sunshine—is needed to warm up the sea.

- **An electric storage heater has 20 kg of ceramic bricks. If the bricks are heated to 100 °C above room temperature, how much extra internal energy is stored?**

Using water to supply heat

In most central-heating systems, water is heated in a boiler and pumped to radiators around the house. There it cools and heats the surrounding air (Figure 2).

- **Where else is water used to supply or remove heat? What advantages does water have? What disadvantages?**

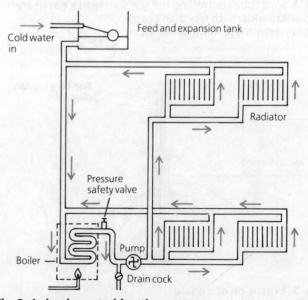

Fig. 2 A simple central-heating system
Why is the tank at the top not sealed (to prevent water from evaporating)? Why does water go in at the bottom of the boiler and radiators and out at the top?

How cold can you get?

Absolute zero—when everything stops

Fig. 1 Minus one hundred and ninty-six degrees Celsius
The flask contains liquid nitrogen. The liquid is boiling. If we cooled it to −210 °C, it would freeze. How much colder could it get?

The colder something gets, the slower its molecules move. Eventually they stop moving altogether. This is the lowest temperature that you can get.

Figure 2(a) shows one way of estimating this temperature. As the air cools and contracts, the sulphuric acid thread moves down the tube. A graph can be drawn of the volume of gas in the tube against the temperature of the gas. The result is shown in Figure 2(b). Two things are the same whatever volume of gas you use:

1 You always get a straight-line graph.
2 The line will always cut the temperature axis at −273 °C.

The temperature of −273 °C at which the gas appears to have no volume is called **absolute zero**. It's as cold as you can get!

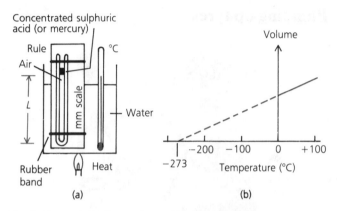

Fig. 2 How gas volume changes with temperature
What would happen to a gas at absolute zero?
What would happen to the gas molecules?
Why is it not possible to cool a real gas down to near this temperature?

Kelvins

If −273 °C is as cold as you can get, then why not call it 0 °? This was Lord Kelvin's suggestion. His temperature scale, now called the **Kelvin temperature scale**, is the recommended SI unit of temperature. It starts at absolute zero:

$$0 \, K \equiv -273 \, °C$$

(Note that we don't usually bother with the degrees sign for kelvin temperatures. We say 'zero kelvins' instead of 'zero degrees kelvin'.)

The Kelvin scale goes up at the same rate as the Celsius scale so that

$$0 \, °C \equiv 273 \, K \qquad 100 \, °C \equiv 373 \, K$$

In other words, to convert a temperature from the Celsius scale to the Kelvin scale, just add 273.

● **The coldest that the Earth ever gets is −88 °C. What is this in kelvins?**

Advantages of the Kelvin scale

1 You don't have negative temperatures.
2 The volume (or pressure) of a gas is directly proportional to temperature. When the temperature doubles, the volume (or pressure) doubles.

More about gases

Pumping up tyres

Fig. 1 Pumping up tyres
Why does the pump get hot when you pump fast? What difference does this rise in temperature make to the air you are putting into the tyre?

How many times should you pump a bicycle tyre to get it up to the right pressure? This isn't an easy question to answer. So many things are happening: the tyre is getting hot, the pressure of the air is increasing, and so is its density.

In physics, we simplify problems by looking at different parts of a problem separately and temporarily ignoring other parts.

Let's start tackling this problem by ignoring the temperature rise. Imagine that we have pumped the tyre up very slowly, so that it has stayed at the same temperature.

Boyle's Law

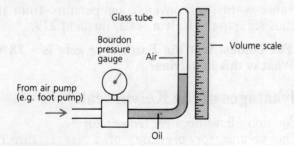

Fig. 2 Apparatus to demonstrate Boyle's law
What is Boyle's law?

Robert Boyle, a wealthy Irishman, studied the compression of gases as long ago as 1650. He found that, if you plot a graph of pressure against volume, you get something like that shown in Figure 3(a). This isn't a very helpful graph, apart from showing that, as you increase the pressure, the volume decreases (surprise, surprise!).

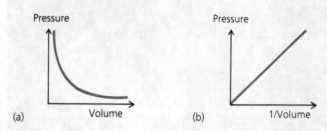

Fig. 3 How gas pressure varies with volume
What can you say about
(a) the pressure when the volume is zero?
(b) the volume when the pressure is zero?

Boyle showed that you can get a much more useful graph by plotting the pressure against the **reciprocal** of the volume ($1/V$). This gives a straight-line graph (Figure 3(b)).

pressure × volume = constant   (1)
provided that the temperature remains constant

This is known as **Boyle's law**.

An example

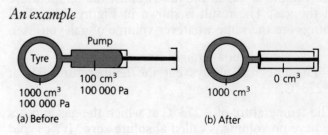

Fig. 4 By how much does the tyre pressure rise?

A pump of volume 0.0001 m³ pumps air into a bicycle tyre with a volume of 0.001 m³. At the start, both the pump and the tyre contain air at a pressure of 100 000 Pa. At the end, all this air is in the tyre.

According to Equation (1),

$$\text{pressure at end} = \frac{\text{pressure at start} \times \text{volume at start}}{\text{volume at end}}$$

$$= \frac{100\,000\,\text{Pa} \times (0.0001\,\text{m}^3 + 0.001\,\text{m}^3)}{0.001\,\text{m}^3}$$

$$= 110\,000\,\text{Pa}$$

Effects of temperature on volume and pressure

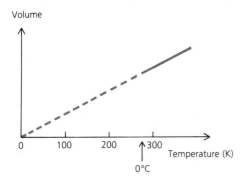

Fig. 5 Gas volume is proportional to the kelvin temperature How would a graph of pressure against (i) the celsius temperature, (ii) the kelvin temperature, appear?

If Figure 3 of Section 8.4 is redrawn in terms of kelvin temperature, then we get the result shown in Figure 5.

> volume = constant × kelvin temperature   (2)
>
> provided that the pressure remains constant

This is called **Charles' law** after the Frenchman who first discovered it.

It is not only the volume which is proportional to the kelvin temperature, the pressure is as well.

> pressure = constant × kelvin temperature   (3)
>
> provided that the volume remains constant

- **How could you demonstrate this in the laboratory?**

- **Find the increase in the pressure of some car tyres when they heat up from 17 °C to 27 °C on a fast journey. (Initial pressure = 130 000 Pa.) What will you assume remains constant?**

Putting it all together—pumping up a tyre at high speed

The three gas laws can be combined:

> $$\frac{\text{pressure} \times \text{volume}}{\text{kelvin temperature}} = \text{constant}$$
>
> or   (4)
>
> $$\frac{P_1 V_1}{T_1} = \frac{P_2 V_2}{T_2}$$
>
> provided that the mass is constant

This is called the **universal gas law**.

Let's go back to the example of the bicycle tyre. Suppose that, in addition to the other changes, the temperature rises from 17 °C to 27 °C. What will the pressure in the tyre be now?

As before,

$$P_1 = 100\,000\,\text{Pa}$$
$$V_1 = (0.0001\,\text{m}^3 + 0.001\,\text{m}^3) = 0.0011\,\text{m}^3$$
$$V_2 = 0.0010\,\text{m}^3$$

Also,

$$T_1 = 17\,°\text{C} = 290\,\text{K}$$
$$T_2 = 27\,°\text{C} = 300\,\text{K}$$

Hence, on rearranging Equation (4):

$$P_2 = \frac{P_1 V_1 T_2}{T_1 V_2}$$

$$= \frac{100\,000\,\text{Pa} \times 0.0011\,\text{m}^3 \times 300\,\text{K}}{290\,\text{K} \times 0.0010\,\text{m}^3}$$

$$= 114\,000\,\text{Pa}$$

If the pressure increases by 114 000 Pa each time that you use the pump, then you will need to pump 3 times to reach a normal tyre pressure of 350 000 Pa (50 psi). **Will it increase by the same amount each time you operate the pump?**

Next time you need to pump up your bicycle tyres— just think! You don't have to guess how many times to use the pump. You can sit down (for a couple of hours or so) and work it all out using the gas laws!

Other types of thermometers

Different thermometers have different uses

Fig. 1 Thermometers come in many forms
If this thermometer is showing degrees celsius, what is the kelvin temperature?

Thermometers come in all shapes and sizes. Look at the thermometers in Figures 1–6. You can make a thermometer with anything that changes with temperature: length, volume, electric voltage, electric current or even colour. However, the most common thermometer is still the liquid-in-glass thermometer invented by Galileo 350 years ago.

The liquid-in-glass thermometer

Fig. 2 The common alcohol thermometer
This is often used for measuring temperatures in people's houses.
Why isn't water used instead of alcohol?

Figure 2 shows a typical home thermometer. Look at its design.

- **Mercury or alcohol is used**—Mercury and alcohol expand in a more regular manner than water and (unlike water) don't stick to glass. Mercury is needed if the thermometer is to be used above 78 °C (the boiling point of alcohol).

- **Most of the liquid is contained in a thin glass bulb**—This allows the liquid to be rapidly heated.

- **There is a narrow capillary tube**—This means that a small expansion moves the liquid a long way along the tube.

The clinical thermometer

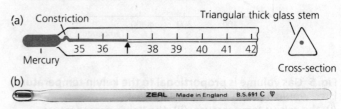

Fig. 3 A clinical thermometer
What is the reading of the thermometer in (a)?

The clinical thermometer is a special version of the liquid-in-glass thermometer.

- The thermometer is small enough to fit under your tongue.

- A constriction stops the mercury from going back into the bulb after you've taken your temperature. This enables you to take the thermometer out of your mouth to read it. You then have to shake the mercury back.

- The capillary tube is even finer than that in a normal thermometer. The glass stem has a triangular cross-section. This makes the mercury thread seem larger, so that the thermometer can be read easily.

- The scale only goes from 35 °C to 42 °C. (A person whose temperature is outside this range is unlikely to be alive!) The average person has a normal body temperature of 37 °C. **Are you an average person?**

- Try measuring the temperature under your tongue, keeping the thermometer there for a couple of minutes. Make sure that the thermometer reads below 36 °C to start with.

The thermocouple

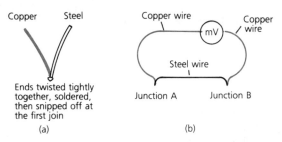

Fig. 4 A thermocouple
(a) A single junction
(b) In practice, there must always be two junctions. Why? If junction A is hotter than junction B, the current will flow one way. If junction B is hotter than junction A, the current will flow the other way. What will happen if the junctions are at the same temperature? (Ideally, the second junction should be in melting ice.)

When two different metals (for example, a piece of copper wire and a piece of steel wire) are joined together, they are said to form a **thermocouple**. They act just like a (very weak) battery to produce a small electrical voltage. This voltage increases with the temperature of the junction. The voltage can be measured with a very sensitive meter, and this thermocouple can be used as a thermometer.

If you have sufficiently thin wires, you can use a thermocouple to measure the temperature under the surface of your skin, or inside the stem of a plant. You can also connect thermocouples (through an amplifier) to a computer.

- If you have a very sensitive voltmeter, try making your own thermocouple. Use it to measure the temperature of some water, and compare this with the result that you get using a normal mercury thermometer.

Thermistors and platinum resistance thermometers

Thermistors and platinum resistance thermometers change in electrical resistance as the temperature changes. The thermometer is connected to a battery, and the current through it is measured. The current changes with temperature. We will look at these thermometers in more detail in Chapter 18.

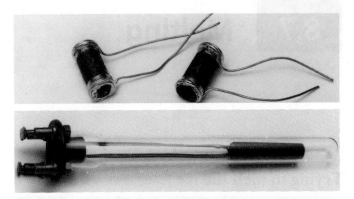

Fig. 5 A thermistor and a resistance thermometer
These measure the temperature by measuring the resistance of the thermistor or platinum wire. This resistance alters with temperature. What is electrical resistance? (See Chapter 18.)

Radiation pyrometer

Fig. 6 A radiation pyrometer
How does it work?

If you tried to use a normal thermometer to measure the temperature of a steel furnace, the thermometer would melt! A better way to find out the temperature is to look at the colour of the furnace. The colour changes as the furnace gets hotter. The furnace glows first red, then orange, then yellow and white. A **radiation pyrometer** is a device which allows you to compare the colour of the furnace with the colour of a light-bulb filament. To do this, you hold the filament in front of the furnace and alter the current through the filament. When the filament is as hot as the furnace, it will disappear. (In other words you won't be able to see any difference between the filament and the furnace.) You can then find the temperature by measuring the electric current.

Every thermometer has advantages and disadvantages. The important thing is to use the right one for the job.

8.7 Melting

Trying to melt the ice

Fig. 1 De-icing agents
The kettle of warm water is less effective than the de-icer. Why?

How can you melt the ice on your car windscreen, or on the path outside your house? You could use warm water. But this doesn't work very well. Very little of the ice or snow is melted—much less than you'd expect. The warm water seems to be of little effect in raising the temperature. **Can you explain why?**

Melting points

The temperature of a solid such as ice stays constant as the ice melts. In other words, solids have a very definite melting point. You can show this by melting stearic acid, a chemical which is a solid at room temperature but which can easily be melted. Figure 2 shows a graph of temperature against time as the stearic acid melts. Notice how the temperature stays constant at the **melting point** even though the heating continues at the same rate. At this stage, a lot of heat is being put in for little obvious reward. We call this **latent heat** (meaning 'hidden heat').

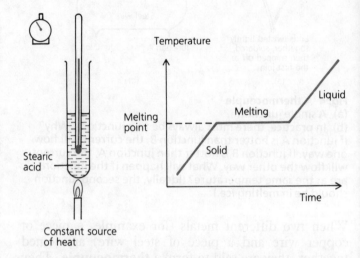

Fig. 2 Melting stearic acid
Why does the temperature stop rising once the stearic acid is melting?

- Allow some molten stearic acid to cool and solidify, and plot a cooling curve—a graph of temperature against time with the temperature decreasing. How does your graph compare with Figure 2?

Why does the temperature stop rising?

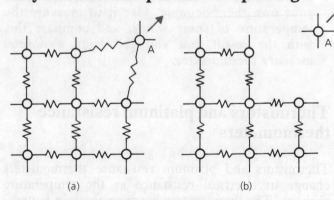

Fig. 3 A model of what happens when a solid melts
The balls represent the molecules.
The springs represent the forces between the molecules.
What represents **latent heat** in this model?

Figure 3 shows what is happening in terms of a simple **model** of the solid. (In science, a model is a simple picture that is easier to understand than the real thing.) This model shows the electrostatic forces between molecules as simple springs.

Consider molecule A in the diagram. The hotter the solid gets, the more this molecule will vibrate. Its speed, and therefore its kinetic energy, will increase. But, to free this molecule, extra energy will have to be provided to break the springs. In other words, to melt the solid (i.e. to free the molecules) extra energy is needed which will not increase the speed of the molecules. We call this energy the **latent heat of melting.**

Since the speed (and therefore the kinetic energy) of the molecules hasn't been changed by this extra energy, the temperature hasn't been changed either. That is to say, the temperature of the solid hasn't been increased by this latent heat.

Losing heat as latent heat

Fig. 4 This car will get colder as the snow melts
Why?

When you travel in a car that is covered in snow, you can sometimes feel the car losing heat. As you travel, the snow melts. As it does so, the latent heat needed for melting is taken from your car. This loss of heat makes the car colder than it would otherwise be.

Getting the latent heat back

When liquids freeze, they give out latent heat. As the molecules of a cooling liquid start to slow down, the electrostatic forces between the molecules pull them together to form a solid. This accelerates the molecules back to their initial speeds. Thus the molecules remain with constant kinetic energy as the liquid freezes, and the substance stays at a constant temperature. The energy that the molecules lost through cooling has been replaced by the **latent heat of fusion** (of freezing). The latent heat of fusion is equal to the latent heat of melting.

How should you melt ice?

To stop liquids from freezing, you need to stop the electrostatic forces from pulling the molecules together. Salt dissolved in water is very effective at doing this. Salty water has a much lower freezing point than fresh water. (This is why the sea seldom freezes. When the sea does freeze, the ice contains very little salt.)

Fig. 5 Gritting pavements with grit salt
Why is this done?
Why does it work?

Alcohol is also effective at keeping water molecules apart. In cars, alcohol is used as antifreeze to prevent water in the engine's cooling system from freezing. It is also used to melt ice on the windscreen.

- **Put some ice in a beaker that is standing in a puddle of water. Now melt the ice rapidly using salt or windscreen de-icer. What happens to the water on the outside of the beaker? Why?**

127

Wet hair on a cold day

Keep your head covered

Fig. 1 What will happen if it snows?
These walkers need to keep their hair covered. This is more important than keeping their hands covered. Why?

Many people have suffered, and even died, from **exposure** (lowered body temperature) because they have been trapped in hills and mountains in cold, wet weather. Those with wet hair have suffered most. Their bodies have cooled down very rapidly indeed. So if ever you go fell-walking in cold, wet weather, make sure that you keep your head covered.

Something similar (though not so dangerous) occurs when you get out of the water at an open-air swimming pool. When first you step out, you feel very cold. Once you are dry, you feel much warmer.

Why does being wet make you cold?

When you are wet, you feel cold because the water on your skin is evaporating. To escape from your wet skin, molecules of water need energy in the form of heat. They take the heat from your skin. We call this heat **latent heat of vaporisation.**

● **Pour some ether or methylated spirits on to the back of your hand. Notice how cold it makes your hand as it evaporates.**

This is why we perspire (sweat) when we get hot—the sweat that evaporates from our skin takes heat with it.

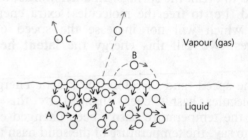

Fig. 2 Molecules take energy as they leave the liquid
What do we call this loss of energy? What happens to the liquid that is left behind?

Figure 2 shows what is happening to the molecules when a liquid evaporates. Molecules such as molecule A start to move more and more rapidly inside the liquid. Some molecules (e.g. molecule B) leave the surface but are not moving fast enough to escape. Other molecules (e.g. molecule C) escape to form a vapour (a gas). Once the faster molecules have escaped, the average speed of the molecules in the liquid is lower than before. The faster molecules have taken their kinetic energy with them. They have removed **latent heat of vaporisation**, so the remaining liquid is colder.

Refrigerators

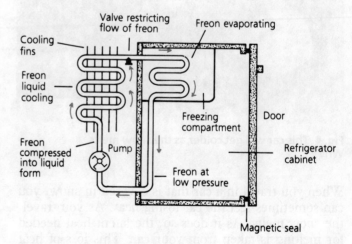

Fig. 3 How a refrigerator works

In most refrigerators, a liquid called **freon** evaporates and takes its latent heat from the refrigerator (Figure 3). A pump compresses the freon back into a liquid, and the latent heat is released from a radiator at the back of the refrigerator.

More about evaporation

How to increase the rate of evaporation

1 Heat the liquid to replace the lost latent heat.
2 Remove the vapour to prevent molecules from condensing back to the liquid.

For example, clothes dry fastest on a hot, windy day.

Fig. 4 Hanging your clothes out to dry
Why do clothes dry better when it is windy?

What is a vapour?

Vapour is the name given to a gas that is at about the same temperature as the liquid that it comes from. The air around us contains water vapour. **Steam,** the invisible gas at the spout of a boiling kettle, is high-temperature water vapour. The white stuff that most of us call steam isn't really steam at all! It's a collection of tiny water droplets.

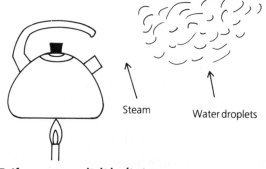

Steam   Water droplets

Fig. 5 If you can see it, it isn't steam
Does steam exist at any temperature other than 100 °C?

Evaporation and boiling

Unlike melting, **evaporation** can occur at any temperature. Water doesn't have to boil for molecules to escape from the surface and form a vapour. But boiling greatly increases the rate of evaporation, because evaporation then occurs throughout the liquid.

Why does water (or any other liquid) boil, and why does this happen at a particular temperature?

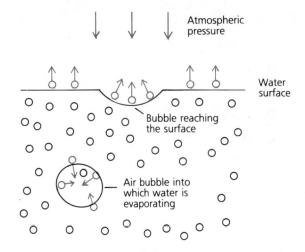

Fig. 6 When will the water boil?
Answer: When the vapour pressure (in the air bubbles) exceeds atmospheric pressure.
How can you alter the boiling point of water?

Water contains dissolved air. If you leave water to stand, some of this air forms bubbles. At room temperature, water starts to evaporate into these bubbles. But the bubbles are prevented from swelling by atmospheric pressure. So the evaporation stops.

If the temperature of the water is increased, the rate of evaporation increases. This increases the pressure inside the bubbles. Eventually, at 100 °C, the pressure inside the bubbles becomes greater than atmospheric pressure. The bubbles expand, with more and more water evaporating into them. They rise rapidly to the surface and burst. This is what we mean by boiling. The temperature at which this occurs is called the **boiling point** of water.

If the atmospheric pressure is decreased, then boiling can occur at a lower temperature. (Don't try making a cup of tea on top of Mount Everest. The air pressure there is so low that water boils at only 70 °C!)

If the atmospheric pressure is increased, then water has to be raised to a much higher temperature before it can boil. For example, water in a pressure cooker boils at a temperature well above 100 °C, and so food cooks much faster.

129

Exercises

1 Which of the following is the SI unit for heat?

 A Degree celsius

 B Joule

 C Kelvin

 D Calorie

 E Watt

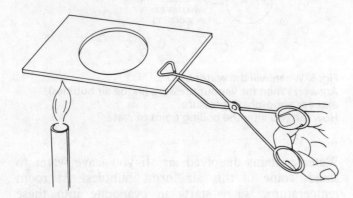

Fig. 1 What happens to the hole?

2 A hole is bored in a sheet of metal (Figure 1). When the sheet is heated, the hole

 A Increases in size

 B Decreases in size

 C Remains the same size

 D Increases or decreases depending on the metal used

3 If you heat a gas inside a sealed container, the molecules

 A Get bigger

 B Move further apart

 C Attract each other more strongly

 D Increase their kinetic energy

 E Become less dense

4 Some water containing melting ice is left in a beaker. Its temperature rises to 10 °C. By how many degrees has its *kelvin* temperature increased?

 A 10

 B 263

 C 273

 D 283

 E −10

Fig. 2 A pressure cooker

5 A pressure cooker cooks food in water at a pressure above atmospheric pressure. It takes less time to cook the food in this way. This is because the pressure

 A Heats the water

 B Increases the power supplied

 C Increases the boiling point

 D Increases the internal energy

 E Heats the molecules

6 Bottle tops can be loosened by holding them under the hot tap for a few minutes. This is because

 A The water reduces the friction

 B The glass bottle expands

 C Air pressure in the bottle increases

D Only the metal bottle top expands

E The metal bottle top expands more than the glass

7 Complete these sentences:

a Temperature is not the same thing as heat. _____ shows the direction in which _____ travels.

b The _____ energy of individual molecules of gas increases as the _____ increases.

c The volume of a mass of gas is proportional to its _____ temperature provided that the _____ remains constant.

8 State and explain three ways in which a clinical thermometer differs from a normal mercury-in-glass thermometer.

9 **a** Explain why motorists should measure the pressure of their tyres **before** going on a long journey and not after they have been travelling for some time.

b A motorist spills petrol on to his hand. The petrol feels far colder than water at the same temperature. Why?

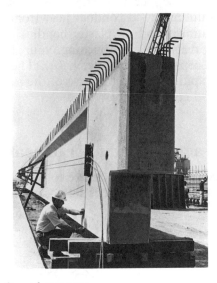

Fig. 3 Reinforced concrete

10 Figure 3 shows some reinforced concrete being made. The steel rods will be covered in concrete. If the steel rods are heated, they expand to the same extent as the concrete. Explain why this is important, stating what would happen if

a the concrete expanded much more than the steel

b the steel expanded much more than the concrete.

11 **a** The water in a car cooling system is usually at high pressure. Why is it very unwise to remove the radiator cap when the engine is hot? (What would happen, and why?)

b If there is a large loss of water from the cooling system, you should not try to refill it with cold water until the engine has cooled down. Why?

12 Kettle heating elements burn out (or trip a safety switch) if they are switched on with no water in the kettle. Why doesn't this happen when the kettle is full of water?

13 Why is it not possible to boil eggs faster by turning up the gas or electricity supply?

Fig. 4 A swimming pool in the tropics
The water is colder than you'd expect. Why?

14 The water in swimming pools in hot but very dry countries can be uncomfortably cold (Figure 4). Why?

15 In a warehouse fire, a sealed but empty oil drum of volume $0.6 \, \text{m}^3$ is heated from $27\,°C$ to $127\,°C$. The air in the drum was initially at atmospheric pressure ($100\,000$ Pa).

a What is the final pressure in the drum?

b If the air at the start had a density of $1 \, \text{kg/m}^3$, what was the mass of air in the drum

i at the start?

ii at a temperature of $127\,°C$?

c If the drum then bursts, to what volume will the air in the drum expand if it remains at $127\,°C$?

16 A 300 g bun is put in a 600 W microwave oven for 1 minute. Its temperature rises from $15\,°C$ to $45\,°C$. what is the specific heat capacity of the bun?

131

9.1 HEAT TRANSFER

9.1 Cold steel

Don't touch the metal!

Fig. 1 Steel cold enough to burn you
The wood on this ship is just as cold as the metal, but it is not as dangerous. Why?

Sailors on ships in Arctic waters have to be careful not to touch any outside metal with their bare hands. If they do, their skin can be badly 'burned'. The metal takes so much heat from their skin that it harms it just like a flame. **Why doesn't wood have this effect?**

In the same conditions, plastic foam wouldn't feel cold at all. It would feel warm.

- **Put a piece of polystyrene foam in the freezing part of a refrigerator for several hours, to make sure that it is really cold. Then take it out and feel it. Does it feel cold? Is it cold? How can you tell for sure?**

Metal, wood and plastics affect your skin differently when they are cold because of the difference in their ability to conduct heat. Metals are good **conductors** of heat. Wood and plastics (such as polystyrene foam) are **insulators**—they don't conduct heat very well.

When you touch a piece of cold polystyrene foam, the heat from your hand soon warms the surface. When you touch a piece of cold metal, the heat from your hand is conducted away through the metal. The surface stays cold and continues to take heat from your hand.

Copper-bottomed saucepans

Copper and aluminium are particularly good conductors of heat. (Copper is best.) Most saucepans are made of aluminium (to conduct heat from the stove) with insulating wood or plastic handles (to prevent heat from reaching and burning your hand). Expensive saucepans have copper bases. These conduct heat very rapidly around the base of the saucepan, so that the food cooks evenly.

Water—a poor conductor of heat

Figure 2 shows how it is possible to boil water at the top of a test-tube while there is still ice at the bottom of the test-tube. **Try this.**

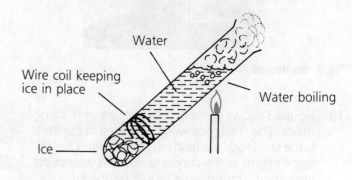

Fig. 2 Water is a poor conductor of heat
Why don't convection currents carry heat down to the ice? (See Section 9.3.)

Air—a good insulator

Fig. 3 Keeping warm with a wet suit
How does it keep you warm?

Air is a good insulator. In other words, it is a very poor conductor of heat. Clothes keep you warm by trapping a layer of air round your body. Divers in cold water wear rubber wet suits that contain bubbles of air. Polystyrene foam and fibreglass are used as insulating materials in buildings because of the air trapped in them.

The Davy safety lamp

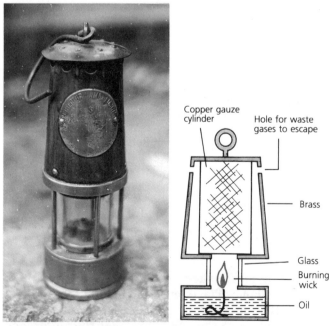

Copper gauze cylinder

Hole for waste gases to escape

Brass

Glass

Burning wick

Oil

Fig. 4 A Davy lamp
What is it for? How does it work?

When coal is cut, methane is given off. If the methane is allowed to build up, an explosion can occur. (Nowadays, the methane is removed, and strict safety measures are taken to prevent sparks from occurring. Explosions do still happen, but only rarely.)

About 1800, Sir Humphry Davy invented a paraffin lamp that wouldn't cause methane to explode (Figure 4). (The lamp is also very useful for showing the presence of methane—when methane enters the lamp, it alters the colour of the flame.) The flame is surrounded by thick, insulating glass, and the hot waste gases escape through a copper gauze. The gauze conducts heat away from the gases and cools them so that they don't set fire to the methane outside.

Davy lamps are still used (alongside electronic sensors) for checking coal mines for explosive methane gas (firedamp). Before electric torches were invented, the Davy lamp was the only lamp that miners could use safely underground.

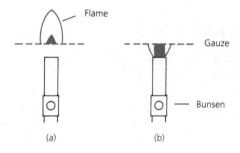

Flame

Gauze

Bunsen

(a)   (b)

Fig. 5 Metal gauze forms a flame trap
(a) Lighting the flame above a gauze
(b) Lighting the flame below a gauze
In each case, the metal gauze stops the flame from spreading above or below the gauze. How does it do this?

Figure 5 shows how you can demonstrate the effect of the gauze. Similar flame traps are used in most gas burners to prevent the flame from travelling back along the gas pipe.

Science isn't enough

The Davy safety lamp is often quoted as a wonderful invention which saved the lives of countless miners. In fact, more miners died after its invention than before! To some unscrupulous mine owners, the lamp was a way of making more money at the miner's expense. Miners could be sent to work in (cheap) old, dangerous mines, full of methane! How many modern inventions, designed to make our lives easier and better, actually make our lives worse?

Fig. 1 Walking through fire
This fireman's safety suit prevents the intense heat from reaching his body.
Why is the outside made of shiny metal foil?

Making a better radiator

In cars, behind refrigerators and in other places where they can't be seen, radiators are always painted black. In houses, radiators can be a variety of colours (to suit the room) but they are never shiny metal. Why?

The reason is that the heat radiated from a hot object depends on the colour of the surface. Dark colours radiate a lot of heat—black radiates most. Light colours (in particular, white) don't radiate much heat, and reflecting, silvery metal surfaces hardly radiate any heat at all. Heat radiation cannot pass through shiny metal surfaces.

However, you can greatly increase the heat radiated into a room by putting a shiny metal surface *behind* the radiator (Figure 2). This reflects back into the room heat that would otherwise be lost into the wall. (Electric fires use similar reflectors, shaped to beam the heat radiation out into the room.)

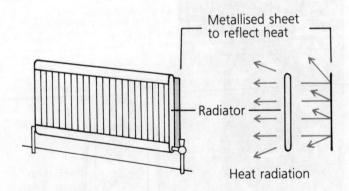

Fig. 2 Making a radiator more effective
How does it work?

• **Place a small sheet of cooking foil behind a bunsen flame. Place one hand behind the foil, and the other in front of the flame to feel the heat reflected from the foil. Now feel the difference when you remove the foil.**

134

Good absorbers of heat radiation

Have you ever got into a car with black seats on a very hot day? The seats are almost too hot to sit on, especially if you are wearing shorts!

Similarly, on a very hot day, black asphalt pavements can heat up so much that the tar starts to melt. The black tar gets much hotter than light-grey paving slabs.

Black surfaces absorb heat radiation much better than light-coloured and polished-metal surfaces. Black surfaces are good radiators of heat and good absorbers of heat. Heat can travel easily in either direction through a black surface. It can't travel as easily through a white surface, and it is reflected by a shiny metal surface.

Solar-heating panels that use sunlight (solar radiation) to heat water are always painted black (see Section 7.5). This makes them absorb or collect more heat.

The vacuum flask

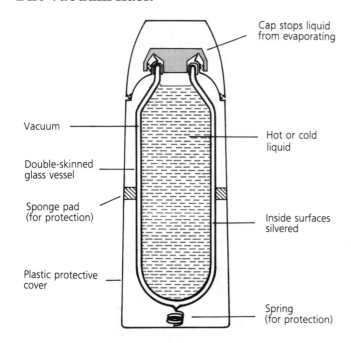

Vacuum

Double-skinned glass vessel

Sponge pad (for protection)

Plastic protective cover

Cap stops liquid from evaporating

Hot or cold liquid

Inside surfaces silvered

Spring (for protection)

Fig. 3 How a vacuum flask works
What steps are taken to reduce heat loss by
(i)   conduction?
(ii)   convection?
(iii) radiation?
(iv) evaporation?

● **Why do hot potatoes stay hot if you wrap them in metal foil? Why do meat and other foods not 'brown' if you cook them in metal foil?**

Vacuum flasks are a very effective way of keeping hot soup hot and cold milk cold. Figure 3 shows the structure of a vacuum flask. The liquid in the flask is (nearly!) surrounded by a vacuum between two glass walls. This prevents heat from being conducted (or convected) out of the flask. A tight-fitting cap prevents heat and vapour from escaping through the top. (The space above the liquid soon becomes saturated so that the liquid stops evaporating— see Section 8.8.)

The only way in which heat could escape from the flask would be by radiation through the vacuum. To prevent this from happening, the inner glass surfaces are silvered to reflect the heat radiation back into the flask.

Heat radiation and the great ice ages

Fig. 4 Black algae growing on rocks high up on a mountain
How does the colour of this algae help it to survive the cold?

The Earth's surface reflects much of the radiation that reaches us from the Sun. White snow and ice reflect more radiation than dark soil and water.

Every few million years, the Earth goes into a very cold **ice age.** As the Earth gets colder, more ice and snow cover the surface. More solar radiation is reflected, and less is absorbed. So the Earth gets colder still.

Once an ice age starts, it is self-perpetuating. The great ice ages in the history of the Earth lasted for millions of years.

It has been suggested that the last ice age was overcome partly by black algae and arctic flowers with black leaves. These absorbed more of the Sun's radiation and warmed the Earth up.

Perhaps when the next ice age comes there will be human beings around who can help. Perhaps they will be able to think of a better way out of the problem. (That is, if they haven't done something to produce a miniature ice-age—a 'nuclear winter'—in the first place!)

The eye of a hurricane

Fig. 1 A hurricane—a giant system of convection currents
From where does the hurricane get its energy?

In 1987, southern Britain was devastated by hurricane-force winds.

A **hurricane** is a huge swirling mass of air with winds of 50 m/s (110 mph) or more, and torrential rain. Yet in the centre (the eye) of a hurricane, it is calm, hot and sunny.

Hurricanes begin over water—usually in the Mexican Gulf. (Those in the Pacific are usually called *typhoons*.) A hurricane is really a giant system of convection currents (Figure 2).

1 The Sun strongly heats the water, causing it to evaporate. The air is heated by the hot sea and made less dense. It rises, and takes the water vapour with it.

2 Cooler, denser air rushes in to take the place of this warm air, causing strong winds.

3 High up in the sky, the water vapour cools and condenses to form clouds which produce torrential rain. The air cools and falls to the base of the hurricane.

4 Because of the rotation of the Earth, the whole system spins (in the northern hemisphere) in an anticlockwise direction.

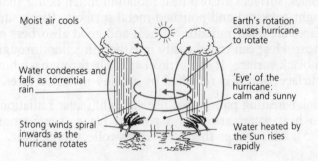

Fig. 2 How a hurricane works
What causes the moist air to rise at the centre of the hurricane?
What causes the rain?
Why does the hurricane rotate?
Why do hurricanes gain energy when they are over the sea, but weaken as they travel over land?

What causes hot air to rise?

When air is heated, it expands and becomes less dense (see Section 8.2). Its large volume gives rise to a large upthrust from the surrounding air. Because of its low density, the air doesn't have enough weight to overcome this upthrust, so it rises above the surrounding, denser air.

Fig. 3 A hot-air balloon
How does the pilot make it go (i) upwards? (ii) downwards?

There are many other examples of hot air rising above cooler air—for instance, ashes rising from a bonfire, or a hot-air balloon lifting off the ground. Glider pilots and birds also make use of upward air currents, or **thermals**, to glide higher and higher into the sky.

- **Make a windmill from aluminium foil, and suspend it above a candle flame. Watch how the hot air rising from the flame causes the windmill to rotate.**

Convection currents and clothes

If we stood around in winter without any clothes, we would soon cool down. Why is this? Why doesn't the air around us insulate us?

The reason is that the air next to our skin is at a lower temperature than our body. Heat therefore flows from our body into the air. But before this air has reached body temperature, it moves away and is replaced by colder air. A convection current is set up, taking heat from our bodies.

Clothes stop this movement of air. They keep the warm air next to our bodies. Only if a strong wind blows through our clothes will we cool down. (This is called the **wind chill** factor.)

Hot-water systems

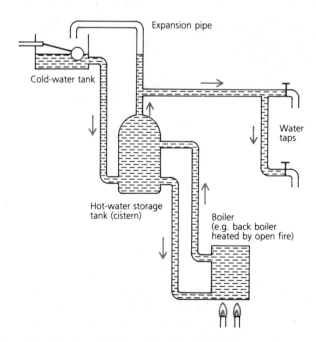

Fig. 4 A domestic hot-water system

Many hot-water systems use thermal convection (Figure 4). Water heated by the boiler rises to the hot-water cylinder. Cooler water falls from the bottom of the cylinder to take its place in the boiler. The water circulates so that eventually all the water in the cylinder becomes hot. **Why does the pipe from the cylinder to the taps come from the top of the cylinder?**

Convection currents in the Earth's core

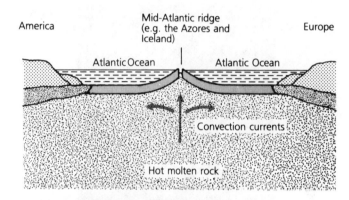

Fig. 5 Convection currents under the ground
What causes the 'ring of fire'—the string of volcanoes and earthquake regions round the Pacific ocean? (What is happening there?)

Over thousands of millions of years, molten rock has been rising up under the Atlantic Ocean. This rock has been pushed up by convection currents within the Earth's core. Gradually, the mid-Atlantic ridge has formed. As the ridge has grown, it has pushed Europe and Africa further away from America.

South America and Africa were once joined together. **Have a look at a world map and see if you can tell how they fitted together.** Most scientists believe that all land masses were once joined in a giant continent which they call Gondwanaland. Convection currents in the Earth's core forced the parts of this continent apart.

These giant underground movements produced the world's earthquakes and volcanoes. (For example, Iceland is a volcanic island on the mid-Atlantic ridge.)

Keeping the house warm

Is double glazing worth having?

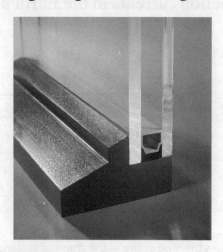

Fig. 1 Double glazing: is it worth it?
How can double glazing reduce your fuel bills?
What other ways are there of doing this? Which is the best value for money?

Some of the heat from our homes escapes through the glass in the windows. Having windows double glazed is an effective way of reducing this heat loss. Double-glazed windows consist of two glass panes with an insulating layer of air in between. Although heat cannot be conducted across the air gap, it can travel across by convection. However, if the air gap is small, the convection currents will also be small.

Double glazing works, but it is expensive. If all you want is to keep the house warm at night, then it is cheaper (and just as effective) to use heavy curtains.

How heat escapes from a house

Reducing heat loss through the windows is just one way of keeping a house warm. Since hot air rises, heat also escapes through the ceilings. If your roof is not insulated, you can lose at least 25% (one-quarter) of your heat in this way (Figure 2). Several inches of fibreglass or other loft insulation material drastically reduce the heat loss.

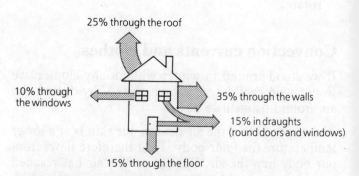

25% through the roof

10% through the windows

35% through the walls

15% in draughts (round doors and windows)

15% through the floor

Fig. 2 How your house loses heat
This shows the heat losses from a pre-war semi-detached house with no extra loft insulation or other forms of insulation.
In what ways would you expect a new house to differ from this? Why?

Fig. 3 Laying fibreglass loft insulation
Why mustn't you lay insulation under the water tank?

Heat loss through the floor can be reduced by using a thick carpet on tightly interlocking floorboards.

Heat loss through the walls

Although the walls of a house are thicker than the windows, there are usually more of them. A lot of heat escapes from a house through the walls. Most modern houses have two external walls with a cavity between them. This prevents moisture from getting into the house from outside. However, convection currents can form in the cavity and carry heat across. This can be prevented by filling the cavity with **cavity wall insulation.** In most new houses the inner walls are made of breeze blocks with a layer of insulation attached, or of special insulating blocks.

U-values

Builders talk about **U-values** when considering how much heat will escape through a wall by conduction and convection. The higher the U-value of a wall (or a door, or a window), the more heat escapes. The amount of heat which can escape increases with both the temperature difference and the surface area:

$$H = UAt(\theta_2 - \theta_1) \qquad (1)$$

where H is the heat getting through area A of wall of U-value U in time t when the temperature is θ_1 on one side and θ_2 on the other side.

Figure 4 gives some examples of U-values. In general, the higher the U-value, the more heat gets through.

Fig. 4 Examples of U-values

	U (W/m^2 °C)
Concrete wall, 150 mm thick	3.5
Solid brick wall, 220 mm thick, unplastered	2.3
Cavity wall without insulation	1.5
Cavity wall with polystyrene in the gap	0.7
Window, single glazed	5.6
Window, double glazed with a 3 mm gap	4.0
Window, double glazed, with a 12 mm gap	3.0
Door	2.3
Classroom ceiling	0.5
Timber floor	0.5

- **What is the heat loss in 1 hour through a bare brick wall 3 m high and 5 m long if the temperature on one side (the inside of the house) is 20 °C and on the other side is 10 °C?**

Draught-proofing

Houses can lose a lot of heat through draughts. But, in addition to removing warm air from a house, draughts remove water vapour. Kitchens, bathrooms and even our bodies give off large amounts of water vapour. If you seal up all the cracks to prevent hot air from escaping (and especially if you cover any ventilation grills), you are likely to have problems with damp.

The water vapour will condense out of the air on to the house walls and windows (Figure 5).

Fig. 5 Is more ventilation needed?
Bad ventilation can encourage the growth of moulds. So can low temperatures. Why?

- **Try to find out the most effective way of insulating your home or school. How much would it cost? How much might you save in fuel bills?**

Mud huts

Fig. 6 Mud-huts have their advantages
This large modern mud-walled building is more comfortable than a concrete-walled building. Why?

Many westerners feel sorry for people in Africa and other parts of the Third World who live in thatched mud huts. But, in fact, mud and thatch are excellent insulating materials and are well suited to hot countries. When problems do arise, they result from the amounts of money or high levels of skill needed to provide really waterproof thatch and large, permanent mud-walled structures that look attractive. Some people have abandoned mud huts and replaced them with concrete-block buildings with metal roofs. But they have found such buildings far less comfortable in the heat. Progress isn't always as easy as it looks—in Africa or anywhere else!

139

Why is it so hot in the greenhouse?

Fig. 1 Keeping plants warm

The Sun is at a very high temperature (6000 °C at the surface). It gives out high-frequency, high-energy heat radiation. This is mainly visible light and high-frequency infra-red radiation (see Section 14.8). This radiation is able to pass through the glass of the greenhouse.

Plants and other things in the greenhouse are at a much lower temperature. They also give out heat radiation, but of lower frequency and lower energy (low-frequency infra-red radiation). This radiation cannot pass through glass, and is reflected back into the greenhouse. This means that energy from the Sun which enters the greenhouse can't escape, so the temperature in the greenhouse rises (Figure 2).

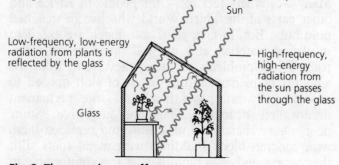

Fig. 2 The greenhouse effect
There are two ways of preventing a greenhouse from overheating in summer. What are they?

Solar heaters make use of the **greenhouse effect** (see Section 7.5, Figures 3 and 4). A solar panel is covered with glass, often double-glazed. Solar energy can get through the glass but low-frequency infra-red radiation can't get out.

Cloudy nights

Glass isn't the only thing that lets high-frequency heat radiation through more easily than low-frequency radiation. Water vapour and carbon dioxide in the atmosphere have the same effect. This is why it is warmer on a cloudy night than on a clear night. The clouds prevent the low-frequency infra-red radiation from escaping into space. This is another example of the greenhouse effect (Figure 3).

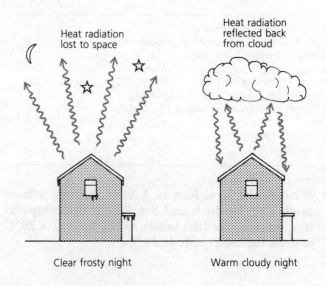

Fig. 3 Clear and frosty nights
Use this diagram to explain why clear nights are more frosty than cloudy nights

If there were no water vapour or carbon dioxide in the Earth's atmosphere, then the Earth's surface would be much colder than it is today.

Fig. 4 Melting the Arctic ice
What have the chimneys got to do with it?
Why is this so important?

Will the Earth flood or fry?

Some people are worried that the level of carbon dioxide in the atmosphere is increasing. Carbon dioxide is produced whenever something burns—for example, when coal and oil are burned in power stations. With every fire, more carbon dioxide goes into the atmosphere. But the more carbon dioxide there is, the more heat radiation is trapped within the Earth's atmosphere. Eventually, if the carbon dioxide level gets too high, the atmosphere will heat up so much that ice will melt from the polar ice caps. This will cause the oceans to rise, and could cause serious flooding in many coastal cities.

The amount of carbon dioxide in the air is a balance between

- the carbon dioxide given out by volcanoes, animals and plants, and
- the carbon dioxide taken in by plants to carry out photosynthesis.

Living things therefore affect the amount of carbon dioxide in the atmosphere. In his book *Gaia—A New Look at Life on Earth*, J. E. Lovelock has suggested that, over the past few millions of years, living things have controlled the carbon dioxide level in the Earth's atmosphere. As the Sun has got hotter, living things have adapted to reduce the level of carbon dioxide. This has kept the temperature of the Earth's surface fairly constant.

Suppose that this is true and that, as the Sun has become hotter, the level of carbon dioxide *has* been reduced by living things. We know that the Sun will go on getting hotter and hotter, but there will come a time when the level of carbon dioxide can be reduced no further. At that point there will be nothing to stop the temperature of the Earth from increasing. Fortunately, this isn't an immediate problem. It will take a few million years for the Sun to make the Earth noticeably warmer. Perhaps by then we will have found an answer.

141

Exercises

1 In an experiment, five stones of equal mass were painted different colours and left in the sun. Which stone would warm up fastest?

   A The black stone

   B The white stone

   C The red stone

   D The silver stone

   E The gold stone

2 The 'vacuum' in a vacuum flask prevents heat loss by

   A Radiation and conduction

   B Conduction only

   C Convection only

   D Radiation only

   E Conduction and convection

3 Heat travels through space from the Sun to the Earth by means of

   A Conduction, convection and radiation

   B Conduction and radiation

   C Convection and radiation

   D Radiation only

   E Convection only

4 It is dangerous to dive down into lakes or rivers because a few metres below the surface the water is much colder. (Many people have been drowned as a result of this.) What is the main reason for the difference in temperature?

   A Water is a poor conductor of heat.

   B Heat radiation cannot travel through water.

   C Convection currents carry cold water down from the surface.

   D The water surface reflects heat radiation.

   E Evaporation at the water surface

Fig. 1 Low-cost African charcoal stoves
Why is a clay stove more efficient than a metal stove?

5 Figure 1 shows African charcoal stoves used for cooking food. Clay stoves (or stoves lined with clay) use less charcoal than metal stoves for the same amount of cooking. The main reason for this is that

   A The clay stoves have a larger mass.

   B Metal is a better conductor of heat.

   C Metal reflects heat better than clay.

   D Clay absorbs heat more than metal.

   E Clay has a higher specific heat capacity.

6 Which of the following is the most accurate description of heat convection?

   A Hot air rises

   B Heat in a moving gas or liquid

   C The movement of hot gases and liquids

   D Heat carried through liquids and gases by currents produced by changes in density

   E The conduction of heat through gases

7 Complete these sentences:

a Heat can travel by _____, _____ and _____ .

b Water is a _____ conductor of heat.

c Hot air rises because it has a lower _____ than cold air.

d Solar radiation is an example of _____ radiation.

8 String vests are full of holes, yet people who wear them say that they keep them very warm. Why is this?

Fig. 2

9 Explain why the house shown in Figure 2 is cooler than a tiled building in summer, and warmer in winter.

Fig. 3 Three ways of carrying apples
What could they represent in terms of heat transfer?

10 Figure 3 shows three ways of carrying an apple across the room. If the apple represents heat, which of these methods corresponds to

a Heat convection?

b Heat radiation?

c Heat conduction?

Give reasons for your answers.

11 Discuss the effectiveness of the following kettles in bringing water rapidly to boiling point:

a A dirty metal kettle

b A polished metal kettle

c A plastic kettle

10 ELECTROSTATICS

10.1 Party balloons and dusty records

Charging things

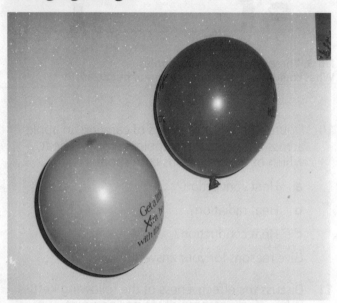

Fig. 1 Why do rubbed balloons stick to a wall?

Have you ever been to a party where you've stuck balloons to the wall? To make them stick, you **charge** them by rubbing them against your jumper. The charged balloon is then attracted to the wall by an electrostatic force. The work that you do against friction produces **electrostatic energy** on the balloon. **Try this.**

If you comb dry hair vigorously with a plastic comb, the comb becomes charged. It will attract your hair. (You can feel the force of attraction if you bring the charged comb close to the small hairs on your arm.) The charged comb will also pick up small pieces of paper, and will attract a stream of water from a tap (see Section 1.1 and Section 10.5, Figure 2). **Try this.**

A cellulose acetate sheet (like those used on overhead projectors) becomes highly charged when it is rubbed with a cloth (Figure 2). In other words, the sheet gains a lot of electrostatic energy. It is better than a charged plastic comb at picking up pieces of paper, attracting hair and bending a stream of water from a tap. **Try this.**

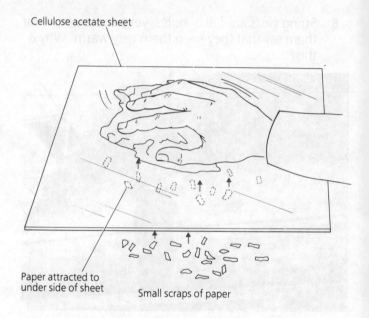

Fig. 2 Charging a sheet of cellulose acetate
Will this work with a sheet of aluminium foil? Explain.

A nylon shirt becomes charged as it rubs against your body. It is then attracted to your body, and this makes it difficult to take the shirt off.

- **What other examples have you come across of things becoming electrostatically charged?**

Electrostatic charge can be useful

The velvet lining in the glove compartment of some cars is applied using electrostatic charge. The glove compartment is first coated with glue and then charged. Fibres of cloth are attracted to the charged surface end on, and are held permanently in place by the glue.

A xerox photocopier uses electrostatic charge to copy printing from one sheet of paper to another. Figure 3 shows how it works.

144

Fig. 4 Bobbin lace
Why must the cover of the pillow be made of natural and not synthetic fibre?

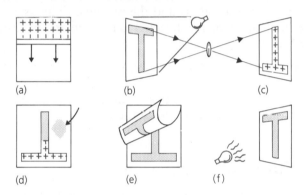

Fig. 3 How a xerox photocopier works
(a) A semiconducting plate is given a positive charge.
(b) Ultraviolet light is reflected on to this plate from white parts of the original (the sheet being xeroxed). The inked parts of the original absorb the ultraviolet light.
(c) Where the ultraviolet light falls on the plate, it removes the charge.
(d) Toner (carbon powder in plastic) is sprinkled on to the plate and sticks to the charged areas.
(e) Paper is pressed against the plate. The powder image transfers to the paper.
(f) The paper is heated. This melts the plastic, fixing the carbon image on the paper.

Electrostatic charge can be a nuisance

Records act rather like acetate sheets. They become charged by friction and then attract dust. If you try to wipe the dust off a record with an ordinary cloth, you merely produce more electrostatic energy. The record attracts even more dust.

There are other ways in which the build-up of electrostatic charge can cause problems. For example, people making bobbin lace must work on a pillow with a cover made of natural fibre. Man-made fibres tend to produce static charge which ruins the lace (Figure 4).

Removing the charge

Once charged, plastics and glass keep their charge so long as they are isolated. However, charge leaks away rapidly through metals. For example, you can remove charge from your hair by using a metal comb.

The microelectronics industry makes use of the fact that metals will remove charge. The electrostatic energy of a charged surface can destroy the tiny **integrated circuits** (silicon chips) in modern electronic equipment. People working with these circuits wear metal bracelets to remove any electrostatic charge from their hands. In addition, they must avoid wearing clothes made from nylon or other man-made (plastic) fibres.

The body of a car can build up electrostatic charge through friction with the air. Some people blame this for car sickness. They hang conducting strips from the rear of their car to carry the charge away to the ground.

Fig. 5 What is the purpose of the conducting strip hanging from the back of this car?

145

Breaking atoms by combing your hair

Fig. 1 Breaking atoms
What is the comb removing from the hair atoms?

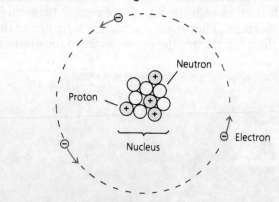

Fig. 2 A simple model of the atom
This is one way of picturing the atom. It has a nucleus (Latin for 'little nut') containing protons and neutrons. Electrons orbit around this nucleus.

To understand what happens when something is charged, we need to look at the tiny atoms from which everything is made (see Section 5.3).

Figure 2 shows a simple model (a simple picture) of the atom. At the centre is a **nucleus** of **protons** and **neutrons.** This is surrounded by a cloud of much smaller particles called **electrons**. In an ordinary atom, the number of electrons is equal to the number of protons. The electrons are attracted to the protons, and remain in orbit around the nucleus. (This is a bit like the planets being attracted to the Sun and orbiting the Sun.)

When you use a nylon comb on your hair, some of the atoms are damaged. Electrons are pulled from the atoms of your hair, and stick to the atoms of the comb. Your hair is then attracted to the comb.

Positive and negative ions

Physicists say that protons have a **positive charge** and electrons have a **negative charge**. Neutrons have no charge—they are neutral.

In a normal atom, the negative charge of each electron balances (and cancels the effect of) the positive charge of each proton. The atom as a whole is uncharged. (This is why the charges are called positive and negative—adding negative charge is like taking away positive charge.)

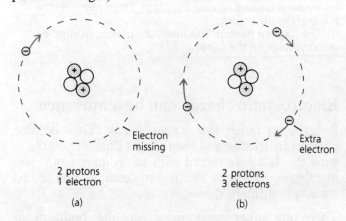

Fig. 3 Positive and negative ions
(a) A positive ion—an atom that has lost an electron
(b) A negative ion—an atom that has gained an electron
This particular atom has two protons. Which element is this?
(See Chapter 17.)

Atoms with too many or too few electrons are called **ions** (not irons!). An atom with some electrons missing has more positive charge than negative charge. It is called a **positive ion**. An atom with too many electrons has more negative charge than positive charge. It is called a **negative ion**.

Attraction and repulsion

When you rub polythene (for example, a polythene bag), it gains electrons and becomes negatively charged. When you rub cellulose acetate (for example, an overhead projector transparency), it loses electrons and becomes positively charged.

If you hang a charged strip of polythene near a charged strip of cellulose acetate, they attract each other. **Try this.**

If you hang two charged strips of polythene near each other, they repel each other. Two charged strips of cellulose acetate will also repel each other. **Try this.**

- **Charge two balloons by rubbing them and then hang them near each other on lengths of thread. Do they attract or repel each other?**

> Like charges repel: unlike charges attract.

+ repels +   − repels −
+ attracts −   − attracts +

Fig. 4 An electrostatic crop-sprayer
What is its advantage compared with an ordinary crop-sprayer?

In some paint-sprayers and crop-sprayers, the tiny droplets of spray are given an electrostatic charge as they come out of the nozzle (Figure 4). Because the droplets all have the same sign of charge (they are either all positively charged or all negatively charged),

they repel each other and remain as a finely separated mist. (If they were not charged, they would tend to join together and to form larger drops.) Their charge also helps them to stick to whatever is being sprayed—for example, a car or some plants. Indeed, cars that are being sprayed are often given the opposite charge to attract the paint.

Why dust sticks to charged surfaces

Dust particles (like everything else) contain positive and negative charges—positive protons and negative electrons. Normally these positive and negative charges cancel each other out.

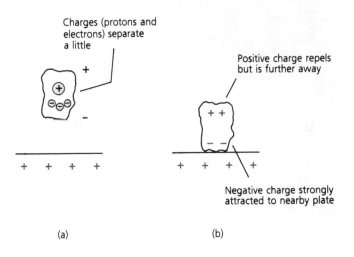

(a)   (b)

Fig. 5 Why dust sticks to a charged plate
Rubbing off the dust can make the plate dustier in the long run. Why?

Suppose that a small dust particle is close to a positively charged surface (Figure 5). The electrons of the dust atoms are attracted to the surface. But the protons are repelled by it. This causes the charges in the dust particle to separate out. The positive charges move away from the surface until they are repelled only weakly. The negative charges move closer to the surface. They are then strongly attracted by it. Overall, the dust particle is attracted to the charged surface.

This process of separating the charges inside an uncharged object—in this case a dust particle—is called **electrostatic induction**.

- **Cover your finger with a cloth, and use it to rub a circle on a cellulose acetate sheet. Scatter fine powder such as pepper on to the sheet and then shake off the excess. What happens? Why?**

Electricity and electrostatics

Fig. 1 A hair-raising experience
This girl is standing on a wax block and is holding the sphere of a Van de Graaff generator. This machine has caused electrons to travel through her body and into her hair. (Only a small amount of energy is involved, so the girl has not been harmed.)
(i)   Why is her hair standing on end?
(ii)   What do we call the movement of electrons?
(iii) Why is she standing on a wax block?

Does electrostatic charge have any connection with electricity? You sometimes get sparks in electrical equipment rather like those you see when you comb your hair vigorously. Also, you can feel sparks if you touch the screen of some television sets or computer monitors. The screens are highly charged even though they haven't been rubbed. In addition, we use the symbols + (positive) and − (negative) on batteries and other electrical equipment.

In fact, the connection between electricity and electrostatics is very simple:

> Electric current is the movement of charge (usually of electrons).

We have already seen that some people attach a conducting strip to the back of their car to remove electrostatic charge (Section 10.1, Figure 5). This conducting strip allows electrons to flow through it to the ground. (The car tyres are insulators—they don't allow charge to flow.) The moving electrons make up a tiny electric current which flows between the car body and the ground.

The negative (−) terminal of a battery or electrical power supply pushes out electrons. So a metal plate connected to this terminal becomes negatively charged. The positive (+) terminal of a battery or electrical power supply pulls in electrons. A metal

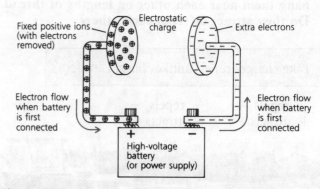

Fig. 2 Using a battery to produce electrostatic charge
The positive terminal takes electrons from the metal. Why does this cause the plate to be *positively* charged?

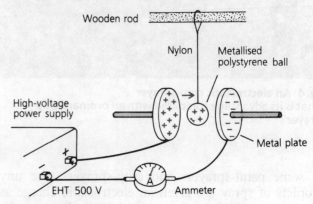

Fig. 3 Electric current is a movement of charge
Why does the metallised ball bounce back and forth between the metal plates?

plate connected to this terminal therefore loses some of its electrons and becomes positively charged. However, you need a very high-voltage battery or electrical supply to produce a noticeable electrostatic force (Figure 2).

Figure 3 shows a way of demonstrating the link between electrostatics and electric current. When you switch on the power supply, the ball bounces back and forth between the metal plates. The meter shows that a current is flowing. (The moving ball must be carrying the current across the gap.) The faster the ball travels, the larger is the current.

The ball is actually carrying electrostatic charge from one plate to the other. First the ball is attracted to, say, the positive (+) plate. Here it loses some electrons and becomes positively charged. The ball is then repelled by the positive plate and attracted to the negative (−) plate. Here it gains enough extra electrons to make it negatively charged. This causes the ball to be attracted back to the positive plate, and so on.

Because electric current is the movement of charge, charged objects are sometimes said to contain **static** (stationary) **electricity**.

Smoky chimneys and electrostatic precipitators

One winter in the 1950s, Britain's cities were hit by a severe smog. This was like normal fog except that it contained a lot of smoke from city chimneys. A lot of people—particularly old people—died as a result of the smog.

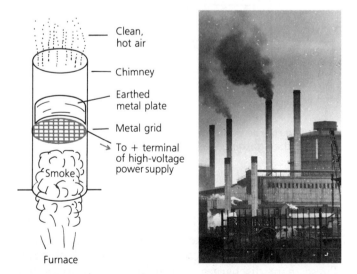

Fig. 4 **This electrostatic precipitator removes smoke from the chimney**
How does it do this?

To prevent the smog from happening again, a clean air act was introduced. People in many areas were allowed to burn only smokeless fuels. Factories and power stations had to reduce the amount of smoke and dust coming out of their chimneys.

An invention that now helps factories and power stations to do this is the **electrostatic precipitator** (Figure 4). A metal grid in the centre of the chimney is connected to the positive terminal of a very-high-voltage power supply. This gives the grid a positive charge. As the smoke particles move up the chimney, they pass through the grid and are charged by it. They are then repelled (because they are now also positively charged). Further up the chimney, the charged particles are attracted to metal plates. They stick to these plates and can easily be removed later. (The metal plates are connected to the ground so that they do not themselves become charged—the charge leaks away.)

Point discharge

If, instead of a wire grid, you connected a highly charged metal point to a terminal of a high-voltage power supply, the smoke or dust particles would be repelled very violently. Figure 5 shows two ways of demonstrating this.

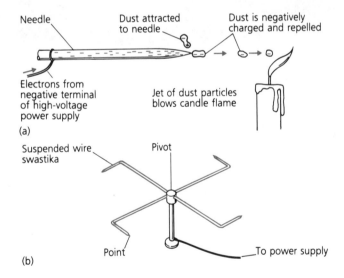

Fig. 5 **Point discharge**
(a) The needle attracts dust particles and then repels them towards the candle flame. The draught blows the flame to one side.
(b) This swastika turns when it is connected to a high-voltage battery. Which way does it turn? Why?

In the next section we will see how this **point discharge** occurs at the top of a lightning conductor during a thunderstorm.

149

Thunder and lightning

Fig. 1 Lightning passing through a car!
Why weren't the people in the car harmed? The discharge is at a temperature of 30 000 °C—five times as hot as the surface of the Sun.
How do you think this temperature was measured? (See Section 8.5.)

When you take off a nylon shirt or blouse, it rubs against your skin and is charged. Sparks jump from the shirt to your body. If you listen carefully, you can sometimes hear the sparks. If it is dark, you can sometimes see them.

Similarly, a thunderstorm occurs when atoms of air rub against one another. The sparks (or lightning) are produced on a larger scale, but the principle is the same.

The build-up of charge

In thunderclouds, the air is moving about very rapidly. Layers of air are moving against each other, producing an enormous build-up of electrostatic charge (positive and negative ions) within the cloud.

As the charging continues, negative charges gather in the lower part of the cloud. Electrons in trees and buildings are repelled by these negative charges, and move away from the cloud into the ground. The trees and buildings therefore become positively charged. This, in turn, attracts more negative charge to the bottom of the thundercloud, and repels positive charge to the top of the thundercloud.

Eventually, the charges on the underside of the cloud pull the cloud down towards the ground. As it nears the ground, there is an even bigger build-up of charge. Figure 2 shows the charge situation just before lightning strikes.

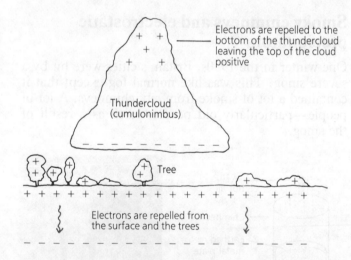

Fig. 2 The charge build-up just before lightning strikes
Where is the lightning likely to strike first? Why?

Lightning

Finally, charges leap down from the cloud to the ground (the leader stroke) and back again (the powerful return stroke) at nearly half the speed of light. These giant discharges (like giant sparks) give out a tremendous amount of energy. The discharges that we can see, we call **fork lightning. Sheet lightning** is what we see when a cloud is lit up as fork lightning goes from one place to another inside the cloud. (**Ball lightning**—a slowly moving fireball—is another form of lightning which happens only occasionally.)

Thunder

Lightning produces tremendous heat. When lightning strikes, the heat produced can destroy trees and houses. This is why it is dangerous to shelter under a tree in a storm. If the tree were struck by lightning, the sudden heat produced could kill you. In Britain, around 12 people are killed each year by lightning.

Fig. 3 A boot from a boy who was struck by lightning
Tom Parkin was lucky. His boots were ruined, but he was unharmed. Others are not so lucky. On average, 12 people a year are killed by lightning in Britain.
How does this compare with other accidents?
Where is (i) the most dangerous, (ii) the safest, place to be in a thunderstorm? Why?

The heat produced by lightning causes the air to expand very rapidly. This results in the noise that we call thunder. When we are close to a lightning strike, thunder sounds like a short, sudden, very loud crack. But when we are a long way away, all that we hear is a low-pitched rumble. This is caused by the reflection of the sound from hills and houses.

Lightning conductors

Because lightning can do so much damage, tall buildings have **lightning conductors** to make a lightning strike less likely (Figure 4). A lightning conductor consists of a copper strip or rod. One end of the rod is buried in the ground. The other end sticks up into the air as a spike. During a thunderstorm, the spike becomes positively charged. It acts as a **point dis-**

Fig. 4 A lightning conductor
How does it protect this tower?

charge, and sprays positively charged particles on to the underside of the thundercloud. This removes some of the charge from that part of the cloud, and so makes a lightning strike less likely (Figure 5).

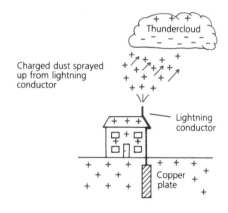

Fig. 5 Spraying a cloud with charge
Why does this work?

If lightning does strike, it usually strikes the conductor rather than something else. Because the lightning conductor is made of thick copper, the huge electric current produced by the lightning can pass up and down the conductor without causing much heat.

However, if the lightning conductor has been damaged or broken, tremendous heat will occur at the break. This heat could destroy the building and could kill someone. So if you see a lightning conductor that is broken, tell someone so that it can be repaired. You may be saving a person's life!

Exercises

1 Ion is another name for which of the following:

A The nucleus of an atom

B A particle that circles round the nucleus

C An atom that has gained or lost electrons

D Electrostatic charge

E A metallic conductor

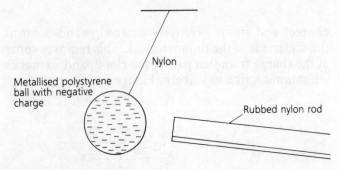

Fig. 1 **A repulsive situation**
What does it show?

2 A metal-coated polystyrene ball is suspended from a nylon thread and given a negative electrostatic charge (Figure 1). A rubbed nylon rod repels this ball. This shows that

A Rubbed nylon has a negative charge

B Rubbed nylon has a positive charge

C The nylon has induced a charge on the ball

D The ball has induced a charge on the nylon

E Metal repels nylon

3 Point discharge describes the fact that:

A Charges cannot exist in metal points

B Charged metal points attract and then violently repel dust particles

C Metal points remove charge from dust particles

D Metal points cause sparks to occur

E Lightning conductors use metal points

4 The conducting strip hanging from the back of some cars is there

A To stop the car from being struck by lightning

B To earth the car's wiring system

C To produce electrostatic charge as it rubs against the road

D To remove any electrostatic charge that has built up in the car

5 Thunder is caused by

A The collision of air molecules

B The sudden expansion of heated air

C Electrons making a noise as they are torn from atoms

D Thunderclouds colliding with each other

E Negative charges being pushed to the top of thunderclouds

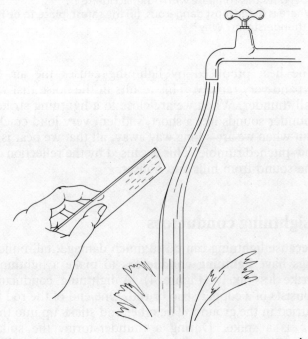

Fig. 2 **What happens if the water touches this strip? Why?**

152

6 Complete these sentences:

a The nucleus of an atom contains _____ which have a _____ charge and _____ that are uncharged. _____ orbit round the nucleus and have a _____ charge.

b A charged atom is called an _____ . It is charged because it has _____ or _____ one or more electrons.

c Like charges _____ ; unlike charges _____ .

7 State two uses and two problems caused by electrostatic charge.

8 When you rub a piece of polythene with a cloth, both become charged. The polythene gains a negative charge.

a Why does it become charged?

b What happens to the cloth? Explain.

9 A rubbed piece of polythene is placed near water dribbling from a tap (Figure 2). At first, the water bends towards the polythene. However, as soon as it touches the polythene, it stops being attracted and falls vertically. Explain this.

10 People who handle electronic integrated circuits wear cotton rather than nylon clothing (Figure 3). They sometimes have a metal bracelet connected to the ground, or touch a metal plate connected to the ground. Explain why.

11 Explain how you could use a positively charged cellulose acetate sheet (from an overhead projector) to test whether a charged balloon had a positive or negative charge.

Fig. 3 Why mustn't she wear nylon?

12 State and explain the difference between combing dry hair with a nylon comb and combing it with a metal comb.

13 What happens when dust and smoke particles get near a charged metal wire? How is this used to reduce the smoke coming from a factory chimney?

14 Explain how a lightning conductor

a makes it less likely that a building will be struck by lightning

b protects the building if lightning does strike.

153

11 ELECTRICITY

11.1 Making a torch

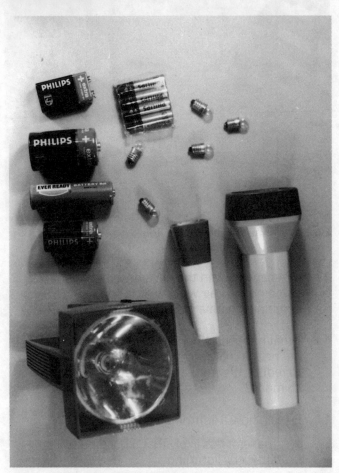

Fig. 1 Torches use bulbs and batteries
What else is needed to make a torch?

To make a torch you need a light bulb, a battery, electrical conductors and a switch.

The light bulb

A light bulb has a very thin tungsten wire filament that glows when an electric current is passed through it. Tungsten is used because of its high melting point. If the filament was kept in air, the tungsten wire would oxidise and would be destroyed. To avoid this, the wire is sealed in a glass container from which all the air has been removed (Figure 2).

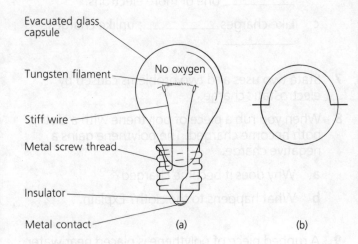

Fig. 2 A light bulb for a torch
(a) The structure of the light bulb
(b) The symbol used in circuit diagrams
Why is tungsten used for the filament?

The battery

A battery is needed to force electricity through the bulb. In fact, a 1.5 V battery should really be called a **cell**. A **battery** is a collection of electrical cells (just as a battery farm is a collection of cages for chickens). (**What is a gun battery?**) A 6 V battery contains four 1.5 V cells. A 9 V battery contains six 1.5 V cells. **How many cells are there in a 4.5 V battery?**

Fig. 3 Inside a 6V battery
A battery is made up of cells.
How many cells are there in a 9 V battery?

Cells turn chemical energy into electrical energy. They act rather like pumps, pumping electrons round a circuit.

Electrical conductors

Electrical conductors are needed to connect the battery to the bulb so that electricity can flow from the battery to the bulb and back again.

Copper is the material most commonly used for connecting wires, but some torches use brass. Any metal will work to some extent, and so will graphite (for example, the lead of a pencil). In contrast, wood and plastics are insulators—they do not conduct electricity.

Only a few liquids conduct electricity. The most obvious examples are mercury (a liquid metal) and (impure) water. (Very pure, **deionised** water does not conduct electricity, but the slightest impurity will change this.) Water and mains electricity are a dangerous combination. For example, children have been killed by shooting water pistols in bathrooms containing electric heaters.

All gases, including air, are insulators.

- **Make a 1.5 V torch cell light a 1.5 V bulb**
  (a) using wires to connect the cell to the bulb
  (b) using something other than connecting wire.
  Do you have to make two connections to the light bulb? Does it matter which way round you have the bulb, or the cell?

The switch

To switch the torch off, you need to break the circuit. In other words, you need to disconnect a part of the copper or brass strip carrying the electricity. Switches are just metal contacts that can be touched together to let current flow or held apart to stop current from flowing.

Different types of switch are designed for different purposes. When the Northern Ireland Minister Airey Neave was murdered, the terrorists used a **mercury tilt switch**. When these switches are tilted, mercury flows between two wires and joins them together. In the Airey Neave murder, the switch operated as the car started to drive up the ramp from the car park at the Houses of Parliament. A more acceptable use of these switches is to enable a severely handicapped person to operate electrical equipment just by nodding their head. (Science can be used for good or for evil!)

Fig. 4 Physics used by a murderer
How can you use mercury switches to help rather than harm people?

Most burglar alarm systems use pressure switches and magnetic reed switches. Magnetic reed switches switch on when a magnet is brought near. For example, a reed switch can be embedded in a door frame, and a magnet fixed into the edge of the door. When the door is opened, the magnet moves away from the switch. The current switches off, and this triggers the burglar alarm.

Switches can be made to react to sound, to light, to the presence of gas, to movement and to a wide range of other effects. But you won't find switches like these in the average torch!

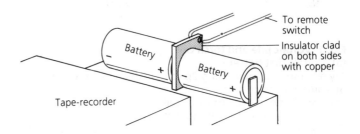

Fig. 5 A simple remote-control switch for a tape-recorder
Does it matter which way round you have the switch? Explain.

Figure 5 shows a way of making a remote switch for a battery tape-recorder (or anything else that runs off batteries). **Can you make an arrangement such that your battery tape-recorder shouts at you, or starts to play a tape of a dog barking, as you try to pick it up?**

155

Getting the voltage right

Buying a new bulb for the torch

A torch bulb has a voltage stamped on it. If you use a much higher voltage battery, you will burn out the bulb. If you use a much lower voltage battery, the bulb will not glow brightly.

- **Try connecting a 2.5 V bulb to (a) a 1.5 V cell, (b) a 3 V battery.**

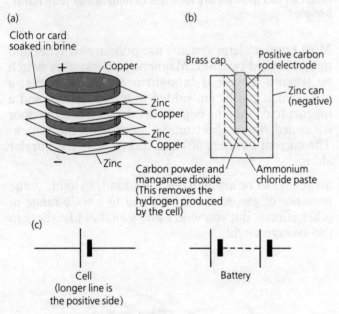

Fig. 1 Voltaic pile and torch cell
(a) Volta's first battery
Try making your own using 2p coins instead of copper and 5p coins instead of zinc.
(b) The cheapest type of torch cell
(c) Circuit symbols for cell and battery
Try making a cell by pushing a piece of copper and a nail into a lemon. Measure the voltage of this cell.

Volts are named after the Italian physicist, Count Alessandro Volta, who invented the first battery—the **voltaic pile** shown in Figure 1(a). Before this, the standard demonstration of electricity was the twitching of dissected frogs' legs when you touched them against different metals. This somewhat unpleasant discovery was made by Luigi Galvani. It is the source of the expression 'galvanised into action'.

An analogy

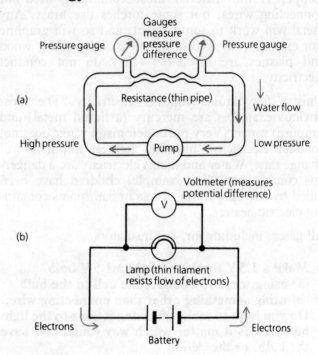

Fig. 2 Voltage acts like water pressure

Consider the simple-pumped central-heating system and the electric circuit shown in Figure 2. There are a number of similarities:

1 In the first diagram, there is a flow of water; in the second, a flow of electrons.

2 The battery in the second diagram acts like the pump in the first diagram.

3 The pressure gauges in the first diagram and the voltmeter in the second diagram have similar functions.

- In the first diagram, the pressure gauges measure the pressure difference produced by the battery.

- In the second diagram, the voltmeter measures the **potential difference** produced by the battery. (The potential difference is measured in volts. It is sometimes called the voltage, but this is not the correct term. It can be measured with a single voltmeter connected across the battery.)

Positive, negative and earth potential

At the negative terminal of a high-voltage battery, electrons are pushed close together. They have a large potential energy. We say that this negative terminal is at a large **negative potential**.

At the positive terminal, the electrons are pulled away from their atoms. Again they have a large potential energy. We say that this terminal is at a large **positive potential**.

In moist ground, the electrons can spread out to just the right distance between them. They have zero potential energy. We say that the Earth (and anything connected to it) is at **zero potential** (zero volts).

A 6 V battery has a **potential difference** (a difference in potential) of 6 V between its terminals. Suppose that the negative terminal is connected to Earth. It must now be at 0 V potential. The positive terminal must therefore be at a potential of +6 V.

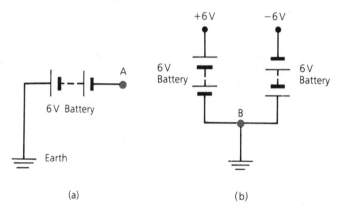

(a)   (b)

Fig. 3 What is the potential at terminal A? What is it at terminal B?

Danger—high voltage!

A lot of electrons at a high potential have a lot of potential energy. This can kill you. Even mains potential (240 V) can kill you, especially if you have wet hands. But 12 V supplies are safe. Even with a

large number of electrons, their potential energy is not enough to harm you.

Strangely enough, a rubbed nylon shirt or the screen of a television can be at a potential of thousands of volts. The reason why they don't harm us is that there are few electrons present. The potential energy of each electron is large, but overall the energy is small. However, these high voltages can destroy tiny silicon chip integrated circuits (see Chapter 18).

Electromotive force (emf)

This is the potential difference across a battery or cell when no current is being taken from it. As you start to take current, some energy is lost inside the battery and the potential difference across the terminals of the battery decreases. **Try this, using the circuit in Figure 4**. In other words, the emf of a battery is also the largest potential difference across its terminals.

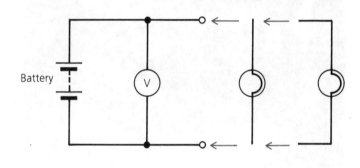

Fig. 4 What happens to the potential difference across the battery?
How does it differ from the emf as you take more current? Why?

The term 'electromotive force' is misleading. It is not a real force—it is measured in volts, not newtons. But the term does remind us that it is the potential difference between various parts of a circuit that forces current to flow between them.

Measuring electric current

Charging a battery

Fig. 1 Charging a car battery
What is the name and purpose of the meter in this battery charger?

Sometimes, a car won't start because the battery is flat. You need to charge the battery—to pass a current through it using a battery charger. The larger the current, the faster the battery will charge. But if the current gets too large, you'll spoil the battery.

A car battery should be charged at the rate of **1 ampere** (usually called **1 amp** (A)). Battery chargers usually charge at between 0.5 A and 1.5 A.

Six million million million electrons per second

We have already seen that electric current is the rate of flow of charge—normally of electrons. One ampere is equal to 6×10^{18} electrons per second! This isn't as large as it sounds. Electrons are very tiny indeed. Most torches use a current of at least half an ampere.

Electric current flows in the wrong direction!

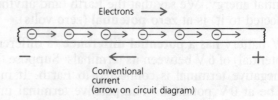

Fig. 2 Current flows in the wrong direction!
We say that electric current flows from plus to minus, even though electrons flow from minus to plus.

You can't see which way current is flowing just by looking at a wire carrying current. In the early days, it was decided that current flowed from positive to negative. This is the **conventional current** direction. We put arrows on circuit diagrams showing current flowing in this direction. Unfortunately, once this convention had become too common to change, it was discovered that electrons flow the other way!

Ampère and the ammeter

There are many ways in which we could estimate the size of the current. One way is to pass the current through a light bulb. The brighter the bulb, the larger the current flowing through it. **What are the disadvantages of this method?**

At the beginning of the nineteenth century, André-Marie Ampère found another way of measuring current. He found that, when an electric current flows near a magnet, it causes the wire or magnet to move. (We will look at this in detail in Chapter 13.) A modern ammeter uses this movement to make a pointer move across a scale. Battery chargers have one of these ammeters built in to check that the current is about 1 A (1 ampere).

Unlike some other scientists, Ampère did his research with very little money. His family's money was taken away when his father was publicly executed during the French revolution. All Ampère's experiments were carried out in his own small flat.

Using an ammeter

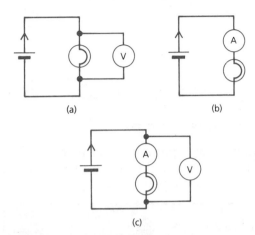

Fig. 3 Using ammeters and voltmeters
(a) The voltmeter is connected across the bulb after connecting the rest of the circuit
(b) You have to break the circuit to fit the ammeter in
(c) Using the ammeter and voltmeter together
If you use a higher-voltage battery, what will happen to
   (i) the voltmeter reading?
   (ii) the ammeter reading?
Why?

Ammeters are not connected to a circuit in the same way as voltmeters are (Figure 3).

With a voltmeter, you can (and should!) connect up the circuit first. *Then* you connect the voltmeter across a part of the circuit to measure the potential difference.

In contrast, ammeters have to be connected in as part of the circuit. An ammeter measures the current that flows through it.

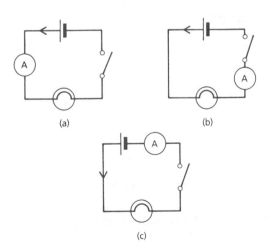

Fig. 4 How does the current change as you go round the circuit?

- Use an ammeter to check the current flowing into a light bulb of the type used in torches. How do you expect the current to differ on each side of the bulb? Measure it and see if you were right.

In the simple (single-loop) circuit of an electric torch, it doesn't matter where you connect the ammeter.

> In a single-loop circuit, the current is the same all the way round the circuit.

No charges—no electrons—are lost. All the electrons that leave the battery travel all the way round and back into the battery again.

Remember, light bulbs don't use up electrons. They only remove their energy. The battery gives the electrons potential energy, and the electrons lose this energy as they travel round the circuit.

Checking for current flow with a voltmeter

A voltmeter connected across part of the circuit can often tell you whether a current is flowing. For example, suppose your voltmeter shows that there is a potential drop across one of the soldered connections in your circuit. This means that the current is not flowing easily (if at all) through this connection. The electrons therefore need extra potential energy to get through. This is similar to the pressure difference of water building up across a blockage in a pipe (Figure 5).

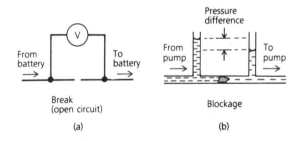

Fig. 5 Finding a disconnection
(a) Finding a disconnection in an electric circuit using a voltmeter
(b) Finding a disconnection in a water circuit using pressure gauges

- Ask a friend to set up a faulty circuit with a bad connection, a break, or a bulb loose in its socket. Then use a voltmeter to identify the fault.

159

Which fuse should you use?

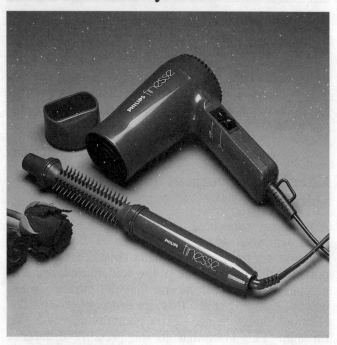

Fig. 1 Which fuse should you use?
How can you find out?

Somebody has given you a hairdryer (Figure 1). It has a 13 amp plug, but no fuse. What rating of fuse should you use? 13 A? 5 A? 3 A?

The fuse rating should always be a little higher than the current that will normally pass through the hairdryer. (The same is true for any other piece of electrical equipment.) If the fuse rating is the same as the normal current, it will blow (burn out) too easily. If the fuse rating is much higher than the current, then it won't provide much protection. (See Section 11.7 for further discussion of fuses.) So you need to know what current the hairdryer will use.

One way of finding this out would be to measure it using an ammeter. However, this would not be very easy (or very safe with mains electricity!). Fortunately there is an easier way. Provided that you know the wattage of your hairdryer (this is normally printed somewhere on it), you can *calculate* the current.

Watts = volts × amps

The watt is a unit of power (see Chapter 7). One watt is one joule per second. But one watt is also one volt multiplied by one ampere.

$$\text{electrical power} = \text{current} \times \text{potential difference (pd)} \quad (1)$$

Suppose, for example, that a 6 V battery is used to drive a current of 2 A through a torch bulb. The power (the energy per second) that the bulb will give out is 6 V × 2 A = 12 W.

● **What is the power output of a torch that uses a 3 V, 0.5 A bulb? Have a look at some torch bulbs. Read the voltage and current from the side of each bulb. How do these bulbs compare with a 24 W car headlight?**

Calculating the current through a hairdryer

Equation (1) can be written as

$$\text{current} = \frac{\text{power}}{\text{pd}}$$

In Britain, the mains electrical supply is at 240 V. So to find the current used by your hairdryer, just divide the power (wattage) of the hairdryer by 240.

For example, if the hairdryer is marked '480 W', then the normal current through it is

$$\text{current} = \frac{\text{power}}{\text{pd}} = \frac{480 \text{ W}}{240 \text{ V}} = 2 \text{ A}$$

In this case, a 3 A fuse would be best.

● **What fuse (1 A, 3 A, 5 A or 13 A) should you use with a 3000 W electric kettle?**

- Find the power consumption of some electrical equipment in your home (including light bulbs). This should be stamped or printed somewhere on them. Calculate the current (assuming that the mains voltage is 240 V). What sort of equipment uses
  (a) the most current?
  (b) the least current?

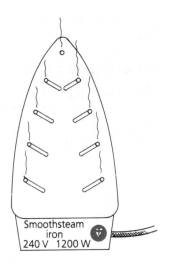

Fig. 2 What current flows through this iron?

Measuring the energy

You can easily measure the energy used by a light bulb, or any other piece of electrical equipment. All you do is to measure the potential difference across it with a voltmeter, the current through it with an ammeter and the time for which the current flows. Then

$$\text{energy} = \text{voltage} \times \text{current} \times \text{time} \qquad (2)$$

- Check the wattage of a torch bulb by measuring the potential difference and the current. Also measure the efficiency of a 12 V electric heater by measuring (a) the electrical energy used and (b) the heat produced. (Use the heat to raise the temperature of some water.)

The electricity meters used in our homes automatically multiply the current and voltage together. A disc inside the meter moves at a speed proportional to current × voltage. The faster the disc spins, the more electrical power you are using. So if this disc goes on spinning fast for a long time, you will have a high meter reading and a large bill! **Why is this?**

- **In what units is electrical energy commonly measured? (See Section 6.6.)**

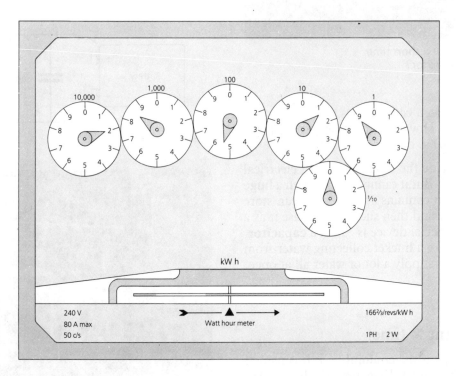

Fig. 3 Measuring the flow of electrical energy
How much energy has been used since this meter was installed (i) in kW h ? (ii) in joules?

161

Charging a flashgun

Fig. 1   A large current for a short time
Why do you need a capacitor?

The electronic flash on a camera uses a huge current, about 100 A or more. However, the flash only lasts for 1/1000 seconds (0.001 s) or less.

A torch cell can provide the small amount of electrical energy that is needed. But it cannot supply such a huge current. The flashgun contains a device that can store charge from a battery and then suddenly release it as a huge current. This special device is called a **capacitor**. (The capacitor acts like a bucket collecting water from a tap. The tap cannot supply a lot of water all at once, but a bucket can.)

Charge = current × time

The SI unit for charge is the **coulomb** (C). It is named after the eighteenth century Frenchman, Charles Augustin Coulomb, who studied the attraction and repulsion of charges. One coulomb is the amount of charge

passing a point in a circuit if one amp of current flows for one second

$$
\begin{array}{ll}
\text{charge} = \text{current} \times \text{time} & \\
1 \text{ coulomb} = 1 \text{ amp} \times 1 \text{ second} & (1)
\end{array}
$$

The capacitor in an electronic flashgun needs to supply a current of 100 A for 0.001 s. How much charge does it need to store?

$$
\begin{aligned}
\text{charge} &= \text{current} \times \text{time} \\
&= 100\,\text{A} \times 0.001\,\text{s} \\
&= 0.1\,\text{A s} \\
&= 0.1\,\text{C}
\end{aligned}
$$

The capacitor therefore needs to be able to store 0.1 coulombs of charge.

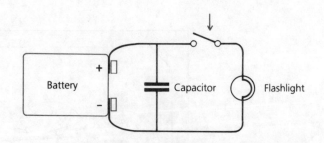

Fig. 2   Inside a flashgun
The capacitor stores charge. What else does it store?

Charge on the electron

You need 6×10^{18} electrons to get 1 coulomb of charge. Thus, each electron carries a charge of only $1.6 \times 10^{19}\,\mathrm{C}$.

Charge in a car battery

Manufacturers of car batteries often use **amp hours** (A h) as units of charge. A typical car battery has a capacity of 20 A h. **What is this in coulombs?** Such a battery can, for example, supply a current of 1 A for 20 hours, or a current of 20 A for 1 hour. (In practice, large currents spoil the battery, so you do not get as much as 20 A h.)

Fig. 3 How long will it take for the battery to go flat?
This car's 20 A h battery was fully charged to start with, and is now supplying a current of 10 A to the lamps. How long (at most) will it take to become completely discharged?

Volts = joules per coulomb

According to Equation (1) of Section 11.4,

$$\text{power} = \text{potential difference} \times \text{current}$$

Hence

$$\text{potential difference} = \frac{\text{power}}{\text{current}}$$

$$= \frac{\text{energy/time}}{\text{charge/time}}$$

or

$$\text{potential difference} = \frac{\text{energy}}{\text{charge}} \qquad (2)$$

If it takes one joule of energy to move one coulomb of charge between the two points, then the potential difference between them is one volt.

$$\boxed{1 \text{ volt} = 1 \text{ joule per coulomb}}$$

In low-voltage circuits, each coulomb of charge (in other words, each 6×10^{18} electrons) has only a few joules of energy. In high-voltage circuits, each coulomb of charge has much more energy.

Energy stored in a car battery

Fig. 4 What would happen if you broke down on the crossing?
Suppose that the engine were to fail when you were halfway across a level crossing. One way of driving the car off the track would be to use the starter motor with the engine in gear. Where does the energy then come from to move the car?

The energy stored in a car battery is the emf of the battery multiplied by the charge stored in the battery. (Remember: the emf of a battery is the potential difference between its terminals when no current is flowing.) For example, the energy stored in a fully charged 12 V, 20 A h car battery is given by Equation (2):

$$\begin{aligned}
\text{energy} &= \text{potential difference} \times \text{charge} \\
&= \text{emf} \times \text{charge} \\
&= 12\,\mathrm{V} \times (20\,\mathrm{A} \times 1\,\mathrm{h}) \\
&= 12\,\mathrm{V} \times (20\,\mathrm{A} \times 3600\,\mathrm{s}) \\
&= 12\,\mathrm{V} \times 72\,000\,\mathrm{C} \\
&= 860\,000\,\mathrm{J}
\end{aligned}$$

This would be enough to drive a friction-free car of mass 860 kg a vertical distance of 100 m up a hill. In practice, there is so much friction that it is barely enough to drive the car 100 m along a flat road!

- **If the flashgun discussed earlier has a 3 V battery, what is the energy of a flash?**

Cells and batteries in series

Fig. 1 Mains light bulbs on a large Christmas tree
Are they in series or parallel? Why?

Renewing the batteries for a radio or a torch can be expensive. The trouble is that you have to renew several batteries at once. Torches and radios don't (normally) use just a single battery. They use several batteries in what is sometimes called a **battery pack**.

The word 'battery' actually means a collection of similar items (see Section 11.1). The 1.5 V batteries that you use in a radio or a torch should really be called **cells**. A 3 V, 4.5 V, 6 V or 9 V battery is a collection of 1.5 V cells.

Putting two 1.5 V cells **in series** (end-to-end, both pointing in the same direction) gives an emf of 3 V. Six cells in series give an emf of 9 V. **How many cells are there in series inside a 6 V battery? What is the voltage of the battery pack shown in Figure 2?**

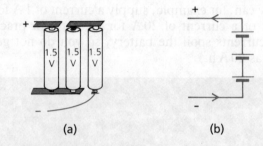

(a)   (b)

Fig. 2 What is the emf of this battery pack?
(a) How the battery pack is wired
(b) A simplified circuit diagram

Cells and batteries in parallel

When you connect cells in series (Figure 2) the voltages add up. But when you connect cells **in parallel**, as shown in Figure 3, the voltages don't add up. The emf of the cells together is the same as that of a single cell.

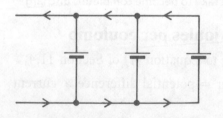

Fig. 3 What is the emf of this battery pack?
In this case, the cells are wired in parallel. What is the advantage of this?

One possible advantage of having two cells in parallel is that each cell has to supply only half the current and so lasts twice as long. However, you have to buy two cells instead of one, so it isn't such a great advantage! It would probably be cheaper just to use a bigger 1.5 V cell in the first place.

A more important advantage of connecting cells in parallel is that they supply more power. One cell on its own will not usually supply a large current. If you try to take a large current from it, the cell will get hot and so waste energy. But several cells in parallel, each supplying a fairly small current, will together supply a large current and last longer.

- **Try using several 1.5 V cells to light a 3 V lamp. First try two cells in series, then two in parallel, then two series pairs in parallel with each other.**

Bulbs in series

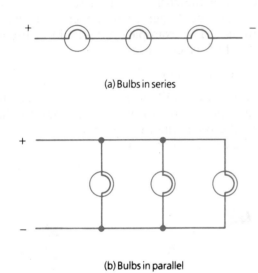

(a) Bulbs in series

(b) Bulbs in parallel

Fig. 4 Bulbs in series and in parallel
Why are house lights wired in parallel?

Bulbs used to light up Christmas trees are often connected in series (Figure 4(a)). The fairy lights that we use on indoor trees typically require a potential difference of 12 V across each bulb. This means that 20 light bulbs need to be connected in series across the 240 V mains supply. The same current goes through each bulb.

Connecting the bulbs in series allows tiny, low-voltage bulbs to be used. However, there is a disadvantage. If one light fails, then they all go out. **How could an electrician check which bulb had failed, other than by replacing each bulb in turn? What will be the voltage across the failed bulb? This is *not* something that you should try yourself at home!**

People have sometimes been known to 'mend' strings of fairy lights by replacing the failed bulb with silver cigarette paper. This is very dangerous, as well as being bad for the other bulbs. It is dangerous because, depending on the bulb that has blown, the potential of the silver paper could be as high as 240 V! Also, it could produce sparks, setting fire to the tree. It is bad for the other bulbs because, with one of the 20 bulbs missing, the others will have an extra potential drop across them. **What will this new voltage be?**

Bulbs in parallel

House lights don't need to be small—they can stand high voltages. And, you don't want them all to go out as soon as one fails. So lights in houses are arranged in parallel (Figure 4(b)). The 240 V mains potential difference is connected across each light. The current is shared between them.

Series and parallel in general

In any series circuit, the same current flows through each item (for example, each bulb or battery). To calculate the total potential drop, you add up the potential drops across each item.

In any parallel circuit, the same potential drop occurs across each item. To calculate the total current, you add up the currents through each item.

We will look at series and parallel circuits again when we discuss resistors and resistance in Chapter 19.

- **Are the lights of a car in series or in parallel? Why?**

11.7 | **Making it safe**

Electricity can be dangerous

Many people are killed by mains electricity—for example, when they cut through the cable of a lawnmower, or use electrical equipment with wet hands. The electric current causes their muscles to contract (just like Galvani's frogs—see Section 11.2). If a large current passes through the heart, it stops it from beating.

Still more lives are lost through fires started by electrical faults. Some fires are caused by **short circuits.** For example, faulty insulation can allow direct connections between supply wires. Other fires are caused by cables overheating as a result of very large currents flowing through them (Figure 1).

Many of these accidents could be avoided by taking a few simple precautions.

Making electricity safer

1 Use cable of the correct current rating. The rating should always be larger than the current that you intend to use. (For example, you shouldn't use a 5 A cable for a 13 A electric fire.)

2 Make sure that the insulation is in good condition.

3 Use **safety plugs**. On these plugs, part of each pin is coated in plastic. This means that if young children play with the plug when it is in a socket they cannot touch the live part of the pins.

Fig. 1 Electrical faults can cause fires
How can you prevent cables in your home from overheating?

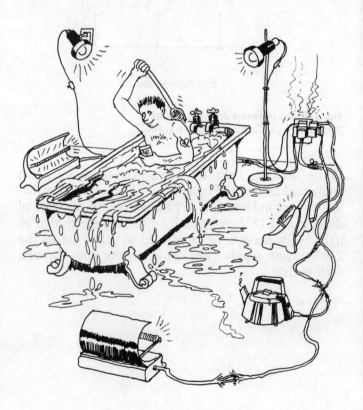

Fig. 2 What is wrong with the way he is using electricity?.
How many dangerous mistakes can you see?

4 Don't put too many plugs into one socket. They can easily overheat and start a fire. Also, don't have leads where people can trip over them.

5 Keep water away from any electrical equipment.

6 Use the correct fuse (see below).

7 Earth the equipment wherever possible (see below).

Fuses

The most common type of fuse consists of a short length of thin wire inside a protective ceramic capsule. When a large current flows, the wire melts and breaks the circuit.

Fuses in plugs protect the flex by preventing large currents from flowing through them accidentally. For example, if you are using a radio with a 3 A flex, then you must use a 3 A fuse in the plug. (It is unfortunate that most plugs are sold with 13 A fuses when, for most equipment, you need a 3 A or 5 A fuse.)

Fuses inside equipment such as radios and electric motors prevent them from being ruined by a small fault. For example, when a motor jams, the current through it increases tremendously. If this current is allowed to continue, it will burn out the motor. A fuse of the correct rating will stop this from happening.

Earthing

Many kettles are made of metal. The heating element in a kettle consists of a thin wire surrounded by insulating material. This is kept inside a metal tube in contact with the water.

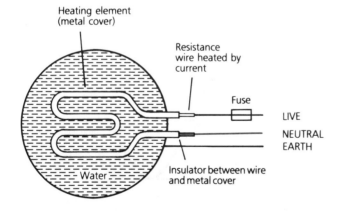

Fig. 3 Earthing a kettle
Plastic kettles are also earthed even though plastic is an insulator. Why are they earthed?

Suppose that the element is damaged so that the heating wire comes into contact with the water. Electric current can now flow from the heating wire to the outside of the kettle. The outer metal will now be at 240 V, and could kill someone.

To avoid this, the outside of the kettle is **earthed** (Figure 3). It is connected by a third wire to the top pin of the mains socket. This, in turn, is connected to the earth (for example, it may be connected to a copper water pipe which goes down into the ground). If electricity now flows from the live wire to the outside metal casing, it will continue on down the earth wire. A very large current will flow which will blow the fuse, and so cut off the supply. The kettle is safe again!

All electrical equipment with an outside metal case should be earthed in this way.

Earth-leakage circuit breakers

Earth-leakage circuit breakers trip as soon as the current flowing into a circuit is greater than the current flowing back to the mains. When this happens, current must be leaking out of the circuit somewhere. For example, if your lawnmower slices through the mains cable, some current will flow out of the cable into the lawnmower and possibly into you! The earth-leakage circuit breaker will switch off the current the instant this happens, so that you aren't electrocuted.

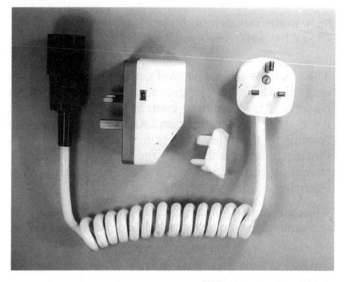

Fig. 4 Ways of making electricity safer
Safety plug on coiled flex, earth-leakage circuit breaker and caps for sockets when not in use.
How does the circuit-breaker work?

● **Find out what you should do if someone does get an electric shock.**

167

Why 240 volts ac?

What does it mean?

Fig. 1 British sockets provide electricity at 240 V ac
Why? What is ac?

The electric current that you get from a mains socket isn't the same as the electric current that you get from a battery. It is **alternating current** (ac). At one instant it's flowing in one direction. At the next instant it's flowing in the other direction. In between, it isn't flowing at all! In the UK, the 240 V mains supply changes direction 50 times a second. (In the USA it alternates 60 times a second, and is at 110 V.)

The current that you get from a battery always flows in the same direction. It is called **direct current** (dc).

Live and neutral

Because mains current is alternating current, we don't talk about positive and negative wires and terminals. Instead, we have **live** (L) and **neutral** (N) wires and terminals. The neutral wire is always kept at about 0 V. The live wire alternates between +340 V and −340 V.

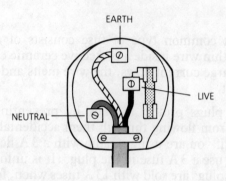

Fig. 2 Wiring a 13 A plug
Why is the fuse on the live side of the plug connecting the live wire to the live pin?

Figure 2 shows the wiring of a 13 A plug. Notice how the fuse is part of the live terminal. **Why is this?**

- **Try wiring a plug. Make sure that**
  (a) the wires are well screwed in to the terminals
  (b) there is as little bare wire as possible inside the plug
  (c) the sheath of the cable is firmly held by the cable grip.

The average voltage

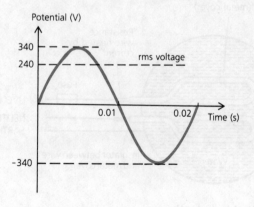

Fig. 3 Mains sinusoidal ac
Why do we call it 240 V ac instead of 340 V ac?

Why do we call it 240 V ac rather than 340 V ac? Because the voltage doesn't stay at 340 V but increases in the smooth (**sinusoidal**) manner shown in Figure 3. 240 V is the (root mean squared (rms)) *average* voltage in each direction. A 240 V dc supply would give the same heating effect. In other words, mains ac behaves more like a 240 V battery than a 340 V battery.

Why do we use high voltages?

If high voltages are dangerous, why are they used?

Although high voltages are dangerous, they allow a lot of energy to be supplied with a fairly small current (see Section 11.4, Equation (1)). This means that thinner, cheaper wires can be used without them overheating (and wasting energy).

In general, the greater the power to be carried by cables, the higher the voltage used. Cables carrying electric power to a town have a potential difference between them of 400 000 V or more.

Figure 4 shows a way of demonstrating the importance of high-voltage transmission (sending electricity at high voltages). The resistance wire has the same effect as the much longer lengths of copper or aluminium cable which are used for carrying electricity. With low voltages, a large current is needed. This causes the wire to become hot and to waste energy. There is not enough energy left to light the bulb. When a high voltage is used, less current needs to be passed through the wire. Little energy is lost as heat in the wire, and the bulb glows brightly.

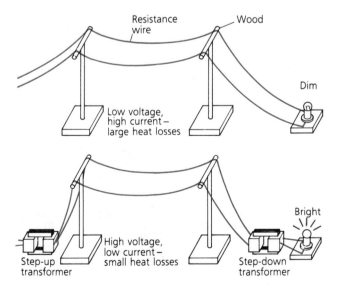

Fig. 4 The importance of high-voltage transmission
If there is an electricity substation or pylon near your house, see if there is a notice stating the voltage.

Why 240 volts?

240 V is about the highest voltage at which most people have a reasonable chance of surviving an electric shock (though many people are killed at this voltage). If the voltage was much higher, then any shock would nearly always be fatal.

In the USA, the voltage is only 110 V, and is therefore a bit safer than in the UK.

Fig. 5 Not everything is bigger in Texas!
What are the differences between the mains supplies in America and the UK?

Why ac?

Alternating current can sometimes be a nuisance. For instance, electronic circuits need to have the current flowing in one direction only.

However, alternating current has one very big advantage. You can use **transformers** to alter the voltage. This means that you can supply electricity to a village at 11 000 V, and then reduce it to 240 V using a transformer. Electronic equipment can reduce the voltage further (for example, to 5 V) by using another transformer. With direct current it is much more difficult to change the voltage. As we shall see in Chapter 19, it is not too difficult to change ac to dc when it is needed.

- **A tungsten-filament light bulb is designed to run off a 6 V torch battery. Will it also run off a 6 V ac supply? Explain.**

169

From power station to 13 amp socket

The national grid

Fig. 1 Carrying high-voltage cables
Where are the insulators? Why are they needed?

The generators of power stations produce alternating current at a voltage of 25 kV (25 000 V).

At each power station, there is a **step-up transformer** that raises the voltage to 400 kV. A **super grid** at this voltage connects all the major power stations to all the major towns and other large users of electricity. The current can travel by several routes from a power station to a town. This allows lines and power stations to be disconnected for maintenance without cutting off people's electricity.

The 400 kV wires have to be carried high above the ground, hanging on long insulators from very large pylons. When they come near to a town, they enter a **step-down transformer** station. This reduces the voltage to 132 kV, allowing smaller pylons and even underground cables to be used (Figure 2).

In each town, there are electricity **substations**. These are further step-down transformers that reduce the voltage to 240 V for houses, 11 kV for light industry and 33 kV for mines, steel mills and other large industrial consumers of electricity (Figure 3).

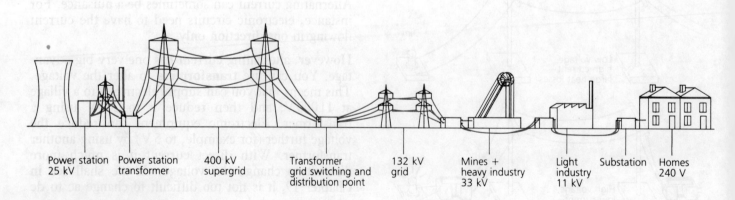

| Power station 25 kV | Power station transformer | 400 kV supergrid | Transformer grid switching and distribution point | 132 kV grid | Mines + heavy industry 33 kV | Light industry 11 kV | Substation | Homes 240 V |

Fig. 2 Step-up and step-down transformers
What do we mean by
(i) a step-up transformer?
(ii) a step down transformer?

Fig. 3 What is happening here?
Why does it hum? (See Section 13.9.)

Up to this stage, the electricity travels in what is called a **three-phase supply.** This is a way of sending the electricity more cheaply and more evenly (it is not switched on and off as with ordinary ac). A full description and explanation is beyond the scope of this book.

Domestic supply

Once the 240 V supply enters your home, it passes through a meter which measures the flow of energy into the house. From there, the electricity passes to the electricity board's fuses. These usually have a rating of 100 A, and are used to protect the board's cables and equipment from any surges of power that might result from you doing something foolish!

After this, the supply passes to the main fuse box. This contains the main switch to cut off power to the house. In the fuse box, the electricity is divided between the different circuits in your house. Each circuit is protected by its own fuse in the fuse box. For example, the lighting circuit has a 5 A fuse, the circuit for wall sockets has a 30 A fuse and the circuit for the cooker has a 40 A fuse.

- **You may wish to find out about the electrical supply in your own home but *don't* try opening or unscrewing anything or in any other way put yourself in any danger! Get an adult to show you the fuses or circuit breakers inside the fuse box. The main switch should be turned off beforehand.**

The ring main

In most houses, the wall sockets are on what is called a **ring main.** This is a single loop of cable going from the fuse box to each 13 A socket in turn and then back to the fuse box. Each socket is connected in parallel (from the live wire to the neutral wire of the loop).

The advantage of a ring main is that there are two routes for the current to follow. This avoids all the currents adding together and producing a high-current bottleneck near the fuse box. The current is about the same all the way round the loop. A new socket can easily be added without having to take the cables all the way back to the fuse box.

A lot of care is taken to get electricity to our electric sockets as safely and cheaply as possible. From then on, it is up to us to make sure that we use it safely and effectively. One way of doing this is to have any wiring alterations or repairs carried out by a qualified electrician.

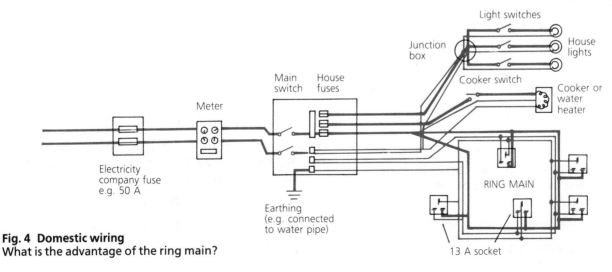

Fig. 4 Domestic wiring
What is the advantage of the ring main?

171

Exercises

1 Electric current is measured in

   A Volts

   B Amps

   C kWh

   D Watts

   E Coulombs

Fig. 1 Why does the torch bulb have only one metal contact?

2 A torch bulb has a single metal contact on its base rather than the two contacts that most mains bulbs have (Figure 1). This is because

   A One terminal is enough for electricity to enter the bulb

   B Torch cells have only one terminal

   C The screwthread provides the second terminal

   D Torch bulbs use dc

   E Torch bulbs work in a different way from mains bulbs

3 Figure 2 shows the circuit for a car's parking lights. The points marked X are connections to the body of the car. The purpose of these connections is

   A To earth the bulbs, to make them safe

   B To remove static charge

   C To make the interior light switch on when the door opens

   D To make sure that the lights are at the same voltage

   E To return the current to the battery

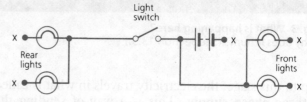

Fig. 2

4 Why are house lights connected in parallel?

   A To make them all equally bright

   B So that they can be switched on separately

   C So that lower-voltage light bulbs can be used

   D Less current is needed when the bulbs are all on together

   E Less power is needed for each bulb

5 Electricity is transmitted across country at a very high voltage. What is the reason for this?

   A Generators produce electricity at a high voltage

   B A big force is needed to push the electricity a long way

   C Transformers can be used

   D More power can be sent without overheating the cables

   E It allows a larger current to flow

6 Suppose that the bulbs in Figure 2 are each marked '12 V, 24 W'. The total current when the lights are switched on is

   A 0.5 A   D 4 A

   B 1 A   E 8 A

   C 2 A

7 Complete these sentences using the following words: energy, electromotive force, potential difference, volts, current, charge, voltmeter, ammeter, parallel, series. You may use each word once, more than once, or not at all.

   a An electric _____ is a movement of _____ .

   b The _____ is the same all the way round a single-loop circuit.

   c The _____ across the terminals of a battery when it is supplying _____ is always less than the _____ . This is because _____ is lost inside the battery when a current flows through it.

   d The _____ across a bulb can be measured by connecting a/an _____ in _____ with the bulb.

   e The _____ through a bulb can be measured by connecting a/an _____ in _____ with the bulb.

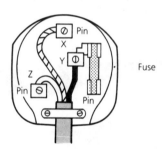

Fig. 3

8 Figure 3 shows a fused 13 A plug. Complete this table for the wires entering the plug:

Wire	Name of wire (e.g. earth)	Colour of insulation
X		
Y		
Z		

9 Why are bathroom switches usually fixed in the ceiling and operated by means of a string?

10 State two reasons why it is very dangerous to repair fairy lights by replacing the bulb with a bit of silver paper.

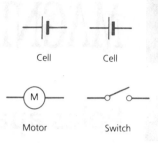

Fig. 4

11 Using the symbols shown in Figure 4, draw a circuit to show how two 1.5 V cells can be used together to drive a 1.5 V motor. What is the main advantage of using the cells in this way?

12 **a** Calculate

   i the charge
   ii the energy
   stored in a fully charged 10 A h battery with an emf of 6 V.

   b These batteries are to be used as a back-up supply to operate the 240 V lights of a hospital operating theatre when the mains power fails.
   i What is the minimum number of batteries required?
   ii How should they be connected together?

13 A radio has a 100 mA fuse inside it and a 3 A fuse in the plug. What is the purpose of each of these fuses?

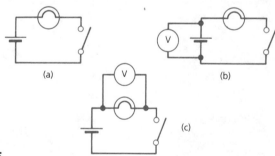

Fig. 5

14 Figure 5 shows a circuit diagram for a torch. The bulb is not working. A voltmeter connected as in diagram (b) shows a reading of 3 V. When the voltmeter is connected as in diagram (c) it shows 0 V.

   a Explain why each of the following could, or could not, be the cause of the problem: an exhausted battery, a faulty bulb, a faulty switch.

   b Explain how you would use the voltmeter a third time to check that you had found the fault.

173

12.1 Poles apart

Magnets everywhere

What do Maglev trains, fridge doors, videotapes, computer discs and oil drain plugs in cars have in common? They are all magnetic.

Fridge doors have a magnetic strip round the edge that sticks to the fridge when you close the door. The magnetic strip keeps the door closed and stops warm air from getting into the fridge.

Oil drain plugs remove steel filings from a car's engine oil (Figure 2.) As an engine is used, it becomes worn. For example, tiny bits of steel may break away from the piston rings. As oil passes through the car engine, it washes these steel filings down into the oil sump under the engine. If the drain plug were not magnetic,

the filings might be carried back into the engine with the oil, and could cause damage. Instead, they stick to the drain plug. This has another advantage—when the oil is drained from the car at the next service; the mechanic can see how badly the engine is being worn.

The surfaces of audio- and videotapes and computer discs are covered with tiny magnets. These magnets can point in any direction. As a tape passes through a recording machine, the magnets are re-aligned to form a pattern. This pattern is used to store information (sounds, pictures, numbers etc.). During playback, the pattern of the magnets is 'read' by the recorder, and the information is sent to the speaker, television screen or computer.

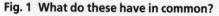

Fig. 1 What do these have in common?

Fig. 2 A magnetic oil drain plug from a car
What is the reason for making it magnetic?

Magnetic poles

Fig. 3 Why aren't there any filings in the middle?

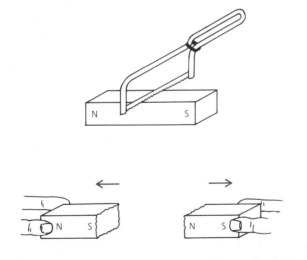

Fig. 4 Making new magnets
If you break a magnet and pull the two halves apart, you get an extra magnet. Where does the extra magnetic energy come from?

When you dip a bar magnet into some iron filings, the filings stick most strongly to two parts of the magnet (Figure 3). This is true of any magnet. **Try it with some other types of magnet. (In some cases, the two places that attract steel are the flat surfaces of the magnet.)**

These areas of greatest attraction are called **poles** (after the Greek word 'polos', meaning pivot or axis). Every magnet has two poles. If you cut a bar magnet in half, new magnetic poles form at the cut ends. You then have two magnets, each with two poles (Figure 4).

This ability of magnets to form new poles at a break is used to test for cracks in welded steel. For example, steel pipes can be made by shaping a steel sheet into a cylinder and welding the join. To test this weld, the pipe is temporarily made into a magnet. If the weld then attracts steel (if there are poles at the weld), there must be a crack there (Figure 5).

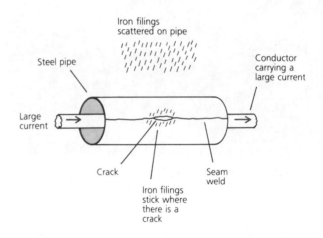

Fig. 5 Using magnetism to check a weld
The electric current magnetises the pipe (see Section 13.1)

Magnetic monopoles

Cutting up a magnet only produces more poles, so you can never have a single pole on its own. Magnetic poles never exist on their own.

Actually, what we should say is that nobody has found a single pole on its own. Some physicists believe that **magnetic monopoles** may exist, and they are still looking for them. The magnetic energy of a monopole would be enormous, and this has worried some scientists. They think that, if monopoles were found, someone might find a way of using their enormous energy to make a bomb far more powerful than a hydrogen bomb!

175

Sailing south

Fig. 1 A modern ship's magnetic compass
Does is point exactly to the north? (See Section 12.5.)

In 1418, some Portuguese ships set sail down the west coast of Africa. The eventual aim was to find a sea route to India. It was a dangerous mission—at that time Europeans believed that the sea boiled as you approached the Equator. But they had with them an instrument which gave them a little more confidence. This device consisted of a lump of magnetic rock called lodestone, floating in a wooden boat. We call it a mariner's compass. The compass was invented by the Chinese, and had probably been brought to Europe some centuries earlier by Arab seamen. However, this was the first time that it had been used as a serious aid to navigation. (The Chinese used it for geomancy—to show them where to build their houses and tombs so as to be in harmony with the forces of nature.)

Magnets point north

If you float a magnet in a small plastic boat, or suspend it from a thread, one end (or pole) of the magnet will always point north. The other pole will point to the south (Figure 2). Because of this, we talk about the north-seeking pole and the south-seeking pole of the magnet. Most people just refer to them as the north and south poles of the magnet.

The pointer of a compass is a magnet—its north-seeking pole is the point of the arrow.

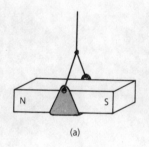

(a)

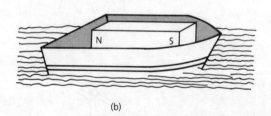

(b)

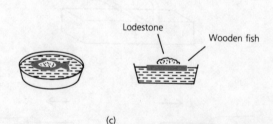

Lodestone

Wooden fish

(c)

Fig. 2 Three ways of making a simple compass
(a) By suspending a magnet
(b) By floating a magnet
(c) By floating a wooden fish carrying a piece of lodestone in a bowl of water (this is the original, Ancient Chinese compass)
How would *you* design a compass?

176

Like poles repel

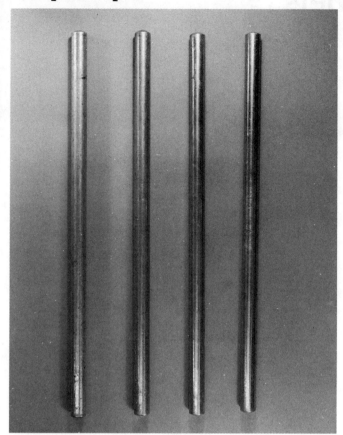

Fig. 3 Which two of these are permanent magnets?
How could you tell which two are magnets and which two are iron without using any other equipment or materials?

Magnets always attract iron and unmagnetised steel. But they do not always attract other magnets. Sometimes magnets repel each other.

If the north-seeking poles of two magnets are facing each other, they will repel each other. The same is true for two south-seeking poles. However, a north-seeking pole attracts, and is attracted by, a south-seeking pole.

> Like poles repel and unlike poles attract.

- If you were given some magnets, some steel rods which looked the same as the magnets, and nothing else, how could you identify the magnets? Try this.

Reed switch

Magnetic reed switches are used in most burglar-alarm systems. These switches make use of the attraction between magnetic poles (see Figure 4). Normally, the two pieces of soft iron inside the switch are not magnetised and do not attract each other. But if you bring a magnet near the reed switch, the soft iron will become magnetised. Whichever way you hold the magnet, the ends of the soft iron facing each other will always become unlike poles. They will then attract each other and stick together. This completes the circuit and switches on the current. When you remove the magnet, the two pieces of soft iron lose their magnetism and spring apart again. The circuit is broken, and the current is switched off.

- If you have a reed switch, try using it to switch a torch bulb on and off. How could you use a reed switch to operate a burglar alarm? (You could make a model of this.)

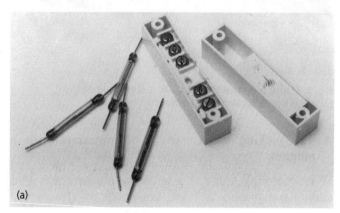

(a)

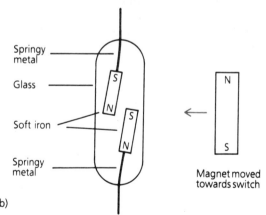

(b)

Fig. 4 A magnetically operated reed switch
How does it work?

177

What materials do you use?

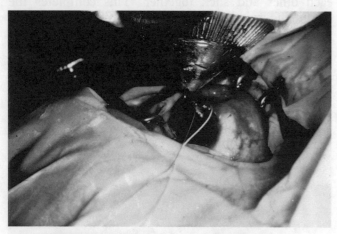

Fig. 1 Using a magnet to remove a steel splinter
Of what material should the magnet be made?

- **Try picking up a variety of materials with a magnet.**

What materials can you use to make a magnet? You cannot use plastic (at least, not on its own), nor can you use wood, or glass, or copper or aluminium foil. None of these can be magnetised. Indeed the only common materials that you can magnetise are what we call **ferromagnetic materials**: iron, steel, nickel and cobalt.

In fact, not all steels can be magnetised. **Stainless steel** was invented during the Second World War, not because it could be used to make attractive cutlery but because it was not magnetic. The idea was that ships made from stainless steel wouldn't attract magnetic mines. Unfortunately, such ships turned out to be too expensive to build.

The oxides and alloys of some ferromagnetic materials can also be magnetised. For example, most recording tapes consist of tiny crystals of iron oxide on a plastic tape.

Magnetising magnetic materials

Having got the magnetic material, how do you magnetise it?

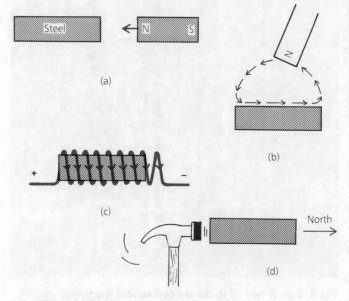

Fig. 2 Ways of making steel into a magnet
Which are likely to be the most efficient and the least efficient methods?
How could you alter methods (c) and (d) so that they demagnetised something that was already magnetic?

1 By magnetic induction

Place the magnetic material next to a magnet. It will become magnetised by what we call **magnetic induction** (Figure 2(a)).

It is by magnetic induction that a magnet can attract a string of nails. The first nail is attracted by the magnet. The nail itself then becomes magnetised and attracts the next nail, and so on. **Try this.**

Figure 2(b) shows a more effective way of magnetising a metal using magnetic induction. The reason why this method is effective will be explained in Section 12.4.

2 Using a magnetic coil

Put the magnetic material inside a coil through which a direct current is flowing (Figure 2(c)). We shall see why this works in Chapter 14.

You must use direct current. If you use alternating current, you will be in danger of removing all magnetism from the material. Indeed, an effective way of *de*magnetising materials is slowly to remove the magnet from the coil while an alternating current is flowing. (The same thing will happen if you leave the magnet inside the coil and reduce the current to zero.)

- **Try this. Use low-voltage dc to magnetise a material and then low-voltage ac to demagnetise it. Do *not* use mains ac. And don't demagnetise any permanent, commercial magnets. You will not be able to magnetise them so effectively again.**

3 By hitting it
You can make a (very weak) magnet just by hitting the magnetic material (Figure 2(d)). In this case, it is the Earth's magnetic field which is inducing the magnetism. Sometimes this happens accidentally—for example, when steel rivets or steel girders are hammered on a building site.

Making magnets lose their magnetism

Once you have magnetised your material, you musn't drop it or let it get hot. This will remove the magnetism. Also, you should keep it away from any other magnets and from any coils through which an electric current is flowing (Figure 3).

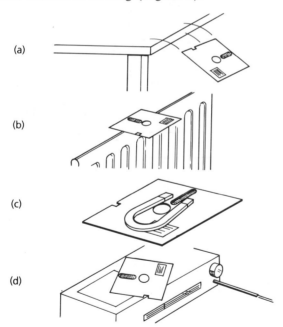

Fig. 3 How to spoil the program on a computer disc (Not recommended!)
(a) By dropping it
(b) By letting it get hot
(c) By leaving it near a magnet
(d) By leaving it on electrical equipment
Why do these spoil the program?

Soft and hard magnetic materials

Some magnetic materials are easy to magnetise, but lose this magnetism very easily. Very pure iron is an example.

Other magnetic materials are very difficult to magnetise, but they keep their magnetism. An example is high-carbon steel.

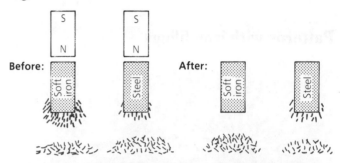

Fig. 4 The different magnetic behaviour of iron and steel Where would this difference make iron more useful than steel? Where would steel be more useful?

- **Try the experiment shown in Figure 4.**

Iron is said to be a **soft** magnetic material, whereas steel is said to be a **hard** magnetic material. Here, soft and hard refer only to the ease of magnetising the materials and not to the physical hardness of the surfaces (Figure 5).

Fig. 5 I thought you said that this was soft iron?! What does 'soft iron' mean? Would soft iron make a good magnet? Why?

Some practical examples

Like the moving parts of reed switches (see Section 12.2), electromagnet and transformer cores need to be easily magnetised and demagnetised. They are usually made of a magnetically soft alloy called **mu-metal**. (This is cheaper and much more effective than very pure iron.)

In contrast, the magnetic coating on recording tape is made of a magnetically hard material—iron oxide. **Why does it need to be magnetically hard? What other situations can you think of in which (a) magnetically soft and (b) magnetically hard materials are needed?**

Patterns with iron filings

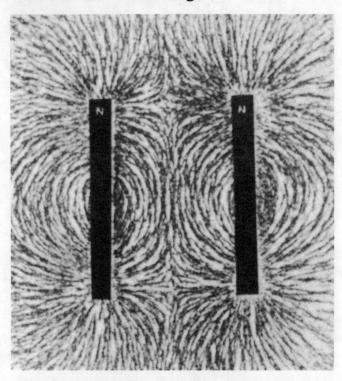

Fig. 1   The flux pattern around two magnets
The flux pattern is sometimes called a **field pattern**. How was this pattern produced?

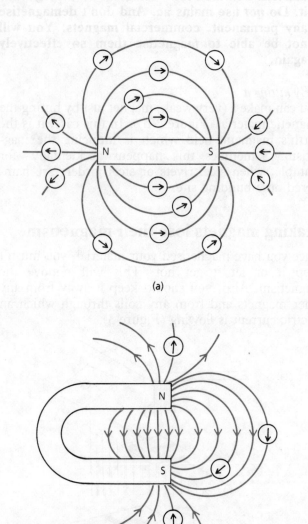

(a)

(b)

Fig. 2   Flux patterns for a bar magnet and a U-shaped magnet
Where do the lines go to inside the magnets?

Iron filings are magnetically soft. They are easily magnetised when they are anywhere near a magnet. This is useful when we are looking at the magnetic field of a magnet.

- Place a bar magnet under a sheet of paper. Scatter iron filings on the paper lightly and evenly. Now tap the paper very gently. Can you see a pattern?

When iron filings are scattered near a bar magnet, they become magnetised. They then link up to form curves like those shown in Figure 2. The pattern of these curves is called a **magnetic flux pattern**. Figure 2 shows the flux patterns for a bar magnet and a U-shaped magnet.

The flux pattern for the bar magnet explains why the method of making magnets shown in Section 12.3, Figure 2(b) works so well. When you stroke the steel with a magnet, the magnet is moving along a line of magnetic flux of the steel. So the magnet is reinforcing the new magnetic field around the steel.

Using a compass

Iron filings scattered near a magnet form a pattern of curved lines. When a compass is placed on top of one of these curves, it always points along it. The compass shows the direction of the magnetic flux. In other words, it shows the direction of the force that would act on any magnetic material at that point.

Flux patterns with more than one magnet

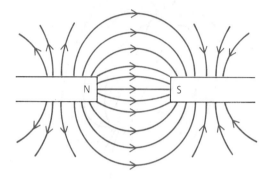

Fig. 3 Magnetic attraction
The lines act like elastic bands pulling the magnets together. What difference would it make if only the left-hand magnet were a permanent magnet and the right-hand 'magnet' was just soft iron?

Figure 3 shows the pattern that you get between the north-seeking pole of one magnet and the south-seeking pole of another magnet. **Try this for yourself with iron filings.**

1 The lines of the pattern act like elastic bands, pulling the two magnets together.

2 Notice how the lines are close together where the field is strongest (near the poles of the magnets). If you put the two magnets closer together, these lines will become straight.

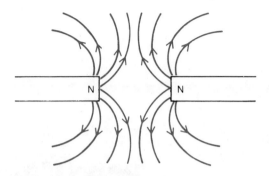

Fig. 4 Magnetic repulsion
What is the pattern like between two south-seeking poles?

Figure 4 shows the flux pattern that you get between two north-seeking poles. The magnets are pushed apart as though the lines were repelling each other. In the middle, between the two magnets, there are no flux lines at all, and here the strength of the magnetic field is (virtually) zero. **Do you get something similar with two south-seeking poles? Try it and see.**

In other situations, we can get an idea of the type and strength of the forces that are acting by looking at the flux patterns and imagining the flux lines contracting and pushing each other apart.

● **Use iron filings to look at the magnetic flux patterns around some other magnets—for example, horseshoe magnets. Use a compass to find the direction of the flux. Check that the compass always points along the flux lines.**

Fig. 1 How could you tell the age of these rocks?

The Earth's flux pattern

Figure 2(a) shows the magnetic flux pattern around a bar magnet. Figure 2(b) shows the magnetic flux pattern around the Earth.

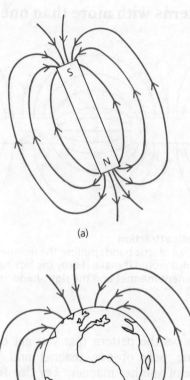

(a)

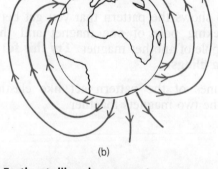

(b)

Fig. 2 The Earth acts like a bar magnet
Like poles repel. Yet the north pole of a magnet points towards the north pole of the Earth. Explain this.

Notice the similarity. The Earth's flux is the same as it would be if there were a giant bar magnet inside the Earth (Figure 3). The bar magnet would lie nearly parallel to the Earth's axis of rotation, but it would point south rather than north. That is to say, the Earth's north pole behaves like a south-seeking pole!

In fact, the Earth's core consists of molten iron and nickel. It is thought that electric currents flowing within this molten core produce the Earth's magnetic field.

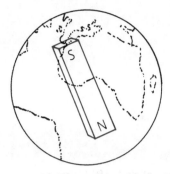

Fig. 3 The Earth behaves as though it were like this
Could there really be a giant bar magnet inside the Earth?
How do you know?

Finding your way with a compass

Over the centuries the compass has enabled travellers to use the Earth's magnetic flux to find their way around. Even now, modern aircraft use magnetic compasses alongside other methods of navigation. **What other methods of navigation do they use?**

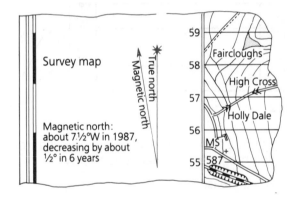

Fig. 4 Magnetic north is not the same as true north
The angle between the two changes with time. How do we know?

Using a compass with a map can be misleading. The direction of the Earth's magnetism is at a slight angle to the Earth's axis. Thus, in most parts of the world, a compass needle points at a slight angle to north. The size and direction of the angle that **magnetic north** makes with **true north** depend on your position on the Earth's surface. In Europe, if it is free to do so, a compass will point not only at an angle to north, but also at an angle into the ground. **Explain this in terms of the Earth's magnetic flux pattern.**

It is not only human beings that navigate using the Earth's magnetic field. For example, some migrant birds have magnetic sensors in their heads that help them to find their way.

Fig. 5 Which way will the compass point?
(i) If you hold it normally?
(ii) If you hold it edgeways?

The Earth's magnetic field is useful

The angle between magnetic north and true north is gradually changing. Over a period of years, it varies very slightly. Millions of years ago, the Earth's magnetic field changed direction altogether. At that time, a compass would have pointed south rather than north! We know that this happened because rocks formed at that time are magnetised in the 'wrong' direction. In fact, this flipping over of the Earth's magnetic field has happened several times.

We can use this fact to date rocks. By finding the direction in which a rock is magnetised, we can tell when it was formed.

Another advantage of the Earth's magnetic field is that it traps dangerous high-speed particles (**cosmic rays**) from the Sun or from outer space. These cosmic rays enter the Earth's atmosphere and are trapped in what we call the **Van Allen belts**. The Earth's field stops these particles from reaching the ground, and so protects us from them.

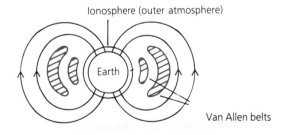

Fig. 6 The Van Allen belts
How are they produced?
How do they help us?

Exercises

1 Which of the following is *not* a ferromagnetic material?

   A Cobalt

   B Nickel

   C Aluminium

   D Steel

   E Iron

2 The north pole of the Earth

   A Attracts both poles of a magnet

   B Attracts the north pole of a magnet

   C Attracts the south pole of a magnet

   D Repels both poles of the magnet

   E Neither attracts nor repels the poles of a magnet

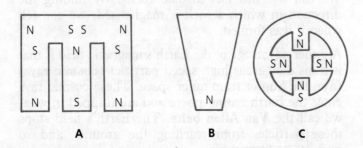

Fig. 1 Which of these couldn't be made?

3 Which of the magnets shown in Figure 1 would be impossible to produce in practice?

4 Soft iron is called 'soft' because

   A It can easily be moulded into the shape of a magnet

   B It is magnetic

   C It can easily be made into a permanent magnet

   D It is easy to magnetise and demagnetise

   E It can easily be compressed

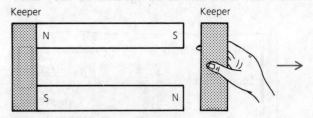

Fig. 2

5 Figure 2 shows a keeper being removed from two magnets. The magnetic energy

   A Increases

   B Decreases

   C Remains unchanged

   D Flows from the north-seeking pole to the south-seeking pole

   E Flows from the south-seeking pole to the north-seeking pole

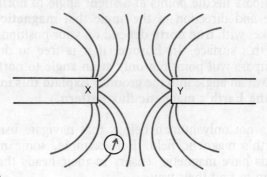

Fig. 3

6 Figure 3 shows the flux pattern (or field pattern) between two magnets. Which of the following describes the poles X and Y?

A X is north, Y is north

B X is north, Y is south

C X is south, Y is north

D X is south, Y is south

7 Complete these sentences:

a Like poles _____ ; unlike poles _____ .

b The Earth acts as a magnet with a north-seeking pole under the geographical _____ pole.

c A line of magnetic flux shows the direction in which a _____ will _____ .

8 State three ways in which a magnet can be made to lose its magnetism.

9 Explain how you would make a compass using only these items: a bottle top, a heavy magnet with the poles marked on it, a steel needle and a bowl of water.

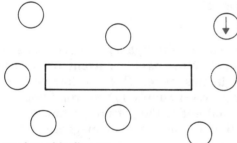

Fig. 4 Complete this diagram

10 Copy Figure 4. Label the poles of the magnet and show the direction in which the other compass needles point.

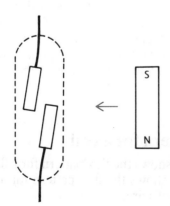

Fig. 5

11 Figure 5 shows a reed switch and a magnet. Explain what happens as the magnet moves nearer to the switch.

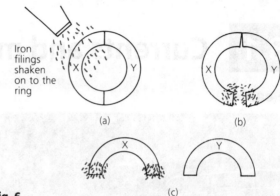

Fig. 6

12 Two metal half-rings join to form a ring as shown in Figure 6. The following observations are made:

- When the ring is dipped into iron filings, a few filings are picked up evenly round the ring.

- As the ring is opened, large numbers of iron filings are picked up at the crack.

- When the two half-rings are fully parted and dipped into iron filings, one half-ring picks up large amounts of iron filings, the other picks up none.

a Explain the above.

b Suggest a possible metal for each half-ring.

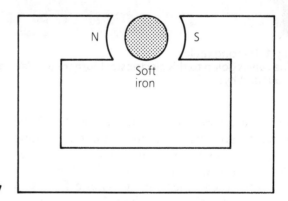

Fig. 7

13 Figure 7 shows the arrangement used to produce a magnetic field in moving-coil ammeters. A cylinder of soft iron is held between the two poles of a specially-shaped horseshoe magnet. Explain what happens to the cylinder and draw the expected flux pattern.

13 ELECTROMAGNETISM

13.1 Currents and magnetism

Live cables

Fig. 1 Dancing cables
The cables going to this electric steel furnace are dancing around. Why?

Some steelworks use electric arc furnaces. When these furnaces are switched on, something strange happens—the huge cables carrying current to the furnace start to jump around (Figure 1). They violently attract and repel each other with **magnetic forces**. Magnetism and electricity are linked: an electric current always produces a magnetic field.

Patterns produced by an electric current

One way of studying the magnetic field produced by an electric current is to study magnetic flux patterns.

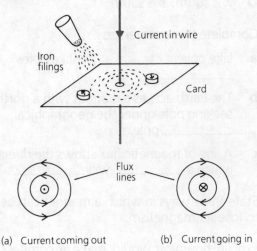

Fig. 2 The magnetic field around a straight wire
How can you show this using
(i) iron filings?
(ii) a compass?

- **Thread a wire through a piece of card as shown in Figure 2. Now pass a current of several amps through this wire. (Use a low-voltage, high-current power supply.) Dust iron filings on to the card, and notice the pattern produced. Check the direction of the lines of magnetic flux using a compass.**

Figure 2 shows the magnetic flux pattern round a wire carrying a current. If you look along the wire in the direction of the current, the lines circle the wire in a clockwise direction. (Note that a dot and a cross are used to show the direction of the current. These represent the ends of an arrow. When an arrow is flying towards you, you see the point (a dot). When it's flying away from you, you see the tail feathers (a cross).)

Flux pattern for a coil

Figure 3(a) shows the flux pattern for a flat coil of wire. Figure 3(b) shows the flux pattern for a stretched-out **helical** coil of wire.

186

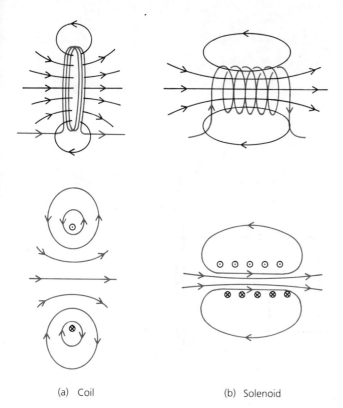

(a) Coil   (b) Solenoid

Fig. 3 Flux pattern through a coil and a solenoid

- **Try making these patterns for yourself, threading the coils through some card and using iron filings and a compass.**

Notice that the field around the helical coil is identical with that around a magnet (see Section 12.4, Figure 2).

Solenoids and security doors

If you place an iron bar at the entrance of a helical (stretched-out) coil and then switch on a current, the iron is pulled into the coil. **Try this**. The coil attracts the iron just as a bar magnet would. When a current-carrying coil is used like a magnet, we call it a **solenoid**. ('Solen' is the Ancient Greek word for a channel. The solenoid is a channel of magnetic flux just as the Solent in Hampshire is a channel of water.)

Figure 4 shows a solenoid as part of a door lock. These electrically operated locks are used for security doors in banks. **Where else are they used?** The current is switched on either by a person inside the bank or by someone with a special security key.

We will come across other uses of solenoids later in this chapter.

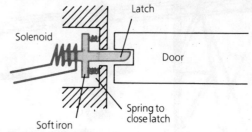

Fig. 4 Banks use magnetic security doors
The latch is released when current is fed to the solenoid (e.g. by a security officer operating a switch).
How does this release the door? How does the door latch close again after the current has been switched off?

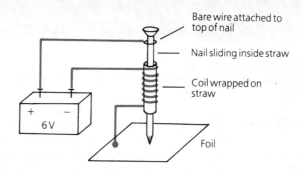

Fig. 5 Making a bouncing nail
As the coil is slowly raised, the nail suddenly starts jumping up and down. Why?

- **Try making the jumping-nail toy shown in Figure 5. Wind thin, insulated wire round a drinking straw to form a solenoid. (Enamelled copper wire is best, but you need to sandpaper the ends to remove the enamel insulation.) Rest a nail just inside the solenoid. Test that the nail is pulled into the solenoid when you switch on the current. Now rest the nail on the foil as shown. Raise the solenoid until the nail starts to jump off the foil. Why does this toy work—why does the nail jump up and down?**

Scrap-yard cranes

Fig. 1 How does this work?
Why is it able to separate ferrous scrap from non-ferrous scrap?

Scrap-yards sort scrap metal into **ferrous** metal (iron and steel) and **non-ferrous** metal (for example, copper). The ferrous scrap is sent to steelworks to be melted down. Electromagnets are used to move the ferrous scrap around. The advantage of this is that electromagnets pick up only iron and steel. This prevents other metals and non-metallic rubbish from getting into the steel furnaces. In addition, electromagnets are very convenient to use. You switch them on, and they lift the steel scrap. You switch them off, and they drop it.

What is an electromagnet?

An electromagnet is a solenoid with a piece of soft iron (or some other soft magnetic material) in the middle. When you pass a current through the solenoid, the soft iron is magnetised. If the current is large, the soft iron

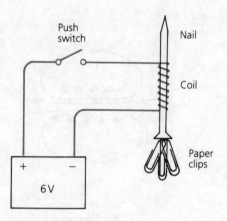

Fig. 2 A nail electromagnet
How many paper-clips or small nails can your nail electromagnet pick up?

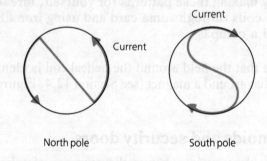

Fig. 3 Which pole is which?
Use this method to decide which end of your electromagnet is a north pole. Test your prediction.

will produce a very strong magnetic field. But as soon as you switch off the current, the electromagnet loses all its magnetism.

- **Make the electromagnet shown in Figure 2. Check the method of finding the poles shown in Figure 3. (How can you find by experiment which pole is which?) Try reversing the current. Does the polarity of the magnet change? (In other words, do the north-seeking and south-seeking poles change ends?)**

A telephone earpiece

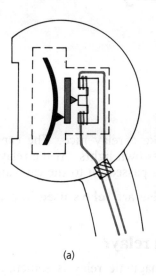

(a)

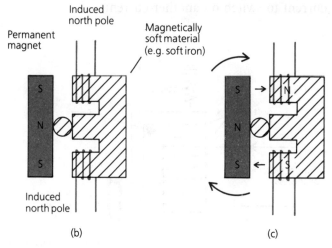

Permanent magnet

Induced north pole

Magnetically soft material (e.g. soft iron)

Induced north pole

(b)   (c)

Fig. 4 Telephone earpieces use electromagnets
(a) An electromagnet causes a soft-iron armature to pivot and push the diaphragm to and fro
(b) The electromagnets when no current flows
(c) The electromagnets when a current is flowing

Figure 4 shows how electromagnets are used in the earpiece of a modern telephone. **Explain from the diagrams how this earpiece works.**

Magnetic recording heads

The recording head in a tape-recorder is a tiny electromagnet which is used to magnetise the tape.

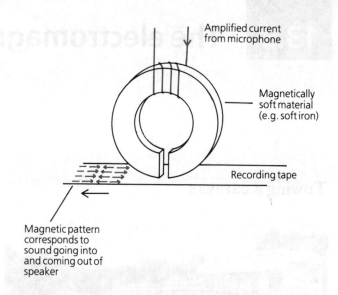

Amplified current from microphone

Magnetically soft material (e.g. soft iron)

Recording tape

Magnetic pattern corresponds to sound going into and coming out of speaker

Fig. 5 The recording head of a tape-recorder
The gap in the electromagnet is very small. Why?

When you record music, the sound is picked up by a microphone. This turns the sounds into a series of tiny electric currents, flowing first one way and then the other way. These currents are made much larger by an **amplifier**, and are then used to operate the electromagnet. The tape is magnetised first one way and then the other way, as the direction of the current changes. This produces a magnetic record of the currents flowing, and therefore of the sounds entering the microphone.

Similar recording heads are used in video-recorders and computer disc drives. In each of these cases, the electromagnet has an extremely small gap (Figure 5). This produces a very strong magnetic field over a very small area of tape or disc. If you should ever look at the electromagnet, be careful not to move it. Never let any metal come into contact with the electromagnet or you are likely to ruin it.

The pattern on the tape or disc can be destroyed by a strong magnetic field (see Chapter 12). A few years ago, according to one newspaper story, some office messengers insisted on travelling round London by taxi. They wouldn't use the underground trains. They said that the magnetic fields produced by these trains would spoil the computer discs that they were carrying. As the paper noted, the magnetic fields on the underground system are much too small to damage a computer disc. The messengers just preferred a taxi ride to the train journey!

The electromagnetic relay

Towing a caravan

Fig. 1 Pulling an extra set of lights
What has this to do with electromagnets?

When someone wants to use their car to pull a caravan, they have to think about the electricity supply. The car's flasher unit is designed only for the lights on the car. It isn't designed for the extra indicator lights on the caravan. In many cases, the current isn't enough for all the lights.

One way of solving this problem is to use a **relay**. This is an electrically operated switch. The current to the car's indicator lights switches on the relay. This in turn switches on a separate current to the caravan indicator lights (Figure 2).

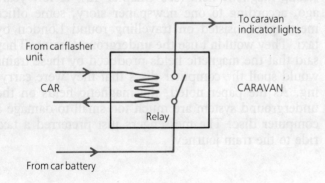

Fig. 2 Using a relay for the caravan's indicator lights

It's a bit like a relay race. The car starts a current moving to its own lights. At the relay, this movement of current is passed on to the caravan lights.

● **Where else are relays used in a car?**

What is a relay?

An electromagnetic relay is something that uses one current to switch on another current.

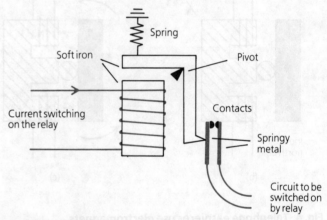

Fig. 3 A simple relay
How does it work?

A common type of relay is shown in Figure 3. The first current switches on an electromagnet. This attracts a piece of soft iron (or other soft magnetic material) on a pivot. The movement of the soft iron pushes two contacts together. This switches on the second current.

A **reed relay** (Figure 4) uses the reed switch described in Section 12.2. A current through the solenoid magnetises two iron strips and causes them to join together. This allows the second current to flow. Reed relays are cheaper than the type of relay shown in Figure 3, but they cannot switch large currents.

There are several other types of relay. Some relays can switch one current on and another current off at the same time (Figure 5).

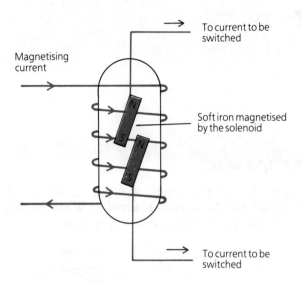

Fig. 4 A reed relay
How does this work?
What are the advantages and disadvantages compared with the simple relay?

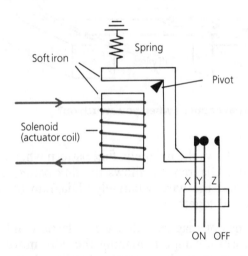

Fig. 5 A double-acting (single-pole, double-throw) relay
When current flows through the actuator coil, contact Y is pushed to the right. The contact between X and Y is broken, but contact is made between Y and Z.
Suggest an application for this relay.

Switching to transistors

In the past, whenever you wanted one current to switch another, you always used a relay. Telephone exchanges and early computers were full of relays. Unfortunately, relays are expensive and tend to break down.

Nowadays, we have another device for switching current—the transistor (see Chapter 18). Transistors are far more reliable, and they are now used much more than relays. However, as we shall see in Chapter 19, there are many situations that need both.

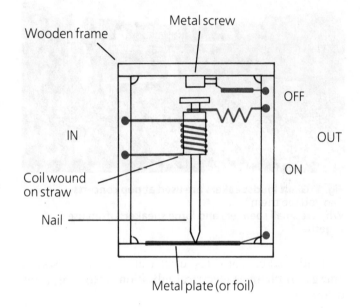

Fig. 6 A home-made relay
The nail rests against the bottom sheet under its own weight but rises to the top contact when the solenoid is switched on.
See if you can design a better version of this relay.

● **Try making your own home-made relay. (Figure 6 shows one way of doing this.)**

Designing a speaker

From electricity to sound

Fig. 1 Giant loudspeakers are used at pop concerts
Can you see them?
Why are small speakers and large speakers often used together?

A loudspeaker converts electrical energy to sound energy. It changes electrical vibrations into vibrations of the air.

How can you make a loudspeaker? You need first to find a convenient way of causing air to vibrate. One way of doing this is to move a diaphragm (for example, a thin sheet of card) backwards and forwards. But how can you get a current to move a diaphragm?

Let's start by considering the simplest way of producing movement with an electric current.

Moving a wire

In Figure 3, the short length of wire rests on two wire rails connected to a power supply. What happens when the supply is switched on? **Try this.**

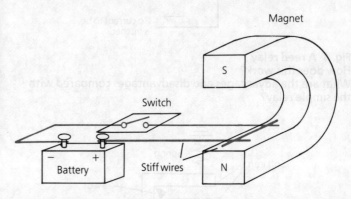

Fig. 3 What happens when you switch on?

Figure 4 shows the magnetic flux pattern when current is flowing. Diagram (a) shows the flux pattern for the magnet and the wire separately. Diagram (b) shows them added together.

If the lines of magnetic flux were elastic bands, they would form a catapult, making the wire move to the right. In practice, the magnetic flux lines have exactly this effect. (Note: magnets don't attract or repel wires that are carrying electric current. They knock them sideways!)

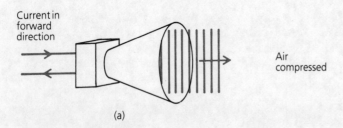

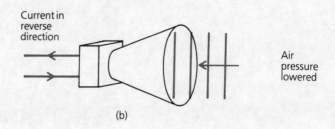

Fig. 2 Turning electrical waves into sound waves
These two diagrams show what any electric speaker must be able to do.
(a) Current flows one way, the speaker pushes the air out
(b) Current flows the other way, the speaker lets the air in
How can you increase the energy of the outgoing sound waves?

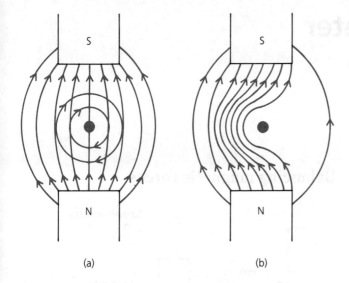

Fig. 4 Flux pattern for a current in a magnetic field
The flux lines act like elastic bands, catapulting the wire to the right.
Why is the magnetic flux zero (why are there no flux lines) just to the right of the wire?

Ambrose Fleming was one of the pioneers of radio at the start of this century. He suggested a 'handy' way of remembering the direction of motion. Put your thumb and the first two fingers of your *left* hand at right-angles to each other in the most comfortable way (Figure 5). If you point your First finger in the direction of the magnetic Field, and your seCond finger in the direction of the Current, then your thuMb will show the direction in which the wire will Move. This is called **Fleming's left-hand rule.** Check that it works in your case.

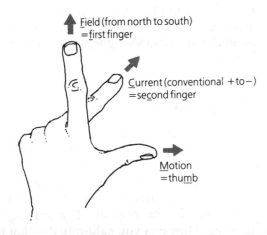

Fig. 5 Fleming's left-hand rule
What would happen if
(i)   the magnet were turned upside down?
(ii) the current direction were reversed?
(iii) both magnet and current were reversed together?

Increasing the force

If you want the wire to move with greater acceleration, then
- use a stronger magnetic field or
- use a larger current.

Try this, if you can.

A moving-coil speaker

To make the speaker, what you now need is some convenient way
(a) of attaching wire to the diaphragm
(b) of holding the wire between the poles of a magnet.

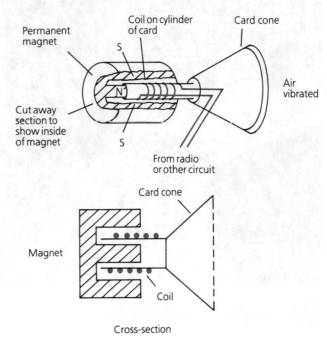

Fig. 6 A moving-coil speaker
Why is card used rather than metal?

Figure 6 shows one way of doing this. The wire is in the form of a coil, wrapped round a cylinder of card attached to the card diaphragm. The magnet is specially designed so that the magnetic field is always at right-angles to the current. The coil moves into or out of the magnet depending on the direction of the current. This **moving-coil speaker** is the most common kind of speaker.

- **Can you design another arrangement? For example, how else can you get an electric current to produce movement? Compare the likely advantages and disadvantages of your design with the moving-coil speaker shown in Figure 6.**

A moving-coil meter

Keeping an eye on things

Fig. 1 Meters in use at a power station
What do these meters have in common?

In power stations, chemical processing plants and many factories, there are control rooms with complicated control panels. Here the staff can check that everything is as it should be. Pressures in boilers and cooling systems have to be checked. Temperatures of furnaces or bearings have to be checked, so do the electric currents flowing in different parts of the system.

Ammeters can be (and often are) used for checking all these things. Sensors at different parts of a factory produce small electric currents that increase with pressure, temperature etc. These currents are measured by ammeters in the control room—the ammeters are marked in pascals, degrees Celsius etc.

The ammeter is therefore a very important meter. In this section we will consider some ways of making one.

Balancing magnetic forces

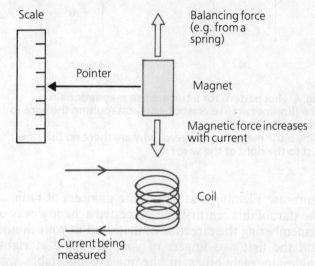

Fig. 2 Measuring currents by balancing forces

As we have seen, an electric current produces a magnetic field. The larger the current is, the greater is the strength of this field and the greater is the force produced. To measure the current, we can balance the magnetic force produced by a current against some other force—for example, that of a spring. As the current increases, it partly overcomes the force of the spring and in doing so causes a pointer to move across a scale (Figure 2).

A simple current balance

In the simple home-made current balance shown in Figure 3, a magnetic force is balanced against a gravitational force. The magnetic force is produced by a solenoid. This attracts or repels a magnet, depending on the direction of the current. This force is balanced against the weight of the magnet. **Try making this current balance. How can you calibrate it—that is to say, how can you mark the scale on it? (You can use a commercial ammeter and other electrical equipment.) Use your current balance to measure the current through a torch bulb.**

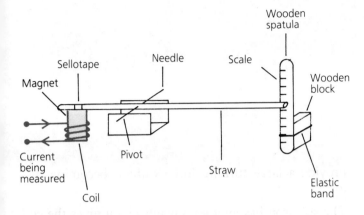

Fig. 3 A simple current balance
Should the pin go through the top part of the straw, the bottom part, or right through the middle? Why?

Current balances with two coils and a very sensitive beam balance are used in some standards laboratories. However, they are not very convenient for general use. **Why not?**

Moving-coil meters

Moving-coil meters turn the magnetic force into a moment, causing a coil to rotate. Figure 4 shows how the poles of a magnet are shaped to produce this circular motion. The field is always at right-angles to the wire as it moves between the poles. The cylinder in the centre is made of soft iron (or some other magnetically soft material). It becomes magnetised by the other magnetic poles.

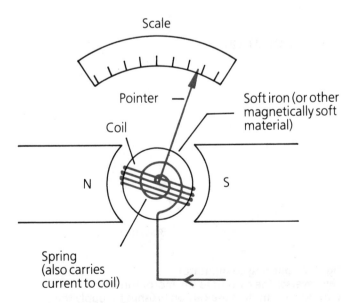

Fig. 4 A moving-coil meter

The wires carrying the electric current pass one way through one of the gaps and the other way through the other gap. One side of the wire coil moves upwards, and the other side moves downwards. The coil as a whole rotates.

Springs at each end of the coil balance this movement. When the current flows, the coil rotates and pushes against the springs. The pointer moves across the scale. The larger the current flowing through the coil, the more it pushes against the springs and the further the pointer moves across the scale.

Making the meter more sensitive

Moving-coil meters can be made to measure very small currents. Three ways of making them more sensitive (of enabling them to measure smaller currents) are
- by using a very powerful magnet
- by having many turns on the coil
- by using very weak springs.

Some ammeters can measure current in millionths of an amp. Ammeters designed for detecting small currents are called **galvanometers** after the Italian scientist Luigi Galvani (see Section 11.2). Most moving-coil meters measure milliamps (thousandths of an amp). As we shall see in Chapter 19, it is easy to convert a milliammeter to read amps, or even volts, just by adding a resistor. (To make a milliammeter read amps, all you do is to provide a bypass so that only one-thousandth of the current flows through the meter.)

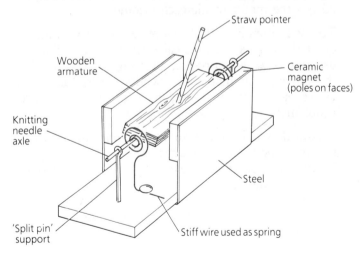

Fig. 5 A home-made moving-coil meter
How can you make this more sensitive?

- **Try making the moving-coil meter shown in Figure 5. How does this meter compare with the simple current balance?**

Model railways

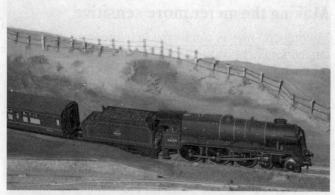

Fig. 1 The cleverest part is the part you can't see
Model trains use electric motors.
Do they use dc or ac motors?

Model railways can be beautifully designed and crafted. But you can't see one of the best-designed parts—the motor inside each locomotive.

The dc motors in these locomotives are very similar to other dc motors, such as car starter motors. They all use moving coils to produce a turning effect—just like the moving-coil meter (see Section 13.5, Figure 4). However, to do this, they have to overcome three problems:

1 How do you keep the coil turning once the wires are no longer between the magnets?
2 How do you feed in electricity without the wires becoming tangled?
3 How do you get the flimsy coil to drive a model locomotive or to turn the massive engine of a car without being distorted?

An armature

The coil in the motor is wound directly on to the centre soft-iron cylinder. This rotates along with the coil. The soft-iron is called an **armature** because it protects the coil just as armour protects a soldier. The coil can thus

provide a large turning force without becoming distorted.

The soft iron has another advantage—it gives the coil greater mass, and therefore greater momentum. This means that the coil and armature keep moving at constant speed, just like the flywheel of an engine. Because of its momentum, the armature continues to rotate even when the wires no longer lie between the poles of the magnet.

Fig. 2 A motor from a model railway

The commutator

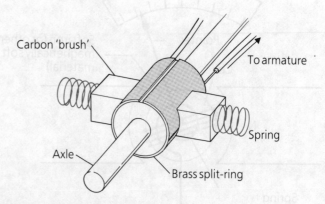

Fig. 3 A split-ring commutator
This reverses the current as the motor turns.
Why do most motors use carbon brushes to supply the current, rather than strips of metal?

196

This supplies current to the coil without the supply wires becoming twisted as the motor spins. A dc motor uses carbon (or flexible metal) **brushes** that run against a split-ring **commutator** (Figure 3).

A commutator is so called because it makes the current **commute.** When **commuters** travel to work in a city, they travel first one way (to work) and then the other way (back from work). The current flowing through the commutator does the same thing. First it flows one way through the coil and then (as the brushes cross the gap in the commutator) it flows the opposite way through the coil.

Figure 4 shows how the coil is made to continue turning by changing the direction of the current at just the right time.

● **Try making a dc motor as shown in Figure 5.**

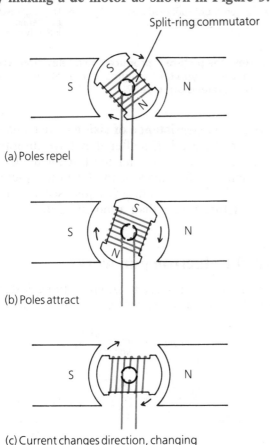

(a) Poles repel

(b) Poles attract

(c) Current changes direction, changing the left-hand pole from a north pole to a south pole

Fig. 4 Reversing the current
What would happen if the current were not reversed?

Multiple-coil and universal motors

Most motors have more than one coil. The armature of a car starter motor has a large number of coils, each one requiring two segments on the commutator.

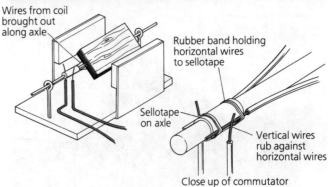

Fig. 5 A simple home-made motor
In this case the split-ring commutator consists of just two wires.
How could this motor be improved?

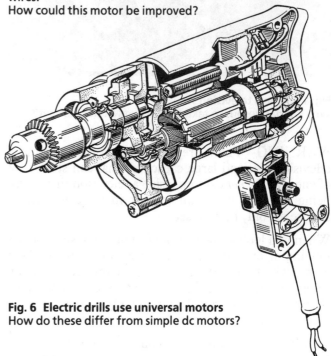

Fig. 6 Electric drills use universal motors
How do these differ from simple dc motors?

Vacuum cleaners and electric drills use **universal motors** that can run on dc or ac. Universal motors are similar to dc motors except that the permanent magnet is replaced by an electromagnet. There are many other types of motor, including the **induction motors** used in washing machines and tape-recorders. However, these are all beyond the scope of this book.

Inside a television

How a television works

Fig. 1 Inside a television set
Why is it dangerous to take the back off a television set?

WARNING There are very high voltages inside a television set, and large capacitors that can store a lot of energy. Do *not* explore inside a television that is still being used. If you want to look inside a television, choose an old, broken set.

When you look at the screen of a television set, you are looking at one end of a large glass tube rather like a giant light bulb. At the far end of this **cathode ray tube**—at the back of the set—is an **electron gun**. This shoots electrons, called **cathode rays**, towards you. They hit the screen and cause it to glow.

In a black-and-white television set, there is just one beam of cathode rays. This forms a white dot on the screen. Electromagnets round the tube deflect the beam, making the spot sweep back and forth across the screen (Figure 2).

As the electron beam scans the screen, it is made stronger (for bright parts of the picture) and weaker (for dark parts of the picture).

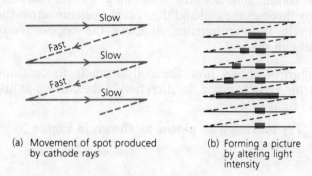

(a) Movement of spot produced by cathode rays

(b) Forming a picture by altering light intensity

Fig. 2 How the picture is produced on a television screen
What happens if you take a high-speed photograph of the picture on a television screen?

Our eyes have **persistence of vision**—we go on seeing things for at least 1/25 s after they have disappeared. The dot therefore moves far too fast for us to see the movement. All 625 lines of the television picture are drawn in 1/25 s. So our eyes just see a complete, square picture rather than a moving dot.

How the electron gun works

When a wire is heated, its atoms vibrate faster. The outer electrons of these atoms also move much more

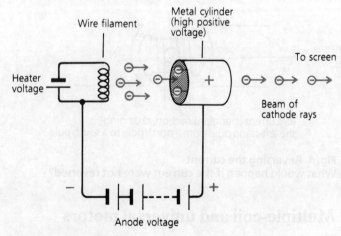

Fig. 3 An electron gun
What causes the electrons to leave the wire filament?
What causes them to form a beam of cathode rays?

rapidly. Some of these electrons move so fast that they leave the wire. Normally, this would cause the wire to become positively charged (since electrons are negatively charged), and the electrons would be attracted back. However, in the electron gun, the wire is connected to a high negative potential. This stops the electrons from returning.

If there were a positively charged metal plate nearby, then this would attract the electrons. In the electron gun, instead of a metal plate, there is a metal cylinder connected to a high positive potential. The electrons are attracted to this, but they go through the hole in the middle of the cylinder and carry straight on. These electrons become the cathode rays that eventually hit the screen.

Using magnets to deflect the cathode rays

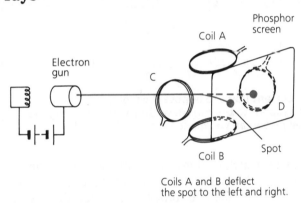

Coils A and B deflect
the spot to the left and right.

Fig. 4 How cathode rays are bent inside a television set
What is the difference from the way in which they are bent in a cathode ray oscilloscope?

An electric current flowing between the poles of a magnet is deflected (moved sideways). This is true whether the electrons are inside a wire (so that the wire as a whole moves) or travelling on their own as cathode rays (Figure 4).

You can distort the picture on a television set using a magnet *but* this temporarily ruins the set! *Don't* do it with your television set at home. (If you do, you will have to send it away and pay for it to be **de-gaussed**.) The Maltese cross tube shown in Figure 5 allows you to see the effect of the magnet without ruining the tube.

In a television, one pair of electromagnets is placed above and below the tube. These magnets move the spot across the screen. Another pair of electromagnets is placed each side of the tube. These magnets cause the spot to move down the screen.

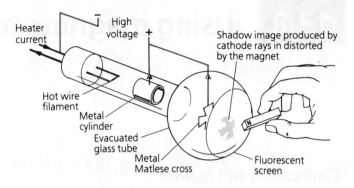

Fig. 5 Don't do this with your television set!
The Maltese cross tube is specially designed to allow you to move the picture with a magnet. *You would spoil your television set doing this.*
How is the picture of the Maltese cross produced on the screen?

A magnetic field is also used in the electron gun to focus the electrons into cathode ray beams. This magnetic field is called a **magnetic lens**.

Colour television

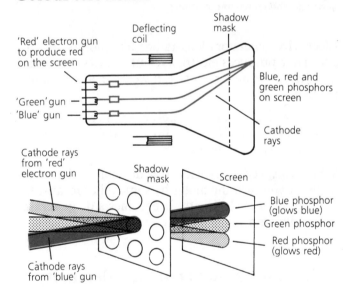

Fig. 6 A colour television uses three electron guns
How do these three electron guns produce all the colours that you see on the screen? (See Section 15.4.)

A colour television uses three cathode ray tubes (Figure 6). These share the same screen. One tube produces red dots on the screen, one produces green dots and the other produces blue dots. The way in which these three tubes together produce all the colours that you see on a television set is explained in Section 15.4.

199

Generators and motors

Fig. 1 A car alternator and starter motor
What do they have in common?

Electricity generators look rather like motors. A car's alternator produces electricity, but it looks very much like the starter motor. In fact, it works in a very similar manner.

- **Connect a small dc motor to a voltmeter or milliammeter. Now try turning the shaft of the motor. What happens?**

When you feed electricity to a dc motor, the motor turns. If you turn the motor by some other means, the motor produces electricity. It becomes a dc **generator** (or dc **dynamo**).

Using a solenoid to produce electricity

You don't need a motor or a generator to make electricity. You can cause an electric current to flow just by moving a magnet near a solenoid.

- **Try this. Connect the solenoid to a milliammeter and move the magnet very quickly. Try moving the magnet**
  (a) past the end of the solenoid
  (b) into and out of the solenoid.

As the magnet moves towards the solenoid, current flows in one direction. As the magnet is pulled out, current flows the other way.

Why does the current change direction?

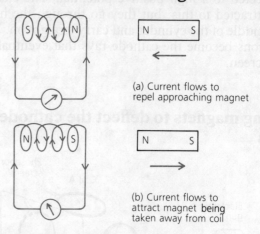

(a) Current flows to repel approaching magnet

(b) Current flows to attract magnet being taken away from coil

Fig. 2 Current flows to oppose the motion
What happens to the current when you stop moving the magnet? How can you make the current larger?

The current always flows in a direction that opposes the motion. A solenoid acts as a magnet (see Section 13.1). So the solenoid repels a magnet that is approaching it. It attracts a magnet that is leaving the solenoid.

This sort of result often occurs in science. Whatever you try to do, nature tries to stop you! Nature usually acts to keep things the way they are.

A mystery

Even though scientists know far more about this effect than they did, it is still basically a mystery. However, it has been given a name: **electromagnetic induction!** (Magnetism has **induced** (caused) an electric current.)

What we do know

1 Whenever a wire is moved through a magnetic field, an emf is produced. (You don't even need a solenoid!) This emf causes a current to flow in the wire.

2 The direction of the current is opposite to that in the motor. In this case, the direction of the current is described by Fleming's *right*-hand rule (Figure 3).

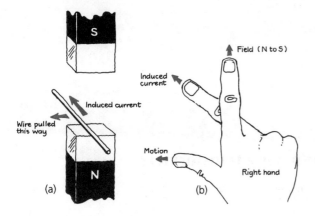

Fig. 3 A way of remembering the direction of the current
You must, however, remember that you use your *right* hand for the current produced by a dynamo, and your *left* hand for the motion of a motor. Think of a way of remembering this.

3 The emf produced is proportional to
- the strength of the magnetic field
- the speed of motion
- (in the case of a coil) the number of turns and the area of the coil.

The faster the change in magnetic flux passing through each turn of the coil, the larger is the emf. This is why generators (including wind generators) always rotate at such high speeds.

The bicycle dynamo

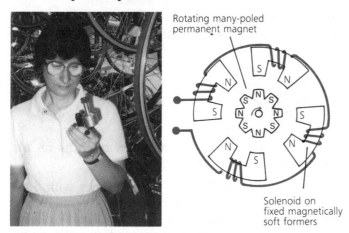

Fig. 4 A bicycle dynamo uses a rotating magnet
Does this need a commutator?

Figure 4 shows a typical bicycle dynamo. A series of magnetic poles passes across the end of each coil. The emf produced is first in one direction and then in the opposite direction. Thus the bicycle dynamo is an example of an ac dynamo.

Tape-recorder playback head

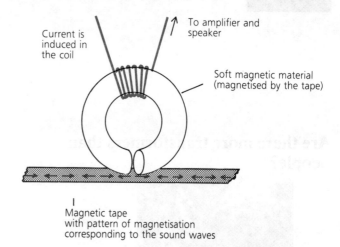

Fig. 5 The playback head of a tape-recorder
How does it work?

In the magnetic head of a tape-recorder, the 'magnets' are magnetised grains of iron oxide on the magnetic tape. These magnets pass across the narrow gap in a ring of soft magnetic material (Figure 5). As each magnet passes the gap, the ring is magnetised. This produces an emf in the coil. The small current produced is then amplified (see Chapter 19) and fed to the speaker.

There are many other applications of electromagnetic induction, one of which is described in the next section.

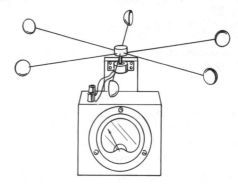

Fig. 6 A table-tennis ball anemometer
This can be used to measure the speed of the wind.

- **Make the wind generator shown in Figure 6. Use it as an anemometer to measure the speed of the wind. You need to calibrate it. In other words, you need to mark the scale of wind speeds. One way of doing this is to hold the anemometer out of the window of a car driving at a known speed (in a safe place!). How else could you calibrate your anemometer?**

Are there more transformers than people?

Fig. 1 Transformers come in many shapes and sizes
Why are they used?

Electrical transformers (not the toy robots of this name!) are found in all sorts of places. Some telephone answering machines, home computers and other devices have separate transformers to provide a low-voltage supply. Larger transformers are sometimes seen on the poles that carry power lines. Even larger transformers are used at electricity substations. These reduce the high voltage from the overhead (or underground) cables to the 240 V needed for our houses (see Section 11.9).

Inside most pieces of electrical equipment you will find a transformer. For example, transformers are used in televisions to provide the high voltage needed for the cathode ray tube. They are also used in some radios so that you can run the low-voltage circuits off the mains supply.

What is a transformer?

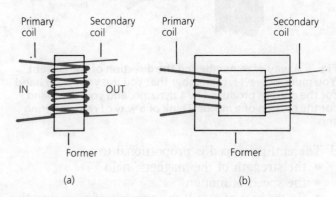

Fig. 2 Two designs for a transformer
(a) The most common design
(b) Separating the coils

The most common design for a transformer is shown in Figure 2(a). The design shown in Figure 2(b) is less common but allows you to see the two coils. The coil on the input side is called the **primary** coil. That on the output side is called the **secondary** coil.

Transformers are (normally) used to change the voltage. The input voltage V_i and output voltage V_o are given by

$$\frac{V_o}{V_i} = \frac{N_s}{N_p} \qquad (1)$$

where N_p and N_s are the numbers of turns on the primary and secondary coils.

Suppose, for example, that a transformer with 1000 turns of wire on the primary coil is to be connected to the mains to provide a 12 V output. Using Equation (1), the number of turns on the secondary coil must be

$$N_s = \frac{N_p V_o}{V_i} = \frac{1000 \times 12\,\text{V}}{240\,\text{V}} = 50 \text{ turns}$$

- **What would the output voltage be if the transformer were connected the wrong way round (with the 1000 turn coil as the secondary coil)?**

How does it work?

The primary coil and core act as an electromagnet. When alternating current flows through the primary coil, the core is magnetised first one way and then the other. This changes the magnetic flux through the secondary coil, producing an (alternating) emf in this coil.

So, overall, the alternating current in the primary circuit produces a separate alternating current in the secondary circuit.

Energy losses

If the transformer is 100% efficient, then the electrical power entering the primary coil is the same as that leaving the secondary coil. Using Equation (1) from Section 11.4, if I_p and V_p are the primary current and the primary voltage, and I_s and V_s are the secondary current and the secondary voltage, then

$$I_p V_p = I_s V_s \qquad (2)$$

In practice, some energy is lost. One way in which this occurs is through **eddy currents** flowing in, and heating, the core. Being an electrical conductor, the core can itself act as a coil.

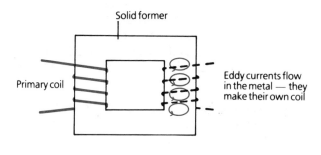

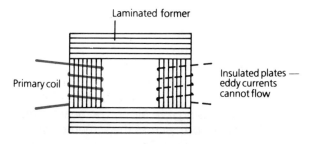

Fig. 3 Why we use a laminated core
Why do all transformers hum? Can any of them have 100% efficiency? How do you know?

To reduce these eddy currents, the cores of most transformers are made from thin plates of magnetically soft material painted with insulation. (We call this a **laminated core**.) The eddy currents are unable to pass through this insulation.

There is one small disadvantage. As the plates become magnetised, they repel each other. This produces the humming sound that you hear when transformers are operating. Electricity itself doesn't hum—it's the metal plates inside the transformer that hum.

- **What is the frequency of this hum? (See Chapter 14 for the meaning of frequency.)**

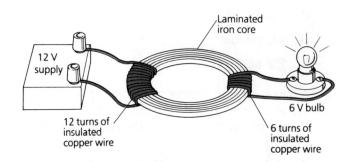

Fig. 4 A home-made transformer

- **Try making and using the transformer shown in Figure 4. After getting this to work, disconnect the ac supply and bulb. Connect a voltmeter to the output and, for a short time, connect the input wires to a battery. What happens as you (a) connect and (b) disconnect the wires to the battery?**

Back emf

Even one coil on its own can act a bit like a transformer. It acts as both the primary coil and the secondary coil. As the current changes, an emf is produced in the opposite direction.

The **back emf** can be very large. It can cause sparking in switches. In Section 19.2 we shall see how it can cause problems in circuits that use relays.

So, if ever you turn off a switch and notice a spark, you'll know what has caused it. It's *just* the back electromotive force produced by electromagnetic induction!

Exercises

1 Which of the following is the best material to use for the core of an electromagnet?

   A Copper

   B Soft iron

   C Steel

   D Aluminium

   E Plastic

2 A particular transformer has more turns on the secondary coil than on the primary coil. How do the **output** voltage and current compare with those of the input?

   A Both are larger than the input values

   B Both are smaller than the input values

   C Voltage smaller, current larger

   D Voltage larger, current smaller

   E Cannot tell without further information

3 A long coil (solenoid) produces a magnetic field similar to that of a magnet

   A Whenever current passes through it

   B Whenever soft iron is put inside it

   C Only when current passes through it *and* it has a core of magnetic material

   D Only during the instant the current flowing through it is switched on

   E Only during the instant the current flowing through it is switched off

4 Cathode rays in a television set are

   A Television waves

   B Rays of white light

   C Rays of red, green and blue light

   D X-rays

   E Fast electrons

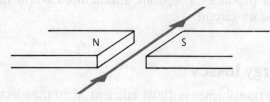

Fig. 1

5 Figure 1 shows a horizontal wire carrying a current and lying between two magnetic poles. The force on the wire produced by the magnet is

   A To the right

   B To the left

   C Upwards

   D Downwards

   E Making the wire rotate

6 Complete these sentences:

   a A _____ is another name for a long (helical) coil of wire through which an electric _____ passes. If a piece of _____ _____ is left in this coil, it becomes _____ . This arrangement is called an _____ .

   b A step-up _____ is a device for increasing the _____ of an electrical supply. It uses two _____ of wire wound on a core of magnetically _____ material. This is _____ to prevent eddy currents from flowing in it.

   c A television has an _____ gun which consists of a heated _____ and a cylinder of metal which is _____ charged. This produces a beam of _____ rays that hit the screen at one point, causing it to glow. The beam is moved back and forth across the screen by a _____ field. The _____ of the beam is increased for _____ parts of the picture and decreased for _____ parts of the picture.

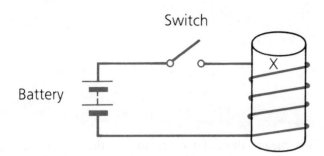

Fig. 2 **Which pole is which?**

7 Figure 2 shows an electromagnet.

   a Which way will the current flow when the switch is closed?

   b Which pole is at the position marked X?

   c What would be a suitable material for the cylinder? Why?

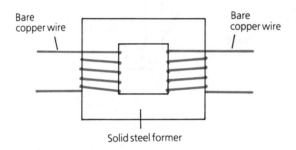

Fig. 3 **What is wrong with this transformer?**

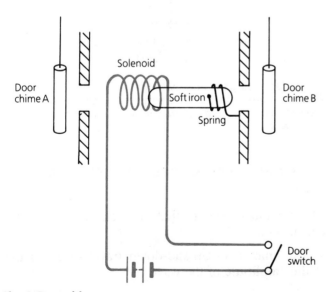

Fig. 4 **Door chimes**
How do they work?

8 Figure 3 shows a design for a home-made transformer.

   a State and explain three things that are wrong with this design.

   b Why are the cores of transformers earthed?

9 Figure 4 shows magnetic door chimes. Explain what happens when the current is

   a switched on

   b switched off.

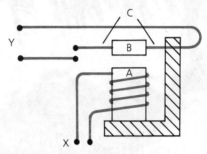

Fig. 5 **What is it and how does it work?**

10 a Name the device shown in Figure 5, and state one use for it.

   b Explain how it works.

   c Explain the physical properties needed for each of the materials A, B, C and D.

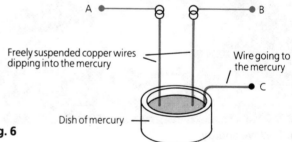

Fig. 6

11 a State what will happen to the copper wires in Figure 6 if

      i Terminal A is connected to the positive side of a battery. Terminal B is connected to the negative side. Terminal C is left unconnected.

      ii Terminals A and B are both connected to the positive side of a battery. Terminal C is connected to the negative side.

   b Explain this behaviour in terms of magnetic flux patterns.

12 Explain, using diagrams, the meaning and purpose of a split-ring commutator.

14 WAVES

14.1 Water waves

Getting energy from the waves

Fig. 1 Wave energy
Where has the energy of these waves come from?

Go to the coast on a windy, stormy day and see (and hear) how the waves crash against the sea-wall. These waves carry a lot of energy as they thunder in towards the shore. How can we make use of this energy?

To us, waves look like hills of water travelling towards the shore. But, in fact, the water itself isn't travelling at all. You may have noticed that objects such as seaweed or beach balls aren't carried along with a wave. They just bob up and down. The same is true of the water itself. It doesn't travel with the wave. It just moves up and down. First one part of the water surface moves upwards, then the next part, and so on. The only thing that travels with the wave is **energy.**

This means that, if we are to use the energy of the waves, we need something that can be pushed up and down by the waves. This up-and-down motion can then drive a generator to produce electricity. Figure 2 shows one of the methods at present being tried.

- **See if you can suggest another method.**

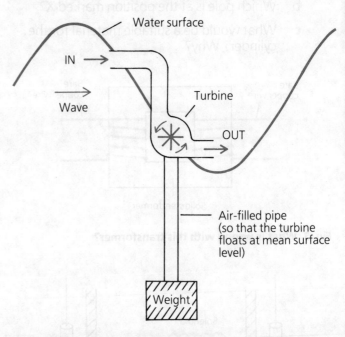

Fig. 2 Harnessing the energy of the waves
These machines convert the energy of the water waves into electrical energy. Suggest a way in which such a machine might work.

How much energy can you get from the waves?

The amount of energy that you can get from waves depends on

- The amount of up-and-down travel—we call this the **amplitude** of the wave.

- The number of waves passing each second—we call this the **frequency** of the wave.

206

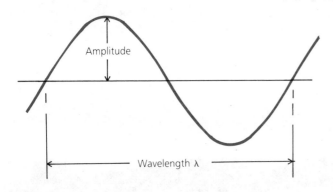

Fig. 3 Amplitude and wavelength

> The frequency of a wave is the number of waves passing a point in one second.

The higher the frequency, the more energy you are going to get from the waves (since each wave brings along its own amount of energy).

Frequency is measured in hertz (Hz) where one hertz is one wave per second. (Heinrich Rudolf Hertz was a German physicist who, in 1880, discovered **electrical waves** in wires.)

Wavelength and wavefront

Wavelength and wavefront are two more terms that help us to describe and study waves.

Wavefront is the name that we use for each wave crest. For example, a wave stretching along a beach is a wavefront. Similarly, the circular ripples which spread out when a stone is dropped into a pond are each called wavefronts.

The **wavelength** is the distance between wavefronts (see Figure 3).

Wave speed, wavelength and frequency

The longer the wavelength, the lower the frequency (provided that the speed of the waves doesn't change).

Suppose that a series of waves has a frequency of 1 Hz. First one wavefront goes past a particular point. Then, 1 s later, a second wavefront passes that point. The first wave will now be one wavelength away. In 1 s, the wave has travelled one wavelength. Its speed must therefore be one wavelength per second.

Now suppose that the series of waves has a frequency of 2 Hz. A wavefront passes a particular point. After 1 s, two more waves will have passed that point. The first wave will now be two wavelengths away. So the speed of travel is two wavelengths per second.

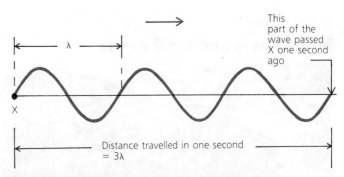

Fig. 4 Wave speed = frequency × wavelength
Draw the situation for waves of frequency 4 Hz. What is the wave speed if the wavelength is 2 m?

Similarly, waves of frequency 3 Hz will travel at a speed of three wavelengths per second. In general,

$$\text{wave speed} = \text{frequency} \times \text{wavelength} \qquad (1)$$

This can be written as a formula.

> If f is the frequency, λ (the Greek letter lambda) is the wavelength and V is the wave speed, then
> $$V = f\lambda \qquad (2)$$

An example
Suppose that you are in a small fishing boat with the engine switched off. The boat is just bobbing up and down. Suppose also that the wave crests near the boat are 10 m apart and that they are travelling at a speed of 2 m/s. According to Equation (1), the frequency of the waves will be

$$\text{frequency} = \frac{\text{wave speed}}{\text{wavelength}} = \frac{2\,\text{m/s}}{10\,\text{m}}$$
$$= 0.2\,\text{Hz}$$

A frequency of 0.2 Hz (⅕ Hz) means a fifth of a wave per second. That means one wave every five seconds.

- **Another boat passes, and produces waves with the same speed but only 2 metres apart. What is the frequency of these waves? How many waves will hit the first boat in 1 minute?**

Bending water waves

Jetties, bays and breakwaters

Fig. 1 Wave patterns in a harbour
(a) Peterhead harbour
(b) Ripple-tank simulation of Peterhead harbour

When plane waves (waves with straight wavefronts) approach the shore, all sorts of things can happen to them.

For example, as plane waves enter a bay, their wavelength gets smaller. If they enter the bay at an angle, they bend towards the shore. As the waves approach the beach, they produce breakers.

When plane waves hit a jetty or a sea-wall head on, they bounce straight back. When they hit the sea-wall at an angle, they bounce back at an angle to produce a diamond pattern. If the sea-wall is curved, the waves can be **focused** back to a point.

Plane waves passing between rocks spread out in the shape of a fan. If they hit a series of posts (such as a breakwater) they can form a pattern of fans.

- **Next time you are at the seashore, see if you can spot these effects.**

Reflection

The diamond pattern produced when plane waves hit a jetty at an angle is caused by **reflection.** The waves

bounce off the jetty at an equal angle as shown in Figure 2(a). Figure 2(b) shows what happens when circular waves hit a straight barrier. The reflected waves seem to be spreading out from a point on the far side of the barrier. Figure 2(c) shows what happens when plane (straight) waves hit a curved barrier. This particular barrier is **concave**—it curves in, like a cave. The waves are focused to a point which we call the **principal focus** of the barrier.

Refraction

The frequency of a series of waves depends on the frequency of the source of the waves. Whatever happens to the waves, their frequency cannot change. For example, if the waves enter a region where they travel more slowly, then their wavelength will decrease.

When waves enter shallow water, they slow down. (This only happens when the water is very shallow—less than five wavelengths deep.) Suppose that the waves enter this region of shallow water at an angle.

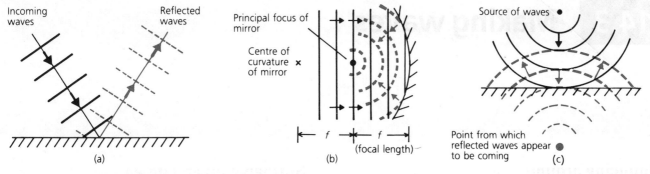

Fig. 2 The reflection of waves
(a) Plane waves and a plane barrier, (b) circular waves and a plane barrier, (c) plane waves and a concave circular barrier
How are plane waves reflected by a convex circular barrier? (Try it and see.)

The first part of each wave to reach the shallow water will slow down before the rest of the wave. This causes the wavefronts to change direction (Figure 3). (Think how a car swerves as the wheels on one side dig into soft mud or snow.) The bending of waves caused by a change in wave speed is called **refraction.**

Changes in the speed of waves can also affect their shape. For example, when a wave slows down, the bottom of the wave will slow down before the top. **Why?** This creates breakers (Figure 4).

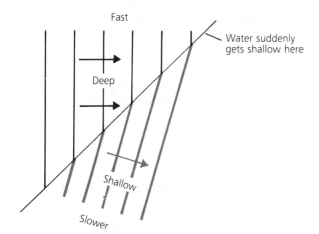

Fig. 3 The refraction of waves
Why do the waves bend?

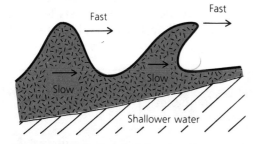

Fig. 4 How breakers are formed
Why do breakers sometimes occur out at sea during very windy weather?

Diffraction and interference

As waves pass through a gap or a hole, they tend to spread out (Figures 1 and 5(a)). The larger their wavelength relative to the size of the hole, the more they spread out. This is called **diffraction.**

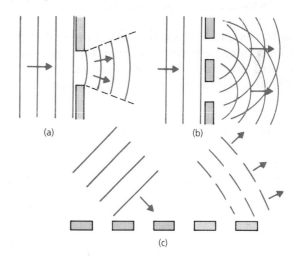

Fig. 5 Diffraction and interference
(a) Diffraction at a single opening
(b) Interference caused by two openings
(c) Interference of waves reflected from regularly spaced objects
What happens in diagram (a) if you alter the width of the opening?

When there are two holes close together, the parts of the waves that get through the holes interfere with each other as they spread out (Figure 5(b)). Interference also occurs when waves are reflected from a regularly spaced set of objects (Figure 5(c)).

Reflection, refraction, diffraction and interference are interesting but not particularly important effects when we are dealing with water waves. But when it comes to designing a concert hall, a microwave transmitter or an electron microscope, these aspects of wave behaviour are of great importance.

Bouncing around

Whenever you get yourself a drink on a train or a coach, you can be sure of one thing. The next few miles will be the bumpiest of the whole journey! The coach will bounce up and down on its springs. This will produce waves on the surface of your drink. If you aren't careful, you'll have the whole lot in your lap!

Waves are always produced by **oscillations** (another word for **vibrations**). All waves consist of up-and-down, side-to-side or to-and-fro oscillations.

- **Send waves down a rope by making the end of the rope oscillate. How many different types of waves can you produce? Increase the frequency of oscillation. Do the waves move any faster?**

- **Send waves along a 'Slinky' spring. Can you make a type of wave on the Slinky that you can't make on a rope?**

- **How can you show that these waves are carrying energy?**

Fig. 1 Train vibrations making coffee waves
Even though the coffee is resting on the table, the vibrations have produced waves that have lapped over the side of the cup.
Do you always need vibrations to produce waves?

Springing up and down

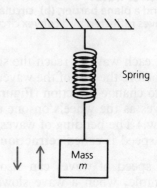

Spring

Mass
m

Fig. 2 Bobbing up and down on a spring or 'vertical oscillations'
What is meant by the 'period of vibration' of the spring? How does it depend on (i) the mass used (ii) the spring constant (the stiffness of the spring)?

Figure 2 shows a simple example of an oscillating (vibrating) system. Imagine that the mass on the spring represents your coach bouncing around while you are drinking coffee. There are two things that you might be interested in:

1 How far the mass moves up or down from its starting position—we call this the **amplitude** of the oscillation.

2 How long it takes for one complete up-and-down movement—we call this the **period** of the oscillation.

The **period** of an oscillation (or wave) is related to its frequency. For example, if there are five up-and-down movements per second, then each lasts for 1/5 s. The frequency is 5 Hz. The period is 1/5 s (= 0.2 s). In general,

$$\text{period} = \frac{1}{\text{frequency}} \qquad (1)$$

You can increase the period of oscillation by
- increasing the mass
- using a weaker spring.

- Hang a mass on a light spring, and make it vibrate vertically. What is the period of oscillation? (It is best to find this by timing several oscillations together. Why?) How does the period depend on the amplitude of the oscillation? Is the period directly proportional to the mass you use? Repeat this for a second, weaker spring.

A simple pendulum

A pendulum oscillates in a more interesting way. At least, Galileo thought so. (See Chapter 2 if you don't know who Galileo was.) Galileo first studied the pendulum during a rather boring church service. His pendulum was a lamp hanging from the roof. The lamp was swinging in a breeze. Galileo timed the period of oscillation of this pendulum using his pulse.

Fig. 3 During a rather boring sermon
What did Galileo discover about the pendulum?

- Repeat Galileo's observations using a ball of plasticine on the end of a piece of string. Use a stopwatch rather than your pulse. Time oscillations of small amplitude. How does the period of swing depend on
  (a) the amplitude of the oscillation?
  (b) the mass of the plasticine?
  (c) the length of the string?

- Make a pendulum with a period of swing of 1 s. Why do you think that pendulums were used in the past to make clocks keep the right time?

Resonance

Have you ever seen an opera singer shatter a wine glass just by singing? If she sings loudly at just the right frequency, she can make the glass vibrate so much that it breaks.

Most things have a **natural frequency** at which they vibrate most easily. If an object is hit by waves of that frequency, it vibrates strongly. This is called **reson-**

ance. An object resonates when it is hit by waves with its natural or resonating frequency.

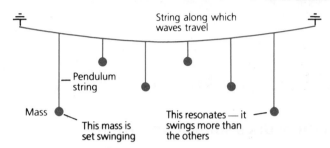

Fig. 4 Demonstrating resonance
How?

- Try making the resonating system shown in Figure 4. Set the first pendulum swinging. This will send waves along the string and cause the other pendulums to oscillate. Which pendulum oscillates most? Why?

Resonance can have disastrous results. For example, the Tacoma bridge shook itself to pieces when it was hit by gusts of wind with its natural frequency of vibration.

Fig. 5 Resonance causes a disaster
The Tacoma bridge swung itself to pieces when gusts of wind hit the bridge at its resonating frequency. Suspension bridges like the Humber and Severn bridges are designed so that they cannot resonate like this in the wind.
Where else is resonance dangerous?

Other examples of resonance are less dramatic. For instance, to make a child on a swing go higher, you don't need to push harder. What you must do is to keep pushing at the correct frequency.

- How do you explain the wheel-wobble that some cars get at a particular speed on the motorway?

211

14.4 Sound's different

Where does sound come from?

Listen to the sounds around you. What is causing them?

Fig. 1 An orchestra produces sound waves
How do the different instruments produce these waves?

Sounds are produced when objects vibrate. For example, when you beat on a drum, the drum skin vibrates. **You can see this by putting some rice or seeds on to the drum. They jump up and down as the drum vibrates.**

In other musical instruments, different things vibrate. For instance to get a guitar to make a noise, you pluck the strings to make them vibrate.

- **What vibrates in**
  - **(a) an oboe or saxophone?**
  - **(b) a cornet or trumpet?**

When we speak, a split membrane in our throat vibrates. The membrane (our vocal chords) is vibrated by air from our lungs. **Try holding your fingers lightly against your throat as you talk or sing. Can you feel the vibration coming from your vocal chords?**

Energy and ultrasonics

Sound waves carry energy. One way in which this energy is used is in **ultrasonic cleaning**. The sound waves used for this are very high frequency. (Ultra-

sonic comes from the Latin words 'ultra' meaning 'beyond' and 'sonus' meaning 'sound'. So ultrasonic waves are 'waves beyond sound'. Their frequency is beyond the range of our hearing.)

Dentists use ultrasonic cleaning to clean our teeth. The vibrations produced by high-intensity ultrasound shake the harmful plaque from the teeth. (Water is used at the same time to prevent the teeth from overheating). Watchmakers use ultrasound for cleaning small pieces of metal in mechanical watches.

Ultrasonic vibrations are also used for cutting and welding metal, and for mixing alloys such as lead–tin–zinc. (Some other uses of ultrasonics are discussed in Section 15.2.)

How sound is different

As a wave travels through water, the water particles move up and down. As a wave passes along a string, the string can move (vibrate) either up and down or from side to side. We call these waves **transverse waves**. (Trans means 'across'.) The direction of vibration is at right-angles to the **direction of propagation** (the direction in which the waves are travelling).

In sound waves the particles don't go up and down or from side to side. They get closer together and further apart. Sound waves consist of **compressions** (when molecules are pushed together) and **rarefactions** (when molecules are allowed to move apart). You can

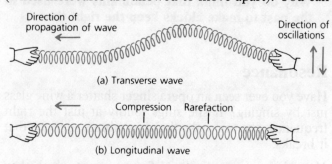

Fig. 2 Transverse and longitudinal waves
Do these waves travel at the same speed along the spring?
Design and carry out an experiment to test your answer.

get an idea of what sound waves look like by sending waves down a long (slinky) spring (Figure 2). **Try this.** Such waves are called **longitudinal waves**.

Sound cannot travel through a vacuum

We know that sound can travel through air. A vibrating object pushes the air molecules nearest to it. These push the molecules next to them, and so on (Figure 3).

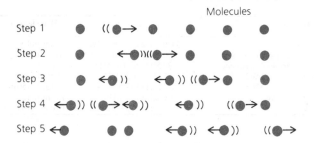

Fig. 3 **A simplified picture of how sound travels through air**
In practice, molecules are always moving and bumping into each other. Sound waves differ in that billions of molecules together bounce against the next lot of molecules.

Sound can also travel through liquids. In liquids, the molecules are closer together than they are in air, so the sound travels faster and further. (Whales can hear each other singing under water even when they are many miles apart.)

Fig. 4 **Whales sing to each other under the ocean**
Whales can hear each other over vast distances. Does sound travel faster or slower under water? Why? How could you check this with an experiment?

If there are no molecules to bump into each other, then sound cannot travel. This means that sound cannot travel through space or any other vacuum. The only ways in which astronauts can talk to each other in space are by making their helmets touch or using a radio.

- Why can they talk to each other when helmets are touching? You can show that sou cannot travel through a vacuum using the ar rangement shown in Figure 5. Why do you think that this works best when you hang the bell from elastic bands rather than from the electric wires?

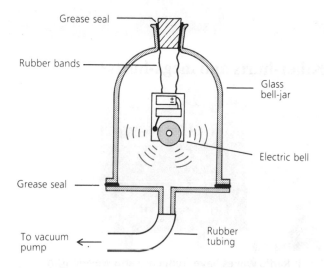

Fig. 5 **A bell in a bell-jar**
What happens to the sound when you pump the air out? Why?

- Do light waves travel through a vacuum? How do you know?

Not so fast!

Sometimes the soundtrack and picture on television get out of step.

One way in which this can happen is that the sound of a person speaking comes just after the person's lips move. We don't usually notice this because we are used to such delays in real life. For example, we hear the sound of a ball on a cricket bat long after we see the batsman hit the ball. We know that sound travels much more slowly than light ($330\,\text{m/s}$ rather than $300\,000\,000\,\text{m/s}$).

Occasionally the soundtrack gets ahead of the picture and we hear the voice just before the lips move. We notice this at once, even if the difference is only a tiny fraction of a second. The effect is confusing and unpleasant. In real life, we never hear the sound of a bat on a ball before we see it. We know that sound cannot travel faster than light.

- How could you measure the speed of sound in
  (a) air?
  (b) water?
  (c) steel?

213

Killer-hurts and mega-hurts?

Fig. 1 Radio waves have frequency and wavelength
What is the wavelength of the medium-wave transmitter advertised on this board?

Radio stations send out waves of a particular frequency. Radio 1 broadcasts on medium wave at 1053 kHz (kilohertz) and on VHF/FM at 88 MHz (megahertz).

If your radio is marked in metres rather than in kHz or MHz, do not despair! You can easily work out this wavelength by remembering that radio waves travel at the speed of light (300 000 000 m/s). For example, we can find the wavelength for Radio 1 on 1053 kHz, using Equation (1) from Section 14.1:

$$\text{wavelength} = \frac{\text{wave speed}}{\text{frequency}}$$

$$= \frac{3 \times 10^8 \text{ m/s}}{1\,053\,000 \text{ Hz}} = 285 \text{ m}$$

(Whether it's quicker to work this out or to look it up in the *Radio Times* is another question!)

- **Use the information in the *Radio Times* to check that waves of all frequencies travel at 3×10^8 m/s.**

Wavebands

Figure 2 shows the wavelengths and frequencies for the different radio wavebands. **See if you can discover the frequencies used for CB (citizen band) radios.**

214

Fig. 2 Radio wavebands

Waveband	Frequency	Wavelength
Microwave	3000 MHz to 30 000 MHz	10 mm to 100 mm
UHF (ultra high frequency)	300 MHz to 3000 MHZ	100 mm to 1 m
VHF (very high frequency)	30 MHz to 300 MHz	1 m to 10 m
Short wave 2 (SW2)	7.5 MHz to 30 MHz	10 m to 40 m
Short wave 1 (SW1)	2 MHz to 7.5 MHz	40 m to 150 m
Medium wave	30 kHz to 2 MHz	150 m to 10 km
Long wave	3 kHz to 30 kHz	10 km to 100 km

The wavelengths affect what aerials you use. Figure 3(a) shows a typical UHF (ultra high frequency) television aerial. The **dipole** (the part of the aerial that picks up the radio waves) is the rectangular frame to which the aerial lead is connected. Ideally, it should be half a wavelength long. (The other parts of the aerial are there to focus the waves on to this dipole.) Figure 3(b) shows a VHF (very high frequency) aerial on a radio.

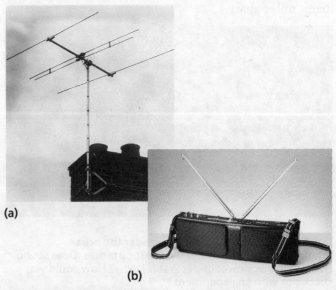

(a)

(b)

Fig. 3 UHF and VHF aerials

VHF and UHF waves travel (more or less) straight from the transmitter to the receiver. Those that go upwards are lost into space. In contrast, short waves bounce off the ionosphere (Figure 4) and medium and long waves bend round the Earth.

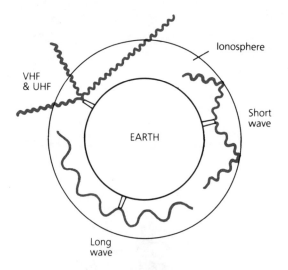

Fig. 4 **Bouncing off the ionosphere**
You can hear short-wave radio stations from other parts of the world, but not VHF stations. Why?

Radio waves are transverse waves

Look again at the UHF aerial in Figure 3(a). Notice that the parts of the aerial are at right-angles to each other. The dipole aerial is set at right-angles to the direction in which the waves are travelling from the transmitter. In other words, it is at right-angles to the direction of propagation of the waves. **If there are television aerials on a number of roofs near you, check whether they are all pointing towards a particular transmitter.**

The amplitude is important

The larger the amplitude, the greater the energy carried by the waves and the better the reception on our radios. Large broadcasting transmitters produce up to a million watts of **effective radiated power**. The radio waves that they produce have very large amplitudes and can be picked up a long way away. In contrast, citizen-band radio transmitters must not, by law, exceed a power of 4 W. They produce waves with much lower amplitudes.

What is waving?

Radio waves make electric currents flow in radio aerials. In fact, an aerial is just a wire, or anything that can carry a current. (Human beings make quite good aerials. Sometimes you get the best picture on the television when you hold the aerial!)

Radio waves also produce tiny magnetic fields. AM radio receivers (normal radios) use small **ferrite rod**

aerials. The ferrite rod is magnetised by the radio waves. This magnetisation causes currents to flow in a coil surrounding the rod (Figure 5). **If you have an old, broken radio, look inside at the ferrite rod aerial.**

Fig. 5 **Picking up the magnetic part of the wave**
As the radio wave passes, magnetic fields pass through the ferrite rod causing currents to flow in the coil.
Should these aerials point towards the transmitter or at right-angles to it? Why?

Because radio waves produce electric currents and magnetism, we call them **electromagnetic waves** (see Section 14.11). The only things that are 'waving' in these electromagnetic waves are voltages and magnetic fields (Figure 6).

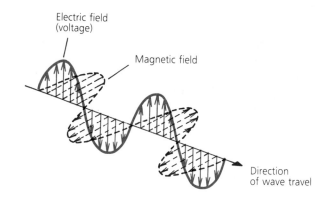

Fig. 6 **An electromagnetic wave**
The electric field (the voltage), magnetic field and direction of propagation are at right-angles to each other.
If this is a radio wave, which way should a wire be placed to receive it?

Radio waves aren't so easy to understand as water waves. You can't see them, and it is difficult to picture voltages and magnetic fields waving about. However, they are very important to us. Without Hertz's discovery of radio waves, our lives would be very different.

Microwaves

Microwave cookers

Fig. 1 Fast foods using microwaves
Why do microwaves heat moist foods so rapidly?

Microwave ovens cook food very quickly. This is because the microwaves get inside the food and heat it from the inside.

Like radio waves, microwaves are **electromagnetic waves.** (They are produced by very-high-frequency alternating currents flowing in the gaps of very powerful electromagnets.) They have higher frequencies than radio waves, and smaller wavelengths (only a few centimetres).

In a microwave oven, microwaves from a very powerful transmitter are absorbed by water inside the food. As they are absorbed, the microwaves give their energy to the water as internal energy. This rapidly heats the food.

Whereas microwaves are absorbed by water, they are reflected by metal. Because of this, you must avoid putting anything metal into a microwave oven. In addition microwaves can produce large electric currents in metal. This could result in sparks inside the oven.

Microwave beams

Microwaves can be reflected and focused into beams by curved metal mirrors. The beams produced by these mirrors travel in straight lines and can be directed towards distant receiving stations. They are used to carry telephone and television signals across the country and up to satellites (Figure 2).

Fig. 2 Microwaves beamed from London's Telecom tower
The concave reflectors are beaming microwaves to other parts of the country. Why?

Radar

Since microwaves are reflected by metal, they bounce off metal aircraft, cars and ships. This means that we can use microwaves to find the position of an aircraft, a car, or a ship. By timing how long it takes for the waves to bounce off an object and come back, we can discover how far away the object is. (By measuring the change in frequency of the reflected waves, we can also tell the speed of the object.)

When microwaves are used in this way, we call them **radar**. (This stands for <u>RA</u>dio <u>D</u>etection <u>A</u>nd <u>R</u>anging.) Police use radar speed checks to detect cars travelling faster than the speed limit (see Section 2.1, Figure 1). Airports use radar to check the position and speed of incoming aircraft (Figure 3).

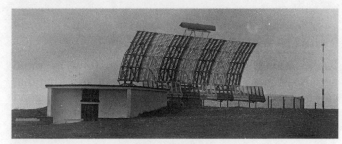

Fig. 3 Watching the planes come in
Why do some military aircraft fly so near the ground?

Infra-red radiation

We are glowing

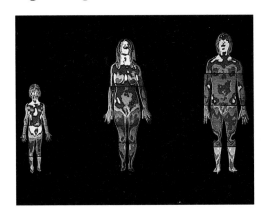

Fig. 1 Glowing with infra-red radiation
Colours have been added to show the regions that radiate most (white/yellow) and least (blue).

In earthquakes and other disasters, people are often trapped alive beneath mounds of rubble. In the past, rescue teams had to rely on hearing buried people shout or tap. They had no other way of knowing where the missing people were. Nowadays, the rescuers use thermal imagers to help them. Thermal imagers detect infra-red radiation given off by survivors and their warmed surroundings. (We shall see the reason for the name infra-red in Section 14.9.)

Anything that is warm gives off this form of electromagnetic radiation. If our eyes could see infra-red radiation, people and animals would appear to be glowing. Some animals can detect infra-red radiation. For example, the rattlesnake has sensitive infra-red sensors which help it to hunt other animals in the dark.

The warmer something is, the more infra-red radiation it gives off. So, thermal imagers can also be used to show whether any part of our body is hotter than it should be, perhaps because of infection.

In addition, infra-red cameras on aircraft and satellites can tell which parts of a crop are too warm or too cold, possibly because of disease (Figure 2).

- **Why do anti-aircraft missiles carry infra-red sensors? Where else are these sensors used?**

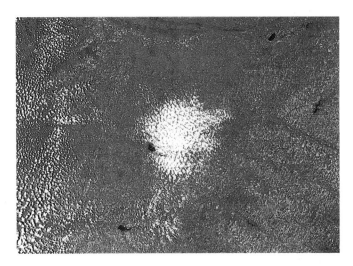

Fig. 2 Remote sensing
This satellite photograph shows slight differences in temperatures. How does the satellite measure these temperature differences?

Radiation that we can feel

Infra-red radiation is the heat radiation that we feel coming from a fire or an electric oven. It is the only kind of electromagnetic radiation that we can feel. Infra-red waves feel warm as they stimulate the nerves in our skin.

- **Put the palm of your hand very near your cheek. Feel the infra-red radiation coming from your hand.**

Heat radiation

All forms of electromagnetic radiation can act as heat radiation. For example, visible light from the Sun helps to warm the Earth. However, most of the heat radiation around us, and the only type that we can feel, is infra-red radiation.

(We know that microwaves, another form of electromagnetic radiation, can heat food. A faulty microwave oven could burn you very badly, but at first you would be unlikely to feel a thing! To avoid this happening, microwave ovens are designed so that they can't be on with the door open.)

Polaroid spectacles

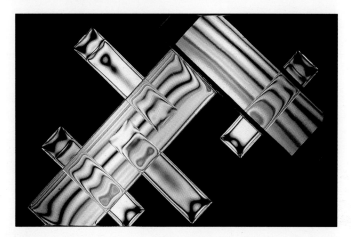

Fig. 1 Stress patterns in a glass plate
These patterns can be seen when the glass is placed between two polaroid filters.

Have you ever tried wearing polaroid spectacles in a car? When you put on the spectacles, coloured patterns seem to appear magically in the windscreen. The glare of sunlight reflected from a wet road disappears.

● If you can find some squares of polaroid film or some old polaroid lenses, try looking through two of them at once. What happens as you rotate one of the lenses? Repeat this with screwed-up polythene, or overlapping strips of sellotape, between the two lenses. See what colours you can produce.

The reason for this strange behaviour is that light consists of waves. Different colours of light have different wavelengths.

Light waves

Some of the light coming towards us is 'waving' up and down. We say that it is vibrating vertically. Other light—such as the sunlight reflected from a wet road—is 'waving' from side to side (horizontally). Polaroid spectacles act like a grid—they remove the horizontal vibrations and let through only the vertical vibrations.

So the glaring sunlight from the wet road is removed (Figure 2).

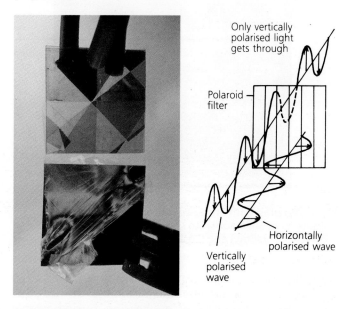

Fig. 2 Light is a transverse wave Polaroid filters absorb light that is oscillating (vibrating) in the wrong direction.
Place a piece of crumpled polythene between two polaroid filters. You will see coloured light. The polythene changes the direction of oscillation of the light by an amount which depends on the wavelength. Since different colours of light have different wavelengths, their direction of oscillation is changed by different amounts.
How else can you produce colours (i) using polaroid squares, (ii) using other methods.

	Mean wavelength (µm)	Mean frequency (x 10^{12} Hz)
	0.41	740
	0.43	700
Blue	0.46	650
Green	0.52	580
Yellow	0.58	520
Orange	0.63	480
Red	0.66	460

Fig. 3 Light of many colours
Each colour of the rainbow has its own frequency band. Which colours are not in the rainbow? How are these produced? (See Section 15.4)

Like other waves, light can be reflected, refracted and diffracted (see Chapter 15):

- We see things only because light is reflected from them.
- The shimmering effect that we see over a fire is caused by refraction in the hot-air currents.
- To see a diffraction pattern of vertical lines, hold your fingers upright and very close together. Now look through the narrow gaps between them towards a light or the sky.

Red light ≡ 460 000 000 MHz

Light is like radio waves in that different frequencies have different effects. With radio waves we have long wave, medium wave, short wave, VHF and UHF. With light, we have red, orange, yellow, green, blue, indigo and violet. **Where have you come across these colours before?** Each colour has a different frequency band as shown in Figure 3. **What is the wavelength of red light?**

White light from the Sun is made up of all the colours of the rainbow added together.

Splitting up white light

Polaroid is not the only thing that splits up white light into different colours. Drops of rain do the same job, and produce a rainbow. In raindrops, each colour is refracted to a different extent. For example, blue light is refracted more than red light (Figure 4).

- **Look at a rainbow through polaroid spectacles or a polaroid filter. What happens if you rotate the filter? What does this show about the rainbow?**

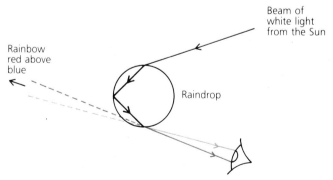

Fig. 4 Raindrops and rainbows
Water refracts different colours of light by different amounts. It splits water up into its separate colour. You can sometimes see a second, fainter rainbow inside the first. Why?

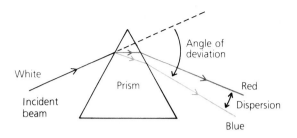

Fig. 5 Using a prism to produce a spectrum
Glass refracts different colours of light by different amounts. This is called dispersion.
Which colour of the spectrum is deviated most?

- **Make your own spectrum using a glass prism as shown in Figure 5.**

Oil films on water produce a coloured **interference pattern**. Light waves are reflected from both the top and the bottom of the oil film. Because the film is so thin, these waves get in each other's way. They interfere with one another to produce a coloured pattern.

Compact discs and video discs produce even more spectacular interference patterns. Light beams reflected from the different grooves interfere with each other to produce vividly coloured patterns (Figure 6).

Fig. 6 Laser discs produce several spectra
These are produced by the interference of light reflected from the different grooves of the disc.
Where else can you see coloured interference patterns?

Coloured objects

The simplest way of producing coloured light is with coloured objects. When white light hits an object, some colours of light are absorbed and some are reflected. The reflected light forms the colour of the object. This is discussed further in Chapter 15.

219

Invisible light

Fig. 1 Getting a suntan
Why can too much exposure to ultraviolet radiation be dangerous?

Some people use ultraviolet sun lamps to give themselves a tan before they go on holiday. Ultraviolet lamps glow with violet light. But the important part of the radiation—the ultraviolet light—is invisible. Ultraviolet light has a higher frequency than violet light. In the spectrum, it forms an invisible band *beyond* the violet light. ('Ultra' means 'beyond'.)

Infra-red lamps are used to treat aches and pains. These lamps glow red. But, like ultraviolet light, the infra-red light itself is invisible. Infra-red light has a frequency *below* that of red light. ('Infra' means 'below'.) Infra-red light is at the opposite end of the spectrum—it forms an invisible band beyond the red.

- **Make a spectrum using a diffraction grating. (A diffraction grating is a slide covered in very fine lines. It produces coloured light in the same way as a compact disc—see Section 14.8.) Now use a sensitive light meter to detect the invisible infra-red and ultraviolet light at each end of the spectrum.**

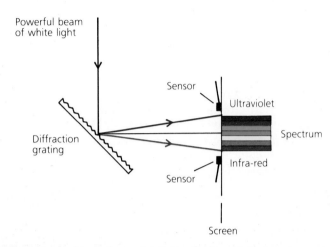

Fig. 2 Detecting infra-red and ultraviolet radiation
Why should a diffraction grating be used rather than a thick glass prism? (See Section 9.6.)

Getting a tan

Ultraviolet light is the invisible part of sunlight that makes our skins go darker. It also produces vitamin D in our skin. Light-coloured skin produces vitamin D more easily than dark skin. It has been suggested that Europeans originally came from Africa and were dark

Fig. 3 Skin colour and ultraviolet light
In what ways do light and dark skins differ in their reaction to ultraviolet light?

skinned. In Europe, there is much less sunlight than in Africa (particularly in winter). The dark skins of the Africans could not produce enough vitamin D from this amount of sunlight. Gradually, their skins lost their colour. (Today, Europeans get the vitamins that they need from a better diet, and so skin colour is less important.)

Unfortunately (as many people know to their cost!), light skin burns more easily than dark skin. It is ultraviolet radiation that causes this sunburn. Too much ultraviolet radiation can also cause skin cancers. Moral: don't overdo the sunbathing!

Fluorescent tubes and uPVC

Ultraviolet light can be a nuisance. It can spoil many plastics. Plastic window frames that spend a long time in the sun have to be made from ultraviolet-resistant PVC (called uPVC).

Ultraviolet light can also be useful. Some chemicals **fluoresce**. That is to say, they turn ultraviolet light into visible white light. **If you have an ultraviolet lamp, place it in a darkened room near a white shirt or some other white object. (It is safer to wear**

Fig. 4 Whiter than white
How do washing powders make shirts 'glow' white?

protective goggles to do this.) What do you notice? You sometimes see this effect in dance halls with ultraviolet lighting.

A fluorescent powder is used inside fluorescent lighting tubes. The electricity inside these tubes produces ultraviolet light. This is converted into white light by the powder.

Fluorescent powder is also added to some washing powders. Shirts washed in these powders absorb ultraviolet light from the Sun and turn it into visible light. They glow whiter than white!

Long-life milk and the ozone layer

Fig. 5 Long-life milk
What has this to do with ultraviolet light?

High-frequency, high-energy ultraviolet light can kill! For example, it is used to kill bacteria in milk. This produces long-life milk (Figure 5).

Ultraviolet light can also harm us. If all the ultraviolet radiation from the sun reached us, there would be a tremendous increase in skin cancers. Luckily, most of the ultraviolet light is absorbed by a layer of **ozone** (a form of oxygen) high up in the atmosphere.

Scientists have found that holes are developing in the ozone layer. These holes may be caused by some of the chemicals that we use, particularly the freon used in aerosol sprays. Scientific research is being carried out—and is urgently needed—to check whether we are harming the ozone layer. If we are, then more research is needed to show what we can do about it.

- **In what other ways could our present technology be threatening our environment? How can science help to overcome these problems? Is the solution to abandon our technology, or to improve it using scientific research?**

14.10 X-rays and gamma rays

Having an X-ray

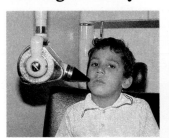

Fig. 1 Taking an X-ray photograph
What are X-rays? Why are they used?

X-rays are very-high-frequency electromagnetic waves. Doctors and dentists use them, in place of visible light, to photograph people's insides.

When a person is X-rayed, most of the X-rays pass straight through his or her body. But some X-rays are absorbed by the flesh and even more by bone. The amount of radiation absorbed by any part of the body depends on the intensity and frequency of the X-rays. By altering the intensity and frequency, it is possible to show up either bone or much softer tissue.

X-rays are dangerous. Cells that multiply rapidly—for example, sex cells—can be damaged by X-rays. So the sexual organs are always protected by lead when an X-ray of the whole body is taken. The person operating the X-ray machine usually stays behind a lead screen. While the occasional X-ray will not do the patient much harm, a large number of X-rays day after day could seriously harm the radiologist operating the machine.

Producing X-rays

X-rays are produced when cathode rays hit metal (Figure 2). Their discoverer, Roentgen, found that photographic film left near a cathode-ray tube became fogged, even if it was in a light-tight box. Roentgen called the rays affecting the film 'X-rays' as he didn't know what they were. Television screens and computer VDUs are designed so that they don't give off X-rays.

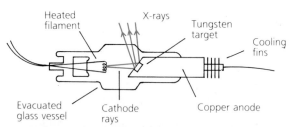

Fig. 2 Using cathode rays to produce X-rays
The cathode rays raise the temperature of the tungsten target sufficiently for it to give off X-rays. (The cathode rays actually knock electrons from the atoms. X-rays are given off as the electrons fall back into the atoms.)
Why does a television cathode-ray tube not produce many X-rays?

Gamma rays

The only real difference between X-rays and gamma rays is their source. If the electromagnetic waves come from a cathode-ray tube, then we call them X-rays. If they come from radioactive material, then we call them gamma rays.

Gamma rays usually have a higher frequency and a higher energy than X-rays. This makes them even more dangerous. Very careful precautions need to be taken when using them. The applications of gamma radiation, and the precautions that need to be taken, are discussed in detail in Chapter 17.

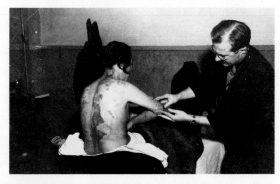

Fig. 3 Radiation burns from the Nagasaki bomb
The surface burns are mainly from infra-red, visible and ultraviolet radiation. Gamma rays pass through the body, and cause more serious damage inside.
How are workers in power stations protected from gamma radiation? (See Section 17.4.)

The electromagnetic spectrum

Hotter and hotter

The type of electromagnetic waves produced by an object depend on its temperature. The coldest objects in the universe just give off radio waves and microwaves. Astronomers use radio telescopes to look at these very cold dust clouds and other objects among the stars.

Warmer objects (around room temperature) give off infra-red radiation. If you switch on a radiant ring on an electric stove, the ring starts to give off more infrared radiation. It feels hotter. Eventually it gets hot enough to give off visible red light. If a fault occurred and it went on getting hotter, it would eventually glow white-hot with all the colours of the visible spectrum.

The Sun is hot enough to give off ultra-violet radiation. But hydrogen bombs are even hotter than the surface of the Sun. They give off gamma rays. So do some distant stars far hotter than our Sun.

What these waves have in common

All electromagnetic waves
- are transverse waves consisting of tiny, changing magnetic fields and voltages travelling through space
- can act as heat radiation, transferring energy from a hot object to a cold object
- travel at the speed of light (3×10^8 m/s)
- can travel through a vacuum
- are produced by vibrating (or accelerating) electric charges.

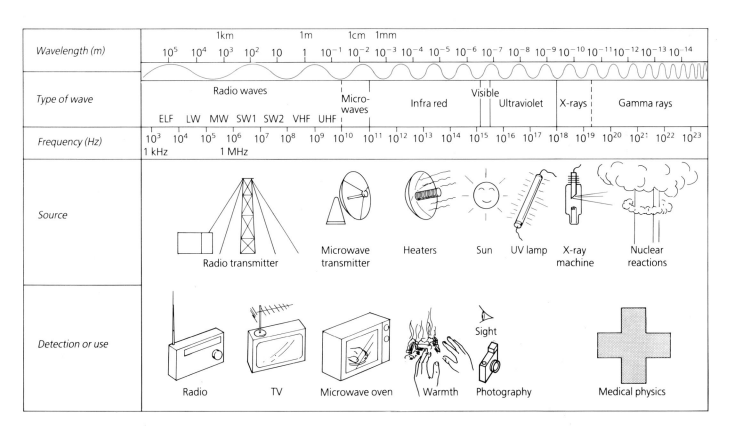

Fig. 1 The complete electromagnetic spectrum

Exercises

1 Sound cannot travel through one of the following. Which one?

   A Water

   B Steel

   C Hydrogen

   D Concrete

   E A vacuum

2 Blue light is different from red light because it

   A Travels faster

   B Has longer wavelength

   C Has higher frequency

   D Has lower energy

   E Isn't refracted or diffracted

3 Which of the following are **not** electromagnetic waves?

   A Microwaves

   B Ultrasonic waves

   C Gamma rays

   D Light waves

   E Heat radiation

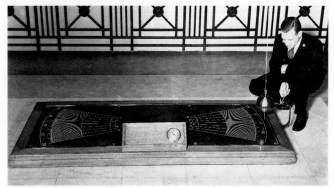

Fig. 1 The 25 m long pendulum in the Science Museum, London
The period of a pendulum depends on its length.
What else?

4 Which of the following is true of X-rays?

   A They are produced by nuclear reactions

   B They are given off by very cold objects in space

   C High-frequency X-rays are the same as low-frequency gamma rays

   D They are not absorbed at all by the human body

   E They are sometimes called cathode rays

5 The period of a pendulum for small oscillations depends on its length and which of the following?

   A Amplitude of swing only

   B Mass suspended from pendulum only

   C Amplitude of swing and mass suspended from pendulum

   D Nothing else

Fig. 2 How does radar spot an aircraft?

6 Air traffic control can use radar to detect aircraft because

   A Aircraft give out microwaves

B Aircraft absorb microwaves

C Aircraft reflect microwaves

D Aircraft use microwaves to send radio messages

7 Which of the following is true of ultraviolet light?

A It appears blue–violet in colour

B It feels warm on your skin

C It makes your teeth glow

D It is absorbed by carbon dioxide in the atmosphere

E It has a longer wavelength than violet light

8 A radio station has a transmitting frequency of 1000 kHz and a wavelength of 300 m. A second station has a frequency of 1500 kHz. What is the wavelength?

A 150 m

B 200 m

C 450 m

D 800 m

E 1500 m

9 Complete these sentences:

a Sound waves are produced by _____ objects.

b All waves carry _____ from one place to another.

c There are two types of wave. In a _____ wave, the vibration is at right-angles to the direction of propagation. In a _____ wave it is in the same direction.

d The number of waves per _____ passing any point is the _____ of the waves and is measured in _____ . The _____ is the distance between wavefronts.

10 State three ways in which sound waves differ from light waves.

11 State three applications of

a Microwaves

b Infra-red radiation

c Ultra-violet radiation

12 State four things that all electromagnetic waves have in common.

13 State two advantages and two disadvantages of mechanical vibrations.

14 Explain what is meant by each of these terms, and give one example of each:

a Reflection

b Refraction

c Diffraction

d Interference

15 Briefly describe three ways of producing a spectrum from white light.

16 a What is meant by the term 'resonance'?

b Describe a method of demonstrating resonance.

c State two situations in which resonance is important.

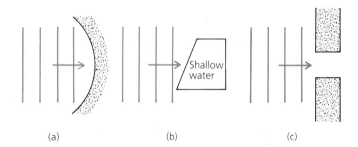

(a)   (b)   (c)

Fig. 3 What happens to these waves?

17 Figure 3 shows plane waves approaching (a) a curved barrier, (b) a region of shallow water, (c) a gap in a barrier. In each case, copy the diagrams and draw these four waves at the instant the last of them has reached the barrier.

18 Some scientific catalogues refer to 'three centimetre wave' equipment. This uses electromagnetic waves with a wavelength of 3 cm. What is

a The speed of these waves?

b The frequency of these waves?

c The type of wave (for example, are they gamma waves)?

d A possible use?

15.1 Communications

Saying hello!

Fig. 1 Stockbrokers communicating with their clients
How many different means of communication can you see in this picture?

Fig. 2 Speech is a kind of music
When we speak, our voice usually changes in pitch. How do we control the pitch?

Suppose that you need to send a message to someone. How can you do it?

- If you are near enough, you can speak to them.
- If you are too far away for them to hear you but they can see you, then you can wave or use sign language.
- If they are out of sight, then you could use the telephone.
- If you are nowhere near a telephone, then you could send a radio message.

- **How else can you communicate with someone?**

In nearly every case, you will be using waves: sound waves, light waves, electrical waves or radio waves.

What is speech?

In some ways, speech is a form of music. Each sound that we make has a definite pitch, a definite loudness, a certain quality and lasts for a definite length of time. In England, we stress certain syllables—we sound some more loudly than others. In China, instead of stressing

syllables, people alter the pitch of their voice. Section 15.3 on music shows how all these factors are related to the sound waves coming from our mouths.

Using colours

Words are usually printed in black ink on white paper. Light waves are reflected from the white paper but not from the black ink. Coloured pictures in books and on colour television sets appear to contain many colours. In fact, they are made up of only three—red, green and blue. This is explained in Section 15.3.

Speaking on the telephone

A device which changes a set of waves from one medium to another, we call a **transducer**. Telephones are devices that take in sound waves and turn them into electrical waves (Figure 3). The electrical waves have roughly the same shape and duration as the sound waves which enter the telephone. They also have roughly the same frequencies. However, the highest frequency notes are missing. This is why voices sound

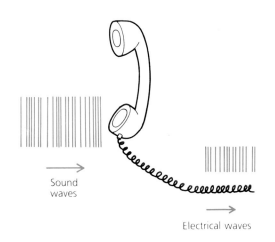

Fig. 3 A telephone converts sound waves into electrical waves
The earpiece converts electrical waves into sound waves. How? (See Section 13.2)

different over the telephone. (By limiting the **bandwidth** in this way, it is possible to send more telephone calls over the same cables.)

Radio waves

The frequencies of radio waves are much greater than those of sound waves. How then can we use radio broadcasts to carry sound?

Medium-wave, short-wave and long-wave broadcasts use **amplitude modulation** (AM) (Figure 4). The amplitude of the radio waves changes with the incoming sound. It forms a second, low-frequency wave called the **signal wave**. The high-frequency radio wave is called the **carrier wave**.

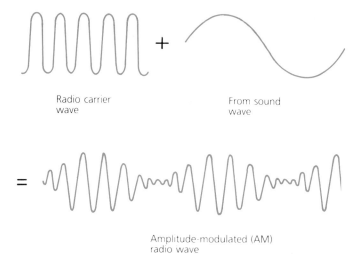

Fig. 4 Amplitude modulation of radio waves
Is this diagram to scale? (How do the frequencies of radio waves and sound waves compare in practice?)

VHF broadcasts use **frequency modulation** (FM). Instead of the amplitude of the waves altering to provide the signal, it is the frequency that is altered.

Using diffraction to explore molecules

Waves allow us to communicate with each other. They also allow us to explore the world around us. For example, scientists use diffraction to study crystals. When crystals are bombarded by X-rays, diffraction patterns are produced. From these patterns, scientists can work out the structure of the molecules which make up the crystals. It was in this way that the structure of DNA was determined, and this has led to genetic engineering. (DNA is the chemical which controls living cells.)

By understanding waves, we are better able to gather or control the information that they are carrying.

● **How can you communicate with someone without using waves?**

Fig. 5 The structure of DNA
What is DNA?
How was its structure discovered?

Bats

Fig. 1 Why do bats have large ears?
Why are they shaped in this way? How does a bat use its ears?

When you go for a walk in a wood, you don't keep bumping into trees. You can see them. Light bounces off the trees into your eyes.

Windows are not so easy to see. Many birds break their necks flying into closed window panes. Yet this never happens to bats. Indeed, bats never bump into anything—even when they fly in pitch darkness. **Why?**

The reason is that bats send out ultrasonic waves and listen for echoes. They can work out where things are from the direction of the echo and the time that the echo takes to reach them (Figure 2). (Ultrasonic waves are sound waves with frequencies too high for us to hear.)

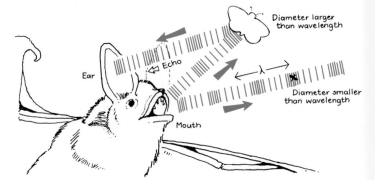

Fig. 2 Bats navigate by echoes
The bat can only detect objects which are larger than the wavelength of the ultrasound.
Given that the velocity of sound in air is 330 m/s, what frequency would be needed to detect a wire 1 mm in diameter?

Distances and the speed of sound

According to Section 2.1, Equation (1), distance = speed × time. So to find out how far the sound has travelled, a bat needs to multiply the speed of sound in air (about 330 m/s) by the time interval between the sound going out and its echo returning. For example, if it takes 0.02 seconds for the echo to return, then the sound has travelled 330 m/s × 0.02 s = 6.6 m. This means that the object is 3.3 m away. (The sound has to travel there and back.)

Of course, bats don't need calculators for this—their brains work it out subconsciously (by instinct).

● **This method can be used to measure the speed of sound. You could do this by timing how long it takes for an echo to return from a wall. You would then need to measure the distance to the wall.**

The disadvantage of doing this is that the time between making the noise and hearing the echo will be very short. So the time will be very difficult to measure. One way round this is to clap two pieces of wood together so that the echo lies midway between the claps. Time 10 claps. What must you divide this time by to get the interval between a clap and its echo?

Try this several times, and get other people to try it. How close are the results
(a) to each other?
(b) to 330 m/s?

Other uses of echoes

Surveyors measuring rooms in houses sometimes use a device that bounces ultrasonic waves off walls. This is quicker and easier than using a measuring tape.

Blind people can be helped to 'see' with ultrasonic 'torches'. These torches bounce ultrasonic waves off nearby objects. They produce a whine which increases in pitch (frequency) as objects get nearer to the torch.

Ships bounce sound waves off the bottom of the sea. This tells them the depth of the sea (Figure 3). Sound waves used in this way are called **sonar**. (SONAR stands for <u>SO</u>und <u>N</u>avigation <u>A</u>nd <u>R</u>anging.) Sonar is also used by warships to detect submarines, and by fishermen to find shoals of fish.

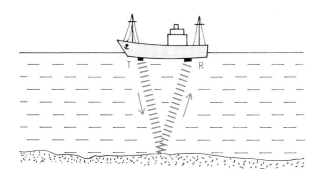

Fig. 3 Using sound to find the bottom of the sea
What else can a ship find using sonar?

Geologists looking for oil sometimes send vibrations down into the Earth by using vibrators or explosions. Such vibrations are called seismic waves. The waves are reflected back to the surface from the various layers of rock deep down in the ground. The time taken for the reflected waves to reach different points on the surface is recorded using special sensors. In this way, geologists find out the shape and spacing of the underground rocks (Figure 4).

Fig. 4 One way of looking for oil!
The lorries are sending vibrations into the ground. Sensors at the side of the road detect the vibrations and any echoes. How does this help geologists to find oil?

Police reflect microwaves off cars to check how fast the cars are travelling. Airports do the same thing with aircraft. We call this **radar** (<u>RA</u>dio <u>D</u>etection <u>A</u>nd <u>R</u>anging). Many traffic lights use radar to detect approaching vehicles.

Fig. 5 Are they driving too fast?
How does a radar speed detector work?

229

Colours that aren't in the rainbow

Fig. 1 Some colours are not in the rainbow
How are they produced?

Whereas every colour in the rainbow has a definite frequency, colours in general only exist in our minds!

Here are two ways of showing this:

- **Place a small piece of strongly coloured red card on a larger sheet of white paper. Stare intensely at it for at least a minute. Now quickly remove it. What do you see?**

- **Shine a beam of red light and a beam of green light on to a screen. What happens where the beams overlap? What happens if you cast shadows of your fingers on this area of the screen?**

How we see colour

In our eyes we have cells of two different shapes:
1 Sensitive rod-shaped cells that help us to see in the dark. These cells cannot detect colours. This is why we only see shades of grey after dark.
2 Three types of cone-shaped cells that allow us to see colours. Some of these cells are mainly sensitive to *red* light, some to *green* light and the remainder to *blue* light.

Physicists call these three colours—red, green and blue—the **primary** colours. **What are the artist's primary colours?**

Additive mixing

So far as our eyes and brain are concerned, yellow equals red + green. Yellow lies between red/orange and green in the spectrum. It therefore has an equal effect on our red cells and our green cells (Figure 2).

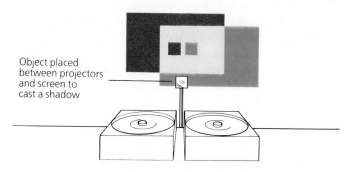

Object placed between projectors and screen to cast a shadow

Fig. 2 What is happening here?
Light from red and green projectors has produced yellow. Where have the red and green shadows come from?

When we see a yellow object, it could be giving off yellow light $(520 \times 10^{12}\,\text{Hz})$ or it could be giving off red and green light together $(460 \times 10^{12}\,\text{Hz}$ and $580 \times 10^{12}\,\text{Hz})$. We have no way of knowing.

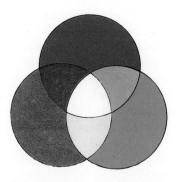

Fig. 3 Additive mixing
This shows what happens when beams from three projectors are shone on to a screen through a red filter, a green filter and a blue filter. What would happen if the red projector were placed nearer the screen than the others? (Try this if you can—perhaps with torches instead of projectors.)

Figure 3 gives some other examples of this **additive mixing**. It shows what happens when you shine red, green and blue lights on to a screen. The colours formed—yellow, magenta (reddish purple) and cyan (greenish blue)—are called **secondary** colours.

Notice that when you add all three primary colours together, you get white light. (You don't have to add all the colours of the spectrum.)

Colour television

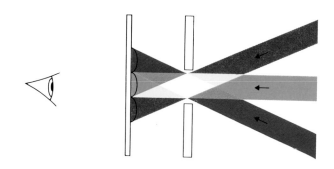

Fig. 4 How a colour television works
Most microcomputer monitors can only produce six colours (other than black and white). What are these six colours? How are they produced?

Figure 4 shows how colour is produced in a colour television. All the colours that we see on the screen are produced by adding the light from red, green and blue **phosphors**.

● **Colour monitors work in the same way. Why do you think that the lead from a computer to a colour monitor is called an 'RGB' lead?**

Subtractive mixing

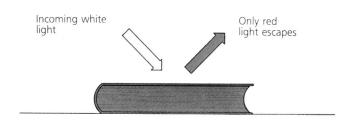

Fig. 5 Why the book is red
The books absorbs blue and green light. What colour would it appear in (i) red light? (ii) green light? (iii) yellow light?

Coloured paints act like filters. They remove some of the light falling on them. For example, cyan paint removes all light except blue and green. Yellow paint removes all light except red, yellow and green.

If cyan and yellow paints are mixed, the only colour of light that the paint doesn't absorb is green. So far as paints (and filters) are concerned, cyan + yellow = green. This is called **subtractive mixing**.

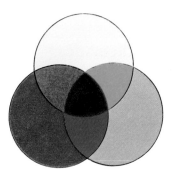

Fig. 6 Subtractive mixing
Light is being removed by the cyan, magenta and yellow inks.
Many leaves are deep green. What colours of light are they absorbing?

Figure 6 shows what happens when you mix the secondary colours cyan, magenta and yellow. Any two of these colours together produce one of the primary colours of physics. All three together remove all light, leaving the 'colour' black. **This is the ideal situation. Is it exactly true in practice? Try it. What happens when you mix blue and yellow paint? Why are the artist's primary colours red, blue and *yellow*?**

A black object absorbs all the light falling on it. A white object reflects all the light. The reason why it appears white and not silvery, like a mirror, is that it scatters the light in different directions.

The colour of an object depends on the light falling on it

If no red light falls on a red object, it cannot reflect red light. The object will then appear black. If only red light falls on a white surface, it will appear red. This is why some people take dress fabrics out of a shop to look at them in daylight.

● **What colour will a yellow object appear in cyan light? Try it.**

These are some of the basic principles of colour mixing. The physics of colour is not simple. But it is of great importance to fabric designers and many other people.

15.4 Making music

Music and mathematics

Fig. 1 Singing the same note an octave apart
What is the ratio of the frequencies?

Music is meaningful sound. Musical notes have a definite **pitch** and sound well together. (Noise is just a lot of random sounds that don't carry any message.)

High-pitched sounds have higher frequencies than low-pitched sounds. **How could you demonstrate this? (One way might be to use the wheels of a bicycle. How?)**

Musical notes that sound well together have frequencies in a simple ratio. Suppose, for example, that a man and a woman sing the same note an octave (eight notes) apart. The frequency of the note sung by the woman is twice that of the note sung by the man. The ratio of the frequencies is 2:1. (The notes C and G on the piano also sound well together. Their frequencies are approximately in the ratio 2:3.)

Musical scales

Music in different parts of the world is based on different scales. A scale is a set of notes of definite, increasing frequency. Most English and European music uses a repeating seven-note scale (the white notes on a piano—Figure 2).

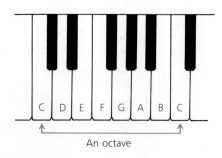

An octave

Fig. 2 A piano keyboard

In the past, there has been disagreement over the actual frequencies used for each note. There is now a standard frequency for A of 440 Hz. This is the note A to which orchestras tune before a concert. If you listen to Radio 3, you will sometimes hear this note between transmissions.

Scottish, and some African, folk songs use a five-note scale (for example the black notes on the piano). In some other parts of the world, different scales are used—some of them with many more notes. We tend to get used to one particular scale and often find that other scales and music sound strange.

Controlling the pitch of an instrument

The pitch of a string instrument depends on the length of the vibrating string. The pitch of a wind instrument depends on the length of the column of air. Long piano strings produce low notes. So do long organ pipes and long brass instruments in which air is vibrating.

The pitch of a stringed instrument depends also on the mass-per-unit length of the string and the tension. The strings that give the lower notes on a guitar or violin are much thicker than those which give the higher notes. The note given by each string can be raised or lowered by tightening or loosening the string. (A man's voice is lower than a woman's voice because his vocal chords are less taut.)

● **Try making a milk-bottle organ. Stand several milk bottles in a row and pour a different amount of water into each bottle. Then blow over the top** of each bottle in turn. The shorter the air column, the higher the frequency and therefore the higher the pitch of the note. Try making some other musical instruments on which you can play a simple tune.

Fig. 3 A West-African xylophone
The gourds underneath resonate when you hit the wooden bars. What does 'resonate' mean?
Some bars have been thinned in the middle to lower their pitch. How does this work? How would you raise their pitch?

Loudness

The loudness of a sound depends on its amplitude (the increase in air pressure as the sound wave passes). But the loudness isn't the same as the amplitude. Doubling or trebling the amplitude makes only a relatively small difference to the loudness. The loudness of sounds is measured in **decibels** (dB) (Figure 4). The quietest sound that we can hear is 0 dB. A pneumatic drill produces about 100 dB, but the amplitude of this is 100 000 times greater than that of the quietest sound!

Fig. 4

Sound	Approximate loudness in decibels (dB)
Enough to cause permanent ear damage	140
Threshold of pain	130
Jet engine	120
Pneumatic drill	110
Someone shouting	100
Noisy office	90
People talking loudly	80
Telephone ringing nearby	70
People talking normally	60
A restaurant	50
A quiet street	40
A whisper	30
A library	20
A pin drop	10
Quietest sound you can hear (threshold of hearing)	0

Waveform

Sounds differ in quality (as you will know from hearing different people sing!) 'Quality' here doesn't just mean 'good notes and bad notes'. The quality (or timbre) of the sound of a piano is different from that of a violin, even though the sounds may be equally pleasant.

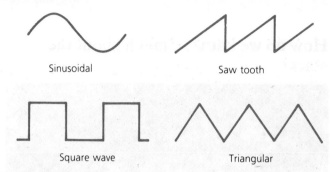

Fig. 5 Different waveforms
If these wave shapes are sent, as electrical waves, to a loudspeaker, what effect do they have on the sound produced?

The quality depends on the shape of the wave (the **waveform**) as shown in Figure 5. You can get an idea of the waveform by using an oscilloscope and a microphone as shown in Figure 6. (The oscilloscope measures the voltage output of the microphone and displays it as a graph.)

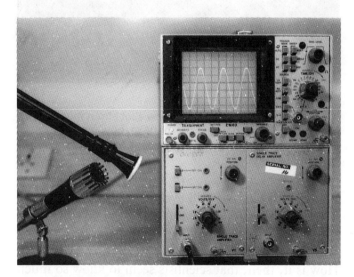

Fig. 6 Looking at the sound of a recorder
Sound is a longitudinal wave. The waves shown on the oscilloscope are transverse. Why is this?

There is a tremendous amount of physics in music. This is a very brief introduction. Try to find out more about this for yourself.

A message from space

How do we know so much about the stars?

Fig. 1 The Andromeda Nebulae
Astronomers believe that they know a lot about most of the stars in the sky—what they are made of, how far away they are, how old they are, and so on.
How do they know?

It's unlikely that we will ever go to the stars. All we know about them is what can see (or detect) through a telescope. We can't even make out their shape, as we can with the Moon. They are just pin-pricks of light.

How is it, then, that scientists seem to know so much about the stars? They believe that they know what the stars are made of, how big they are, how far away they are and how fast they are travelling. How do they know this?

The only thing that reaches us from these stars is electromagnetic radiation but this can tell us a tremendous amount.

Spectroscopy

Fig. 2 A spectrometer used to study spectra
This instrument produces a very clear spectrum that can then be measured.
How can white light from the Sun or a star be split into a spectrum?

The light from the stars can be split up to form a coloured spectrum using a machine called a **spectrometer** (Figure 2).

When different elements are heated until they glow, the spectrums that they produce are slightly different. Not all frequencies of light are present. Some frequencies are given off more strongly than others. For example, the hot sodium in streetlights gives off more yellow light than any other colour. Very hot copper gives off mainly green light.

By carefully sorting out the total spectrum of light (and other electromagnetic radiation) from a star, you can tell what it is that is glowing on that star. You can tell which elements are present on the star, and which of them are most abundant.

Measuring the temperature of a star

The hottest stars give out mainly X-ray radiation. The coldest objects in space give out only radio waves. By seeing which type of radiation a star gives out most strongly, you can work out the temperature of the star.

Measuring the speed of a star

When a fire-engine is racing towards you with its siren blaring, you hear a high-pitched sound. As it passes you, the pitch falls. The faster it travels away from you, the lower in pitch the sound becomes. (This is called the **Doppler effect** after the nineteenth century Austrian physicist, Christian Doppler, who explained why it occurs.)

The same effect occurs with light. If a star is travelling away from us, the spectrum that it produces decreases in frequency. (We call this the **red shift**—the colours shift towards the red end of the spectrum.)

Astronomers have found that the light from *all* stars has this red shift. This suggests that they are speeding away from us! Astronomers believe that the whole universe is expanding like a giant balloon. This suggestion arose from the work of an American astronomer, Edwin Hubble. We call it the **Hubble theory** (Figure 3).

The stars furthest away from us are moving away fastest. So by measuring the speed at which a star is travelling away from us, we can tell how far away it is. Since light from these distant stars takes a very long time to reach us, we are also looking back into history. Scientists believe that when they look at some of the most distant stars they may be looking back to the dawn of history—the **big bang**.

Following Newton

Newton believed that the same forces exist in space as on Earth. (In other words, he believed that gravity exists in space—see Chapter 1.) Today, we believe that most of the physics of our world is also true for the most distant stars. Using our knowledge of physics and chemistry, we are able to work out the mass of each star, the reactions occurring in it and its probable age.

So next time you are at the coast and see waves coming in to the shore, just think: it is waves coming to us from space that tell us all we know about our universe.

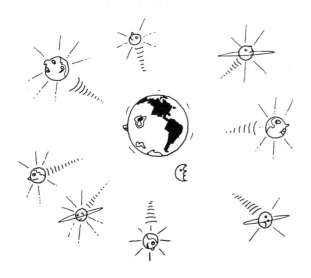

Fig. 3 The rest of the universe is rushing away from us
What reason do we have for believing this? Does it mean that there is something special about us?

Fig. 4 We can learn a lot from waves
What sort of waves can we use to explore the universe?
What can we learn from waves coming to us from space?
From things around us? From the people around us?

235

Exercises

1 The pitch of a note is determined by its

   A Wave speed

   B Wave shape

   C Amplitude

   D Frequency

   E Wavelength

2 An echo is produced when waves are

   A Focused

   B Refracted

   C Diffracted

   D Reflected

   E Made to interfere

3 Ultrasonic waves are

   A Any waves that produce echoes

   B Sound waves of frequency above the audible range

   C Waves produced by high-speed aircraft

   D High-frequency electromagnetic waves

   E Low-frequency electromagnetic waves

Fig. 1 What affects the frequency?

236

4 Which of the following does *not* affect the frequency of sound produced by a violin?

   A The mass per unit length of the strings

   B The length of the strings

   C The amount by which the string is pulled from its mean position

   D The tension in the string

5 Sound travels through seawater with a velocity of 1500 m/s. A ship sends a pulse vertically downwards. An echo is received from the sea bottom 2 s later. The depth of the water under the ship is

   A 375 m

   B 750 m

   C 1500 m

   D 3000 m

   E 6000 m

6 A card appears to be dark blue when it is seen in white light. In yellow light, it will appear to be

   A Green

   B Blue

   C Yellow

   D Black

   E White

7 Complete these sentences:

   a Bats navigate using _____ waves. They send out pulses of these waves that are _____ by trees and buildings. The distance between a tree and the bat is equal to _____ the _____ of the waves multiplied by the time taken between sending out the waves and receiving the echo.

   b The screen of a colour television has three types of phosphors (chemicals that glow when cathode rays hit them). These phosphors glow with the colours _____, _____. and _____. The colour yellow is produced when the _____ and _____ phosphors glow together at any part of the screen.

8 **a** List the primary colours of physics.

b List the secondary colours of physics.

c List the colours of the spectrum in order of increasing wavelength.

9 A man sees an explosion in a nearby quarry. Two seconds later he hears the sound. Another two seconds later, he hears an echo from a cliff behind the quarry.

a Given that sound travels through air at 330 m/s, how far is the man from
i the quarry?
ii the cliff behind the quarry?

b The man sees the explosion because light waves have reached him from the explosion. Why, then, is it not necessary to use the speed of light when answering **a**?

Fig. 2

10 A '16-foot' organ pipe produces sound with a wavelength of 10 m.

a What is the frequency of the sound produced, given that the speed of sound in air is 330 m/s?

b What would be the frequency from an '8-foot' organ pipe sounding the same note in a different octave?

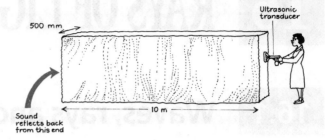

Fig. 3

11 The strength of concrete can be determined from the speed of sound in the concrete. An engineer sends a pulse of ultrasound through a wall of concrete 500 mm thick and receives an echo from the opposite face 0.0002 s later.

a What is the speed of sound in the concrete?

b She now sends a pulse lengthways through the wall, travelling 10 m to the far end as shown in Figure 3. If the speed of sound is the same as before (in other words, if the concrete is of uniform quality), how long will the echo take to return?

12 How do

a the loudness

b the pitch

c the quality

of a note from a plucked stringed instrument depend on
i the sound waves coming from the instrument?
ii the string being plucked, and the way it is plucked?

Fig. 4 Silk-screen printing

13 Explain the difference between the way colours are produced in a colour television set and the way they are produced by the mixing of pigments (dies) to make a screen print.

16 RAYS OF LIGHT

16.1 Waves, rays and laser beams

Using lasers

Fig. 1 A laser
How are lasers used in medicine, in industry and in homes and shops?

Lasers are an important part of modern technology. They have many different uses:

• They are used in the check-outs of some supermarkets for reading bar-code labels.
• They are used in compact disc players.
• They are used to cut cloth in some clothing factories.
• They are used for eye operations in hospitals, and for other operations where there is a danger of too much bleeding. (The heat from the laser seals the wound and stops it from bleeding.)
• Tiny semiconductor lasers are used to send telephone messages along optical fibres.
• Soldiers use lasers for range finding. (The Strategic Defence Initiative ('Star Wars') proposals include X-rays and powerful infrared lasers capable of shooting down rockets.)

What is a laser?

A laser beam is a light beam. (LASER stands for Light Amplification by the Stimulated Emission of Radiation.) Unlike the light from a torch, the light from a laser forms a very narrow, very powerful beam. Scientists can bounce light from a laser off the Moon and back to Earth. This isn't possible with a torch!

Laser beams are narrow and powerful because the light waves are in step. All the light waves have the same wavelength, and they are all **in phase** (they all start at the same time—Figure 2). Each atom in a laser gives out a train of waves in step with the waves from other atoms.

In contrast, the light from a torch contains waves of many different wavelengths. Individual atoms in the bulb of a torch give out short bursts of light waves. The waves from different atoms are of different wavelengths, and are not in phase.

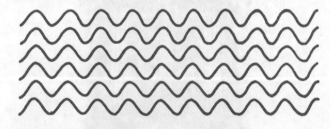

(a) Laser beam

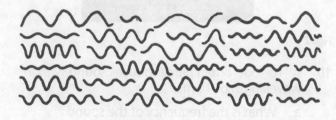

(b) Torch beam

Fig. 2 Laser beams are light beams
But laser beams are very different from ordinary light beams. In what way?

A laser is like a ray of light

In physics, a ray of light is represented by a line. Light rays show the direction in which light waves are travelling. Figure 3 shows what this means for **plane** and **circular** waves. When you are looking at a ray diagram, it is sometimes useful to picture the rays as laser beams. Rays of light behave in the same way as laser beams.

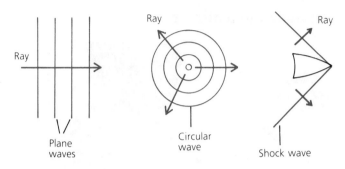

Fig. 3 Waves and rays
The rays show the direction in which the waves travel.

Ray boxes

Lasers are expensive. They are also dangerous. If a powerful laser beam enters your eye, it can seriously damage your retina and may blind you. Ray boxes are a lot cheaper and a lot safer. A ray box consists of a light bulb placed behind one or more slits in a piece of metal (Figure 4). Although the light beams produced don't behave quite as well as laser beams, they demonstrate the reflection and refraction of light quite well.

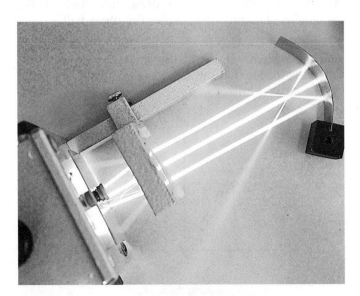

Fig. 4 A ray box being used to demonstrate reflection
How else could you demonstrate the reflection of light?

• Try using a ray box to see what happens when a light ray
  (a) hits a plane (straight) mirror at an angle
  (b) passes at an angle through a rectangular block of glass.

Why use rays?

Why bother using rays? Why not stick to waves? The reason is that wave diagrams soon become very complicated. Ray diagrams make it easier to understand how cameras, microscopes, telescopes, projectors and other pieces of optical equipment work.

To take a simple example, consider the bent ruler shown in Figure 5. In terms of waves, it is difficult to understand why the ruler appears to be bent. Using rays, it is much easier. The light coming from the lower part of the ruler is refracted at the water surface. So this part of the ruler appears to be higher up than it really is. For the same reason, the water looks shallower than it really is.

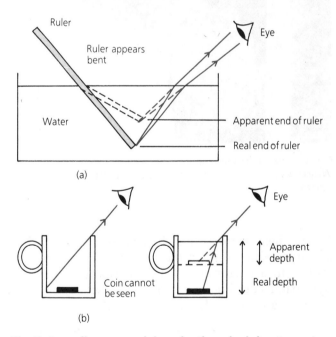

Fig. 5 A ray diagram explains why the ruler is bent
What relevance does this have to someone about to wade across a shallow-looking river?

• **The water in a swimming pool looks much shallower than it really is. So does water in a bowl or a fish tank. How could you measure the apparent depth of a fish tank? (The apparent depth is how deep it seems when seen from directly above.)**

239

Mirror, mirror on the wall

O wad some Pow'r the giftie gie us
To see oursels as others see us!
Robert Burns, *To a louse*

Fig. 1 Looking in a mirror
Why does your right hand appear as your left hand in the mirror?

Mirrors help us to see ourselves as others see us—but not quite. Our image in the mirror is the wrong way round. In a mirror, our left-hand side becomes our right-hand side (Figure 1). In science, we say that our image in a mirror is **laterally inverted**.

- **What is mirror writing? How does it differ from ordinary writing?**

- **Have a look at yourself in a mirror. What do you notice about your image? Does it look larger or smaller than you? How far away is it? What happens to your image as you move nearer to the mirror? What about the image of your feet? How much do you have to angle the mirror to see your feet? If you keep the mirror upright instead of angling it, where do you have to put it to see an image of your feet?**

An image in a mirror

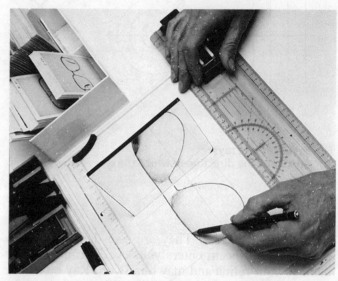

Fig. 2 A spectacle designer making use of a mirror
How can you use a mirror to draw one line perpendicular to another?

Figure 2 shows a spectacle designer using a plane mirror. He only needs to draw one half of the spectacles. The mirror provides the other half.

Figure 3 shows what happens to a ray of light when it reaches a mirror. If the ray hits the mirror at an angle, then it is reflected at the same angle. This is true even with a curved mirror.

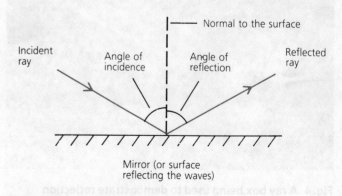

Fig. 3 The laws of reflection

- The **normal** to the surface is a line drawn at right-angles to the surface
- The **angle of incidence** is the angle between the incoming (incident) ray and the normal
- The **angle of reflection** is the angle between the reflected ray and the normal

> 1 The incident ray, the reflected ray and the normal are in the same plane. (If you hold a piece of card so that the two rays lie along the surface, then the normal will also lie along the surface.)
>
> 2 The angle of incidence is equal to the angle of reflection.

These are called the **laws of reflection. Check them, using a ray box. Do rubber balls obey these laws of reflection? Do snooker balls? Try it and see.**

Figure 4 shows how the mirror produces an image of the spectacles. Rays of light from each part of the spectacles are reflected by the mirror into the designer's eyes. These rays seem to be coming from behind the mirror. The image isn't real. There aren't really any rays coming from behind the mirror. We call such an image a **virtual image**.

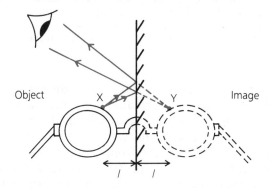

X is a point on the object distance *l* in front of mirror.

Y is the corresponding point on the image distance *l* behind mirror.

Fig. 4 How the mirror copies the picture
The image it produces is virtual. What does this mean?

Figure 4 also shows why the image in the mirror is the same size as the object, but laterally inverted.

- **Why, when you look in a mirror, do you see yourself flipped over from side to side, but not from top to bottom (as though you were standing on your head)?**
- **Use a ray box to look at rays forming an image in a mirror. Draw lines back along the reflected rays to find the position of the image.**

Other uses for mirrors

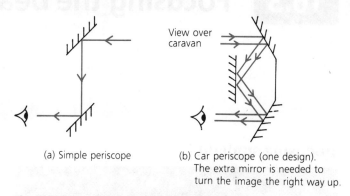

(a) Simple periscope

(b) Car periscope (one design). The extra mirror is needed to turn the image the right way up.

Fig. 5 Using reflection to produce a periscope
The periscopes used in submarines use prisms rather than mirrors. What is the advantage of this? (See Section 16.6.)

Cars have several mirrors which allow the driver to see the road behind. These have to be set at the correct angles. Cars towing caravans are sometimes fitted with a periscope. This enables the driver to see over the top of the caravan. Figure 5 shows how this periscope works.

- **Try making such a periscope. Then try making the kaleidoscope shown in Figure 6. How does this work? Where else are plane mirrors used?**

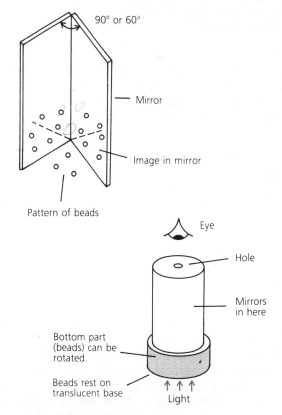

Fig. 6 A kaleidoscope makes beautiful patterns
How does it work?

Focusing the beam

Focusing sunlight

Fig. 1 Cooking with sunlight
This simple solar cooker was able to cook a cake! Why do the curved mirrors increase the temperature of the food? Why aren't there many solar cookers in tropical countries?

Fig. 2 Most astronomical telescopes use curved mirrors
This photograph shows the final polishing of the giant 4.2 m diameter mirror of the William Herschel telescope. It is believed to be the most accurately shaped mirror in the world.

Have you ever noticed what happens to a sandwich left out in the sun after a picnic? The bread goes dry and the butter becomes liquid. Suppose that the Sun were much hotter than it really is. Instead of drying out the sandwich, it would cook it!

In fact, sunlight *can* be used to cook food. If rays of sunlight are concentrated on to a small area, then that area becomes very hot. One way of concentrating sunlight is to focus it using a concave (inward curving) mirror (Figure 1). Ideally, the mirror should be parabolic (it should have a parabolic rather than a circular section). Parallel light from the Sun is reflected from the mirror to a point. This point, called the **principal focus** of the mirror, is where you put your food.

A solar cooker like this sounds ideal for people living in the Tropics. Just think of all the gas and electricity you'd save! If people in developing countries didn't need wood or charcoal to cook with, then they wouldn't have to cut down so many forests. Unfortunately, it's not that simple. Most people want a hot meal after the Sun has set, not in the middle of the day. **How could you overcome this problem?**

The amount of light reaching us from very distant stars is so small that we cannot normally see them. Many of the telescopes that scientists use to look at these stars have large concave parabolic mirrors (Figure 2). These mirrors concentrate the light from a star on to one point—the principal focus of the mirror. A very sensitive photographic film is placed at the principal focus for several hours. Over this time, an image of the star is built up.

Satellite stations use parabolic mirrors to collect very weak radio signals from satellites. Telecommunications relay stations use parabolic mirrors to focus microwaves coming from other distant stations. In both cases, the rays are focused on to a small receiver at the principal focus of the mirror.

- **Try using a concave mirror to cast an image of a distant light on to a sheet of paper.**

- **Look at yourself in a concave mirror**
  (a) with it held near your face
  (b) holding it some way from your face.
  Does it act like a plane mirror? Try to explain what is happening.

Headlight beams

Car lights use concave mirrors in a different way. The source of light—the headlamp bulb—is placed near the principal focus. Light from the bulb is reflected from the parabolic mirror as a beam of light (Figure 3).

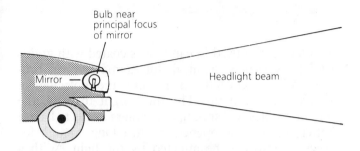

Fig. 3 Headlights use parabolic mirrors
Why?

Torches also have curved reflectors. On some torches, you can move the position of the reflector by screwing the end of the torch in or out. When the bulb is at the principal focus of the reflector, the torch gives a narrow, parallel beam. But when you move the bulb a short distance from the principal focus, the beam spreads out.

Parabolic reflectors are also found in some small electric and gas heaters. Heat is reflected into the room as a beam of infra-red radiation (Figure 4).

Similarly, the Post Office Tower and other telecommunications stations have parabolic transmitters (see Section 14.6). These send parallel beams of microwaves to the receiving dish at the next station.

Fig. 5 Concave mirrors can cause problems
What has this got to do with domed concert halls?

Fig. 4 Focusing the heat
What is the heat radiation that we can feel coming from this heater? How does this differ from the solar cooker described in Figure 2?

Concave reflectors can occur where we don't want them. For example, domed buildings like the Royal Albert Hall in London focus sound (Figure 5). This can be a nuisance—you don't usually want the sound from an orchestra to be focused into one part of the concert hall. The focusing effect of concave reflectors is something that architects and a lot of other people need to take into account.

- **Have a look at someone's ears. Why do we have big, ungainly ears rather than just simple holes in our heads? Which parts of the ear might be acting as parabolic reflectors? Is there any advantage in our ears having such a complicated shape? (Would it be better if they were just like microwave receivers, focusing sound to a point inside our heads?)**

A pinhole camera

Fig. 1 How does a camera work?

The simplest type of camera is a pinhole camera. It consists of a box with a small hole in it (Figure 2). Rays from the top of the object being photographed reach only the bottom of the film. Rays from the bottom of the object reach the top of the film. Thus the film receives an inverted (upside down) picture of the object being photographed.

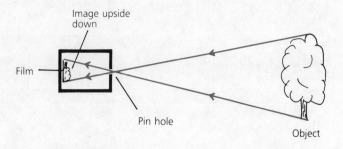

Fig. 2 A pinhole camera
This has one advantage over a lens camera. What is it?

244

The type of film used in cameras is coated with grains of a light-sensitive chemical (for example, silver bromide). When light falls on the film, the molecules of this chemical split up. The more light there is, the more molecules will split up. A camera needs to have a shutter that can be opened for just long enough for sufficient grains to be affected by the light. With a pinhole camera, the hole needs to be open for about a second. You can do this with your finger.

Once it has been exposed, the film needs to be processed. First it is **developed** to bring out the image. Then it is **fixed** so that light no longer affects it.

- **Try taking some photographs with a pinhole camera using photographic printing paper instead of normal film.**

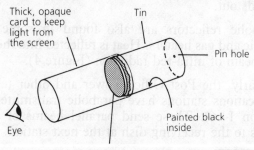

Fig. 3 A pinhole camera with a viewing screen
See if you can design a better version of this

- **Instead of a film, try using a screen as shown in Figure 3. If you keep the back of the camera shaded, it is possible to see an image of a very bright object (for example, a sunlit tree or a candle flame) on the screen. Once you have seen this image, make a second pinhole so that you have two holes instead of one. What do you see on the screen this time? Now make a large number of holes, covering an area the size of a 5 pence piece. What do you see now? What do you see if you punch out this area to leave a large, 5-pence-sized hole? Is there a way of producing a single, bright but unblurred, image?**

A lens camera

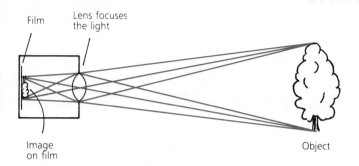

Fig. 4 How a lens camera works
Does it matter what lens you use? Why?

A convex (outward-bulging) lens allows you to use a larger hole that lets in more light. You can then use shorter exposure times. (This is essential for photographing moving objects.)

The lens focuses the rays passing through the hole (Figure 4). It produces a clear inverted image a certain distance from the lens. This is where you place your film.

When distant objects are being photographed, the distance from the image to the film is called the **focal length** of the lens. The lens of a modern camera has a very short focal length. This gives you a small, compact camera. (The focal length also affects the magnification. Telephoto lenses used for photographing objects a long way away have very long focal lengths.)

- **Bottles containing liquid act as very powerful lenses with short focal lengths. Why, when you look through such bottles from a distance, do they seem to turn things the wrong way round (Figure 5)? Why is the image distorted?**

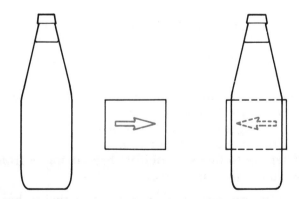

Fig. 5 Why is the arrow the wrong way round?
The bottle of water turns the arrow the wrong way round. How does it do this? Would it turn a vertical arrow upside down? Why?

Which camera is best?

The pinhole camera doesn't let much light on to the film. It needs long exposure times, and so it cannot be used for moving objects. However, it has the advantage that it doesn't need focusing. Every part of the image is always in focus. We say that the camera has a large **depth of focus**.

A camera with a large lens can be used in dull weather, and it can take photographs of moving objects. Its disadvantage is that it needs careful focusing.

In practice, most cameras are somewhere between these two extremes. Cheap cameras have a small lens that allows you to photograph slowly moving objects, but with a reasonable depth of focus. More-expensive cameras allow you to adjust the size of the hole (or **aperture**) using an **iris diaphragm** (Figure 6).

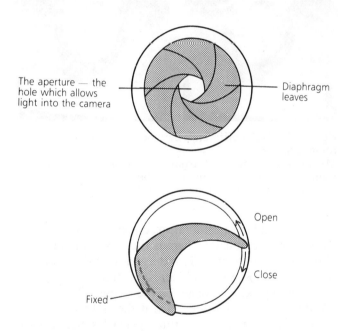

Fig. 6 How an iris diaphragm works
Why do expensive cameras use iris diaphragms? These cameras use a stop number to describe the aperture. For example, a stop of f/8 means that the aperture diameter is one-eighth of the focal length of the lens.
What do we mean by the focal length?

- **Explain the size of aperture—large or small—that you would use for the following:**
  - **(a) A photograph in a dark wood**
  - **(b) A photograph of a friend, with a waterfall some way behind him**
  - **(c) A portrait where you wanted to see the person, but not the background**
  - **(d) A photograph of a speeding car.**

245

The eyes have it

Fig. 1 What is the difference between these two photographs?
Many people think that the girl looks more attractive in the right-hand picture. Why might this be?
What relevance does this have to the use of cameras?

Eyes are similar to cameras except that they have two lenses. On the outside, there is the clear bulging front of the eye—the cornea. This does most of the focusing. Inside the eye is a second lens. This finishes the job of focusing to produce images on the retina. The image is upside down—our brains turn it the right way up. A researcher once tried wearing spectacles that turned things upside down. At first, he saw things upside down but after several months his brain adapted. He then only saw things upside down when he took the spectacles off!

The more a lens bulges, the more powerful it becomes (the shorter its focal length becomes). The lens in our eye can be stretched and made thinner to focus distant objects. It can also be made thick to focus near objects. Short-sighted people cannot stretch their lenses enough. Long-sighted people cannot bulge them enough. These people need extra lenses so they wear spectacles or contact lenses.

Our eyes have an aperture (a hole) called the pupil, surrounded by an iris diaphragm. At night or in a dark

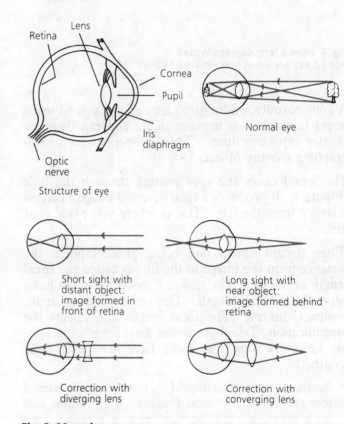

Fig. 2 Many lenses
Our eyes have two lenses each. Where are they?
What is meant by short-sightedness and long-sightedness?

room, this aperture dilates (gets larger). This also happens when we are concentrating on something or someone when it doesn't matter that everything else is out of focus.

- **Have a look into someone's eyes. Watch what happens to the pupils when**
  (a) the light is turned on or off
  (b) they concentrate on you.
  Then try to focus on objects behind and in front of you at the same time.

- **In pictures, girls appear more attractive to boys (and boys to girls) when their pupils are made larger. Is this because the girl, or boy, seems to be more interested in you?**

A magnifying glass

A camera lens produces a small image of whatever is being photographed. However, lenses can be used to make things appear larger. The magnifying glass is an example.

● **Hold a powerful lens so that its distance from your eye is about twice the focal length of the lens. Now put your other hand just behind the lens. Move it slowly away from you, keeping the lens still. What happens to the image of your hand seen through the lens? Why?**

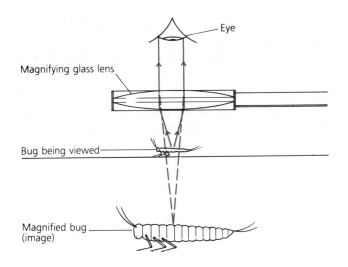

Fig. 3 How a magnifying glass works
Why isn't the image inverted as it was in Section 16.4, Fig. 5?

Figure 3 shows how a magnifying glass works. With the lens very near the object, the image is different from that in a camera. It is the right way up, and it is larger than the object.

Unfortunately, the image seen in a magnifying glass cannot be shown on a screen or on a photographic film. This is because there isn't really anything there. The image is where the rays of light *seem* to be coming from—like an image in a mirror. It is called a **virtual image**.

A projector

A projector produces a real, magnified image of a slide on a screen (Figure 4). The slide is strongly lit and placed upside down near the lens (just beyond the principal focus). The lens produces a large image on the distant screen. The lens also turns the image the right way up (the lens **inverts** the image).

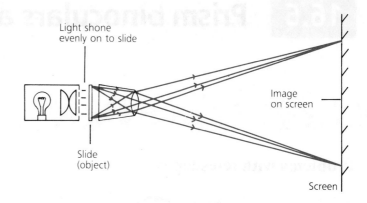

Fig. 4 How a projector works

Microscopes and telescopes

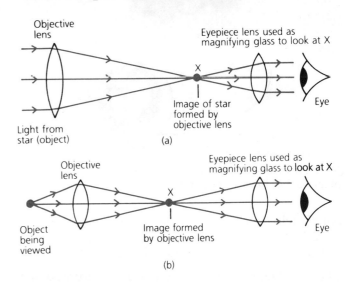

Fig. 5 Using two lenses together
(a) An astronomical telescope
(b) A microscope
Why are they different?

If you hold a lens some distance in front of another lens, you can get extra magnification (enlargement). The second lens magnifies the image produced by the first lens. This is how microscopes and telescopes work (Figure 5). The only difference between microscopes and telescopes is in the power of the lenses. In telescopes, the **eyepiece lens** nearer your eye is much more powerful than the **objective lens** nearer the object. In microscopes, both lenses are powerful.

● **Using Figure 5 as a guide, try making**
  (a) a telescope with a short-focal-length lens and long-focal-length lens
  (b) a microscope using two short-focal-length lenses.

247

Problems with telescopes

Fig. 1 Prism binoculars and optical fibres
What do they have in common?

Simple telescopes have two big disadvantages:
1 To be powerful, they need to be very long
2 They turn everything upside down.

These problems aren't very serious if you are studying the Moon or stars using a telescope on a stand. (Indeed, maps of the Moon are printed upside down.) But, for a tank commander or a bird-watcher, a pair of binoculars 1 metre long that turned things upside down might not be ideal! One way of overcoming this problem is by using **total internal reflection**.

Fig. 2 Problems with telescopes

248

Total internal reflection

When light passes from a dense material to a less-dense material (for example, from glass to air), we always find that

1 Light bends away from the normal as it leaves the denser medium
2 Some of the light is reflected back. (See Section 16.2.)

As the angle of incidence increases, so does the angle of refraction. The refracted light gets weaker, whereas the reflected light gets stronger (Figure 3).

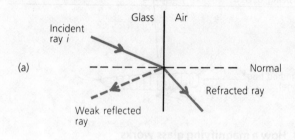

(a)

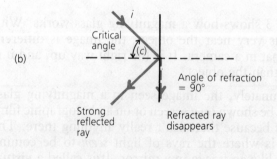

(b)

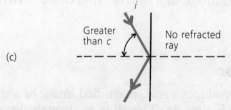

(c)

Fig. 3 Refraction of light when leaving glass
(a) Reflection and refraction
(b) The critical angle
(c) Total internal reflection
Why total *internal* reflection? Why *total* internal reflection?

Eventually the refracted ray would be along the surface but by this stage it has faded away altogether. At this point (when the angle of refraction is 90°) we say that the angle of incidence is equal to the **critical angle**. For glass, the critical angle is about 42°. (For water, it is about 49°.)

For angles of incidence larger than this critical angle, there is no refracted light. All the light is reflected. This is called **total internal reflection**.

- **How can you show this using a semicircular glass block? What is the advantage in using this rather than a rectangular glass block?**

Fig. 4 Demonstrating total internal reflection
Can you see
(i) a ray that is reflected and refracted?
(ii) a ray that is totally internally reflected?

(Notice the word 'internal'. The light is in the denser material, not outside in the air. Total internal reflection only occurs if the light is travelling from a denser to a less-dense medium—for example, from glass or water to air.)

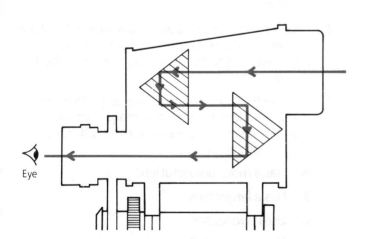

Fig. 5 How prisms are used in prism binoculars
Why aren't mirrors used instead?

Binoculars—folded telescopes

Total internal reflection enables telescopes to be made shorter. Binoculars are, in effect, folded telescopes. Prisms are used to reflect the light back and forth inside the binoculars (Figure 5). The prisms also turn the image the right way up.

You could do this using four mirrors but the image would be very dark. Mirrors are not very efficient reflectors. Some light is reflected from the front glass surface of the mirror as well as the silvered surface. Also a lot of light is absorbed at the silvered surface.

This problem doesn't arise with prisms. Very little light is reflected on entering and leaving the prism. (The light hits normal (at right-angles) to the surface and not at a glancing angle.) At the other surface we have total internal reflection (all light is reflected).

- **Set up the prism arrangement shown in Figure 5. First check that you have got it in line by using a ray box, then try looking through it. Are things seen through it inverted?**

Fibre optics

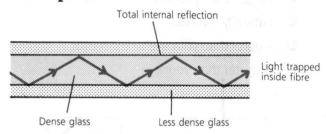

Fig. 6 Fibre optics
Where are fibre optic cables used? What is their advantage?

Optical fibres are glass fibres that act as light pipes. Light put in at one end is totally internally reflected by the fibre walls and so cannot escape until it reaches the other end.

Optical fibres are used to send telephone messages. They are much cheaper than copper wires and can carry far more messages. They can also be used to look inside people's bodies.

- **What would happen to the light passing through an optical fibre if, at one point, the fibre were folded fairly sharply back on itself (but not enough to break it)? What would you notice if you had an instrument to measure the amount of light reaching the end of the fibre? Suggest a technological use for this.**

- **If you have a suitable kit, try sending radio signals down an optical fibre.**

249

Exercises

1 A ray of light is

 A A beam of light

 B A line drawn perpendicular to the wavefronts

 C The part of the light that is reflected and refracted

 D The part of the light that carries radiation

 E The same thing as a light wave

2 The image of your eye seen in a plane mirror is

 A Smaller than your eye

 B Larger than your eye

 C Laterally inverted

 D Nearer than your eye to the mirror

 E Brighter than your eye

3 Figure 1 shows what can happen to a ray of white light directed towards one surface of a prism. Which of the rays coming from the prism is split into separate colours?

4 Which of the following does *not* use a concave mirror?

 A A microwave aerial

 B A radiant heater

 C A camera

 D Car headlights

 E A reflecting telescope

5 Which of the following is *not* true for a pinhole camera?

 A The image is smaller than the object being photographed.

 B The image is inverted.

 C The image is dimmer than that produced by a lens camera.

 D It is not suitable for photographing fast-moving objects.

 E The camera can only focus on one object at a time.

6 Figure 2 shows curved waves about to hit a plane barrier. Which of the diagrams A to E shows what happens to these waves after they have hit the barrier?

7 A projector produces an image larger than the object. In a lens camera, the image is smaller than the object. The reason for this difference is that the projector

 A Has a more powerful lens

 B Has a larger lens

 C Uses two lenses

 D Uses a brightly lit object

 E Has the lens nearer to the object

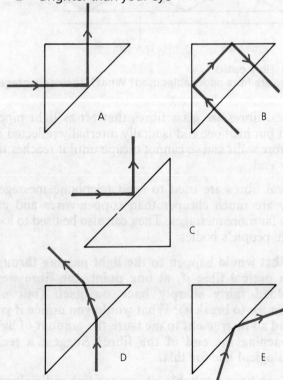

Fig. 1 Which of the rays is coloured?

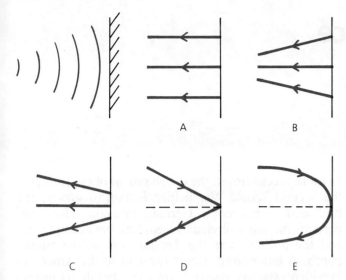

Fig. 2 **Which rays show how the waves are reflected?**

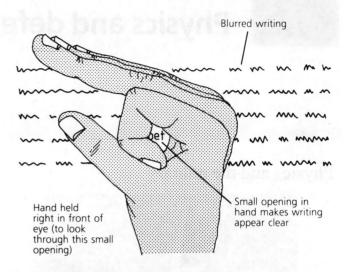

Fig. 3 **How to read from 50 mm
How does it work?**

Blurred writing

Hand held right in front of eye (to look through this small opening)

Small opening in hand makes writing appear clear

8 Short-sighted people can read distant posters more easily on a bright day than on a dull day. This is because on a dull day

A Their eyes are darker.

B The light doesn't reach the back of their eyes.

C Their pupils dilate.

D Their rod cells are less sensitive.

E The lens in their eyes is not powerful enough.

9 Complete these sentences:

a When light is reflected, the _____ ray, the _____ ray and the _____ at the point of incidence are all in the same plane. The _____ of _____ is equal to the angle of _____.

b For light to be totally internally reflected, it must be travelling from a _____ medium to a _____ _____ medium. The angle of _____ must also be greater than the _____ angle.

10 State four uses for lenses. Describe two of these uses in more detail, showing the function of the lens and how it works.

11 Explain the following:

It is impossible for most people to read something ony 50 mm from their eyes (Figure 3). However, if they look at it through a tiny hole then they can read it.

Try it for yourself.

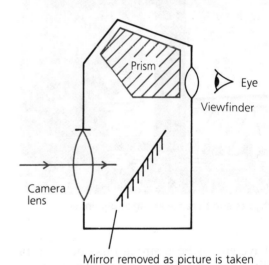

Prism

Eye

Viewfinder

Camera lens

Mirror removed as picture is taken

Fig. 4 **How does the ray pass through this camera prism?**

12 Figure 4 shows a common type of camera that uses a five-sided prism. A ray of light is passing through the lens of the camera towards a mirror underneath the prism. Copy the diagram and show how the ray continues to the photographer's eye.
(This system allows the photographer to see the object through the camera lens, but the right way up. The mirror is removed when the picture is taken.)

13 Show how two prisms can be used to make a periscope.

14 What is an optical fibre? How does it work? State two uses for such a fibre.

Physics and defence

Physics and the military

Fig. 1 Physics and defence are strongly linked

There have always been strong links between physics and military science. Even Archimedes (287–212 BC) was employed mainly for military research. (His detective work with the fraudulent goldsmiths (discussed in Section 5.4) was very much a sideline.) Archimedes worked for the King of Syracuse at a time when Syracuse harbour was under siege. One of his main tasks was to design machines that could destroy the warships besieging the harbour.

Many other prominent scientists have been involved in military science. For example, Galileo was a professor of physics and military research. His work on the motion of projectiles helped to revolutionise European gunnery. This enabled Europeans to conquer the world.

In the nineteenth century, the research into heat and work by the English physicist James Joule also owed its origin to military research. Joule based his work on Count Rumford's experiments on cannon-boring at the munitions factory in Munich.

In more recent times, the development of radar during the Second World War helped Britain to survive the blitz and to prevent a German invasion. However, perhaps the most obvious recent link between physics and the military was the development of the atomic bomb. A letter from Albert Einstein to the American President started research into the bomb. (Einstein feared that the Nazis were developing their own atomic bomb.) A second letter from Einstein, in which he urged the President not to drop the bomb on the Japanese, was ignored.

In the 1980s, large numbers of physicists are employed in the Strategic Defence Initiative(SDI). **See what you can find out about this project in scientific journals such as *New Scientist*.** At present, more than half the money spent on research and development in Britain is allocated to projects directly related to armaments and defence. **How does this compare with other countries?**

A moral dilemma

There are arguments for and against this link between physics and military defence.

One argument in favour of military research is that we constantly need new and more-efficient weapons to defend ourselves. Such modern armaments form an effective deterrent to warfare. So they reduce the number of people killed in wars.

Against this is the argument that spending a lot of money on military research actually encourages warfare. It also wastes precious resources which could be used for more worthy causes.

- **What do you think about this?**

Some of the results of military research seem easy to justify. In the Second World War, physicists used clever tricks with radar to confuse enemy bombers. The bombers dropped their bombs on to empty fields, thinking that they were big cities.

Other research is less easy to excuse. For example, scientists have developed bombs which will destroy people but not buildings.

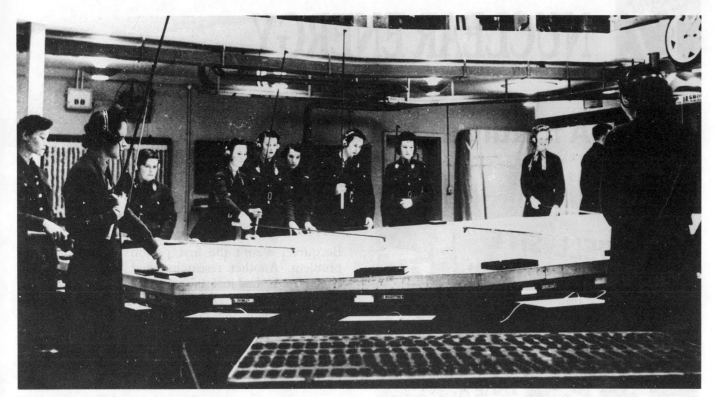

Fig. 2 Military defence can save lives
Radar helped to save lives in the early years of the Second World War

Some people lay the blame for such horrific weapons on scientists. But scientists develop new weapons only because there is a demand for them. Nations and governments are constantly demanding new weapons with which to defend themselves. So, rather than blaming scientists, it is up to each of us to make up our mind how much military research should be carried out for our defence.

Other kinds of defence

Physics can also help people in the battle against starvation, disease, unemployment and other evils.

- Modern transport and communications, new energy sources, new materials and new equipment for agricultural research have made it possible to fight starvation throughout the world.

- X-rays, nuclear physics, ultrasonics, electronics and many other aspects of physics have made people in Britain and other developed nations healthier than ever before.

- New discoveries and inventions based on the use of physics and enabling scientists to study many natural and man-made problems, ranging from earthquakes to pollution.

Many scientists would like to spend more time on such research. But who will pay for it? That is not just a question for scientists, nor for politicians, but one which concerns us all.

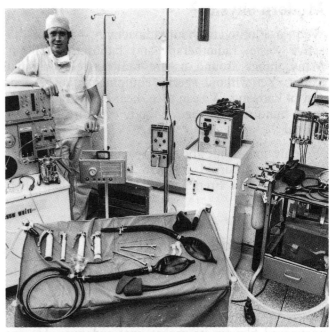

Fig. 3 Defence against poverty, illness and starvation
Physics can also help with this.

17 NUCLEAR ENERGY

17.1 A fortunate accident? Radioactivity

Fig. 1 Many people are concerned about nuclear energy Why?

Modern physics?

We hear a lot today about radioactivity—about radioactive waste, radiotherapy and radioactive fall-out. Many things around us are radioactive to a small extent. Yet without special equipment, we have no way of knowing. We can't see, hear or feel radioactivity. A hundred years ago, nobody even dreamt that it existed.

We only found out about radioactivity because of an event that occurred in 1896. It happened in the laboratory of a French physicist called Henri Becquerel.

Becquerel's discovery

Becquerel had been using some photographic film to study the effect of X-rays on a uranium–potassium salt. (See Section 14.10 on Roentgen's discovery of X-rays.) At the end of the day, Becquerel put the unexposed film (in its packet) into a drawer. He put the lump of salt on top of it.

254

Next day, Becquerel found that the part of the film on which the salt had been standing was totally exposed as though it had been in the light. **How would you explain this?**

Becquerel wasn't the first person to have had this problem. Another researcher had noticed a similar effect, but he had just thrown the film away. Becquerel was more careful. He thought about what had happened. Perhaps the salt itself had given out some radiation, just like an X-ray machine. When he tested this theory, he found that the uranium *was* giving out radiation. So it was the uranium salt that had affected the film.

Fig. 2 It could have turned out differently Becquerel's film was exposed even before he'd taken it out of the packet. Why? How did Becquerel know it wasn't just a bad film?

Where was the energy coming from?

The X-rays discovered by Roentgen got their energy from electricity. But where was the uranium getting its energy from? It hadn't been heated. It wasn't converting some other form of radiation (like the powder in a fluorescent tube).

Fig. 3 Danger! Radiation!
What type of radiation is coming from this salt that doesn't come (in such large amounts) from cooking salt?
Where does the energy come from for this radiation?

Becquerel had discovered not just a new form of radiation, but a new form of energy. He had discovered **nuclear energy**. The energy was coming from deep inside the nucleus of the uranium atom. This is why we call the radiation given off **nuclear radiation**.

Marie Curie

Fig. 4 The only person to win two Nobel Prizes
Who was she? What did she do to win the first of these prizes?

The term 'radioactivity' was invented by Marie Curie. She is famous as the only scientist to have received two Nobel Prizes. She received the first prize for identifying a new, highly radioactive, element called radium. This involved years of hard work. She had to treat many tons of pitchblend to get a few grams of radium. It was a labour of love—she had very little help from the university in which she worked. All that they allowed her was a cold, leaking wooden shed!

Marie Curie called elements such as radium 'radioactive' because they were *active* in giving out radiation (not because they affected radios—they didn't exist at that time).

The danger

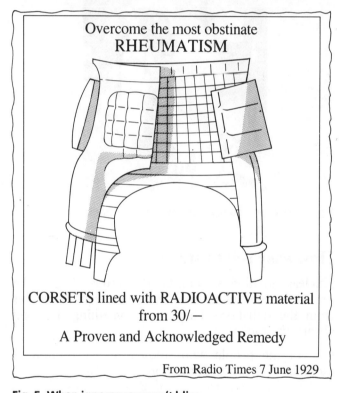

Overcome the most obstinate
RHEUMATISM

CORSETS lined with RADIOACTIVE material
from 30/−

A Proven and Acknowledged Remedy

From Radio Times 7 June 1929

Fig. 5 When ignorance wasn't bliss
An early recommended use for radium.
Why wasn't this a good idea?

One thing that none of them—Roentgen, Becquerel or Marie Curie—realised was the danger of radioactivity and nuclear radiation. All three of them carried out their experiments without worrying about the effects of the radiation. They all suffered terrible injuries as a result.

None of them dreamt how important their discoveries would be in the future. **How does nuclear energy affect us today?**

255

17.2 Absorbing radiation

Fig. 1 How can you protect yourself from radiation?

How easy is it to stop?

Nuclear radiation is useful but dangerous. People who use radioactive materials need to protect themselves from the radiation. They need something that will absorb the radiation.

One of the people who studied the absorption of radiation was Ernest Rutherford. Lord Rutherford (as he later became) was one of Britain's most famous physicists this century. His experiments on bombarding atoms eventually led (with the work of a colleague Sir John Cockroft) to the splitting of the atom. At the time, some people thought that this would immediately bring about the end of the world. Rutherford himself had some equally mistaken beliefs:

> The energy produced by the breaking down of the atom is a very poor kind of thing. Anyone who expects a source of power from the transformation of these atoms is talking moonshine.

How wrong you can be!

Rutherford tried passing nuclear radiation through various materials to see how much was absorbed. He found that materials with a high atomic weight (for example, lead, gold and barium) absorbed a lot of radiation. Materials with a low atomic weight (for example, boron and carbon) didn't.

He then tried using different thicknesses of aluminium foil. As he increased the thickness, more radiation was absorbed. But the results were rather odd.

For very thin foil (up to a fiftieth of a millimetre in thickness), Rutherford's results were as he expected. The amount of radiation getting through the foil decreased rapidly with the thickness of the sheet. But for thinner sheets, the decrease was much slower (Figure 2). Most of the radiation that got through a fiftieth of a millimetre (0.02 mm) of foil still got through sheets up to half a millimetre (0.5 mm) thick.

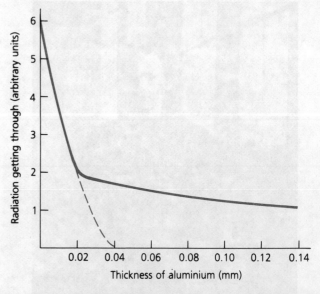

Fig. 2 The thicker the metal, the less radiation gets through
Why does the shape of this graph suggest that there is more than one type of nuclear radiation?

- **If you have a suitable radioactive source and a Geiger counter, check this for yourself. Try using other materials—for example, paper.**

Three types of radiation

Rutherford argued that there must be at least two types of radiation. **How does this explain his observations?**

He called these two types of radiation **alpha radiation** and **beta radiation**. (Alpha (α) and beta (β) are the first two letters of the Greek alphabet.) Later, a third type of radiation was discovered. It is even more penetrating—and can pass through a centimetre of lead. This was called **gamma radiation**. (Gamma (γ) is the third letter of the Greek alphabet.)

Captured on film

We are now able to 'see' the tracks left by alpha and beta radiation as it travels through a photographic plate (Figure 3). The rays act like light, blackening the photographic plate as they pass through.

(a)

(b)

Fig. 3 Photographic tracks left by alpha and beta radiation
Which is alpha and which is beta? Why are they so different?

Alpha rays force their way straight forwards, pushing the atoms out of the way. This soon brings them to a halt. Beta rays bounce off the atoms, and keep going much further.

The radiation given off depends on the source

Some materials give off beta and gamma radiation but no alpha radiation, whereas other materials give off alpha and gamma radiation but no beta radiation, and so on.

Does the type matter?

One reason for checking the type of radiation is that the different types have different effects on us. So we need to take different precautions.

Alpha sources are safe in sealed containers. The alpha radiation cannot escape. Even in air, the radiation can only travel a few centimetres. The only danger is if we get the alpha sources on or inside our bodies — for example, through contaminated clothes, air or food. If alpha radiation reaches our body, it is rapidly absorbed and does a lot of damage. (It is more likely than other forms of radiation to give us cancer.)

Fig. 4 Why bother taking precautions?
This man was foolish — he wasn't safe!
Why did he think that the radiation couldn't reach him?
Why and how is he now likely to be harmed by it?
What should he have done to avoid this?

A beta source needs a thick metal container (preferably lead) to absorb the radiation.

Gamma radiation passes easily through most materials. It is the most difficult radiation to avoid. Of the three types of radiation, it releases the least energy when it is absorbed. However, it can reach important and easily damaged cells deep inside our bodies. For example, it can reach and damage the bone marrow that supplies our red blood cells.

This question of safety and protection is considered in more detail in Section 17.4.

- **Section 14.10 described the use of lead to protect people working with X-rays. Is this protection needed for people working with**
  (a) gamma radiation?
  (b) alpha radiation?
  Why?

257

What are alpha, beta and gamma rays?

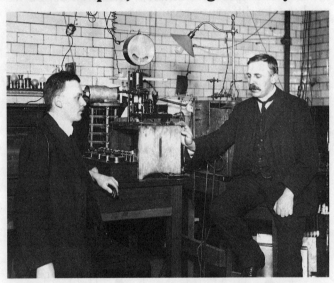

Fig. 1   The early days of nuclear research: Geiger and Rutherford
What did these, and other, scientists carrying out early research on nuclear physics discover about alpha, beta and gamma radiation?

All the scientists working with radiation wanted to find out what alpha, beta and gamma rays consisted of. They carried out many experiments and made the following discoveries.

Alpha rays

- are attracted to a negatively charged plate
- go round in circles when placed between the poles of a magnet (the circles are much larger than for electrons, showing that they have a much larger mass)
- behave as helium gas when collected in a glass vessel.

From this, they were able to work out what alpha radiation is.

> Alpha particles are helium nuclei. They consist of two protons and two neutrons stuck together.

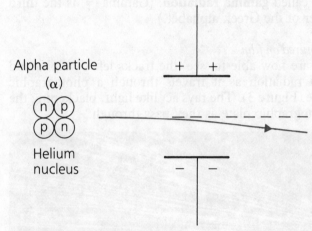

Fig. 2   Alpha radiation

Beta rays behave just like cathode rays (Section 14.10) except that they have more energy. For example, they are attracted to a positively charged plate and they circle like electrons when they are between the poles of a magnet.

> Beta particles are fast electrons (like cathode rays but faster).

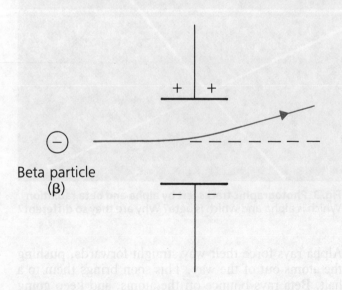

Fig. 3   Beta radiation

Gamma rays aren't affected by electric or magnetic fields. They are diffracted by crystals in the same way as X-rays.

> Gamma rays are electromagnetic radiation similar to X-rays (but they are usually of higher frequency and energy).

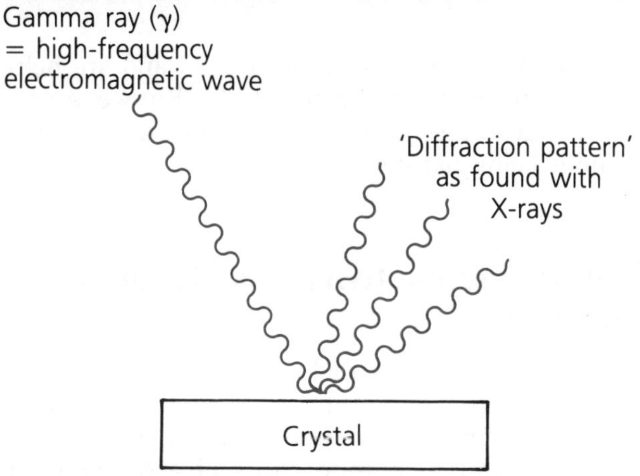

Gamma ray (γ)
= high-frequency
electromagnetic wave

'Diffraction pattern'
as found with
X-rays

Crystal

Fig. 4 Gamma radiation

'Beware, ionising radiations'

DANGER!
IONISING
RADIATION

Fig. 5 What is meant by ionising radiation?

You see this sign where radioactive isotopes are being used. What does it mean?

When alpha particles (helium ions) or beta particles (fast electrons) hit atoms, they damage them. They knock some of the electrons away from the atoms. So alpha and beta particles leave a trail of positive ions behind them. This is why alpha and beta rays are called **ionising radiation**.

Alpha particles are the largest and most highly charged type of radiation. **Why are they more highly charged than beta particles?** In addition, they cause the most ionisation. They charge straight forwards, ionising any atoms in their path.

Beta particles don't cause so much ionisation. They are more easily deflected out of the way by the atoms that they come across.

Even gamma rays and X-rays cause some ionisation but very much less than alpha and beta particles. Ionisation only occurs when the gamma ray or X-ray is finally absorbed. The outer electron of the absorbing atom is given a large amount of energy. In fact, it gets so much energy from the incoming ray that it flies off, leaving a positive ion.

By ionising atoms, the radiation causes chemical reactions to occur. This is why nuclear radiation exposes photographic film.

The rays also affect the chemicals in the genes of our body cells. Some of the cells are killed. Others go out of control and become cancerous. The effect is greatest with rapidly multiplying cells. These include red blood cells, hair and sex cells. This is why people exposed to high levels of radiation can suffer from anaemia, hair loss and sterility.

The ionisation caused by these rays helps us to detect them. Some methods of detecting them are described in Section 17.5.

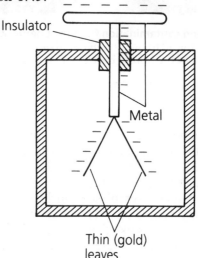

Insulator

Metal

Thin (gold)
leaves

Fig. 6 A charged gold-leaf electroscope
What happens if a radioisotope is placed near the plate?
Why?

Figure 6 shows a leaf electroscope that can be used to demonstrate ionisation. It consists of a couple of very thin metal leaves (gold or aluminium) suspended from a metal rod. If the plate at the top of this rod is given a negative charge (see Chapter 10), then the charges travel down into the leaves and cause them to part. If some radioactive material is now brought near the electroscope, the leaves rapidly fall together again. **Why? Try this if you have an electroscope and a weak radioactive source.**

259

Why don't we ban it?

Fig. 1 Removing contamination from the Chernobyl disaster
This truck was found to be contaminated by radioisotopes when it arrived at the border between East and West Germany.
How did it get contaminated?

Nuclear radiation is dangerous. You may have seen films about the atomic bombs dropped on Hiroshima and Nagasaki, and the terrible effects of nuclear radiation. Most people feel that the world would be a better place if there weren't any nuclear weapons. In addition, many people are worried about accidents at nuclear power stations like that at Chernobyl. There is also concern about increased radiation levels near nuclear power stations and nuclear waste dumps.

So why don't we get rid of nuclear energy and radioactive materials altogether? Why not forget that Becquerel ever discovered radioactivity?

Dangerous, but useful

Even if we did get rid of all radioactive materials, people would still die. For example, it would be much more difficult to treat cancer patients and to diagnose diseases. Medical and agricultural research would grind almost to a halt. So would many other important areas of modern industry.

Radioactive isotopes have helped us, and are helping us, in many ways (see Section 17.8). But we must take safety precautions so that we can use these materials without being harmed by them.

Natural radioactivity—background radiation

There is another reason why we can't just ban nuclear radiation. Look at Figure 2. Most of our radiation comes from natural sources inside us and all around us. For example, granite rocks give off radioactive radon gas.

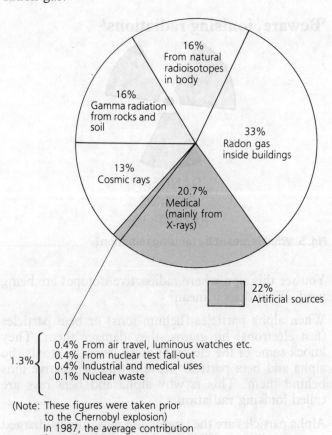

Fig. 2 Where the radiation comes from
What is our main source of radiation?
Why does this depend on there we live and work?

Next to smoking, radon is probably the single biggest cause of lung cancer. In some places in Cornwall, the air inside people's homes is so radioactive that it would not be allowed inside a nuclear power station. In America, one worker at a nuclear power station set off radiation alarms every day on his way *into* the building. His home contained so much radon gas that the air he was breathing was said to be as risky as smoking 135 packets of cigarettes!

We are all constantly being bombarded by **cosmic rays**. These are tiny particles from outside the Earth's atmosphere. Many of them are the result of nuclear reactions. They all have the same effect on us as nuclear radiation.

- **If you have suitable equipment, try measuring the level of background radiation at your school.**

How much radiation over what period?

We are all exposed to some radiation. But we should *not* be exposed to higher levels of radiation *unless* we are gaining some benefit from it. X-ray diagnosis or radiation treatment for cancer is usually worth the increased risk from extra radiation. So perhaps is a job working with radioactive materials. Figure 3 shows the maximum levels of radiation that are regarded as acceptable in such circumstances.

Fig. 3 Permitted levels of radiation for workers exposed to nuclear radiation

Area category	Dose rate ($\mu Sv/h$)	Maximum annual dose (mSv)
Unsupervised areas	Less than 2.5	5
Supervised areas (medicals and monitoring optional)	2.5 to 7.5	15
Controlled areas (medicals and monitoring compulsary)	7.5 to 25	50
Restricted areas (protection required)	More than 25	50

1 sievert (Sv) is equal to 1 joule of energy absorbed per kilogram of body tissue. A dose of 1 Sv of X-rays, gamma rays or beta particles is sufficient to cause nausea and vomiting (radiation sickness) after 2 hours. A dose of 0.05 Sv of alpha particles has the same effect. Is it correct to say that lower levels of radiation cannot do you any harm?

If we are exposed to higher levels of radiation, it should only be for a short time. The higher the dose of radiation and the longer we are exposed to it, the more likely we are to be harmed (the more likely we are to develop cancer).

Taking precautions

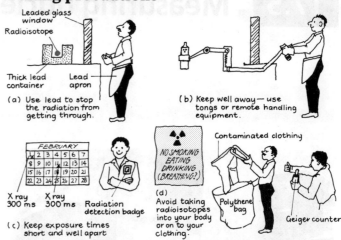

Fig. 4 Taking safety precautions
What are the dangers if you don't?

Suppose that you were a radiation worker. These are some of the precautions that you would have to take to protect yourself from a radiation overdose.

1 Keep all radioactive materials in sealed containers which, for beta and gamma radiation, should be made of thick lead. If you are working with beta or gamma radiation, use lead screens and a lead apron to protect your reproductive organs (the most easily damaged part of your body). Any windows for viewing the material should be made of glass containing lead.

2 Keep as far away from the radioactive materials as you reasonably can. Handle the materials by remote control or using tongs.

3 Keep the times for which you are exposed to the material as short and as few as possible. (Dentists often ask you to hold the X-ray film in place while they keep well away or behind a screen. This may seem unfair— you get all the radiation and they hide from it. But you only have an occasional X-ray. They take lots of X-ray photos, and so have a far higher chance of being harmed.)

4 Avoid contaminating food, clothing or the air you breathe. (Any alpha-particle sources held against your skin or inside you are particularly deadly.) Wear disposable clothing and don't eat, drink or smoke when dealing with radioactive materials. Check your take-home clothing with a radiation detector to make sure that it is not contaminated.

5 Wear a radiation badge that glows when exposed to radiation. If this shows that you have received too much radiation, then you should keep away from any sources for some time. Have a holiday—but not too near a granite quarry!

Measuring nuclear radiation

Fig. 1 Using a Geiger counter to check for contamination

Using photographic film

Nuclear radiation leaves tracks on (exposes) photographic film. This was how Becquerel discovered radiation (Section 17.1). Today we usually just photograph tracks in bubble chambers.

How scintillating!

Some chemicals will glow for a very short time after nuclear radiation hits them. These glints of light (or **scintillations**) can be used to count the number of rays coming from radioactive material. Unfortunately, the scintillations are very difficult to see. You have to be in complete darkness for some time before you can see them. Early nuclear scientists spent hours in dark rooms counting these scintillations. In Rutherford's experiments on radiation absorption (Section 17.2), his assistants Geiger and Marsden counted over 100 000 scintillations while looking down a microscope! **Would you have liked to have been one of these scientists?**

Fig. 2 Another way of detecting radiation
This was the main way of detecting radiation before the Geiger counter was invented.
Where else are chemicals (phosphors) used to change invisible radiation into visible light?

Geiger counters

No doubt Hans Geiger became heartily sick of counting scintillations. So he invented an easier method. The **Geiger counter** is an electronic counter. The part of the counter that detects radiation has two terminals—a wire and a cylinder—with a very high voltage between them. A scientist called Müller worked with Geiger on this part of the counter. We call this a Geiger–Müller or GM tube.

Radiation passes into one end of the tube through a very thin piece of mica. The radiation ionises the gas in the tube and allows a current to flow between the two

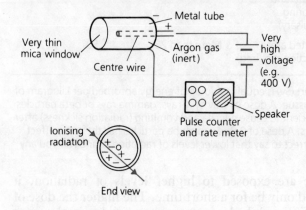

Fig. 3 How a Geiger counter works
Why does the mica at the end of the tube need to be very thin?

terminals. This current triggers an electronic counter. The counter records the number of times that a current flows and so counts the number of times that radiation passes through the tube (Figure 3).

Most Geiger counters have a meter to show the count rate (the number of counts per minute). They also have a speaker that makes a sound each time radiation passes through the tube.

Using a Geiger counter

Using a Geiger counter is fairly straightforward provided that you take two precautions.

1 Write down the count rate that you get with the radioactive sample well out of the way (for example, with it in its lead box). The GM tube will now be picking up background radiation from natural radioactive materials. (Everything around us is radioactive to some extent.) You will need to subtract this background reading when you measure the count rate from a radioactive sample.

2 Take your readings over a reasonably long period of time (for example, a minute). Radiation is given off at random. At one moment, several atoms may give out radiation together. The next moment, there may be no atoms giving out radiation, then perhaps one, then four and so on. You need to average out this changing count rate.

- **If you have a Geiger counter, try this. See how the radiation rate gets more constant when measured over longer periods of time.**

Other methods

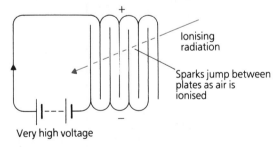

Fig. 4 A spark chamber
What advantage does a spark chamber have compared with a Geiger counter?

Spark chambers work in a similar way to Geiger counters (see Figure 4). They have the advantage that, by photographing the sparks, you can see the path followed by the radiation.

Cloud chambers also show the path of the radiation. They contain air that is supersaturated (more than saturated) with water or alcohol vapour. Alpha, beta or gamma rays ionise the gas and cause the vapour to condense along the path of the rays (Figure 5).

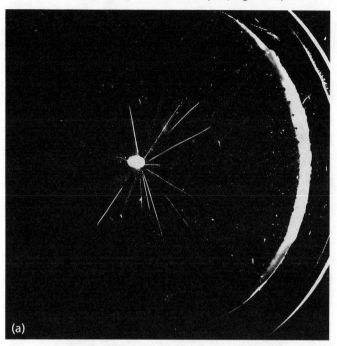

(a)

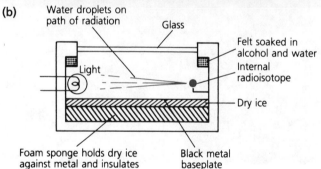

(b)

Fig. 5 α-particle tracks in a cloud chamber
The photograph shows trails of water droplets coming from the central radioisotope. Moist air in the cloud chamber is suddenly cooled or lowered in pressure. This saturates the air with water vapour. Where the air is ionised, water droplets form.
Why does low pressure or low temperature saturate the moist air?

Bubble chambers are similar to cloud chambers except that liquid hydrogen is used instead of supersaturated air. They rays leave a trail of bubbles that can be photographed.

- **If your school has a cloud chamber, use it to show how beta radiation is deflected by a magnet or an electric field.**

17.6 Isotopes—radioactive and otherwise

Fig. 1 The Chernobyl explosion released caesium-137
Clouds of caesium-137 drifted over Europe.
What is caesium-137?
What does the 137 stand for?

Radioiodine

In 1957, an accident occurred at Britain's Windscale reactor. Several tons of uranium fuel rods melted. Iodine gas was released. The gas spread down wind across 200 square miles of farmland. Cows ate the grass on to which it fell, and the iodine passed into the milk. Once this happened, milk supplies from the region were stopped.

Why were supplies of milk stopped? All milk contains iodine. Our bodies need iodine. So what was wrong with this iodine?

The Windscale iodine was radioactive. It contained iodine-131. Far from helping our bodies, this form of iodine can cause cancer of the thyroid gland. (This is the gland where the iodine that we take into our bodies is concentrated.)

In the Chernobyl disaster of 1986, a Russian nuclear reactor exploded. Caesium-137, a radioactive form of caesium, was released. The wind spread the radioactivity over much of Europe. Many animals, including most Lapp reindeer, soon became unfit to eat because of the caesium-137 in their bodies.

Different isotopes of the same element

What do we mean by iodine-131 and caesium-137?

The central part of an atom is called the nucleus. It contains protons and neutrons (see Section 10.2). The number of protons determines the element. For example, all iodine atoms have 53 protons. But the number of neutrons can vary. The number of neutrons in an atom affects the mass of the atom, but it doesn't affect the chemical properties.

Group 6	Group 7	Group 0
All isotopes of helium belong in this box ▷		Atomic number 2 He Helium
Atomic number 8 O Oxygen	Atomic number 9 F Fluorine	Atomic number 10 Ne . Neon
Atomic number 16 S Sulphur	Atomic number 17 Cl Chlorine	Atomic number 18 Ar Argon

Fig. 2 Isotope means 'same place' in the Periodic Table
What is the Periodic Table?
What do the different isotopes of an element have in common?

264

Most iodine atoms contain 74 neutrons, but a few contain 78 neutrons. Chemically, these atoms behave in exactly the same way. We call these different forms of iodine **isotopes** of iodine. (*Isos* means 'same' in ancient Greek and *topos* means 'place'. The isotopes of an element occupy the same place in the Periodic Table of the elements.)

Iodine-127 is the common isotope of iodine. Its atoms contain 127 **nucleons**: 53 protons and 74 neutrons ($53 + 74 = 127$). (A nucleon is either a proton or a neutron.)

Iodine-131 is a less-common isotope of iodine. Its atoms contain 131 nucleons: 53 protons and 78 neutrons. In fact, iodine has 23 different isotopes ranging from iodine-117 to iodine-139.

- **Caesium atoms contain 55 protons. How many neutrons are there in an atom of caesium-137?**

Hydrogen has three main isotopes. 99.99% of hydrogen is hydrogen-1 (which has no neutrons). Most of the rest is hydrogen-2. Less than one atom in a million is hydrogen-3. Hydrogen is the *only* element for which we give the isotopes different names. Hydrogen-2 is called **deuterium** and hydrogen-3 is called **tritium**. As we shall see in Section 17.12, these may one day be our main source of nuclear energy.

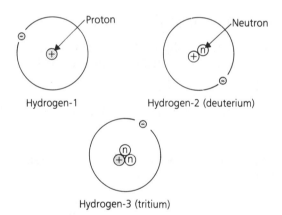

Hydrogen-1

Hydrogen-2 (deuterium)

Hydrogen-3 (tritium)

Fig. 3 The isotopes of hydrogen
Heavy water is water made with deuterium rather than with hydrogen. How much heavier is this water than ordinary water? (A molecule of water consists of one atom of oxygen—mass number 16—and two atoms of hydrogen.)

Atomic number, nucleon number and nuclide notation

The clearest way of describing an isotope is to use **nuclide notation**. We talk about the **nuclide**:

$$^A_Z X$$

Here X is the chemical symbol of the element
Z is the atomic number (the number of protons in the nucleus)
A is the nucleon number (the number of nucleons in the nucleus).

Using this notation, iodine-131 and caesium-137 become

$$^{131}_{53}I \quad \text{and} \quad ^{137}_{55}Cs$$

- **Describe the deuterium and tritium nuclides using this notation. (The symbol for hydrogen is H.)**

Radioactive isotopes

In most elements, some of the isotopes are stable. Others are radioactive. They are called **radioisotopes**. Iodine-131 and caesium-137 are both radioisotopes. Tritium is also a radioisotope, whereas deuterium and hydrogen-1 are stable isotopes.

Fig. 4 Iodine-131 being used in a hospital
How can this help in the treatment of cancer (see Section 17.8)?
Will radioiodine taste any different from ordinary iodine?

Stable isotopes of light elements tend to have about the same number of protons as neutrons. Heavier nuclei need to have more neutrons than protons.

Radioisotopes with too many neutrons compared with the number of protons normally give off beta and gamma radiation. Radioisotopes with too few neutrons usually give off alpha and gamma radiation. However, this is only a general guide.

- **Carbon has atomic number 6. How would you expect (a) carbon-9, (b) carbon-14 to decay?**

Sellafield

Fig. 1 The Sellafield reprocessing plant
What is being reprocessed, and what does this involve?

The reprocessing plant at Sellafield (Figure 1) deals with the spent fuel rods from nuclear power stations. Useful radioisotopes (including plutonium) are removed. The remainder is separated into high-level and low-level waste for disposal or long-term storage.

These isotopes weren't present in the uranium when it was first put into the power stations. They were created by the nuclear reactions that occurred in the fuel rod.

We live in a changing world

Many centuries ago, alchemists dreamed of changing one element into another. In particular, they wanted to change lead into gold. These two metals have a similar mass but different properties (and value). The alchemists wanted to know why. (They weren't just interested in a quick way of getting rich!)

Today, we *can* change one element into another. The free neutrons in a nuclear reactor are constantly doing this. It is still not easy to turn lead into gold. But we are already turning uranium into the man-made element plutonium, and producing many other radioisotopes that are needed in industry and medicine.

New elements are also formed when radioisotopes **decay** by giving out alpha or beta radiation.

Fig. 2 The alchemists
Who were they? What were they trying to do?

An example of alpha decay

Beryllium-8 is the lightest radioisotope to undergo alpha (α) decay. The nuclide equation for this is

$$^8_4\text{Be} \rightarrow \,^4_2\text{He} + \,^4_2\alpha$$

In this case, beryllium has decayed into helium (Figure 3).

- **What is the nuclide equation for uranium-238 decaying by alpha decay?**

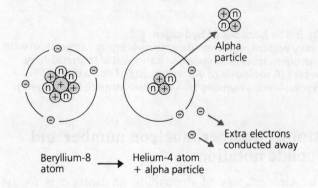

Fig. 3 Alpha decay
There is no way of telling when an atom is about to decay. Nor is there any way of making it decay, or of stopping it from decaying.

An example of beta decay

Hydrogen-3 is the lightest isotope to undergo beta (β) decay. The nuclide equation for this is

$$^3_1\text{H} \rightarrow {}^3_2\text{He} + {}^{\ 0}_{-1}\beta$$

(The -1 on the beta particle is not its atomic number but its charge. It is useful to put this in to make the numbers balance.)

The way in which this nuclear reaction takes place is as follows.

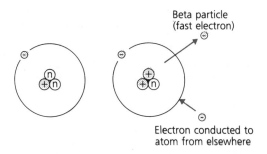

Beta particle
(fast electron)

Electron conducted to
atom from elsewhere

Fig. 4 Beta decay
Could an isotope of hydrogen decay by alpha decay? Explain.

1 At some instant (for a reason we don't understand), one of the neutrons suddenly splits into a proton and an electron. The overall charge hasn't altered. The charge on the proton is equal and opposite to the charge on the electron.

2 Instead of this electron sticking to the proton (as we would expect for a positive and negative charge), it is thrown out of the nucleus at very high speed. It becomes a beta particle.

- **What is the nuclide equation for the beta decay of iodine-131?**

A complicated problem

Most radioactive decay is more complicated than this. Usually, some gamma radiation is given off as well as the alpha or beta particle. Also, the new isotope may itself be radioactive. One of the most common radioisotopes—uranium-238—decays from one element to another more than half a dozen times before it ends up as a stable isotope of lead (lead-206).

In nuclear power stations, uranium-238 is bombarded by neutrons. After two beta decays, it turns into plutonium-239. This is suitable for use in nuclear power stations and for nuclear weapons.

Fig. 5 The alchemist's dream come true?
This machine replaces the used fuel rods in a nuclear reactor. The used rods contain new chemicals which were not there when the rods were put into the reactor.

A lot of other radioisotopes are produced in a nuclear reactor (Figure 5). Some are produced by absorbing free neutrons. (The coolant passing through the reactor becomes radioactive in this way and so must be kept in an enclosed system. It mustn't be allowed to escape.) Other radioisotopes are formed as a result of the fission process (see Section 17.10).

From time to time, these radioisotopes have to be removed. Some of them can be used to great benefit, as is shown in Section 17.8. Others can be a menace, forming the nuclear waste that nobody wants. Low-level waste can be dumped. Some of the high-level waste can be kept in cooling tanks until its activity has dropped to a safe level. Other waste will go on being highly radioactive and therefore dangerous for thousands of years. This material needs careful, long-term storage.

- **See if you can find out what the present plans for storing this nuclear waste are.**

Great care is needed when dealing with these man-made isotopes, particularly with their long-term storage and disposal. If we are not careful, then the alchemist's dream may become our nightmare!

267

Using radioisotopes

Tracer techniques and radioisotope labelling

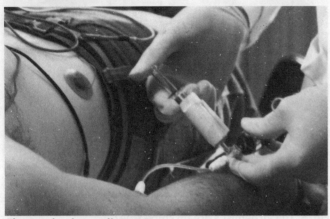

Fig. 1 Injecting sodium-24
This enables the flow of salt through the body to be traced. How?
The sodium-24 used by the hospital becomes unusable after a while. Why?

Sodium is just one of a great variety of minerals needed by the body. Our main source is common salt (sodium chloride). But too much salt can be bad for us, causing high blood pressure and some heart conditions. Tracing the movement of sodium round the body can help in the diagnosis of some diseases. This can be done by giving the patient salt containing the radioisotope sodium-24. As it moves round the body the sodium-24 gives out radiation. Its movement can then be traced using a Geiger counter.

This technique can also be used to check whether people are bleeding inside. The blood is made slightly radioactive. A Geiger counter is then used to check for a build-up of radiation in any part of the body. Such a build-up of radiation would indicate a build-up of blood caused by bleeding.

Sodium-24 is ideal because

- it is a beta emitter, which causes less damage than an alpha emitter
- it has a short **half-life** (it decays away quite quickly) so it doesn't do much harm. (See Section 17.9 for further discussion of half-life.)

Other examples of radioactive tracer techniques

Radioactive tracer techniques are not only used in hospitals, but in many other areas of science and industry.

1 The radioisotope phosphorus-32 is often used to study how plants take up and use different fertilisers.

2 In the oil industry, several companies will sometimes use the same oil pipeline. They need to know where one company's oil stops and another company's oil starts. They can tell this by labelling the first part of each batch of oil with a suitable radioisotope. A Geiger counter fixed to the pipe will show when this isotope passes.

3 Radioisotopes can be used to detect leaks in underground pipes and sewers. A suitable radioisotope is put into the water. A Geiger counter is then used to check for a build-up of radiation.

Cancer therapy

The main difference between cancer cells and ordinary cells is that the body cannot control cancer cells. They multiply far too fast and in the wrong places. Nuclear

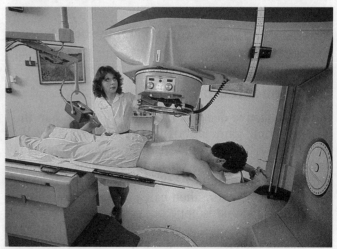

Fig. 2 Using gamma radiation to kill a tumour
How is it that the cancer cells are affected more than the other cells?

268

radiation can stop them from multiplying, and can therefore reduce the problem. Methods of treatment must avoid damaging other cells and causing too many side effects. Here are two examples.

1 A narrow beam of gamma rays is passed through the cancerous growth (Figure 2). Other parts of the body, especially the sexual organs, are protected with lead.

2 The patient eats a radioisotope that goes straight to the cancerous part of the body. For example, iodine-131 is given to patients suffering from cancer of the thyroid gland. (This gland uses more iodine than any other part of the body.)

Sterilisation

Fig. 3 Using radiation to sterilise food
The strawberries which are free from fungus have been irradiated.
What does this mean?
What is the radiation doing to the food?

High-intensity nuclear radiation kills living cells. It is used to sterilise medical instruments (knives, scalpels etc.). The radiation kills off any bacteria, so that the instruments can be used without causing infection.

Radiation is sometimes also used to sterilise food (Figure 3). It destroys the bacteria and fungi that cause food to go bad. This allows the food to be stored for a long time while still tasting fresh. **Why are some people not happy about this? If you don't know, see if you can find out.**

Thickness measurement and control

The thickness of a sheet of plastic can be measured by placing a suitable radioisotope above the sheet and a Geiger counter underneath. (The thinner the sheet,

the more radiation gets through.) This information can then be fed back to the machine which controls the thickness of the sheet (Figure 4).

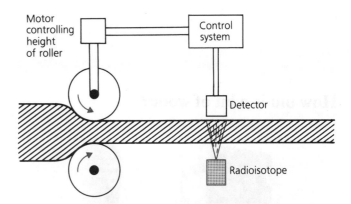

Fig. 4 Using radiation to keep the thickness constant
What is the advantage of this method?

A similar process is used to control the coal shearer in some coal mines. A Geiger counter is attached to the top of the shearer. When the shearer reaches the top of the coal seam, there is an increase in the natural background radiation. (The rock contains more natural radioisotopes than the coal.) The Geiger counter controls the shearer. When it detects this increase in radiation, it prevents the shearer from cutting any higher (Figure 5).

Fig. 5 Using radiation to find the top of the coal seam
How does this work?

These are just some of the benefits that we can gain from the use of radioisotopes. **See how many more uses you can discover.**

17.9 Half-life and radiocarbon dating

How old is a bit of wood?

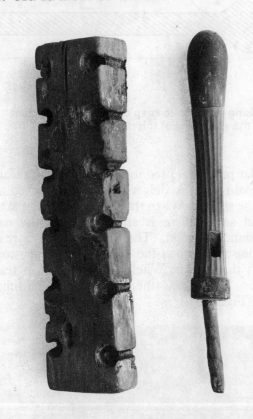

Fig. 1 A 5000-year-old fire-making tool taken from Tutenkhamen's tomb
How could carbon-14 be used to check its age?

You can tell an old piece of wood from a new one just by looking at it. But you can't tell *how* old a piece of wood is. Scientists use a process called **radiocarbon dating** to find the age of wood. This process makes use of the fact that wood naturally contains the radioisotope carbon-14. As wood gets older, less radiation is given off by the carbon-14. (Similarly, when a torch has been on for some time, the bulb starts to glow less brightly.) The age of the wood can be found by measuring the amount of radiation given off.

Radiocarbon dating is used by archaeologists to date ancient remains. To understand how it works, we need to look at the nature of radioactive decay.

When will it decay?

The atoms of a radioisotope don't all decay (give off radiation) at once. Some decay straight away. Others can last for a very long time. The atoms give off their radiation at random. Nothing that we do seems to affect this. All we can tell is that

- overall, one particular isotope will always decay more rapidly than another
- the more atoms there are, the more likely it is that one of them will decay in the next instant.

As the atoms decay, there are less atoms of that particular radioisotope left to decay. This means that the **activity** (the rate of decay) decreases as time goes on. Figure 2 shows how it decreases. (It is fairly easy to demonstrate this for radon gas—see Figure 4.)

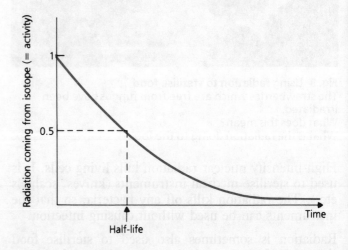

Fig. 2 Half-life
What is meant by the half-life of an isotope?
Why does the activity of a radioactive isotope get less as time passes?

Half-life

We cannot say how long a particular radioactive isotope will last. The last few atoms may suddenly decay together or they may last for a very long time.

What we can predict with reasonable certainty (after a few tests on the material) is the **half-life**.

> The half-life is the time taken for half the atoms of that isotope to decay.

But half the atoms means half the activity. So the half-life is also the time taken for the isotope's activity to drop to half its starting value. Notice that the half-life doesn't depend on the amount of material. **Why not?**

The half-life is very different for different isotopes. For example, beryllium-10 has a half-life of 2.5 million years whereas beryllium-8 has a half-life of less than a thousand million millionth of a second! Beryllium-8 has decayed away before we can even look at it, whereas we would have a long wait to see any change in the activity of beryllium-10!

Why do we still find radioisotopes with short half-lives? Why didn't they all decay long ago? The reason is that they are constantly being produced. They are formed by the decay of radioisotopes with very long half-lives.

For example, radon gas has a half-life of 52 seconds. It is produced by the decay of thorium-232 which has a half-life of 1.4×10^{10} years.

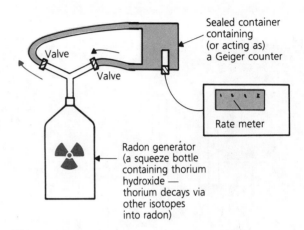

Fig. 4 Measuring the half-life of radon
Why radon?

Radiocarbon dating

The carbon-14 in the atmosphere is constantly being renewed by cosmic rays. These hit stable carbon-12 atoms in the upper atmosphere and turn them into carbon-14 atoms.

Trees take in this carbon-14 together with carbon-12. Once a tree dies (or is cut down), no further carbon-14 enters the wood. Carbon-14 has a half-life of 5730 years. This means that, 5730 years after it was cut down, the tree will have half its original carbon-14 activity. By checking the radiation level, you can tell the age of the tree. (You can do the same for any plant or animal remains.)

- **Suppose that you have two pieces of wood—one freshly cut, the other 17 190 years old. How much more radioactive would the fresh wood be than the old wood (considering only the decay of carbon-14)?**

(a)   Beryllium-8 (half-life 0.000 000 000 000 000 2 seconds (2×10^{-16} s))

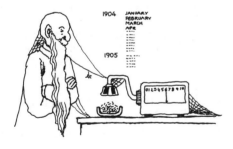

(b)   Beryllium-10 (half-life 2 500 000 years)

Fig. 3 Some half-lives are very short, others are very long
Does a radioisotope really disappear when it decays (as in Fig. 3(a)?

Fig. 1 A peaceful use of nuclear power?
In what ways are nuclear power stations different from coal-
and oil-fired power stations?
In what ways are they the same?

Nuclear fission

When a radioisotope decays, it releases some nuclear
energy (enough to power some very tiny electronic
circuits). But if the nucleus is bombarded with a
neutron and smashed to pieces, much more energy is
released (Figure 2). This is called **nuclear fission**.

The most common **fissionable materials** (materials
with breakable nuclei) are uranium-235 and plu-
tonium-239. These materials always have some neu-

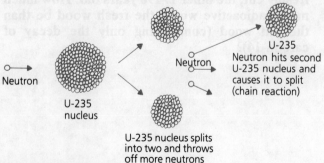

Fig. 2 Nuclear fission
What is meant by (i) a chain reaction? (ii) 'going critical'?

272

trons flying around in them. All that you need is a
sufficiently big lump of material (a **critical mass**), and
fission of vast numbers of atoms will take place.

Nuclear weapons

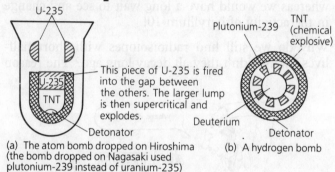

(a) The atom bomb dropped on Hiroshima
(the bomb dropped on Nagasaki used
plutonium-239 instead of uranium-235)

(b) A hydrogen bomb

Fig. 3 Atomic bombs and hydrogen bombs
(a) The atomic bomb explodes once there is a large enough
lump of uranium-235 or plutonium-239 for the fission
reaction to become supercritical.
(b) In the hydrogen bomb, deuterium (hydrogen-2) is
heated by an atomic bomb to the temperature at which
nuclear fusion can take place.
Whereas a hydrogen bomb explodes in a ten-millionth of a
second, a neutron bomb takes a full millionth of a second.
What difference does this make to the blast? Why?

The atomic bomb that destroyed Hiroshima used
uranium-235. The Nagasaki bomb used plutonium-
239. Figure 3 shows the construction of the bombs.

The atom bomb was made up of three lumps of
fissionable material. Each lump was below the critical
mass, so there were too few neutrons for (much) fission
to occur. When the bomb was detonated, a chemical
explosion took place. This forced the three lumps of
material together to form a critical mass. There were
now plenty of neutrons. Fission occurred on a tremendous scale, releasing vast amounts of nuclear energy.
In what form was this energy released?

The hydrogen bomb uses an atomic bomb to heat
hydrogen to 100 000 000 °C. At this temperature, hydrogen behaves like the hydrogen in the Sun (see
Section 17.12), releasing a massive amount of energy.

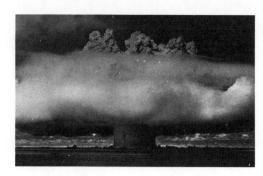

Fig. 4 A nuclear explosion
What produces the blast? (See Section 8.2.)

Nuclear power stations

In the reactors of nuclear power stations, the fission reaction is kept just **critical**. That is to say, there are just enough neutrons to keep the reaction going but not enough for an explosion to take place. (The extra neutrons are absorbed by control rods made of boron, and by uranium-238.)

The heat from the nuclear reactor is used in the same way as the heat obtained from burning coal or oil in a coal-fired or oil-fired power station (see Section 7.1).

Advantages of nuclear power stations

1 A nuclear power station needs very little fuel compared with a coal-fired or oil-fired power station. A tonne of uranium gives as much energy as 25 000 tonnes of coal. This lowers the cost of the fuel. It makes disruption in fuel supplies less likely. It also means that you can build a smaller and cheaper power station for the same power output. Nuclear power is (or can be) cheap power.

2 Unlike power stations that use coal and oil, nuclear power stations don't release large quantities of carbon dioxide and sulphur dioxide into the atmosphere. So they don't cause **acid rain**.

3 In Britain, a switch from coal to nuclear power means fewer mining accidents and fewer coal tips. (But it also means fewer jobs.) On a world scale, for the same energy output, uranium mines produce just as much environmental pollution as coal mines and as many accidents.

4 If **fast-breeder reactors** are used, then our present uranium supplies will last far longer than our supplies of oil or coal. But fast-breeder reactors are difficult to control. At present, Britain has only one experimental fast-breeder reactor, at Dounreay. With ordinary nuclear reactors, uranium resources are likely to be used up long before coal resources.

Problems of nuclear power

Fig. 5 Brockdorf nuclear power station in West Germany
This power station is defended like a military base. Many people feel that we should get rid of nuclear power stations. Why?
What are the advantages of nuclear power?
What are the disadvantages?

1 A serious accident at a nuclear power station is a major disaster. British nuclear reactors cannot blow up like an atomic bomb, but even a conventional explosion like that at Chernobyl can release tonnes of radioisotopes into the atmosphere. (Actually, the reactor at Chernobyl nearly did blow up like an atomic bomb.) Careful design and safety precautions can make the risk very small but it can never be removed entirely.

2 Even minor faults and accidents at nuclear power stations cause some release of radioisotopes into the environment.

3 Nuclear power stations produce radioactive waste, some of which is very difficult to deal with (see Section 17.9).

4 After a few decades, nuclear power stations will themselves have to be disposed of. This will not be easy. At first, they will be sealed off to allow some of the radioisotopes to decay. There is the danger that they could be left like this for a very long time!

● **Suppose that you were living in an isolated coastal area with high unemployment. There is a proposal to build a nuclear power station nearby. What arguments are likely to be raised by your neighbours for and against its construction?**

273

Controlling the temperature

Fig. 1 Controlling a nuclear power station
How is the fission reaction controlled?

The fission reaction in a nuclear reactor releases energy and gives it out as heat. Where does this energy come from? The nuclei and neutrons produced by the fission reaction have less total mass than the original uranium or plutonium nuclei. The energy released in the reaction comes from this lost mass. Einstein showed that, when a mass m disappears in this way, the energy released is

$$E = mc^2 \qquad (1)$$

where c is the speed of light (3×10^8 m/s).

Thus a small loss in mass produces vast quantities of energy. **How much energy do you get from a loss of 1 g?** This energy raises the reactor to a very high temperature.

In a nuclear reactor, fission occurs as a chain reaction (Figure 3). The neutrons released by nuclei in one reaction collide with other nuclei. This causes these nuclei to split, releasing more neutrons. One way of slowing down the reaction (and therefore of reducing the temperature) is to remove some of these neutrons.

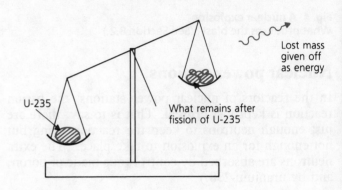

Fig. 2 Energy produced by a loss in mass
What is the mass loss per day from the fuel of a thousand million watt nuclear reactor?

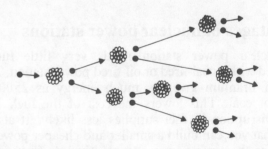

Fig. 3 A chain reaction
What must be true for the material to become critical?

Neutron absorption

99.3% of natural uranium is uranium-238. Only 0.7% is uranium-235. Uranium-238 can absorb the fast-moving neutrons produced by the fission process. In doing so, it turns into plutonium-239.

Unfortunately, if natural uranium is used in the reactor, too many neutrons are absorbed. There are two ways round this:

1 Use highly enriched uranium which contains a much higher proportion of uranium-235 than natural uranium does.

2 Slow the neutrons down to normal *thermal* speeds (about 1000 m/s). Uranium-238 doesn't absorb such slow(!) neutrons.

Fast-breeder reactors

(a)

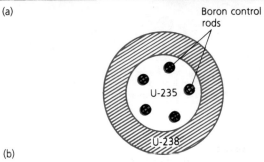

(b)

Fig. 4 The Dounreay fast-breeder reactor
Why is it called (i) fast? (ii) a breeder reactor?

Fast-breeder reactors, use highly enriched uranium. Uranium-235 is separated from the uranium-238 in natural uranium. The uranium-238 is then used as a blanket round the uranium-235 (Figure 4(b)). Nuclear fission takes place in the uranium-235 with fast-moving neutrons. Only the neutrons that reach the uranium-238 outside are absorbed. These neutrons turn the uranium-238 into fissionable plutonium-239. This plutonium can be used to replace the used uranium-235. The reactor **breeds** more fuel.

The only British reactor which uses this method is at Dounreay in northern Scotland (Figure 4(a)). Because of the high neutron speeds, changes in reaction rate occur much faster than in other types of reactor. This makes the reactor much more difficult to control.

Thermal reactors

Thermal reactors use **moderators** to slow down the neutrons. The earliest reactors, and most British reactors, use a graphite block as a moderator (Figure 5). This contains holes for the cylinders of uranium fuel. Most of the world's reactors are **pressurised-water reactors** (PWRs). These use water as a moderator. **Why do you think the water is kept under high pressure as it passes through the very hot reactor? (See Section 8.8.)**

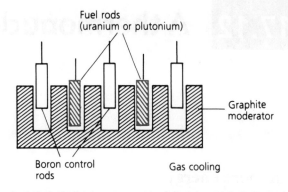

Fig. 5 A thermal reactor using graphite as a moderator
What is a moderator?
What is the difference between this type of reactor and a pressurised-water reactor?

Control rods

In order to control the reaction, we need to be able to control the number of neutrons absorbed. This is done by using control rods made of boron or cadmium. (These are both materials that absorb neutrons.) To slow down the reaction, the control rods are lowered between the fuel rods. To speed up the reaction, the control rods are raised.

In the Chernobyl disaster, the reaction was going far too slowly—like a fire going out. The operators tried to speed up the reaction by removing control rods. But they removed far too many. It was like throwing petrol on to a fire. The sudden increase in temperature, together with other factors, caused an explosion.

Cooling

A cooling system is needed
(a) to cool the reactor and
(b) to transfer the heat to the boilers in order to generate electricity.

British gas-cooled reactors use carbon dioxide gas as a coolant. Pressurised-water reactors use water as a coolant (as well as a moderator). If the coolant leaks from a pressurised-water reactor, the nuclear reaction will stop. But there may be enough internal energy (heat) left to melt the reactor. This happened at Three-Mile Island in America. **See what you can find out about this accident.**

- **The Chernobyl reactor used water as a coolant and graphite as a moderator. Why was this a particularly dangerous design?**

- **Find out what you can about the different designs of nuclear reactors in Britain.**

275

A thermonuclear future?

Far more energy

Fig. 1 Designing a thermonuclear reactor
This is a test model. It will be decades before a full-scale thermonuclear reactor is built.
What is a thermonuclear reactor?
What is its advantage?
What are the main difficulties in designing it?

Nuclear fission (splitting the atom) produces a tremendous amount of energy—far more than in any chemical reaction. But sticking hydrogen nuclei together to produce helium releases even more energy. This process is called **nuclear fusion**. (The nuclei of hydrogen *fuse* together to form helium.) Far more nuclear energy is released from nuclear fusion than from nuclear fission.

The fusion of deuterium nuclei

A deuterium (hydrogen-2) nucleus consists of one proton and one neutron. Suppose that you force two deuterium nuclei together. To start with, they repel

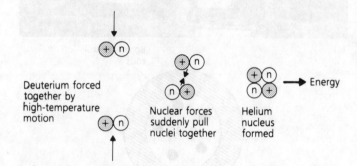

Fig. 2 Nuclear fusion
Where is this reaction taking place on a large scale at the moment?

each other very strongly because they both have a positive charge. But as you force them closer and closer together they suddenly start to attract each other. The deuterium nuclei rush towards each other to form a helium nucleus. As they do so, a tremendous amount of (nuclear) energy is released (Figure 2).

A thermonuclear reaction

Nuclear fusion is often called a **thermonuclear process**. (*Therme* is the Greek word for heat.) The reason for this is that heat is required to start the reaction. The only way of forcing hydrogen nuclei together is to heat the hydrogen to about 100 million degrees Celsius. At this temperature, the atoms move around so violently that they lose all their orbiting electrons. (The separate, high-speed nuclei and electrons form a **plasma**.) The hydrogen nuclei are moving so fast that they bang together and fuse into helium.

The Sun is a thermonuclear reactor, turning hydrogen into helium. The hydrogen bomb is also a very short-lived thermonuclear reactor. In this case, an atomic bomb provides the tremendously high temperature that is needed for the fusion reaction.

Designing a thermonuclear reactor

If thermonuclear reactions could be controlled in a power station, then our energy needs would be more than filled for thousands or even millions of years. We could use the hydrogen in seawater as fuel. Unfortunately, it is very difficult to design a thermonuclear reactor:

- How do you heat the hydrogen to 100 million degrees Celsius?
- How do you keep it at this temperature without it vaporising everything around it?
- How do you get the energy out safely?

These are very difficult problems, but there may be solutions. Powerful lasers could be used to heat the gas. The hot gas could then be kept in a magnetic bottle. That is to say, the material could be held in a vacuum and kept away from the walls of the container using magnetic fields (Figure 3).

Research has been carried out on this for many years. Perhaps at some time well into the next century a thermonuclear power station may be a possibility. Let us hope that, if we are to have a thermonuclear future, then it will be with safe, environmentally beneficial, thermonuclear power stations, and not with thermonuclear weapons!

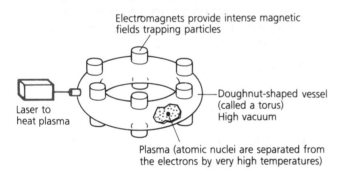

Fig. 3 Heating a plasma in a magnetic bottle
What is a plasma?
What is a magnetic bottle?

Fig. 4 What sort of thermonuclear future will there be?
How can physics help, and how can you help, to make the future better than the present?

277

Exercises

1 An alpha particle is

A A proton

B A neutron

C An electron

D A positron

E A helium nucleus

2 The half-life of an isotope is

A Half the time taken for that isotope to decay completely

B Half the time taken for one atom to decay

C The time taken for one atom to split into two

D The time taken for the activity to fall to half its initial level

E The time taken for the activity to fall to half that of a standard isotope

3 The different isotopes of the same element have the same

A Mass

B Nucleon number

C Atomic number

D Type of radioactive decay

E Abundance

4 The graphite moderator of a nuclear reactor is there

A To absorb the neutrons

B To slow down the neutrons

C To prevent the reactor from exploding

D To produce the heat

E To cool the reactor

5 In an experiment, some radiation passes through a sheet of paper but is completely stopped by a thin steel sheet. The radiation is most likely to be

A Alpha radiation

B Beta radiation

C Gamma radiation

D X-radiation

E Ultraviolet radiation

6 When a plutonium-239 nucleus is hit by a neutron, a reaction occurs. More neutrons are released and a large amount of energy is given out. This is called

A A chain reaction

B Nuclear fusion

C Nuclear fission

D Neutron decay

E Alpha decay

7 Plutonium-239 has a half-life of 24 000 years. How long will it take for the activity of 1 kg of this isotope to fall to one-eighth of its initial level?

A 3000 years

B 72 000 years

C 96 000 years

D 192 000 years

E 129 000 years

8 Carbon-14 (atomic number 6) decays by beta decay into one of the following. Which one?

A Beryllium-10 (atomic number 4)

B Boron-14 (atomic number 5)

C Carbon-13 (atomic number 6)

D Nitrogen-14 (atomic number 7)

9 Complete these sentences:

a Each element has several different _____, differing in _____. Some do not decay, but are _____. Some, called _____, decay and give out nuclear radiation. Those with _____ half-lives have higher activity than those with _____ half-lives.

b In British gas-cooled reactors, _____ is used as a _____ to slow down the neutrons. This makes the neutrons less likely to be absorbed by the uranium-_____. Instead, they cause uranium-_____ atoms to undergo _____. As the nuclei split in two, they give out more _____ and _____.

10 State two advantages and two disadvantages of nuclear power stations compared with coal-fired power stations.

11 What is meant by a tracer technique? Describe one medical example and one industrial example.

12 Uranium-238, uranium-235 and plutonium-239 are radioisotopes. They all undergo alpha decay. Suppose that you had
- a new uranium fuel rod completely encased in metal
- a used uranium fuel rod
- a sealed plastic packet of plutonium.

a Which (if any) of these would it be safe to hold in your hand?

b Would it be safe to hold any of them with tongs? If so, which one?

c Which of them (if any) could safely be kept in a far corner of your room? Explain your answers.

13 State three precautions to be taken by people employed in the use of radioisotopes.

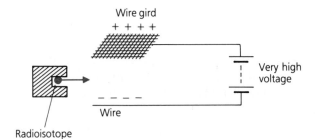

Fig. 1

14 Figure 1 shows a wire grid held near a single wire. There is a very large potential difference between the wire and the grid.

a What happens when a radioisotope is held nearby?

b Why?

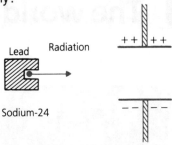

Fig. 2 What happens to the beam between the charged plates?

15 Sodium-24 decays into magnesium-22, giving out two different kinds of radiation. Figure 2 shows a sodium-24 source placed near some charged metal plates. Copy the diagram, and continue the beam of radiation from the isotope showing what happens as it passes between the plates.

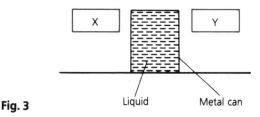

Fig. 3

16 The system shown in Figure 3 is using a radioisotope to check some cans made of thin metal. The system is used to check whether or not the cans are completely full of liquid as they come out of a filling machine.

a What are X and Y?

b What type of radiation should the radioisotope emit? Why?

17 Explain the differences between a fast-breeder reactor, a thermal reactor and a thermonuclear reactor.

18 What is meant by a nuclear reactor 'going critical'? How is this controlled?

19 Describe an experiment to measure the half-life of radon. Why is this radioisotope relevant to the air flow in granite houses?

18 ELECTRONICS

18.1 The world of electronics

High tech

Fig. 1 High tech
This picture shows radios, televisions and tape-recorders in a shop window. What do these have in common?

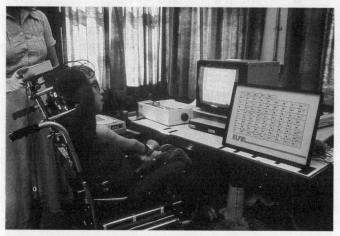

Fig. 2 Where the body fails, electronics takes over
This person is able to do things that would have been impossible without microelectronics.
What other uses of electronics can you think of?

What do you think about when you hear the word electronics? Digital watches? Video recorders? Computers? Electronic sewing machines? Industrial robots? **How many more can you add to the list?**

What do these things have in common? What is so special about electronics that makes it, apparently, so important?

1 It's up to date. New types of electronic equipment are coming on to the market all the time. They are cheap but very effective.

2 It's clean and easy to use. All it needs is electricity, and not much of that! All you do is to press a button, and the silicon chips sort everything else out—telling the time, washing the clothes, recording the television programme . . . .

3 Electronics is changing people's lives in many ways. Some people are losing their jobs because of it. Others are training for jobs and tasks that didn't exist before the silicon chip. The lives of many handicapped people have been improved by microelectronics. Similarly, microelectronics has been of great benefit in hospitals. In fact, most of our lives have been affected by electronics in some way. **How different would your life be without electronics?**

Electronic systems

You may have heard people talking about electronic systems. What do they mean by this? What exactly is a system?

From our point of view, a television is a **system** for turning radio waves into sound and pictures. A cassette recorder is a **system** for storing sounds on tape, and then playing them back again. A burglar alarm is a **system** for ringing an alarm bell when a burglar enters a building.

Electronic systems all have three parts:
1 **Input sensors** to detect radio waves, sound, light, temperature, magnetism, the pressing of keys on a keyboard etc.
2 **Output devices** such as television screens, speakers, motors etc.
3 **Processing circuits** that process the electrical signals from the input sensors, and send appropriate voltages and currents to the right output devices at the right time.

Figure 3 gives some examples of electronic systems and details of the input sensors, output devices and processing.

Fig. 3 Electronic systems

Equipment	Input sensors	Output devices	Processing
Public address system	Microphone	Loudspeaker	Amplify (increase) the electric power coming from the microphone and send it to the speaker
Television	Aerial Control switches	Television screen Speaker	Take the signal from the radio waves for the required television station. Send the vision part of this signal to the screen and the sound part to the speaker
Washing machine	Control switches	Pump Motors Heater	Read the wash program from the control switches, and use it to switch the motors and heater on and off at the appropriate times

- What other examples of electronic systems can you think of?

Looking inside

Fig. 4 Artificial intelligence
Computers can carry out some of the simpler tasks of the human brain. From our point of view, there could be tiny people inside the computer doing all the work.
What do computers do really well compared with people?

- **Ask your teacher if he or she has any electronic equipment that you can look inside. Make sure that the electrical supply is DISCONNECTED first.**

From each of the input and output devices, there are wires going to one or more **printed circuit boards** (PCBs). These boards carry out the processing.

On one side of each PCB, there is a printed solder pattern called a **printed circuit**. This is part of the wiring. It connects together the different **components** of the circuit (Figure 5).

(a)

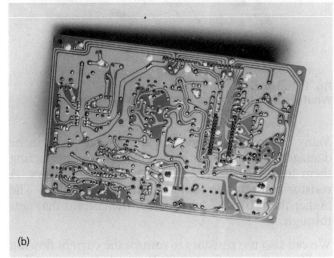
(b)

Fig. 5 A typical printed circuit board
(a) Component side
(b) The components are soldered underneath
Should the boards themselves be made of a conducting or an insulating material? Why?

The most important components are the **integrated circuits** or ICs (sometimes called silicon chips). These do most of the processing. (You should be able to spot these—they look a bit like centipedes, with many legs along each side of a tiny black plastic box.)

Transistors are another important part of many circuits. (These are usually tiny black squares or metal cylinders with three legs.)

- **Have a look at an old printed circuit board and see how many components you can name.**

We will look at all these components, and others such as diodes and capacitors, in these last two chapters. We will start by looking at resistors—by far the most common component of electronic circuits.

Resistance and resistors

Resistors and Ohm's Law

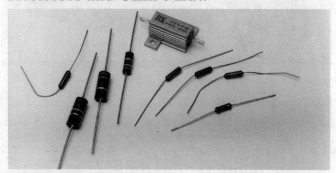

Fig. 1 Resistors
What are they for?   How are they made?

Many electronic components are delicate and can be damaged by large currents. One way of protecting them from such large currents is to use **resistors**. A resistor restricts the flow of current through it. The higher the resistance, the smaller the current that gets through.

We can also use resistors to control the current flowing in different parts of a circuit. But to do this we need to know how much current gets through a resistor.

The nineteenth century physicist Georg Simon Ohm carried out experiments to measure this. He discovered the following law which we now call **Ohm's law** (Figure 2).

$$\text{potential difference} = \text{current} \times \text{resistance}$$
$$\text{or} \qquad V = IR \qquad (1)$$

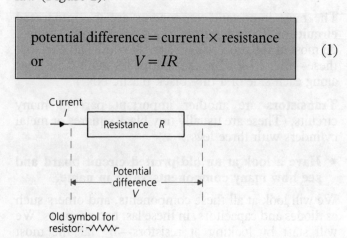

Old symbol for resistor: ⌇⌇⌇⌇⌇

Fig. 2 Ohm's law

The current depends not only on the resistance but also on the potential difference. For example, we can make more current pass through a resistor by increasing the potential difference across it.

Resistance is measured in ohms (Ω), kilohms (kΩ), or megaohms (MΩ). (Ω is the Greek letter omega.)

An example
From Equation (1), the current through a 1 kΩ resistor when a potential difference of 3 V is placed across its terminals is

$$\text{current} = \frac{\text{potential difference}}{\text{resistance}} = \frac{3\,\text{V}}{1000\,\Omega}$$
$$= 0.003\,\text{A} = 3\,\text{mA}$$

- **What resistance must a resistor have to pass a current of 2 mA when placed across a 6 V battery?**

Why use resistors?

*Typical LED has current $I_F = 20$ mA when pd across it is $V_F = 2.4$ V. The pd across the resistor must therefore be $V_R = 3.6$ V, and the resistance $R = V_R/I_F = 3.6/0.02\,\Omega = 180\,\Omega$

Fig. 3 Resistors are used to protect components
How do they give protection?

We use resistors:

1 To protect delicate electronic components—a resistor can prevent too much current from going through a component. For example, a light-emitting diode (the small red light on some electronic equipment) needs to have a resistance of at least 180 Ω in series with it when it is used with a 6 V power supply (Figure 3).

2 To control the voltages at different points of a circuit. Controlling the voltages allows you to control the electronic currents flowing in the circuit (see for example Section 18.5).

Common types of resistor

The cheapest but least-accurate type of resistor is the **carbon composition resistor**. This is made of carbon powder mixed with a gluelike binder. The more carbon there is, the more easily electricity can pass through (the lower the resistance).

Carbon-film resistors and **metal-film resistors** are more accurate but more expensive than carbon composition resistors. They consist of a ceramic (clay) cylinder coated with a film either of carbon or of tin oxide. The electricity flows through this coating. The thinner the film, the higher the resistance.

The most accurate type of resistor is one that you can make yourself! **Wire-wound resistors** consist of a length of nichrome (nickel–chromium) resistance

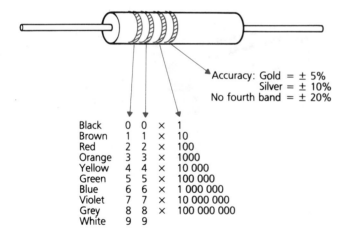

Accuracy: Gold = ± 5%
Silver = ± 10%
No fourth band = ± 20%

Black	0	0	× 1
Brown	1	1	× 10
Red	2	2	× 100
Orange	3	3	× 1000
Yellow	4	4	× 10 000
Green	5	5	× 100 000
Blue	6	6	× 1 000 000
Violet	7	7	× 10 000 000
Grey	8	8	× 100 000 000
White	9	9	

Fig. 4 The resistance colour code
Try working out the resistance of some resistors from their colour code. Then measure the resistance using an ammeter and voltmeter.
How accurate is the resistance?
How accurate was your measurement?

wire. The longer and the thinner the wire, the higher the resistance.

● **Try making a 10 Ω wire-wound resistor. How can you be sure that it has this value?**

Resistance colour code

The coloured bands that you see round most resistors show the value of the resistance. Figure 4 explains how this colour code works. **What are the resistance and tolerance of resistors with the following bands:**
(a) brown, black, red, silver?
(b) grey, blue, green?

You can't buy just any value of resistor. The resistors that are normally available are listed in Figure 5. These are enough for most purposes. You don't usually need to be very precise when choosing a resistor. (See Section 18.4 if you need a value of resistance in between those available.)

Fig. 5 Commonly available resistors

Resistors with 10% tolerance	1.0 1.2 1.5 1.8 2.2 2.7 3.3 3.9 4.7 5.6 6.8
Resistors with 20% tolerance	1.0 1.5 2.2 3.3 4.7 6.8

In addition, resistors with these values multiplied by a power of 10 are available. (For example, you can get a 270 k resistor with 10% tolerance but the nearest available resistor with 20% tolerance is 220 k.)

Modern notation

The symbol Ω is not very convenient for printing. Neither is the decimal point. Because of this, the symbol Ω is often omitted (or replaced with an R) and R, k or M is used instead of the decimal point. For example, 33 Ω becomes 33R, 0.47 kΩ becomes k47 and 5.6 MΩ becomes 5M6. **Write 1.5 kΩ and 220 Ω in this notation.**

Resistance elsewhere in the circuit

In fact, all circuit components have some resistance—not just resistors. In some components, Ohm's law is not obeyed. The resistance changes with the voltage that is applied. As we shall see, this makes these components extremely useful.

Heating elements

Fig. 1 An electrical heating element
This uses resistive heating.
Where else are heating elements used?

A light bulb has a tungsten filament which glows when the bulb is switched on. The filament is acting as a resistor. When current flows through it, it becomes very hot and starts to glow.

Similarly, the heating element of an electric oven, a toaster or an iron consists of a length of resistance wire. (In an oven, this is surrounded by a ceramic insulator and then by a metal cyclinder—see Section 11.7.) When an electric current flows through the wire, it glows red hot.

In fact, whenever a current flows through a resistance, it produces heat.

Heat in electronic circuits

When a large current flows through a resistor, the resistor gets hot. A transistor or a silicon chip integrated circuit will also get hot. (Technicians looking for faults in *low-voltage* electronic equipment sometimes touch transistors and other components to see if they are over-heating. If they are, the current is too large.)

We don't really want all the resistors in a circuit to glow like a light bulb. Nor do we want to fry eggs or grill toast using our integrated circuits. (Indeed, heating on this scale would completely destroy these components.) So we must keep the current through these components small enough to avoid this problem.

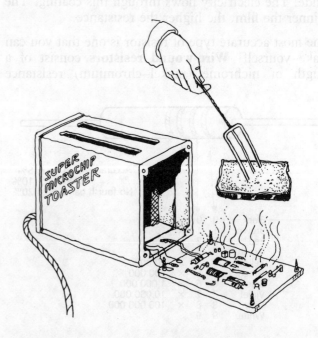

Fig. 2 Why do some circuit components get hot?

How much heating?

How much heat do you get for a particular current flowing through a particular resistance?

According to Section 11.4, Equation (1), the heating power is given by

heating power = potential difference × current

Substituting the expression for potential difference from Section 18.2, Equation (1) gives

$$heating = resistance \times current^2$$
$$P = RI^2 \qquad (1)$$

Thus the heat produced by a current of 2 A flowing through a 100 Ω resistance will be

heating power = 100 Ω × (2 A)^2 = 400 W

- What heat will be given off if
  (a) the current doubles to 4 A?
  (b) the current remains at 2 A but the resistance doubles to 200 Ω?

  Notice that a fractional increase in current has much more effect on heating power than a fractional increase in resistance.

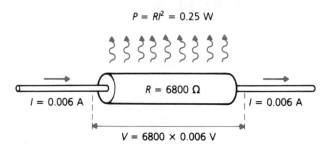

$P = RI^2 = 0.25$ W

$I = 0.006$ A $R = 6800$ Ω $I = 0.006$ A

$V = 6800 \times 0.006$ V

Fig. 3 A 6800 Ω, quarter-watt resistor
What is the maximum voltage that can be used?
Why?

Overheating

How do you stop electronic components from overheating?

1 Choose components to fit the currents that you will be passing through them. Electronic catalogues state the maximum power (or sometimes the current) that the components can stand. Don't try to save money by using a resistor designed for up to 0.25 W of heating power when you need one that can stand 0.5 W.

2 Use a **heat sink** for components that are likely to get hot. A heat sink is just a large piece of metal which removes the heat. **Why is metal used for this?**

3 If you need to pass a large current through low-power resistors, then connect the resistors in parallel (see Section 18.4).

Fig. 4 What is the purpose of the metal plate?

Why use resistors in series or in parallel?

Fig. 1   Resistors in series and in parallel
How would you work out the resistance of such a network of resistors?
Why do some circuits use resistors in series or in parallel?

Two resistors connected in series or in parallel act just like a single resistor (of a different value). So why not use an **equivalent resistor** in the first place?

One reason is that you can't always get the resistor that you want (see Section 18.2). Another reason for putting resistors in parallel is that this reduces the current through each resistor. This helps to avoid overheating (see Section 18.3).

It is very important to be able to work out what happens when resistors are connected in series and in parallel. Other electronic components are frequently connected in these ways and it is often very important to know their combined resistance.

Adding resistors in series

Figure 2(a) shows two resistors, R_1 and R_2, in series. The same current I flows through each resistor. The equivalent resistor shown in Figure 2(b) behaves in the same way as the two in series. For this resistor to carry the same current I, the same potential difference V must be connected across it.

The value of this equivalent resistor R is

$$R = R_1 + R_2 \qquad (1)$$

Thus a $1.2\,\text{k}\Omega$ resistor and a $1.8\,\text{k}\Omega$ resistor in series have an effective resistance of

$$1.2\,\text{k}\Omega + 1.8\,\text{k}\Omega = 3\,\text{k}\Omega$$

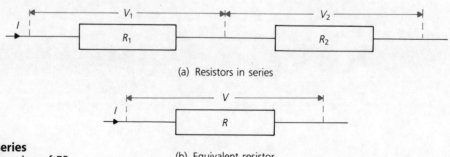

(a) Resistors in series

(b) Equivalent resistor

Fig. 2   Resistors in series
How do you find the value of R?

286

- **What is the effective resistance of a 1 kΩ resistor in series with a 100 Ω resistor?**

Derivation of Equation (1)
Consider the first resistor R_1. According to Ohm's law (Section 18.2), the potential difference between the ends of this resistor is

$$V_1 = R_1 I$$

Similarly the potential drop across resistor R_2 is

$$V_2 = R_2 I$$

The total potential drop across the two resistors (and therefore across the equivalent resistor) is

$$V = V_1 + V_2$$
$$= R_1 I + R_2 I$$

Applying Ohm's law to this equivalent resistor, we have

$$V = RI$$

These two expressions for V must be equal to each other. Therefore

$$RI = R_1 I + R_2 I$$

On dividing both sides of this equation by I, we are left with Equation (1).

Adding resistors in parallel

Figure 3(a) shows two resistors R_1 and R_2 in parallel. In this case, the effective resistance R is given by

$$\frac{1}{R} = \frac{1}{R_1} + \frac{1}{R_2} \quad \text{or} \quad R = \frac{R_1 R_2}{R_1 + R_2} \qquad (2)$$

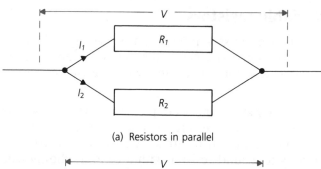

(a) Resistors in parallel

(b) Equivalent resistor

Fig. 3 Resistors in parallel
How do you find the value of R?

Suppose, for example, that we connect a 1.2 kΩ resistor in parallel with a 1.8 kΩ resistor. Then, according to Equation (2),

$$R = \frac{(1200\,\Omega) \times (1800\,\Omega)}{(1200\,\Omega) + (1800\,\Omega)}$$

$$= 720\,\Omega$$

- **What is the effective resistance of a 1 kΩ resistance and a 100 Ω resistance connected in parallel?**

Notice that for resistors connected in parallel the effective resistance of the combination is always less than that of each resistor on its own. Normally, the resistances R_1 and R_2 are equal. When these resistors are connected in parallel, the effective resistance is half the value of the resistors.

- **Use Equation (2) to show that this is so, and check it experimentally.**

Derivation of Equation (2)
The potential drop V across each resistor is the same. The current through R_1 is

$$I_1 = \frac{V}{R_1}$$

Similarly, the current through R_2 is

$$I_2 = \frac{V}{R_2}$$

The current I through the equivalent resistor shown in Figure 3(b) must be the sum of these currents. Therefore

$$I = I_1 + I_2$$

But

$$I = \frac{V}{R}$$

Hence

$$\frac{V}{R} = I_1 + I_2$$

$$= \frac{V}{R_1} + \frac{V}{R_2}$$

By dividing both sides of this equation by V, we get Equation (2).

18.5 The potential divider

Controlling the voltage

Fig. 1 A potential divider
Why is it called an input voltage unit?

Suppose that you want to use batteries for a 5 V circuit. The only batteries that you can get are 4.5 V and 6 V. What do you do? Answer: you divide the 6 V potential difference from the battery into 5 V and 1 V using a **potential divider**.

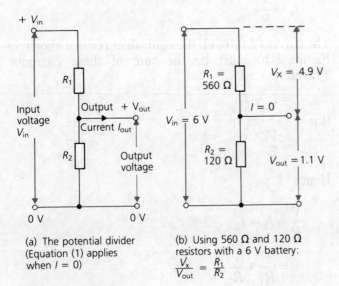

(a) The potential divider (Equation (1) applies when $I = 0$)

(b) Using 560 Ω and 120 Ω resistors with a 6 V battery:
$$\frac{V_x}{V_{out}} = \frac{R_1}{R_2}$$

Fig. 2 How the potential divider divides the potential
What is the output voltage?
What happens to this voltage if you connect a resistor across the output?

Figure 2 shows such a potential divider. The two resistors R_1 and R_2 divide the input voltage into two parts. We use one of these parts.

The output voltage from such a divider depends on the current that we take from it. If we do not take any current, then the output voltage is

$$V_{out} = V_{in} \frac{R_2}{R_1 + R_2} \qquad (1)$$

(In practice, this equation still works when there is a small output current provided that the output current is much less than the current through R_2.)

For example, if R_1 is a 560 Ω resistor, R_2 is a 120 Ω resistor and the input voltage is 6 V, then according to Equation (1)

$$V_{out} = \frac{V_{in} \times R_2}{R_1 + R_2}$$

$$= \frac{6\,V \times 120\,\Omega}{560\,\Omega + 120\,\Omega} = \frac{6 \times 120}{680}\,V$$

$$= 1.1\,V$$

Variable resistors

If you wish to use a different output voltage, then you need different resistances. Alternatively, you can use a **variable resistor**—a resistor whose resistance can be changed.

The **rheostat** is one example of a variable resistor (Figure 3). Rheostats are (or were) sometimes used to dim stage lights in theatres. A rheostat consists of a large wire-wound resistor with a central, sliding contact. This allows you to choose the length of wire you wish to use.

For smaller currents you can use the cheaper variable resistors that are found in radios. Most of these are also wire wound, though some use the resistance of a ring of carbon.

(a)

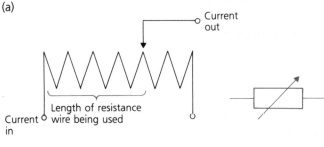

(b) How it works

(c) Circuit symbol for a variable resistor

Fig. 3 A rheostat

Potentiometer

(a)

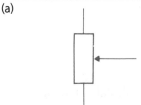

(b) Circuit symbol
(also used for a rheostat when it is used as a potentiometer)

Fig. 4 Potentiometers
How can they be used as variable resistors?

The most common variable resistor is that used for the volume control on a radio or a television. It is called a **potentiometer** (Figure 4). It has three terminals: one at each end and a central sliding contact.

When you want to use a potentiometer as a variable resistor, you must make your connections to the central terminal and one of the end terminals. However, a potentiometer can also be used directly as a potential divider. This is how it is normally intended to be used (hence the name). A rheostat also has three terminals, and can be used in the same way.

Using a potential divider for measuring resistance

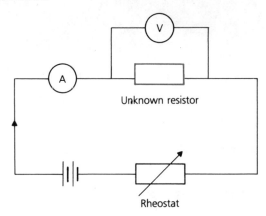

Fig. 5 Measuring an unknown resistance

We now have a way of measuring resistance for a range of voltages. Figure 5 shows a suitable circuit for resistances of less than $100\,\Omega$. **Why is this circuit not suitable for larger resistances? What circuit would you use for these?**

Several measurements of V and I are taken for different settings of the rheostat. $R = I/V$ is worked out in each case and the results are averaged.

- **Use this method to find the resistance of**
  (a) a length of resistance wire
  (b) a pencil lead.

This is only one of many uses of a potential divider. Another use is described in Chapter 19.

Capacitors

Fig. 1 Capacitors
What do they do?
Where are they used?

Short-term storage

Capacitors store charge—rather like batteries. But whereas a car battery is used to store thousands of coulombs of charge for many months, a typical capacitor is used to store about a millionth of a coulomb for a fraction of a second. Capacitors are used for short-term storage of small amounts of charge.

For example, a camera flashgun uses a capacitor (see Section 11.5). A battery **charges** the capacitor by putting charge into it. When the flashgun is set off, this charge flows out through the flashbulb. The capacitor **discharges** with a large current. On its own, the battery could not supply this amount of current!

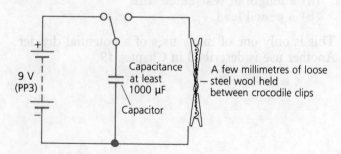

Fig. 2 A homemade flashgun
Why is the capacitor needed?

9 V (PP3)

Capacitance at least 1000 μF
Capacitor

A few millimetres of loose steel wool held between crocodile clips

290

- Try making the homemade flashgun shown in Figure 2. What is the advantage of using the capacitor and switch rather than connecting the steel wool directly to the battery?

How it works

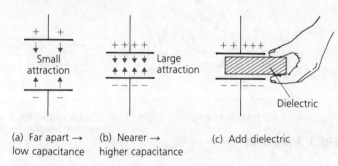

(a) Far apart →
low capacitance

(b) Nearer →
higher capacitance

(c) Add dielectric

Fig. 3 How a capacitor works
Would paper soaked in salty water make a good dielectric? Why?

A capacitor consists basically of two metal sheets with a space between them. The larger the metal sheets are, and the closer they are, the more charge they can store.

When the capacitor is connected to a battery (as in Figure 2), one sheet becomes positively charged and the other negatively charged. The positive charge on one sheet attracts the negative charge on the other sheet (Figure 3). (The positive charge is caused by a shortage of electrons. When a negatively charged sheet is brought near, this drives away even more electrons.)

Another way of increasing the amount of charge that a capacitor can store is shown in Figure 3(c). An insulating material such as polyester is placed between the two metal sheets. This increases the amount of charge that the sheets can carry. We call such materials **dielectrics**.

A capacitor with a large **capacitance** (one which can store a lot of charge) therefore consists of two large metal sheets close together with a dielectric in between them.

Practical capacitors

In practice, it is inconvenient to handle large flat metal sheets. We need capacitors which are small and easy to use.

Polyester capacitors—These are made by rolling two sheets of metal foil (or metallised plastic) between three polyester sheets (Figure 4).

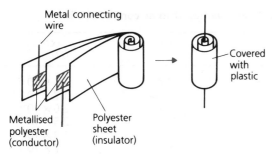

Fig. 4 A polyester capacitor
Why is it necessary to use three polyester sheets rather than just one?

● **Try making your own capacitor using kitchen foil and polythene sheeting. Use it for some of the circuits described in Section 19.7.**

Ceramic disc capacitors—These are used more frequently than polyester capacitors for storing small amounts of charge. (They have a much smaller capacitance than polyester capacitors.) They consist of a disc of ceramic (clay) separating two small metal plates.

Electrolytic capacitors—These have the highest capacitance. A single metal sheet is coated with a very thin layer of aluminium oxide. This is the dielectric. In place of the second metal sheet, the dielectric is covered with a layer of conducting jelly. Electrolytic capacitors must be connected the right way round. The plate with the oxide must be connected to the negative side of the power supply or battery.

Ac gets through; dc doesn't

When you charge a capacitor, electrons flow into one of the metal sheets and out of the other. It looks as though an electric current is flowing through the capacitor. If you now discharge the battery, the electrons will flow back. Current will appear to flow back through the capacitor in the opposite direction.

If this change from charging to discharging happens quickly, before the capacitor is fully charged, then the circuit will behave as though the capacitor wasn't

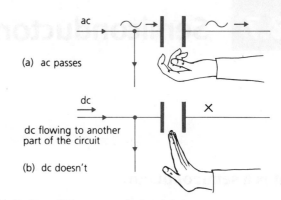

Fig. 5 Capacitors pass ac but not dc
Why is the frequency of the ac important?

there. This means that an alternating current of sufficiently high frequency can pass through a capacitor as if the capacitor wasn't there.

In contrast, direct current charges the capacitor in the first tiny fraction of a second and then stops. In other words, capacitors can pass alternating current but not direct current. They can pass changes in electric currents but not constant electric currents (Figure 5).

This has many advantages in electronic circuits. Some of these are described in Chapter 19.

● **Try passing first alternating current and then direct current through a polyester capacitor. Does the frequency of the ac matter?**

A word of warning

Capacitors store energy as well as charge. You can get a nasty electric shock from electrolytic capacitors in high-voltage electrical equipment. This can sometimes happen even when the equipment is no longer connected to the mains supply. So *don't* meddle inside high-voltage equipment even when you've pulled the plug out!

Fig. 6 Capacitors store energy as well as charge!
What sort of energy?

18.7 Semiconductors

What is a semiconductor?

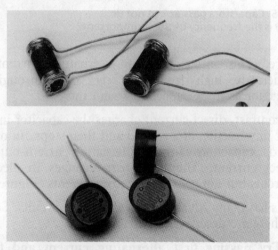

Fig. 1 Thermistors and light-dependent resistors are made with semiconducting materials

Metals and carbon have low resistance. They conduct electricity very easily. They have lots of 'free' electrons that move from atom to atom carrying the electric current.

Insulators such as plastics have extremely high resistance. The electrons are all tightly bound to their atoms and aren't free to move.

Semiconductors such as silicon, germanium and gallium arsenide have resistances in between the resistances of metals and of plastics (Figure 2). They conduct electricity better than insulators but not so well as conductors. They have some free electrons but not so many as metals have (Figure 3).

What makes semiconductors so useful is that we can control the number of free electrons. We can therefore control the resistance of the semiconductor. Most modern electronics is based on this. In most cases, the semiconductors are **doped** with special impurities to alter their behaviour (see Section 18.8). But there are two electronic components in which doping is not necessary. These are the **thermistor** and the **light-dependent resistor** (LDR). Thermistors rely on the change in semiconductor resistance with temperature.

Fig. 2 Resistivities of some common solids

	Solid	Electrical resistivity* $(\Omega\,m)$
Metals:	Silver	1.4×10^{-8}
	Copper	1.7×10^{-8}
	Gold	2.0×10^{-8}
	Aluminium	2.5×10^{-8}
	Tin	1.3×10^{-7}
	Steel	1.7×10^{-7}
	Nichrome	1.1×10^{-6}
Semiconductors:	Graphite	3×10^{-6} to 5×10^{-5}
	Germanium	0.003 to 0.5
	Silicon	0.1 to 50
Insulators:	Wood	10^{9}
	Glass	10^{10}
	Concrete	10^{10}
	Wax	10^{13}
	Hard rubber	10^{14}
	PVC	10^{16}

*The resistance of a wire is equal to the resistivity multiplied by the length and divided by the cross-sectional area:

$$R = \frac{\rho L}{A}$$

where ρ is the resistivity, L is the length and A is the cross-sectional area.

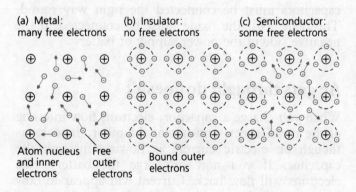

(a) Metal: many free electrons (b) Insulator: no free electrons (c) Semiconductor: some free electrons

Atom nucleus and inner electrons Free outer electrons Bound outer electrons

Fig. 3 How free are the electrons?
How do the differences shown in these diagrams cause the difference in electrical resistance?

Effect of temperature on resistance

If you use a computer in a very hot room, it sometimes goes haywire. (Large mainframe computers have air-conditioning to avoid this problem.) The high temperature causes electrons to be shaken from the vibrating atoms of the semiconductors. This increases the number of free electrons in the semiconductors, and so lowers the resistance.

> Semiconductors pass more current at higher temperatures.

This isn't true of metals. However much you heat a metal, the number of free electrons stays constant. All that happens is that the movement of electrons between the vibrating atoms is hindered. This increases the resistance.

> Metals pass less current at higher temperatures.

Thermistors

Thermistors are pieces of semiconductor (normally silicon) that decrease very markedly in resistance when they get hot. In Figure 4 the current–voltage characteristics of a thermistor are compared with those of a metal filament from a light bulb.

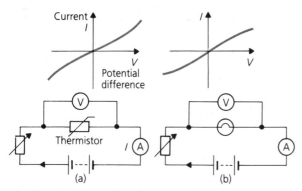

Fig. 4 What happens when it gets hot?
Current–voltage characteristics for a thermistor and a light bulb
How does the resistance of each change as it gets hot?

When you increase the current through the light bulb, the filament gets hotter. Its resistance increases. To increase the current further, you need to increase the potential difference across the filament to overcome this resistance.

In a thermistor, the resistance decreases as the current increases. So you need less increase in potential difference for the same increase in current.

- Try plotting the current–voltage characteristics for a torch bulb and a thermistor.

Thermistors have at least two uses:
1 They can be used to measure (or at least to detect) a change in temperature.
2 They can compensate for the increased resistance of metal filaments when they get hot. For example, in a television set a thermistor is connected in series with the cathode-ray tube filament. As the current builds up, the resistance of the filament increases but that of the thermistor decreases. The overall resistance stays the same.

- See if you can make a thermometer using a battery, a thermistor and a milliammeter.

Light-dependent resistors

Light-dependent resistors (LDRs) are used to detect light. For example, some bedside clocks have an LDR which senses how bright the room is. The LDR automatically changes the brightness of the display. It makes the display dimmer at night (so that it doesn't disturb you) and brighter during the day (so that you can still see it).

LDRs rely on the fact that light can increase the number of free electrons in a semiconductor. In an LDR, the semiconductor forms a zigzag between two pieces of metal (Figure 5). As soon as light falls anywhere on the semiconductor, it produces free electrons. This allows current to flow more easily between the two pieces of metal. The more light that falls on the LDR, the lower its resistance becomes.

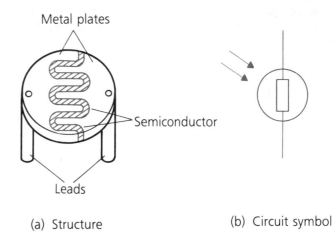

(a) Structure

(b) Circuit symbol

Fig. 5 A light-dependent resistor
Why does the semiconductor form a zigzag?

- See if you can make a light meter using a battery, an LDR and a milliammeter.

One way only

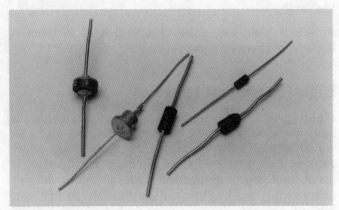

Fig. 1 Diodes made from doped semiconductors
What is 'doping'?

A semiconductor diode is a device which allows current to flow through it in one direction only. Most diodes look like resistors except that they have only one dark-coloured band near one end. For current to flow through a diode, this end must be connected to the negative side of a power supply. This is called **forward bias**. If the diode is connected the other way round, no current flows. This is called **reverse bias** (Figure 2).

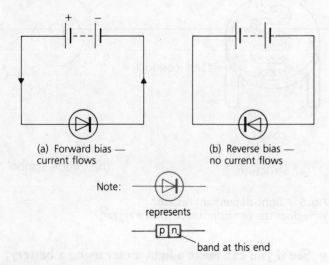

(a) Forward bias —
current flows

(b) Reverse bias —
no current flows

Note: represents

band at this end

Fig. 2 Diodes only pass current in one direction

- **Show this, using a bulb, a battery and a diode.**

To make a diode, special impurities are added to the semiconductor. This process is called **doping**. The end with the coloured band is doped with phosphorus to produce what we call **n-type semiconductor**. The other end is doped with boron to produce **p-type semiconductor**. Electric current can flow from p-type to n-type but *not* from n-type to p-type. For current to flow, the p-type end must be connected to the positive side of the power supply, and the n-type to the negative side of the power supply.

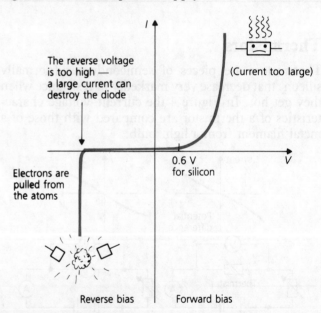

The reverse voltage is too high — a large current can destroy the diode

(Current too large)

0.6 V
for silicon

Electrons are pulled from the atoms

Reverse bias   Forward bias

Fig. 3 Diode characteristic
What is the difference between this curve and that for a thermistor which also curves upwards for large forward currents?

Figure 3 shows the current–voltage graph for a typical diode. No current flows for reverse voltages (unless they are large enough to pull electrons from the atoms). Current flows in the positive direction provided that the voltage exceeds 0.6 V. The resistance then gets less as the current increases.

- **Try measuring the current–voltage characteristics for a diode, applying up to 6 V in either direction.**

Using a diode

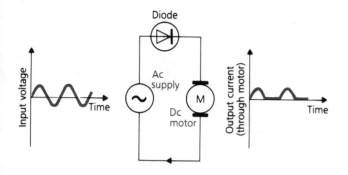

Fig. 4 Half-wave rectification
How does it work?
What would you notice with a very low-frequency ac supply?

Figure 4 shows how you can run a dc motor from an ac supply using a diode. The current is jerky, but allows the motor to keep turning in the same direction. The diode is said to be acting as a **half-wave rectifier**. **Why half-wave?**

- **Try this using (for example) a 3 V ac power supply and a 3 V dc motor.**

A simple power supply

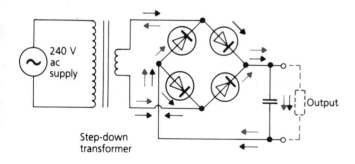

Fig. 5 A power supply circuit

A simple power supply circuit is shown in Figure 5. It uses four diodes in what is called a **bridge rectifier**. Whichever the direction of the current from the transformer, it always leaves the bridge rectifier flowing in the same direction.

The transformer reduces the voltage from the mains voltage (240 V) to a safe output voltage (for example, 12 V). **Why is the core of the transformer earthed? What is the purpose of the fuse?**

The capacitor smooths the output from the power supply. The current from the bridge rectifier continually builds up and dies away to zero. These changes in current are smoothed out by the capacitor (see Section 18.6). The output then receives a steady current.

This smoothing is only completely effective when *no* current is being taken from the power supply! Some power supplies have a voltage regulator connected to the output. This ensures that the final output voltage is constant even when a sizeable current is taken.

We will look at some other uses for diodes in Chapter 19.

A light-emitting diode (LED)

When a current flows through a diode, light is given out at the junction. This may be either visible light or infra-red light, depending on the material. Normally, even the visible light is not noticeable. LEDs are designed to make it noticeable. An LED glows (usually red) when electric current flows through it (Figure 6).

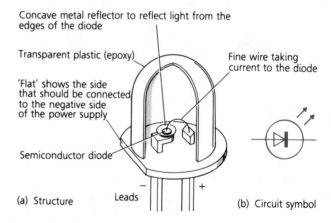

(a) Structure   Leads   (b) Circuit symbol

Fig. 6 A light-emitting diode
Does this work as a diode?
Try it and see. (Remember to use a protective resistor in series—see Section 18.2, Figure 3.)

Light-emitting diodes are often used as indicators, in place of light bulbs. They last longer than light bulbs, and use much less power. Digital clocks often use LEDs as glowing red lines to show the time. **The arrangements of LEDs in this case are called seven-segment displays. Why?**

LED lasers are used for sending telephone messages along optical cable. **Why can't a light bulb be used for this?**

These are only some of the many types and uses of a very important electronic component, the semiconductor diode.

18.9 Transistors and integrated circuits

Transistor radios

(a)

(b)

Fig. 1 Transistors and integrated circuits
Which are which?

We call portable radios 'transistor radios'. At one time (when transistors were new), people were willing to pay more for radios with a lot of transistors. Some manufacturers put in more transistors than were needed, sometimes just using them as resistors!

Today, transistors are less glamorous and less obvious. (They are usually hidden inside silicon chips.) But they are still the most important part of most electronic circuits. Some simple transistor circuits are considered in Chapter 19.

What is a transistor?

A **transistor** is a device that allows one current to control another. Many transistors are used as electrically operated switches. They can be used instead of relays (see Section 13.3) and are far faster and more reliable.

A simple (npn junction) transistor has three terminals (Figure 2).

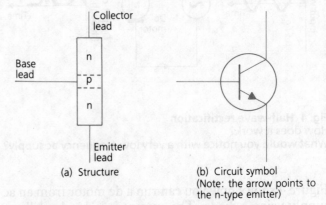

(a) Structure

(b) Circuit symbol
(Note: the arrow points to the n-type emitter)

Fig. 2 Most transistors have three terminals
You have to look in the manufacturer's catalogue to tell which is which.
Does it matter? Why?

1 The emitter—This is so called because it emits electrons into the transistor. It is usually connected to the negative side of both the input and the output circuits (see Figure 3).

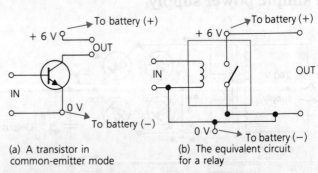

(a) A transistor in common-emitter mode

(b) The equivalent circuit for a relay

Fig. 3 A transistor acts as an electrical switch
How does it differ from that other electrical switch, the relay?

2 The collector—This is furthest from the emitter terminal. It is so called because it collects electrons from the transistor. The collector is connected to the positive side of the output.

3 The base—This terminal is known as the base because it formed the bottom of the first transistors. The input current is connected to this terminal. It can only take a very small current, and therefore a protective resistance of at least 1 kΩ is needed.

How it works

When a small current flows into the base terminal, the transistor switches on. Current is now able to flow through from the collector to the emitter. (Remember—conventional current flows the opposite way to electrons (see Section 11.3).)

When no current flows into the base terminal, the transistor switches off. Current is no longer able to flow through the transistor from the collector to the emitter (Figure 4).

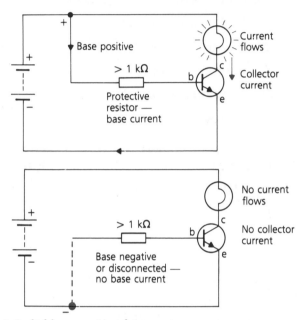

Fig. 4 Switching on a transistor
The transistor switches on when a current flows into the base. For this to happen, the base must have a positive potential (it must be connected to the positive side of the supply).
What do we mean when we say that the transistor is 'switched on'?

The current flowing into the collector is thousands of times greater than the current which flows into the base. So a transistor allows very tiny input currents (for example, from a microphone or a computer) to control much larger output currents (for example, to a speaker or the printing mechanism of a computer printer).

From this point of view, a transistor is a bit like the valve of an aerosol container. When you press gently on the valve, high pressure gas escapes. A small pressure releases a much larger pressure. In a transistor, a small current releases a much larger current from a battery. It is the battery that supplies the energy—the transistor merely controls the flow of this energy.

Silicon chips

These days, very few transistors are used on their own. Instead, they are made together in a single crystal of silicon called an **integrated circuit** (IC). (These are better known to most people as silicon chips or microchips.) A single integrated circuit may contain anything from half-a-dozen to a few thousand transistors, together with a similar number of diodes, capacitors and resistors. The crystals themselves are seldom bigger than the head of a match. But they are usually mounted in larger black boxes with two rows of terminals. This makes them easier to handle (Figure 5).

Fig. 5 A packaged crystal
The tiny silicon crystal can be seen in the middle of this EPROM integrated circuit. Fine gold wires connect it with the metal terminals down each side (the 24 legs).
Why is gold used for this?
Why is the crystal packaged in this way?

- **Where are integrated circuits used on their own and not in a box—probably in something you or a friend are wearing?**

- **An EPROM is an encased integrated circuit with a window which allows you to see the crystal inside. Have a look at an EPROM, perhaps through a microscope.**

Integrated circuits were first used in electronic circuits guiding missiles and space rockets. They were particularly useful because they were very small and used very little electricity. It was soon found that ICs could be made on a large scale as cheaply as single transistors.

Today manufacturers of integrated circuits are competing with each other to produce more and more complex and useful circuits on smaller and cheaper chips. But there is still a long way to go before they can produce circuits which can match the human brain in power, compactness and complexity.

- **What advantage do ICs have compared with single transistors? See what you can find out about the manufacture of ICs.**

297

Exercises

1 Electrical resistance is measured in

   A Volts

   B Watts

   C Newtons

   D Ohms

   E Amps

Fig. 1

2 The device shown in Figure 1 is

   A A thermistor

   B A light-dependent resistor

   C A light-emitting diode

   D A phototransistor

   E A photodiode

3 Which of the following statements about a capacitor is *not* correct?

   A It stores charge

   B It stores energy

   C Alternating current can pass through it

   D Direct current cannot pass through it

   E Direct current can flow through it, but in one direction only.

4 A device that decreases markedly in resistance as the temperature rises is called

   A A thermistor

   B A light-bulb filament

   C A resistor

   D A transistor

   E A diode

5 A light-dependent resistor is in a darkened room. The light is switched on. This causes the resistor

   A To decrease in resistance

   B To increase in resistance

   C To produce an emf

   D To produce a current

   E To glow

6 A current of 2 A flows through a heating coil of resistance 10 Ω. Heat is produced at the rate of

   A 5 W

   B 20 W

   C 40 W

   D 200 W

   E 400 W

7 Complete these sentences:

   a The potential difference across a resistor is equal to the _____ of the resistor multiplied by the _____ through the resistor.

   b With resistors in _____, you add the currents through each to give the total current.

   c An npn junction _____ allows a small current to switch on a larger current. A small change in current to the _____ terminal causes a large change in the current flowing from the _____ terminal to the _____ terminal.

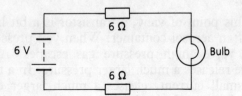

Fig. 2

8 What is the current through the lamp in Figure 2?

9 Give the name of the circuit shown in Figure 3 and state one applicaton of this circuit.

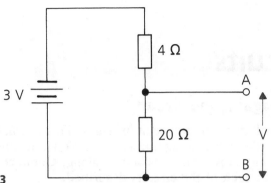

Fig. 3

10 a State two ways of increasing the capacitance of a capacitor.

b Briefly describe two uses for a capacitor.

11 An electric kettle is marked '240 V, 2400 W'.

a What is the current through the element of this kettle?

b What is the resistance of the filament?

c How is the electric current prevented from flowing through the water in the kettle
i Normally?
ii If the element is damaged?

12 a Name the devices producing the current–voltage characteristics shown in Figure 4.
b What is the potential difference *V*?

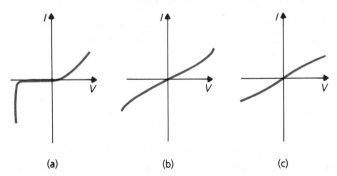

(a)   (b)   (c)

Fig. 4

13 a What is the resistance of the light bulb in Figure 5?

b What is the power output from the light bulb?

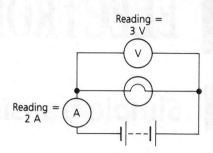

Fig. 5

14 Figure 6(a) shows an electronic component (labelled p–n) connected to a battery. Figure 6(b) shows the same circuit with the battery reversed.

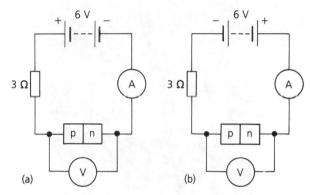

(a)   (b)

Fig. 6

a What is the name and purpose of the component?

b Assuming that this component has zero resistance, what would you expect to be the reading of the ammeter in each of the diagrams? Give reasons for your answers.

c What would you expect to be the reading of the voltmeter in each of these diagrams? Give reasons for your answers.

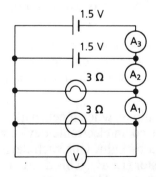

Fig. 7

15 What would you expect to be the reading of the voltmeter and each of the ammeters in Figure 7?

19 ELECTRONIC CIRCUITS

19.1 Simple transistor circuits

Automatic street lights

Fig. 1 A streetlight on in the daytime
Can you prevent this using electronics?

Have you ever seen street lights on in the middle of the day? They were probably controlled by a timer that had gone wrong (perhaps because of a power cut). This wouldn't have happened if, like many modern street lights, they had been controlled by a light sensor. The sensor switches the street lights on automatically when it gets dark, and off again when it gets light.

You can easily make your own automatic light control. In this section, we will consider one for a small 6 V bulb (suitable for street lights for a model village, perhaps?).

To switch the bulb on when it gets dark and off when it gets light, we need an electronic device whose properties are changed by light. One such device is the light-dependent resistor (LDR). This decreases in resistance when light falls on it. The change in resistance can be used to trigger a transistor that switches the light on or off.

Designing the circuit

We will develop the circuit in stages. This is usually a good idea when designing circuits. You can quickly spot and correct faults as you go along. **Connect and try out each of the circuits described.**

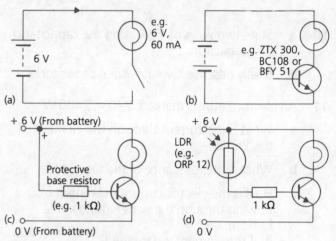

Fig. 2 Using a transistor switch
What is the purpose of the base resistor?

1 Connect the bulb across the battery with a switch in series, as shown in Figure 2(a). This is the normal way of switching the light on and off.

2 Replace the switch by a transistor, as shown in Figure 2(b). (Remember to connect a protective resistor to the base (Figure 2(c))—see Section 18.9.)

The transistor will not allow current to pass unless the base is connected to the *positive* side of the power supply. Once that is done (as in Figure 2(c)), the transistor switches on and the light bulb lights.

3 (A wrong move!) The LDR can control the transistor if it is connected (as in Figure 2(d)) between the base terminal and the positive side of the supply. Unfortunately, this works the wrong way round. In the dark when the LDR has high resistance, the transistor switch will be off. In the light when the LDR has low resistance, the transistor switch will be on. The bulb will be on in the day and off at night! This isn't what we want!

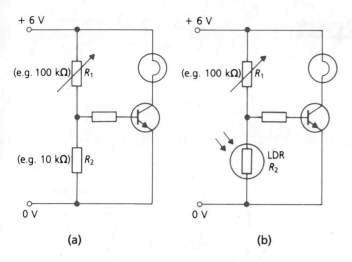

(a)   (b)

Fig. 3 Using a potential divider
Diagram (b) is the circuit required to switch on the light
when it gets dark.
How does this circuit work?

4 (A step in the right direction.) What we do is to use a
potential divider as shown in Figure 3(a). R_1 is a
variable resistor. It enables us to change the output
voltage of this potential divider.

- **Try this. What happens when you adjust the
  variable resistor? See Section 18.5 for the theory
  of the potential divider.**

The higher the value of R_2, the greater the output
voltage of the potential divider, and therefore the
greater the positive potential of the transistor's base
terminal. Large values of R_2 turn the transistor on.
Small values of R_2 turn it off.

5 By replacing R_2 with the LDR (as shown in Figure
3(b)), we have the circuit we need.

    High light level (daytime) ⇒ low LDR
                       resistance (R_2)

                    ⇒ transistor switch off

                    ⇒ bulb off

    Low light level (night-time) ⇒ high LDR
                       resistance (R_2)

                    ⇒ transistor switch on

                    ⇒ bulb on

Our circuit works, at least in theory! **See if it works in
practice.**

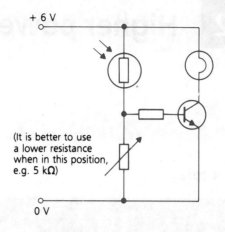

Fig. 4 What happens in this case?

By using a variable resistor for R_1, we can adjust the
light level at which the transistor will switch on and
off.

Note: it is important that you put the LDR and the
variable resistor the right way round. If they are
connected as in Figure 4, the light bulb will light in the
daytime and not at night. **Why?**

A multipurpose control circuit

The same circuit can be used with other sensors and
other output devices. For example, you could make a
fire alarm by replacing the LDR with a thermistor and
using a buzzer instead of the light bulb.

- **Draw this circuit and explain how it works. Figure
  5 shows the symbols for the thermistor and
  buzzer.**

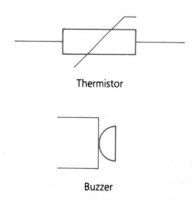

Fig. 5 Making a fire alarm
How can you do this using these components?

19.2 Higher power output

Adding a relay

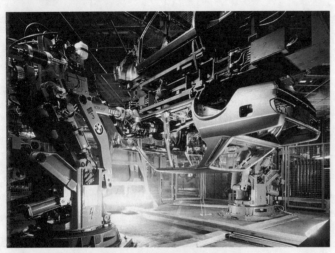

Fig. 1 Robots need a high power output!
Industrial robots use low-power electronic circuits but high-power motors and hydraulic systems.

The circuit described in Section 19.1 allows you to switch a torch bulb on and off. But you could not use this circuit as it is to operate street lights. You couldn't even use it to operate a low-voltage motor. To do this, you need to add a relay.

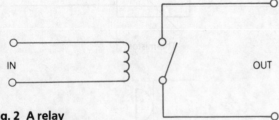

Fig. 2 A relay
Why is it needed?
How does it work?

The way in which a relay works is described in Section 13.3. The current controlling the relay flows through the **activating coil** of an electromagnet (Figure 2). This forces two contacts together, thereby switching on a larger current.

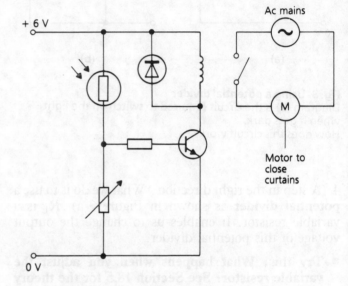

Fig. 3 Using a relay to control a motor

Figure 3 shows how you could (in theory!) close the curtains when it gets dark. A light-dependent resistor switches on a motor which pulls the curtains together. Compare this circuit with the circuit for switching on a torch bulb when it gets dark (Section 19.1, Figure (3(b)). The relay has taken the place of the torch bulb. (The purpose of the diode is described below.)

When it gets dark, the transistor switches on (see Section 19.1). This activates the relay. The relay switch is closed, connecting the motor to the mains ac supply.

Notice that the transistor circuit and the motor circuit are completely separate. The motor can run off ac or dc of any voltage without affecting the transistor circuit.

- **Try out this circuit using a low-voltage dc motor and a low-voltage dc supply rather than the mains supply.**

- **How would you alter the circuit to switch on a fan when it gets hot?**

Using a diode to protect the transistor

When the current through the relay coil is switched off, it produces a large **back emf** (see Section 13.9). If this sudden high voltage passed through the transistor, it could ruin it. The diode prevents this by short-circuiting the current (Figure 4). The current flows round the small loop, missing out the transistor.

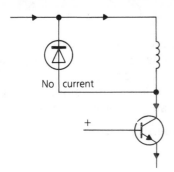

(a) The transistor is on. Current flows through the coil, not the diode (wrong direction)

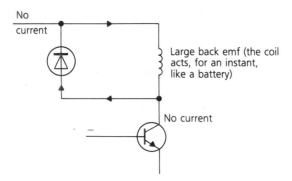

(b) The instant after the transistor is off, the coil tries to push a large current through it, but this short-circuits through the diode

Fig. 4 Using a protective diode
What causes the back emf?

A short length of wire would work just as well as the diode in short-circuiting this current. But it would also allow current to flow straight from the positive side of the battery to the transistor, missing out the relay. The diode does not allow this reverse current to flow through it (see Section 18.8).

Using a driver

A **driver** is an integrated circuit that allows a low-current circuit to drive a higher current device. If your transistor can only pass a very small current, you may need a driver to allow it to operate even a relay.

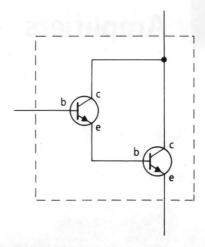

Fig. 5 A Darlington driver
What is it used for?
How does it work?

One common type of driver is the Darlington driver shown in Figure 5. This consists of two transistors. A low-current circuit switches on the first, lower-power transistor. This in turn switches on a high-power transistor.

Some electronic circuits, particularly those in computers, need **display drivers** just to operate the LED displays. A driver is also used to supply current to a **bus**—a set of wires carrying data inside the computer. Guess what this is called!

Fig. 6 A transducer driver
Why does it have metal fins?

- Some electronics kits use transducer drivers that can switch large currents to operate solenoids and motors (Figure 6). They usually have metal fins attached. Why? Try using one of these transducer drivers to switch on a motor or a solenoid when it gets dark.

303

Different types of amplifiers

Fig. 1 A hi-fi system
What are the different parts of this system?
What is the purpose of the amplifier?

Hi-fi systems use amplifiers. In fact the amplifier that you buy for the system usually contains several amplifiers. Some of these are **voltage amplifiers**. They increase the small potential differences produced by the record player, cassette player and tuner (Figure 2). You then need **power amplifiers** to operate the speaker—you need to boost the current as well as the voltage.

Both kinds of amplifier are used to increase alternating voltages and currents. The tiny signal from the record player is an alternating current. So is the amplified signal going to the speaker. This amplified signal makes the speaker vibrate and produce music.

- **Where else are amplifiers used?**

An example of a voltage amplifier

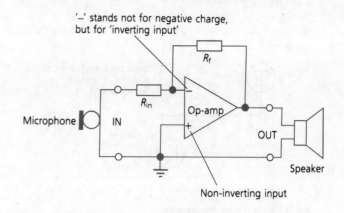

Fig. 3 Using an operational amplifier
What is the voltage gain for this amplifier?

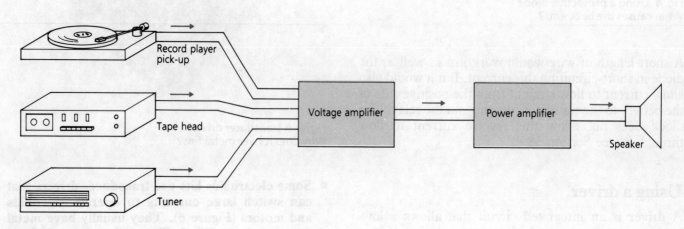

Fig. 2 How a hi-fi system works
Why do you need the two amplifiers? (In practice, both are in the same box.)

The **operational amplifier** (or op-amp) is one of the simplest voltage amplifiers to use. Figure 3 shows an operational amplifier being used to amplify the voltages from a sensitive microphone. One advantage of this particular amplifier is that you can alter the amount of amplification just by altering the resistance R_f.

The amount of amplification produced by a voltage amplifier is called the **voltage gain** or **amplification factor**.

$$\text{voltage gain} \equiv \frac{\text{change in output voltage}}{\text{change in input voltage}}$$

(This only applies for small changes in voltage. If the input voltage becomes too large, the output voltage will reach that of the power supply and won't be able to increase any further.)

For the operational amplifier shown in Figure 3,

$$\text{voltage gain} = \frac{R_f}{R_{in}} \qquad (1)$$

For example, if R_{in} is $1\,k\Omega$ and you require a voltage gain of 100, then R_f should be $100\,k\Omega$. **What will the gain be if R_f is then increased to $330\,k\Omega$?**

- **Set up this circuit, and connect the output to an oscilloscope (Section 19.4). See how the voltage of the output increases as you increase R_f.**

Using an op-amp as a comparator

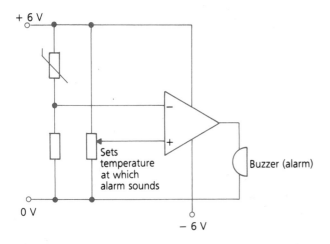

Fig. 4 Using an operational amplifier for a fire alarm
What is the advantage of this operational amplifier circuit compared with a simple transistor circuit?

In Figure 4, the operational amplifier is being used in a very sensitive fire alarm. It amplifies the difference between the voltage across the thermistor and the **reference voltage**. The reference voltage is set such that the alarm is just about to turn on. The slightest increase in the temperature of the thermistor will then switch on the alarm.

- **How would you alter this operational amplifier to sound an alarm as soon as it heard a noise? See if you can connect up these circuits and get them to work.**

Power amplifiers

Fig. 5 What you need to make a radio
Battery, speaker, tuned circuit, receiver circuit and power amplifier.
How should they be connected? What is the purpose of the power amplifier?

Power amplifiers increase the power. That is to say, they increase the current as well as the voltage. Power amplifiers are needed for loudspeakers (see Figure 5). The output from an operational amplifier or another voltage amplifier may have a sufficiently high voltage to drive the speaker but not sufficeint current.

- **Suppose that you connected this circuit, or the system shown in Figure 2, differently. Suppose that you connected the amplifiers the other way round, with the signal passing first through the power amplifier and then through the voltage amplifier. Would these circuits work just as well? Why?**

There are many other types of amplifier. All amplifiers are used to increase either the voltage or the power of an electrical signal.

What is an oscilloscope?

Fig. 1 A cathode-ray oscilloscope
Why is it more useful than a simple voltmeter?

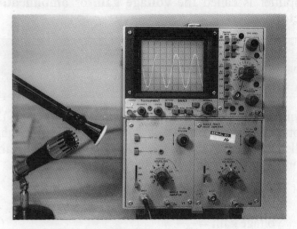

Fig. 2 Displaying an ac signal
What can you find out about this signal using the oscilloscope?

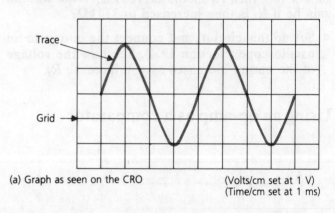

(a) Graph as seen on the CRO   (Volts/cm set at 1 V)
                                                              (Time/cm set at 1 ms)

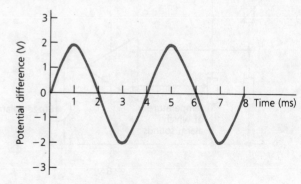

(b) Graph as you would draw it with scales and axes

Fig. 3 The CRO produces a voltage–time graph
What parts of the graph are *not* shown on the CRO?

Most electronics workshops use cathode-ray oscilloscopes (CROs). A CRO is a kind of voltmeter. It is used for looking at and measuring changing voltages in electronic circuits.

An oscilloscope can be connected across parts of a circuit just like a voltmeter. But unlike a voltmeter, the CRO doesn't just tell you the present voltage (which may be changing rapidly in a typical circuit). Instead, the screen displays a graph of voltage against time. A spot moves from left to right across the screen, then whips back and starts again. The spot is deflected upwards (or downwards) when there is a positive (or negative) voltage across the input.

A CRO takes much less current from the circuit being measured than even the best ordinary voltmeter. You can safely use a CRO on very sensitive circuits without causing any disturbance at all.

Displaying waveforms

Figure 2 shows an oscilloscope being used to display the ac signal from a microphone. Figure 3(a) shows the graph as seen on the screen. Figure 3(b) shows the same graph as you would draw it on graph paper.

There are three things that you can measure from the graph:
1 The maximum voltage of the signal (2 V).
2 The period of the wave (4 ms) and therefore the frequency of the wave (1/4 ms = 250 Hz).
3 The shape of the wave.

- **What are the maximum voltage and frequency of the waves shown in Figure 4?**

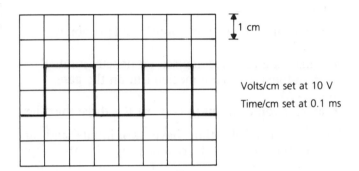

1 cm

Volts/cm set at 10 V
Time/cm set at 0.1 ms

Fig. 4 Another wave on a CRO screen
Two ways of making this type of wave are described in Section 19.7.
What do we call this wave?

Using the controls

One problem in using an oscilloscope is that the axes of the graph are not shown, nor is there any labelling on the grid. To work out the axes, you need to use the CRO controls.

To start with, have the 'Volts/cm' control set to 1 V and the time base, or 'seconds/cm' control, set to 1 ms.
1 The 'sync' and 'trig level' controls allow you to start the trace (to start the spot moving across the screen) at the right time. If you set the sync to 'auto' and the trig level at a minimum, then the trace will start as soon as you switch on.
2 You need to get the graph in the right position on the screen. (You may find that it's off the screen altogether to start with!) The X shift and Y shift controls allow you to alter its position.
3 You can now display your graph and choose any scales by altering the volts/cm and seconds/cm controls.

- **What settings would you use for a signal of amplitude 3 mV and frequency 1 kHz?**

How it works

A CRO works in a similar way to a television set (see Section 13.7), but there are just two differences.
1 Instead of electromagnets, charged metal plates are used to deflect the cathode rays.
2 The spot on the screen produced by the cathode rays sweeps across the same path each time. It sweeps out a line rather than a square picture.

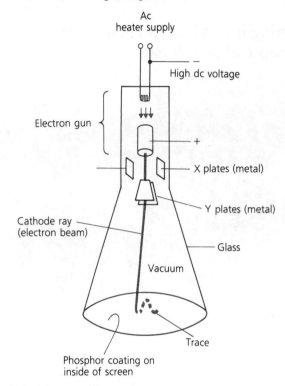

Ac heater supply

High dc voltage

Electron gun

X plates (metal)

Y plates (metal)

Cathode ray (electron beam)

Glass

Vacuum

Trace

Phosphor coating on inside of screen

Fig. 5 Inside an oscilloscope
Using an electric field to deflect the beam.
How does this differ from a television tube? (See Section 13.7.)

The X plates (Figure 5) form the time base. They move the beam to the right at constant speed, and then move it back again much more quickly.

The voltage that you apply to the oscilloscope is amplified and connected across the Y plates. A positive voltage applied to the top Y plate makes the cathode rays move upwards. This makes the spot move up the screen.

- **Why does this cause the spot to move up the screen? Another control allows you to alter the brightness of the spot on the screen. How do you think it makes the spot brighter?**

307

Logic gates

Getting into a football match: an example of an OR gate

Fig. 1 The gates of a football ground
In what way do these act as an OR gate?

To get into a football ground, you have to pass through a gate. There are two ways of getting through. Either you pay money *or* you show a season ticket. Either money *or* a ticket will get you in. (If you wished, you could do both. The football club wouldn't complain!)

The departure gate at an airport: an example of an AND gate

There's only one way of getting through the departure gate at an international airport. You have to show your passport *and* your plane ticket. Just showing one or the other isn't enough.

Automated football ground and airport departure gates

Suppose that a football club decides to replace its gatekeepers with electronic controls. The club doesn't want to make any other changes. How could this be done?

They would need

- a machine to take and count people's money (input A)
- a machine for checking season tickets (input B)
- an automatic release mechanism on the gate (output Q)
- an electronic circuit to connect the three together.

The circuit would thus have two inputs and one output. Its task would be to send a signal to the output when it received a 'yes' signal from input A OR from input B.

Such a circuit is called an **OR gate** (Figure 2). When you apply a voltage to one input OR the other, you get a voltage at the output Q.

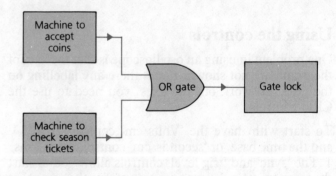

Fig. 2 Using an electronic OR gate
Where else could an OR gate be used?

The control circuit for an automatic airport departure gate would be slightly different. This circuit should send an output signal to the gate lock only if it gets a 'yes' signal from the passport machine *and* from the ticket-checking machine. The electronic circuit needed for this is the **AND gate** shown in Figure 3.

'Yes' = 5 volts!

For common TTL gates (transistor–transistor logic gates), the 'yes' signal from the input should be a voltage of at least 4.5 V. The input is then said to be

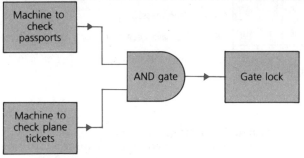

Fig. 3 An airport departure gate
In what way does this act as an AND gate?

high. If there is no voltage or if the voltage is very small, then the input is said to be **low**. This is the 'no' signal. For example, for a football gate, 5 V means 'Yes, this person's ticket or money is OK'. 0 V means 'No, it isn't!'. The 5 V output signal then triggers the gate-opening mechanism.

How a gate works

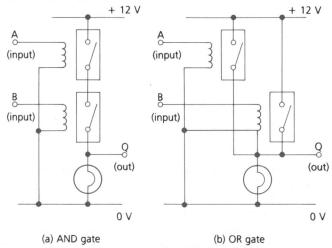

(a) AND gate   (b) OR gate

Fig. 4 Simple AND and OR gates using relays
How do they work?

Figure 4 shows how you could make AND and [OR] gates using relays. In practice, such an arrangement [is] too slow, uses too much current and soon wears out. Instead, integrated circuits are used in which transistors do the switching.

A NOT gate

This gate has only one input. When there is NOT an input signal, it gives an output. So if the input is **low**, then the output is **high**. If the input is **high**, then the output is **low**. (The NOT gate is often called an **inverter** because the behaviour of the output is upside-down to the behaviour of the input.)

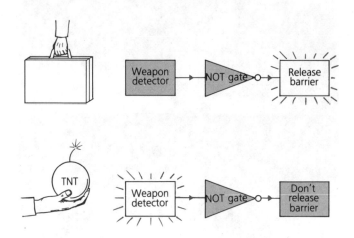

Fig. 5 NOT gate for airport security
If you are carrying a weapon, you canNOT pass through. Where else could you use a NOT gate?

A NOT gate could perhaps be used for controlling a security check (Figure 5). If the passenger is carrying a weapon, do NOT open the gate. If the passenger is NOT carrying a weapon, then do open the gate.

- **Can you suggest another use for this gate?**

There are other types of gate (NAND gates, NOR gates and Exclusive OR gates), but all these can be made from AND, OR and NOT gates.

- **How would you make a gate for which the output was always high *unless* both inputs were high? (This is called a NAND gate.)**

More complicated uses for electronic gates

Fig. 1 What is the truth table for this crossing?
What is a truth table?

A central-heating system needs an electronic circuit to control the boiler. The task of such a circuit might be as follows: *If* it is a time when the house should be warm *and* if the house is *not* warm, *then* switch on the boiler.

A pelican crossing also needs an electronic control circuit. *If* a pedestrian has pressed the button *and* the lights have been green for a long time, *then* the control system makes the lights change to red.

Truth tables

A	B	Q
0	0	0
0	1	0
1	0	0
1	1	1

A = button pressed

B = lights have been green for a long time (timer)

Q = make lights red (output)

Fig. 2 Truth table for the green man
What electronic gate is needed for this pedestrian crossing?

Engineers who design these and more-complicated control systems find it easier to describe them in terms of **truth tables**. Figure 2 shows the truth table for the pelican crossing.

In this table, a high input or output is represented by a 1. In other words, a 1 in column A or column B means that the answer to the corresponding question is 'Yes'. A low input (or 'No!') is represented by a 0. Such tables are called *truth* tables because we are in effect saying 'Yes it is true, there is a signal' or 'No it isn't true, there isn't a signal' (there isn't any traffic, the water isn't hot etc.) The fact that we use two digits—0 and 1—is why we talk of **digital electronics**.

- **Show the truth table for the boiler, where input A answers the question 'Is it time for the house to be warm?' and input B answers the question 'Is the house warm?'. The output Q switches on the boiler.**

Matching truth tables with electronic gates

Which electronic gate or gates do we need to control the pelican crossing and the central-heating system? To answer this question, we need the truth tables for AND, OR and NOT gates. These are shown in Figure 3.

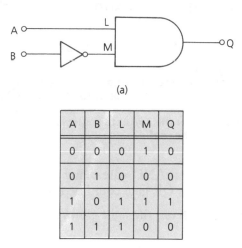

A	B	Q
0	0	0
0	1	0
1	0	0
1	1	1

(a) AND gate

A	B	Q
0	0	0
0	1	1
1	0	1
1	1	1

(b) OR gate

A	Q
0	1
1	0

(c) NOT gate

Fig. 3 Truth tables for single electronic gates

Compare the truth table for the AND gate with the truth table for the pelican crossing. They are identical. So what we need for this problem is an AND gate.

(a)

A	B	L	M	Q
0	0	0	1	0
0	1	0	0	0
1	0	1	1	1
1	1	1	0	0

(b) Columns L and M are added so that we can deal first with the NOT gate and then with the AND gate.
(This is the easiest way to analyse combinations of gates.)

Fig. 4 A combination of gates
How does it work?
Where could it be useful?

- Figure 4 shows a combination of gates and the corresponding truth table. Compare this with your truth table for the central-heating system. Would this circuit be suitable for the central-heating system?

Microprocessors

We have looked at some very simple control systems. In practice, the control systems needed for washing machines and automated equipment in factories are too complicated to use individual gates. They would require too many gates. In such cases, it is better to use a **microprocessor** (Figure 5). This is essentially a programmable gate. It has many inputs and outputs and you can program it to give whatever truth table you want.

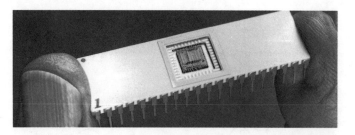

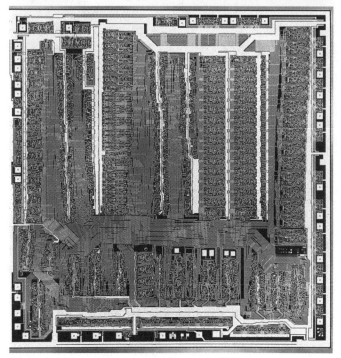

Fig. 5 A microprocessor—a programmable gate
Where is it used?

We will look at this again when we discuss computers in Section 19.8.

311

Using a gate as an electronic switch

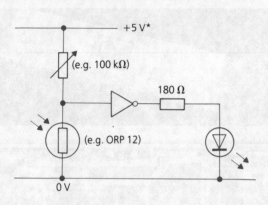

* For TTL gates we need 5 V.
  For CMOS gates we can use, say, a 6 V battery.

Fig. 1 Using a gate as an electronic switch
What else could be used instead of the gate? (See Section 19.1.)

A NOT gate can be used in place of a transistor. Figure 1 shows a NOT gate used with a light-dependent resistor to switch a light-emitting diode on and off.

- **How would you modify this circuit to allow a thermistor**
  (a) to switch the LED on and off?
  (b) to switch a fan on and off using a relay?

Using a gate as a buffer

Commercial gates take very little current from the input. They act as **buffers**. Just as buffers in a railway siding can stop a train, electronic buffers can stop the input current.

A NOT gate works as an **inverting buffer**. The output is low when the input is high.

An AND gate with both inputs connected together acts as a **non-inverting buffer**. The output is high when the input is high. **Is this also true for an OR gate with both inputs conected together?**

A delay circuit using a capacitor and gate

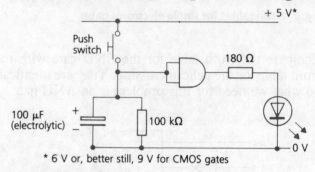

* 6 V or, better still, 9 V for CMOS gates

Fig. 2 Delayed action
The light goes off some time after it has been switched off.
What is the purpose of (i) the capacitor, (ii) the AND gate in this circuit?
How could you alter this circuit to control a mains light bulb? Where might this be useful?

Figure 2 shows an AND gate being used as part of a delay circuit. (An OR gate could be used just as well.)

When you switch on, the light glows and the capacitor charges.

When you switch off, the LED doesn't go off straight away because charge is stored in the capacitor. This charge keeps the gate input high. The charge cannot leak into the gate. Only when the charge leaks away through the resistor will the gate input become low and the LED switch off.

- **Try making this circuit. How does the time delay depend on**
  (a) the resistance of the resistor?
  (b) the capacitance of the capacitor?
  Suggest a use for such a circuit—perhaps using a mains light bulb (via a relay) rather than an LED.

An oscillator circuit

In Figure 3(a), a series of delay circuits causes a 'high' to continue moving round the circuit, followed by a 'low'. The output is a square-wave alternating voltage (see Section 19.4, Figure 4). The circuit acts as a **square-wave oscillator**.

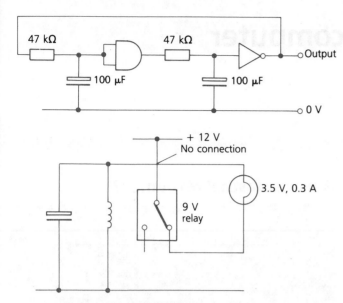

Fig. 3 **Square-wave oscillator circuits**
Which is best? Why?

Figure 3(b) shows how the same effect can be produced using a relay. This method does work, but it is not nearly so cheap, durable or convenient as that using gates.

● **Make and compare these circuits.**

A latch circuit

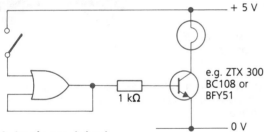

Fig. 4 **An electronic latch**
Why is it called a latch?
Where can it be used?
How does it work?

Look at the circuit shown in Figure 4. Once the light is switched on, it will stay on, whatever you do with the switch. The gate is acting as a **latch**, like that on a door or a garden gate.

Latches are used a lot in electronics. For example, computer keys operate latches. This means that the computer doesn't have to keep 'looking' at the keyboard switches. It can carry out a calculation and then check to see which keys have been pressed while it was calculating.

● How would you alter the circuit shown in Figure 4 to allow you to reset the latch? Try out your circuit to see if it works.

A bistable or flip-flop

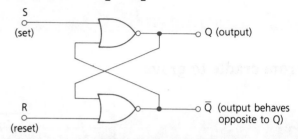

Fig. 5 **Using two NAND gates to make a bistable**
A bistable is often called a flip-flop. Why?
How does this circuit work?

Figure 5 shows what is known as a **bistable** or flip-flop. When one of the outputs is high, the other must be low. **Why?**

Suppose that both switches are off to start with. When you operate the upper 'Set' switch, the output of the lower gate goes (or stays) low, and the output of the upper gate goes (or stays) high.

If you now operate the lower 'Reset' switch, the output of the lower gate goes low and that of the upper gate goes high.

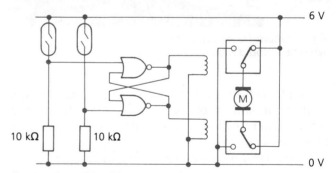

Fig. 6 **Using a bistable to operate a motor**
What is the purpose of the bistable in this case?
Which switch starts the motor? How do you know?

Figure 6 shows how this bistable and two reed switches can be used to control a motor. If a magnet is brought near to the first reed switch, the motor turns in one direction. If the second reed switch is operated, the motor turns in the opposite direction. **Try making this system. Suggest a practical applicaton.**

Bistables (ready made as integrated circuits) and latches play an important role in microprocessors and computers.

313

The world of the computer

From cradle to grave

Fig. 1 A main-frame computer
What tasks could it be carrying out?

Computers affect every part of our lives. They are used to monitor and record our birth. They help us at school. Later, they may provide us with work, assist us in our job or even compete with us for work. They are used to record who we marry, and when and how we die.

Not only do computers keep records of *when* we live, but they also influence *how* we live. For example, computers can be used to help to prevent crime. They are also used in defence and in times of war.

On a day-to-day basis, computers can be used to help to design and make many things that we rely on, such as cars, televisions, washing machines, dress fabrics and so on. They can help to print our newspapers and books, to make music and entertainment for us and to arrange our holidays. They even monitor our progress when we are ill.

● **Where in your town are people using computers?**

A new industrial revolution?

▲
Woollen mills in
Halifax

The processor of a ►
supercomputer

Fig. 2 Are we in the middle of an industrial revolution?
What effect does the electronic age have on the way in which we live?

The steam engine was at the heart of the first industrial revolution. It allowed a small number of people to make vast quantities of cloth and other goods. The steam engine replaced muscle power.

Computers are at the heart of our modern technological revolution. In some industries, computers have made it possible for a few people to do the work of thousands. In addition, the speed with which computers can process information has made possible many things that were previously impossible. Computers replace brain power.

● **What other similarities and differences are there between the industrial revolution and industry today?**

Processors of information

The first computers 'computed'—they carried out mathematical calculations. For example, they worked out companys' payrolls or calculated the direction for aiming guns.

This is still true today. But computers can now carry out such a vast number of tasks that it is better to think of them as processors of information. A computer takes the information in at an input. It processes the information and then sends it out to wherever we want it to go.

More important, computers can be programmed. You can give them a set of instructions to follow. At a later date, you can change those instructions.

To us, 'information' can be stories, poetry, pictures, music or even just letters and numbers. To a computer, all 'information' is a pattern of 1s and 0s (see Figure 3). 1 means 5 V, 0 means 0 V.

The heart of the computer

Figure 4 shows the structure of a computer. At its heart is a processor or microprocessor. This has 8, 16 or 32 wires going into it (depending on whether it is an 8-bit, 16-bit or 32-bit computer). Each input wire can be 'high' (5 V) or 'low' (0 V).

The processor acts as a programmable gate. For every pattern of input voltages, it gives the required pattern of output voltages. In effect, the computer program provides the computer with the required truth table.

A kind of clock (actually a square-wave oscillator—see Section 19.7) changes the information at least once every millionth of a second.

Finally, a computer has several memories, consisting of bistables and latches (see Section 19.7). The memories allow the computer to get on with a task without having to keep asking you for more information.

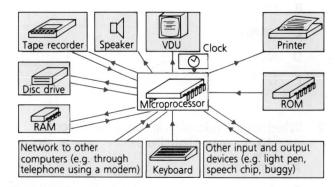

Fig. 4 Inside a computer
What is the purpose of
  (i)   the microprocessor?
  (ii) the clock?
  (iii) the memory?

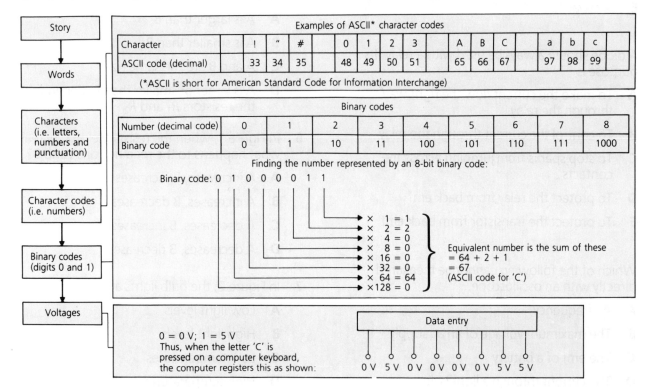

Fig. 3 Levels of information
At what level does the computer operate? At what level do we usually operate?

Exercises

1 Which of these gates is also called an inverter?

   A AND

   B OR

   C NAND

   D NOR

   E NOT

2 Which of the following allows a transistor to switch on a mains light bulb?

   A A resistor

   B A diode

   C A relay

   D A rheostat

   E A capacitor

3 A diode should always be used with a relay. Its purpose is

   A To make the current flow the right way through the relay

   B To control the current through the relay

   C To stop sparks from jumping across the contacts

   D To protect the relay from back emf

   E To protect the transistor from back emf

4 Which of the following *cannot* be measured directly with an oscilloscope.

   A Ac frequency

   B The maximum voltage of an ac supply

   C The emf of a battery

   D The current through a light bulb

   E The time interval between electrical waves

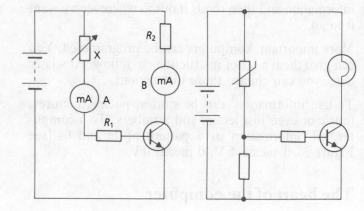

Fig. 1   **Fig. 2**

5 In Figure 1, the readings on A and B are related to each other as follows:

   A A is larger than B

   B A is smaller than B

   C A and B are the same size

   D A is larger or smaller than B, depending on the resistors R_1 and R_2

6 In Figure 1, when the resistance of X increases, what happens to the readings on A and B?

   A A increases, B increases

   B A increases, B decreases

   C A decreases, B increases

   D A decreases, B decreases

7 In Figure 2, the bulb lights at

   A Low light levels

   B High light levels

   C Low temperatures

   D High temperatures

   E All times

316

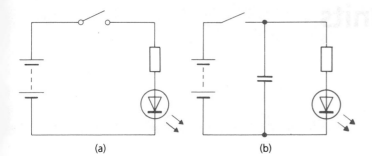

Fig. 3

8 In Figure 3(a) the LED lights when the switch is closed. In Figure 3(b), a capacitor has been added. The LED now lights

A All the time

B Only when the switch is open

C Only when the switch is closed

D When the switch is open and for a short time after it has been closed

E When the switch is closed and for a short time after it has been opened

9 Complete these sentences:

To make an automatic street light you can use a resistor whose _____ changes with _____ _____. This is called a _____ _____ _____. It is placed in one arm of a _____ _____ that controls the voltage of the _____ terminal of a transistor. When current flows into the _____ terminal of the transistor, a larger current is allowed to flow through a bulb connected to the _____ terminal of the transistor. Large ac currents to the street lamp can be controlled by putting a _____ in place of the _____.

10 State one advantage and one disadvantage of a transistor compared with a relay for using a small current to switch a large current.

11 A solenoid is used at a bottling factory to remove bottles that have not been properly filled. One sensor checks whether there is a bottle in front of the solenoid. A second sensor checks whether the bottle is full.

a Draw the truth table for this situation.

b Suggest a circuit diagram using gates that would give this truth table.

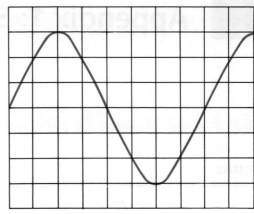

Fig. 4

12 Figure 4 shows the screen of a cathode-ray oscilloscope. The controls are set at 10 V/cm and 1 ms/cm.

a Describe the waveform.

b What is the maximum (peak) voltage?

c What is the ac frequency?

13 Describe how gates can be used

a to keep a light on once a button has been pressed.

b to switch on the light when one button is pressed, and switch off the light when a second button is pressed.

c to keep a light switching on and off at regular, short intervals.

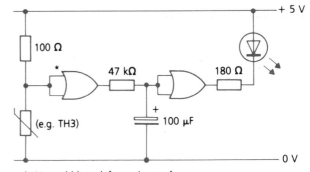

* We could have left one input of the OR gate disconnected and it would still have worked

Fig. 5

14 Figure 5 shows a circuit for a fire alarm. The temperature must remain high for a short time for it to operate.

a Explain how the circuit works.

b State two ways of increasing the time taken for the alarm to sound.

317

Appendix 1: SI units

Base units

Quantity	Name of unit	Symbol
Length	metre	m
Mass	kilogram	kg
Time	second	s
Electric current	ampere	A
Temperature	kelvin	K
Luminous intensity*	candela	cd

* Not used in this book.

Derived SI units

Quantity	Name of unit	Symbol	Equivalent units
Force	newton	N	$kg\ m/s^2$
Frequency	hertz	Hz	$1/s$
Energy	joule	J	$N\ m$
Power	watt	W	J/s
Charge	coulomb	C	$A\ s$
Electric potential	volt	V	J/C
Electric resistance	ohm	Ω	V/A

Prefixes

Prefix	Symbol	Multiplier	Prefix	Symbol	Multiplier
kilo	k	$\times 10^3$	milli	m	$\times 10^{-3}$
mega	M	$\times 10^6$	micro	μ	$\times 10^{-6}$
giga	G	$\times 10^9$	nano	n	$\times 10^{-9}$
tera	T	$\times 10^{12}$	pico	p	$\times 10^{-12}$

Appendix 2: Using mathematical formulae

Shorthand

Formulae are a form of mathematical shorthand. For example,

$F = ma$

is just a shorthand way of writing

force = mass × acceleration

Each letter in the formula stands for some quantity (mass, time etc.). Usually the connection is obvious — for example, v stands for velocity, A for area and m for mass. But sometimes the connection is not so obvious — for example, I is used for current, and θ for temperature.

Multiplication signs are not used in formulae. When two letters are written next to each other, this means that one is to be multiplied by the other.

Using formulae

To solve a problem

1 Find a formula that has
  ● what you are trying to find on the left-hand side (this is called the **subject** of the formula)
  ● what you already know on the right-hand side.

2 Write down the formula.

3 Replace the letters on the right-hand side with numbers and SI units.

4 Write the numbers in the form of a sum. Then write down the overall SI unit (the unit for the quantity on the left-hand side of the formula).

5 Work out the sum to get a single number. Again follow it with the appropriate SI unit.

6 Repeat step 5, correcting the number to a sensible number of significant figures (usually one or two only).

For example To find the potential energy gained by a 1300 g box lifted 1200 cm:

1 $E = mgh$

2 $= 1.3 \text{ kg} \times 10 \text{ N/kg} \times 12 \text{ m}$

3 $= 1.3 \times 10 \times 12 \text{ J}$

4 $= 156 \text{ J}$

5 $= 160 \text{ J}$ (to 2 significant figures)

Changing the subject of a formula

Many formulae are of the form

$A = BC$

For example,

force = mass × acceleration

power = voltage × current

voltage = current × resistance

You will often find that the quantity you want is on the right-hand side of the formula. An easy way of changing the subject of a formula is to draw a triangle. If you then take any one of the letters, you will be able to see the form that the other two should take:

   $A = BC \qquad B = \dfrac{A}{C} \qquad C = \dfrac{A}{B}$

For example Find the current through a lamp, given the power and the voltage.

Use the fact that $P = VI$, and draw a diagram. Then, since you want to find the current (I), write the current as the subject of the formula:

   $I = \dfrac{P}{V}$ (current $= \dfrac{\text{power}}{\text{voltage}}$)

Appendix 3:
Constant acceleration formulae

We shall use the constant acceleration formulae to show how formulae can be combined and rearranged to solve a range of problems. These formulae can be used to solve any problem involving constant acceleration.

For example   How deep is a well if it takes 3 seconds for a stone to reach the bottom?
How far will a car, travelling at 30 m/s, continue to travel before coming to a halt if the driver brakes with a deceleration of 2 m/s²?

Symbols

The symbols used in the constant acceleration formulae are

a for acceleration
t for time
u for the initial or old velocity
v for the final or new velocity
s (not d!) for the displacement.

Formula 1

Using the definition of acceleration (Section 3.1)

$$a = \frac{v - u}{t}$$

we find that

$$v = u + at$$

Formula 2

Using the definition of average velocity (Section 2.1)

$$\text{average velocity} = \frac{u + v}{2} = \frac{s}{t}$$

we find that

$$s = \frac{(u + v)\, t}{2}$$

Formula 3

Replacing v in formula 2 by the expression for v in formula 1 gives

$$s = \frac{u + (u + at)t}{2}$$

Hence

$$s = ut + \frac{at^2}{2}$$

Formula 4

Rearranging formula 1,

$$u = v - at$$

Substituting this for u in formula 2 gives

$$s = \frac{([v - at] + v)t}{2}$$

Hence

$$s = vt - \frac{at^2}{2}$$

Formula 5

Rearranging formula 1,

$$t = \frac{v - u}{a}$$

Substituting this for t in formula 2 gives

$$s = \frac{(u + v)}{2} \frac{(v - u)}{a}$$

This can be rearranged to give

$$v^2 = u^2 + 2as$$

Example of using the constant acceleration formulae

Find the depth of a well if it takes 3 seconds for a stone dropped down the well to reach the bottom.

We know that

a = 10 m/s^2 (gravitational acceleration)
t = 3 s (time of fall)
u = 0 m/s (the stone was dropped from rest)

v we do not know, or wish to know
s is what we are trying to find

The formula that involves a, t, u and s but not v is formula 3. It already has s as the subject, so we can go ahead and substitute values for a, t and u:

$$s = ut + \frac{at^2}{2}$$

$$= (0 \text{ m/s} \times 3 \text{ s}) + (10 \text{ m/s}^2 \times 3 \text{ s} \times 3 \text{ s})/2$$

$$= \{(0 \times 3) + (10 \times 3 \times 3)/2\} \text{ m}$$

$$= 45 \text{ m}$$

The well is therefore 45 m deep.

- **A car travelling at 30 m/s starts to brake, and decelerates at 2 m/s^2. Use the constant acceleration formulae to find out how far the car will travel before it stops.**

Answers

Answers are given only for multiple-choice and numerical questions.

Chapter 1 Exercises
1 B
2 B
3 C
4 A
5 C
12 **a** 3.5 N, 1.6 N
    b 200 g, 350 g, 160 g
13 **a** 620 g
    b 6.2 N

Chapter 2 Exercises
1 A
2 A
3 D
4 C
5 E
6 A
11 50 s
12 **a** 100 m
    b 200 s
    c 400 s
    d 0.5 m/s
13 **b** 22 m/s
15 10 s

Chapter 3 Exercises
1 D
2 A
3 E
4 C
5 D
6 B
11 **a** 20 s
    b 400 m
    c 1000 N
12 3.8 m/s^2
13 10 m/s^2
14 **a** 30 m/s
    b 45 m
15 **b** 2 per second
    d B
    e 40 m/s

Chapter 4 Exercises
1 C
2 E
3 B
4 D
5 D
6 B
14 **b** 2 m
17 **a** 1005 N
    b 17 m/s^2

Chapter 5 Exercises
1 D
2 A
3 C
4 E
5 B
6 A
7 **a** 50 kPa
11 **a** $60\,000 \text{ N/m}^2$
    b $6\,000\,000 \text{ N/m}^2$
12 **a** 3.2 N
    b 64 Pa

Chapter 6 Exercises
1 D
2 E
3 D
4 C
5 C
6 A
10 **a** 2000 J
    b 2000 J
12 **i** 0.1 J
    ii 10 J
    iii 990 J gain

Chapter 7 Exercises
1 B
2 C
3 C
4 E
5 D
6 E
9 **b** **i** 8p
        ii 48p
10 **a** 500 J
    b 0.5 m/s
    c **i** 250 J
        ii 0.25 m/s
11 **a** 120 000 J
    b 33 W
    c 33%
12 **a** **i** 0.5 m
        ii 100 m
    b 1 N
    c 100 J
    d 100 J
    e 10%

Chapter 8 Exercises
1 B
2 A
3 D
4 A
5 C
6 E
15 **a** 130 000 Pa
    b **i** 0.6 kg
        ii 0.6 kg
    c 0.8 m^3
16 4000 J/kg K

Chapter 9 Exercises
1 A
2 E
3 D
4 A
5 B
6 D

Chapter 10 Exercises
1 C
2 A
3 B
4 D
5 B

Chapter 11 Exercises
1 B
2 C
3 E
4 B
5 D
6 E
12 a 36 000 C
   b 220 000 J
   c 40

Chapter 12 Exercises
1 C
2 C
3 B
4 D
5 A
6 D

Chapter 13 Exercises
1 B
2 D
3 A
4 E
5 D

Chapter 14 Exercises
1 E
2 C
3 B
4 C
5 D
6 C
7 C
8 B
18 a 3×10^8 m/s
   b 10 GHz

Chapter 15 Exercises
1 D
2 D
3 B
4 C
5 C
6 D
9 a i 660 m
    ii 990 m
10 a 33 Hz
    b 66 Hz
11 a 5000 m/s
    b 0.004 s

Chapter 16 Exercises
1 B
2 C
3 D
4 C
5 E
6 C
7 E
8 C

Chapter 17 Exercises
1 E
2 D
3 C
4 B
5 B
6 C
7 B
8 D

Chapter 18 Exercises
1 D
2 C
3 E
4 A
5 A
6 C
8 0.5 A
9 b 1 V
11 a 10 A
    b 24 ohms
13 a 1.5 ohms
    b 6 W
14 b In (a), 2 A
    In (b), 0 A
   c In (a), 0 V
    In (b), 6 V
15 $V = 1.5$ V
   $A_1 = 0.5$ A
   $A_2 = 1$ A
   $A_3 = 0$ A

Chapter 19 Exercises
1 E
2 C
3 E
4 D
5 B
6 D
7 D
8 E
12 a 30 V
    b 125 Hz

Index